JOHN ROBOTTOM

A Social and Economic History of Industrial Britain

LONGMAN

Acknowledgements

We are grateful to the following for permission to reproduce photographs and other illustrations: B. T. Batsford, Olsen, *The Growth of Victorian London*, page 145 above, and Perry, *A Geography of Nineteenth Century Britain*, page 289; BBC Hulton Picture Library, pages 22, 100, 103 left, 120, 121, 124 above, 157, 193 and 269 right; Beamish North of England Open Air Museum, page 88; Birmingham Public Libraries, page 207 left; Bodleian Library, page 118 below; Bristol Museum and Art Gallery, page 175; British Leyland, page 229 below; British Library, page 32 centre, 47, 77, 118 above, 162, 184, 189 and 219; British Museum, pages 171 and 199 below; British Rail, page 236; Cambridge and County Folk Museum, page 124 below; Cheshire Record Office, page 217; Derby Local Studies Library, page 29; *Derby Evening Telegraph*, page 256 below; *Farmers Weekly*, page 301 (photo Ben Tyrer); J. H. Farr, pages 231; Greater London Council Photographic Library, pages 129 and 310; Guildhall Library, page 105 below left; Michael Heath, page 307; Her Majesty's Stationery Office, page 226; ICI, page 83; Illustrated London News Picture Library, pages 115 below and 244 above; Imperial War Museum, pages 244 below, 256 above left and right and 298 above; Ironbridge Gorge Museum Trust/Elton Collection, pages 39, 58 above, 103 right and 107; Peter Jackson, page 139 left; Lancashire Record Office, page 95; London Express News and Feature Services and the estate of David Low, page 273 above; Manchester Central Library, Local History Library, pages 172 and 249; Mansell Collection, page 169; Marks and Spencer, page 246; Mary Evans Picture Library, page 292; Museum of London, page 212; National Library of Ireland, page 160; National Motor Museum, Beaulieu, page 229 above; National Union of Agricultural Workers, page 191, Northamptonshire Libraries, page 215; *The Observer*, page 273 below, Photosource/Keystone, page 253; Post Office, page 223; Frank Power, page 24 below; Public Record Office, page 255; *Punch* Picture Library, pages 91 above, 105 above, 115 above, 139 right and 209; Jeffrey Richards, page 166; Rochdale Local Studies Library, page 113 below; Salvation Army, page 127 above; Science Museum, pages 16 below, 42 above, 80, 91 below, 93 and 101; Society of Apothecaries, page 154; Staffordshire County Council, page 24 above; STC, page 262; Topham, pages 259 above, 283 (photo Fox), and 298 below (photo Fox); Trinity College Cambridge/Munby Collection, page 207 right; University of Reading, Institute of Agricultural History and Museum of English Rural Life, pages 14, 16 above and centre, 18 below and 163; Michael Ware, page 65; Wedgwood Museum, Barlaston, page 52; Wellcome Institute Library, London, pages 136 and 151; West Yorkshire Passenger Transport Executive, page 85 centre.

We are also grateful to the following for permission to redraw artwork: Philip Allan Publishers, Aldcroft, *British Economy Between the Wars*, 1983, page 247 above; B. T. Batsford, Pawson, *The Early Industrial Revolution*, page 20; BBC Publications, Longmate, *Milestones in Working Class History*, 1979, page 195; David and Charles Publishers, Gale, *British Iron and Steel Industry*, 1967, page 80 and Aldcroft, *British Transport Since 1914*, 1975, page 236 above; Leicester University Press, Dyos and Aldcroft, *British Transport*, 1969, page 90 and Simmons, *The Railways in England and Wales*, page 96; Methuen and Co, Matthias, *The First Industrial Nation*, page 242 above and 160 above; Thomas Nelson and Sons, Gregg, *A Social and Economic History of Britain*, inside back cover; Oxford University Press, Morgan, *Rebirth of a Nation*, 1981, page 75 and Patterson, *Immigration and Race Relations in Britain*, 1969, page 295 above; Penguin Books, Townsend, *Poverty in the UK*, 1979, page 283 right; Osprey Publishing/George Philip and Son, Partridge, *Farm Tools Throughout the Ages*, 1973, page 40; Times Books, *The Times Concise Atlas of World History*, 1982, page 242 below.

We are grateful to the following for permission to reproduce copyright material: Associated Book Publishers (UK) Ltd for an abridged extract from 'Unemployment in the West Midlands' by S. Taylor pp. 69–70 *Unemployment* 1982, ed. B. Crick, pub. Methuen; Centerprise Trust Ltd for an abridged extract from 'Interview by Ida Rex' pp. 24–9 *Working Lives* Vol. 1 1905–45; Guardian Newspapers Ltd for an extract from article by Lena Jeger *The Guardian* 1964; the Controller of Her Majesty's Stationery Office for an abridged extract from 'The Preface' by Sir G. Crowther pp. 10–11 *Traffic in Towns (Buchanan Report)*; Routledge & Kegan Paul Ltd for an abridged extract from pp 132–3 *Family and Kinship in East London* (1962) by Young and Willmott. We have unfortunately been unable to trace the copyright holders of an abridged extract from *The NHS: Your Money and your Life* by L. Garner, and would appreciate any information which would enable us to do so.

Source information

1B: P. Horn, *A Georgian Parson and His Village*, Beacon Publications 1981; 14A: R. Fitton and A. Wadsworth, *The Strutts and the Arkwrights*, Manchester University Press 1958; 16B: T. S. Ashton, *Iron and Steel in the Industrial Revolution*, Manchester University Press 1924; 33B: G. Williams, *The Age of Agony*, Constable 1975; 39A: R. A. S. Hennessy, *The Electric Revolution*, Oriel Press 1972; 40B: L. T. C. Rolt, *George and Robert Stephenson*, Longman 1960: 43D: J. Simmons, *The Railway in England and Wales 1830–1914*, A. & C. Black 1978; 57C: R. W. Harris, *National Health Insurance in Great Britain*, Allen & Unwin 1946; 62F: R. Dubois, *Pasteur and Modern Science*, Heinemann Educational 1963; 63A: C. Woodham-Smith, *Florence Nightingale*, Constable 1950; 63B: S. Bingham, *Ministering Angels*, Osprey 1979; 66B: P. Matthias, *The First Industrial Nation*, Methuen 1969; 88A: M. K. Ashby, *Joseph Ashby of Tysoe*, Cambridge University Press 1961; 93C: S. Davis, *Memories of Men and Motor Cars*, Seeley 1967; 95A: C. Buchanan, *Traffic in Towns*, Penguin and HMSO 1964; 97C: K. Hudson and J. Pettifer, *Diamonds in the Sky*, Bodley Head and BBC 1979; 100B: D. H. Aldcroft, *The British Economy Between the Wars*, Philip Allan 1983; 103A: J. Stevenson and D. Cook, *The Slump*, Jonathan Cape 1977; 104D: H. Dalton, *The Fateful Years*, Muller 1952; 105A: A. Marwick, *British Society since 1945*, Penguin 1982; 107C: B. Crick (ed.), *Unemployment*, Methuen 1981; 111D: J. Stevenson, *Social Conditions in Britain Between the Wars*, Penguin 1977; 111E: J. Gathorne-Hardy, *Doctors*, Weidenfeld & Nicolson 1984; 112B: J. Beveridge, *Beveridge and His Plan*, Hodder & Stoughton 1956; 112C: W. S. Churchill, *The Second World War IV*, Cassell 1951; 113B: L. Garner, *The NHS. Your Money and Your Life*, Penguin 1979; 114D: P. Harrison, *Inside the Inner City*, Penguin 1984; 115A: M. K. Ashby, *Joseph Ashby of Tysoe*, Cambridge University Press 1961; 116E: D. Gershon (ed.), *We Came as Children*, Gollancz 1966; 117B: P. Addison, *Now the War is Over*, Jonathan Cape and BBC 1985; 117C: S. Patterson, *Immigration and Race Relations in Britain*, Oxford University Press 1969; 120A: M. Spring-Rice, *Working Class Wives*, Penguin 1939; 121D: S. Rowntree and G. Lavers, *Poverty and the Welfare State*, Longman 1951; 122C: M. Bragg, *Speak for England*, Secker & Warburg 1976; 123C: T. Burgess, *A Guide to English Schools*, Penguin 1964.

Cover: Part of a certificate for members of the Amalgamated Society of Engineers, Machinists, Millwrights, Smiths, and Pattern Makers, 1852. Photograph courtesy of Amalgamated Union of Engineering Workers.

Contents

Introduction

1
Two hundred and fifty years ago

Each unit in this book begins with a quick guide to the two parts: the narrative and sources. This unit explains why the book begins in the time of Daniel Defoe, and how to make sense of money before decimalisation.

The 1720s

You could start a book about modern Britain with the Romans who gave us much of our language, or the Anglo-Saxons who founded many of our villages. But this story begins in the 1720s and there are two reasons for that. By looking for evidence about the 1720s we find traces of a time when village people grew food mostly for their own use, goods were made in workshops or living-rooms, horses were far more important than stage-coaches and few people got married until their mid twenties. Yet young people of the 1720s would live long enough to see factories, steam-engines, canals and fast mail coaches, as well as the first town slums.

Daniel Defoe (1660–1731)

The second reason is that we can find out a great deal about the 1720s from a book written by Daniel Defoe. It is *A Tour Thro' the whole Island of Great Britain*, which was published in three volumes between 1724 and 1726. Great Britain had been a whole island only since 1707 when Scotland was united with England and Wales. The *Tour* is a good starting-point for social and economic history, which is the study of how people have lived and earned their living.

Daniel Defoe was well qualified to write about how livings were earned. As a young man he had gone into business as a stocking merchant and then into shipping insurance. After some years he went bankrupt and turned to writing political books and pamphlets. This was a risky business as governments were quite ready to put authors in prison for attacking them. That is what happened to Defoe, which is perhaps why he turned his hand to novels, such as *Robinson Crusoe*. He wrote the *Tour* near the end of his life. He made special journeys to collect some information but other parts were based on his earlier travels as a merchant.

Money

One journey took him to Derbyshire, and Defoe describes how he and some other travellers met a poor family. The husband earned fivepence a day digging lead ore and his wife got threepence a day for washing it. The travellers collected a crown to give them. That story shows how the system of money before 1971 was utterly different from our decimal system. It would be silly to try to change it into our money. You would find, for instance, that the man in Defoe's story earned 2.05p and the woman 1.23p. So, for events up to 1971 this book uses the old money.

These examples are taken from the middle of the period, in the early 1800s. Ordinary people would usually reckon in pennies as well as half-pennies and farthings, which were a 'fourthing' or a quarter penny. They knew that twelve pennies made a shilling and that twenty shillings made a pound (though the pound gold *coin* was called a sovereign). If they could write they would know that pennies were shown by a 'd' (1d, 4d, 2½d, 7¼d and so on), shillings by as 's', or a sign like this /-, and pounds by an 'L'. (Gradually the L changed into the £ sign.) If they could add up they would know that it was important to set money out in columns as is done in Source B. From the table below you can see how much the value of money has changed in the last two hundred years. It will be a good idea to turn back to this table whenever you are not sure whether a sum of money was a lot or a little.

Weekly earnings

Unskilled labourer				*Skilled craftsman*		
1800	About	10s	0d	About £1	0s	0d
1900	About	15s	0d	About £2	10s	0d
1930	About £2	0s	0d	About £4	0s	0d
Today	?			?		

Measurements

The systems of measurement used in Britain have been changing since the 1970s but for all times up to then this book uses the imperial measurements which go back to Saxon days. This table can be used if you need to understand any of the sources or the narrative where 'imperial' measurements are quoted.

Imperial measures	*(Approximate metric equivalent)*
Length	
1 inch	2.5 cm
12 inches (1 foot)	30.0 cm
3 feet (1 yard)	1.0 m
1,760 yards (1 mile)	1.6 km
Weight	
1 ounce (oz)	28 grams
16 oz (1 pound(lb))	0.45 kg
14 lbs (1 stone)	6.30 kg
28 lbs (1 quarter)	12.75 kg
4 qtrs (1 hundredweight (cwt))	50.00 kg
20 cwts (1 ton)	1 tonne
Capacity	
1 pint	0.56 litres
8 pints (1 gallon)	4.50 litres
Area	
1 acre	0.40 hectares

A

The title-page at the beginning of the first volume of Daniel Defoe's book as it was printed in 1724.

1 *How many examples can you find of*
   (a) different spellings from today?
   (b) different ways of printing letters?
2 *Who might be tempted to buy Defoe's book after reading the title-page?*
3 *What do you think there is in the list of contents which might be useful for students of the social and economic history of Britain?*

A

TOUR

Thro' the whole ISLAND of

GREAT BRITAIN,

Divided into

Circuits *or* Journies.

GIVING

A Particular and Diverting ACCOUNT of Whatever is CURIOUS and worth OBSERVATION, *Viz.*

I. A DESCRIPTION of the Principal Cities and Towns, their Situation, Magnitude, Government, and Commerce.

II. The Customs, Manners, Speech, as also the Exercises, Diversions, and Employment of the People.

III. The Produce and Improvement of the Lands, the Trade, and Manufactures.

IV. The Sea Ports and Fortifications, the Course of Rivers, and the Inland Navigation.

V. The Publick Edifices, Seats, and Palaces of the NOBILITY and GENTRY.

With Useful OBSERVATIONS *upon the Whole.*

Particularly fitted for the Reading of such as desire to Travel over the ISLAND.

By a GENTLEMAN.

LONDON;
Printed, and Sold by G. STRAHAN, in *Cornhill.*
W. MEARS, at the *Lamb* without *Temple-Bar.*
R. FRANCKLIN, under *Tom's* Coffee-house, *Covent-Garden,*
S. CHAPMAN, at the *Angel* in *Pall-Mall.*
R. STAGG, in *Westminster-Hall,* and
J. GRAVES, in St. *James's-Street.* MDCCXXIV.

Daniel Defoe, *A Tour Thro' the whole Island of Great Britain,* 1724

B

Part of the accounts kept for 1791 by the Revd David Davies, a country parson in a Berkshire village (who was rather better off than many parsons of the time).

4 *Can you explain how David Davies added up his total spending for June and July?*

5 *Who do you think the black silk stockings were for?*

6 *What does he mean by 'Plate at the Sacrament'?*

7 *Who did the parson's odd jobs?*

8 *Write three more questions like those above (and try to be fairly sure you know the answers) and give them to someone else to work out.*

			l	s	d
June	7	Paid Collier work &c. &c.		6	–
	12	Plate at the Sacrament		2	6
		Paid for a Hat (to Mr. Chase)	1	2	–
		Paid I. Spier, for T. Marlow's Schooling to Midsumr. next		6	–
		Paid Mr. J. Simmonds 1 B. Pollard, & ½ Sack Bran for Pigs		6	2
			2	2	8
July	3	Paid Farmer John Hobbs, Highway Rate up to last Michs.		8	6
		Journey to Town and expences	1	5	–
		Dinner at the Globe Tavern		6	6
		Mr. Spence, for drawing a Tooth		10	6
		Paid Mr. Wallen, for Bread &c. to 17th June		13	9¾
		Paid Mr. Chase, his Bill		7	–
		Paid Collier for work in Garden &c.		2	4
		Washing 1/––Powder–Sugar 1/––Eggs 6d.– Lems. &c. 6d		3	–
	25	Paid for making 8 Shirts & marking them at 2/–		16	–
		Paid for a piece of cloth for a Sleeve to one of the shirts		2	3
		3 Pans of milk 1/–		3	–
		Paid for black currents 1/– – for a Rubber for the Scythe 4½		1	4½
		Journey to Town & back again	1	3	–
		2 pair black Silk Stockings	1	10	–
		Smelling-Bottle 2/6 – Tooth Brushes &c. 2/–		4	6
		Lost at Cards		6	–
		Paid Winter & Shee, Taylors, their Bill, to 8th July Inst.	10	4	3
		Paid for a Pair of Gloves		1	6
		Paid for Washing in Town		1	–
		Paid Mrs. Browne for washing &c. omitted		6	4
		Paid Ab. Toby, Smith, his Bill to 29th Jan. 91	1	14	10
	28	Paid same time for news-papers to 31st inst.	1	–	2
	30	Paid Dame Payne for children's Schooling to this day		5	6
		Paid Mr. Crutwell his Bill to 17th June	2	15	6
		Paid Mr. Fennemore, repairing an Umbrella		4	6
			24	16	4¼

D. Davies, 1791, in P. Horn, *A Georgian Parson and His Village*, 1981

2 Britain's food in Defoe's time

In the 1720s people ate mostly food which came from near by, which meant their diet was different from one part of Britain to another. It was not possible to move meat long distances and keep it fresh, so it either had to be preserved, like bacon, or taken live, like beef.

Grain

Most of us still eat more grain than anything else (even if it is disguised in breakfast cereals or hidden in our sausages). In Defoe's time grain was much the biggest part of nearly everyone's daily diet. Almost every home had an oven. Women in southern England baked wheat into light brown loaves but further north they used rye to make coarse black bread. Scots ate their grain mostly as oatcakes or porridge.

Potatoes

Today the potato is the second largest part of our diet. In the 1720s it was the main food in Ireland and some parts of the Scottish Highlands. It was beginning to be grown as well in fields around Glasgow and Lancashire towns.

Beef

For country people beef was a rare (and tough) treat after they had killed an ox which was no longer fit to pull a plough. Beef for better-off townspeople walked to town on the hoof. Cattle drovers in the mountains of Scotland or Wales fitted the animals with iron shoes before setting off. Scottish drovers sold some beasts at Falkirk and Dalkeith. They drove the rest on down the Pennines, living on oats and black pudding. The drive ended at the yearly fair at St Faith's near Norwich. Local farmers fattened up the cattle before the last walk to the London slaughterhouses.

Mutton

Sheep grazed on all the low hills but they came to market in the same way. The meat was tough and stringy and good only for pies and stews.

Bacon

Bacon was the most common meat because pigs were cheap to feed. They were kept in woods around dairy farms where they were given the wheys, the watery part of milk left over from cheese making. They could also be fed the remains of barley used to make ale in the thousands of small breweries. Owners killed their pigs on the spot and salted or smoked the bacon so that it would keep and could be carried by pack-horse or wagon.

Food and markets in the 1720s
A

This modern map shows all the main specialist food districts and the most important fairs for corn and cattle. The three extracts are from Daniel Defoe's Tour Thro' the whole Island of Great Britain, *1724–6, and show how different foods reached London.*

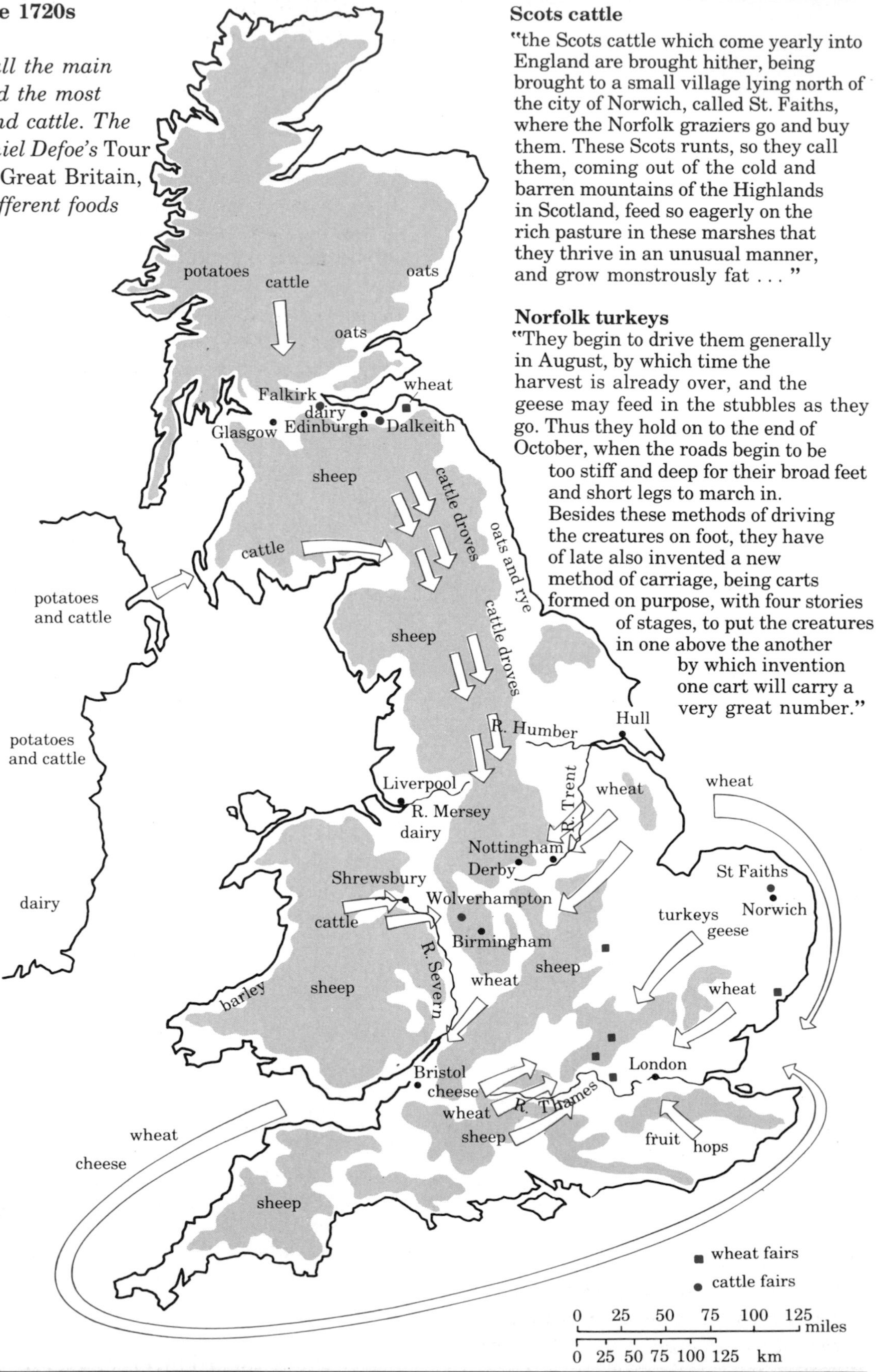

Wiltshire produce

"All the lower part of this county, and also of Gloucestershire adjoining, is full of large feeding farms which we call dairies, and the cheese they make. . . . Of this a vast quantity is every week carried to the river of Thames by land carriage, and so by barges to London.

Besides this, the farmers . . . send a very great quantity of bacon up to London . . . the hogs being fed with the vast quantity of whey, and skimmed milk, which farmers have to spare, and which must, otherwise, be thrown away.

But this is not all, for . . . they sow a very great quantity of barley, which is carried to the markets of Abingdon, at Farrington and such places, where it is made into malt and carried to London."

Scots cattle

"the Scots cattle which come yearly into England are brought hither, being brought to a small village lying north of the city of Norwich, called St. Faiths, where the Norfolk graziers go and buy them. These Scots runts, so they call them, coming out of the cold and barren mountains of the Highlands in Scotland, feed so eagerly on the rich pasture in these marshes that they thrive in an unusual manner, and grow monstrously fat . . ."

Norfolk turkeys

"They begin to drive them generally in August, by which time the harvest is already over, and the geese may feed in the stubbles as they go. Thus they hold on to the end of October, when the roads begin to be too stiff and deep for their broad feet and short legs to march in. Besides these methods of driving the creatures on foot, they have of late also invented a new method of carriage, being carts formed on purpose, with four stories of stages, to put the creatures in one above the another by which invention one cart will carry a very great number."

Map labels: potatoes, cattle, oats, oats, wheat, Falkirk, dairy, Glasgow, Edinburgh, Dalkeith, sheep, cattle, cattle droves, oats and rye, cattle droves, potatoes and cattle, sheep, potatoes and cattle, R. Humber, Hull, Liverpool, R. Trent, wheat, wheat, R. Mersey, dairy, Nottingham, Derby, St Faiths, dairy, Shrewsbury, Wolverhampton, turkeys, Norwich, cattle, Birmingham, geese, sheep, R. Severn, wheat, wheat, barley, sheep, wheat, sheep, London, Bristol, cheese, R. Thames, wheat, sheep, fruit, hops, wheat, cheese, sheep

■ wheat fairs
● cattle fairs

```
0   25   50   75   100   125
                           miles
0  25 50 75 100 125  km
```

■ land over 200 metres

Dairy foods

As today, townspeople ate cheeses made in Gloucester, Cheshire and places in the west of Britain. Milk, butter and vegetables went bad quickly so most towns had nearby market gardens and a riverside area where cows were kept. In many towns some cows were kept in stables squeezed between houses and shops. Milk was sold from open pails.

Markets and fairs

There were a thousand towns which had a weekly market. The stall-holders obtained some goods locally. The rest were supplied by merchants who had filled their warehouses with goods they had bought at the annual fairs held in only a few dozen places.

Imports

Today, half of our food comes from abroad. In Defoe's time the only important foreign items were sugar and tea. Sugar was grown by slave labour in the Caribbean and sent in ships to Britain in barrels as brown sticky muscovados. Refinery workers in Bristol and Glasgow boiled the muscovados to produce sugar crystals.

Tea came mostly from China. In the 1720s it found its way only into the cups of the wealthy. Fifty years later it was drunk by nine-tenths of the British. The government put high customs duties on tea, so thousands of people helped to smuggle it in small waterproof bags from ships to the towns.

Health hazards
B

You can learn much about the past from novels. Tobias Smollett wrote Humphrey Clinker *in 1771. Here Mr Bramble, who is a countryman, explains his disgust at the way milk is sold in London.*

1 *What do you think Mr Bramble meant by 'foul rinsings'?*
2 *Supposing you were doing a project on eighteenth-century health, how would you use this extract as evidence of health conditions?*

"... carried through the streets in open pails, exposed to foul rinsings discharged from doors and windows, spittle, snot and tobacco-quids from foot passengers, overflowings from mud carts, spatterings from coach wheels, dirt and trash chucked into it by rogueish boys for the joke's sake, the spewings of infants ..."
T. Smollett, *Humphrey Clinker*, 1771

3 *Look at Source A opposite. Where did people eat mostly a) wheat, b) oats, c) rye, d) potatoes?*
4 *After London, which were the two most important food-consuming districts?*

Sources A–B
7 *One eighteenth-century man described London as the stomach of Britain. Use the sources to explain what he meant.*

5 *Why did Wiltshire farmers specialise in cheese and bacon rather than butter and pork?*
6 *Why was Norwich the main cattle market for London and not London itself?*

3
Food producers in Defoe's time

Seven out of every ten people earned their living from agriculture. This unit shows how the ways of making a living changed as you moved down the social scale. The explanations of the words in the margins will help you to understand the other units on agriculture.

Landowners

The great families

In Defoe's time the wealth of the richest families came from the land they owned. There were just about four hundred of these top families. They were those who made about £10,000 a year from renting their lands to tenant farmers. Source A shows all the land the Coke family owned in Norfolk. They also had thousands of acres in other parts of England. Together these lands made up the Coke 'estate'.

At different times the head of the Coke family was an old lady and a young boy. But the rents were still paid to the steward who managed the estate. Some landowners left everything to the steward and spent most of their time in London. These men had great influence in Parliament. Those with titles were members of the House of Lords. Their sons and relatives made up the greatest number of MPs in the House of Commons. Two of the Cokes' neighbours in the 1720s were the Prime Minister (Sir Robert Walpole of Houghton) and the minister in charge of foreign affairs (Lord Townshend of Raynham).

The gentry

After the few hundred great landowners came a few thousand gentry families. Most had small estates in one or two parishes and they, too, lived by renting land. If he owned most of the land in a single village, the gentleman would be thought of as 'the squire' and his home as 'the hall'. Such members of the gentry became Justices of the Peace (JPs) for their county. From the hall the squire would combine his work as a JP and a landowner. On the same day he might be fining the local poacher and seeing one of his tenants about a new barn.

Husbandmen

In the 1700s, when people spoke of growing crops or keeping animals they called it husbandry. A man who did these things was a husbandman.

Farmers

The word 'farmer' was used for the husbandman (or sometimes his widow) who paid rent for farmland. The amount was fixed in a lease agreement, which would last for a number of years, and was signed by the farmer and the landowner or his steward. The landowner promised to keep the farm buildings, roads and fences in good repair while the farmer agreed to keep the land and animals in good condition.

Freeholders

There were a small number of husbandmen (and a few women) who did own their own land so they were not farmers but freeholders. Their numbers went down in the eighteenth century.

Labourers

Some farmers and freeholders worked their lands with help only from their families but most had a team of workers. A fairly small farm would need at least a cowman, a shepherd, a ploughman, a dairymaid and a thresher as well as a kitchen maid.

Farm servants

Many of these workers were farm servants who were taken on for twelve months at a very low wage because they slept and ate in the farmhouse. A farmer might go to a 'mop' or hiring fair for a new servant. There he would look out for people looking for work and a sign of their trade, such as a piece of cow hair or straw stuck in their hat.

Day labourers

Farm servants were single young men and women. When he married, a skilled and healthy man would take regular work as a day labourer and, if he was lucky, live in a small cottage which was tied to the job. Less skilled and less healthy men might find work only at harvest time or as part of a gang which hired itself out to mend roads or buildings.

Commoners

Some of these families, where the adults had no regular work, could keep themselves because they had common rights. This meant that the family had been allowed to keep a cow and a few other animals on the village common land for longer than anyone could remember. It was generally understood that commoners would collect dead timber for firewood and glean, or rake up, the ears of corn left after the harvest.

Women

A woman's working life depended on her husband's position in society. The main task of wives of great landowners and gentry was to see that the household was run smoothly by servants. In London they were important in fashionable society but in the country they rarely left the home because the only means of travel was by horseback which was thought unsuitable for gentle ladies.

Farmers' wives

Wives of tenant farmers were usually hard-working and business-like because they took charge of the dairy work, the poultry and the orchards. The dairy had to be run like a factory. Milkmaids were sent into the fields to milk before dawn and then put to work turning heavy wooden churns to make butter or cheese. From mid afternoon to mid evening the whole job was done again. The farmer's wife would travel to market with the butter, cheese, eggs, and fruit and keep the accounts for this side of the farm's work. Many records show that, if their husbands died first, women often took charge of the whole farm themselves.

Labourers' wives

A day labourer's wife or cottager's wife had no servants, so that she spent much of her time making bread and looking after the children. It was quite common to have five or six living at any time, although not all would survive to be teenagers. But such a woman also had to contribute to the family's keep. She would grow food and keep animals in the garden or on the common and earn money as a field worker at harvest and other busy times.

Countryside classes

A

This map shows the land owned by the Coke family at the end of the eighteenth century.

1 *In how many villages were the Cokes important landowners?*
2 *What would have been a major problem for the steward managing the Coke estate?*

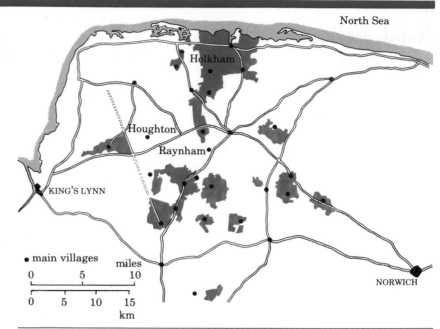

B

Parson David Davies, whose accounts were printed in Unit 1, collected information about the standard of living of labourers in his parish in 1787.

3 *What was the price per lb of candles?*
4 *There is no mention of money for rent or for fuel. Suggest reasons for this.*
5 *Which items would not have appeared in this family's diet in Defoe's time (fifty years before David Davies wrote this)?*
6 *Why do you think the village labourer had regular work for only eight months of the year? What jobs might he have done in the other four?*

Weekly Expences of a Family, consisting of a Man and his wife, and five Children, the eldest eight years of age, the youngest an Infant.

	s	d
FLOUR: 7½ gallons, at 10d. per gallon	6	3
Yeast, to make it into bread, 2½d.: and salt 1½d.		4
Bacon, 1 lb. boiled at two or three times with greens: the pot-liquor, with bread and potatoes, makes a mess for the children		8
Tea, 1 ounce, 2d.; – ¾ lb. sugar, 6d.; ½ lb. of butter or lard 4d.	1	0
Soap, ¼ lb. at 9d. per lb.		2¼
Candles, ⅓ lb. one week with another at a medium, at 9d.		3
Thread, thrum, and worsted, for mending apparel, &c.		3
Total	8	11¼

Weekly Earning of a Man and his Wife, viz.

	s	d
The man receives the common weekly wages 8 months in the year	7	0
By task-work the remaining 4 months he earns something more; his *extra* earnings, if equally divided among the 52 weeks in the year, would increase the week wages about	1	0
The wife's common work is to bake bread for the family, to wash and mend clothes, and to look after the children; but at bean-setting, haymaking, and harvest, she earns as much as comes one week with another to about		6
Total	8	6

D. Davies, *The Case of Labourers in Husbandry Stated and Considered*, 1795

4 Husbandry – old and new

Here we look at the differences between husbandmen who used traditional methods and those who were called 'improvers'. An improver could make each acre of land produce more food and earn him more money than his old-fashioned neighbour.

Old-fashioned husbandry

Imagine a traditional husbandman who did things in the way his father and grandfather had taught. He has three kinds of land: pasture, meadow and plough-land. The pasture was grassland for sheep and cattle. He could not remember anyone ever ploughing it up and sowing new grass seeds. The meadow was left for grass to grow until he could cut it for hay. The plough-land (or arable) was used for growing grain such as oats, wheat and barley. It was divided into three areas which were sometimes made up of strips and sometimes of fields. He kept his land divided in this way so that he could follow the ancient three-course rotation:

Three-course rotation

	area 1	area 2	area 3
1720	wheat	barley/oats	fallow
1721	barley/oats	fallow	wheat
1722	fallow	wheat	barley/oats
1723	?	?	?

He knew that every third year arable land must lie fallow when nothing should be sown. Unless he did this there would soon come a time when he would reap no more grain than he had sown as seed. He did not know that this was because the land became starved of chemical plant foods, especially nitrogen. He did know that animal manure would help the next crop so he put cattle or sheep on the fallow to eat the stubble and the weeds. But the weeds could not feed many animals and so he had only a little manure.

Alternate husbandry

Now imagine an improving husbandman. He would plan for more years ahead so that he could use the new alternate husbandry. The idea was to bring the meadows *and* pastures *and* plough-lands into *one* rotation system. That way all the land would be used alternately for grains and grass. When it was time to grow grass the husbandman used specially selected seeds of grass or clover. This gave fresh summer food and hay for the winter.

Turnips

Alternate husbandry was used in all parts of Britain but the leaders were the husbandmen of Norfolk. Their light sandy soil was just right for the turnip. This humble vegetable was brought to Norfolk from Holland in the 1650s and it was the key to longer rotations. These were often six or seven years long but the one which got the most publicity was the Norfolk four-course system:

Four-course rotation

	area 1	area 2	area 3	area 4
1720	wheat	turnip	barley/oats	grass/clover
1721	turnip	barley/oats	grass/clover	wheat
1722	barley/oats	grass/clover	wheat	turnip
1723	grass/clover	wheat	turnip	barley/oats
1724	?	?	?	?

The turnip appears where the traditional husbandman would have left land fallow. Turnips did not add to soil starvation and they actually drew in some nitrogen from the atmosphere. And, whatever humans thought of them, sheep and cattle enjoyed turnips as winter food. So the improver could keep more animals and have more manure to spread. He was not so lucky if his farm was on clay soils because the turnips rotted in the wetter earth. Europe came to the rescue again in the late eighteenth century with the turnip's tough cousin, the swede.

Marling

Every so often, the improver had his land marled. He paid a gang of labourers to dig a pit down to the clay below the light topsoils. The men then spread the clay over the fields to make the earth firm. A good marling was expensive but it helped to hold in the roots of grain or grass for about twenty years.

Fertilisers

Improvers also spread fertilisers on their land. These included crushed bone-meal from butchers, combings from wool known as shoddy, seaweed and night-soil, which was carried in carts out of towns in the days before sewers and WCs.

Water-meadows

A husbandman who owned land near a river could improve his grass by making a water-meadow. He dammed the river in the early spring so that it flooded. This made the grass grow early, which meant that he could turn his cattle out on to the meadow up to six months earlier than his neighbours.

Improvements in Norfolk and Suffolk

A

This account appeared in a handbook on husbandry published in 1750.

1 *According to the writer, when were turnips first used in these counties?*
2 *Explain the ways in which he says turnips can bring profits to husbandmen.*

"It is in these two Counties beyond all others in *England*, that some fine improvements in Husbandry may be seen, to the infinite Profit of both Landlords and Tenants: Which have been brought to pass within these fifty Years, ever since they learned the Way of sowing and houghing Turneps in their open, common, sandy, Fields, which has not only proved a Preparative to their succeeding Crops of Barley, but such Turnep-Crops give them a vast first Profit besides, by feeding their horned Beasts with them to the Degree of Fatting; so as to fit them in a compleat Manner for a *Smithfield* Market, where Thousands of them are sold in a Year ..."
W. Ellis, *The Modern Husbandman*, 1750

5
Meat for the market

In Unit 2 we saw that most meat in Defoe's time came from small cattle and sheep which were tough enough to live on high ground. In other parts of the country animals were kept mainly for their manure, wool, leather and milk. In this unit we look at the specialist animal breeders who first showed how to produce meat for the market.

Breeding

It was common for the upper classes to spend heavily on hunting and going to the races. By Defoe's time many towns had their own racecourses and, by 1780, the St Leger, the Oaks and the Derby had all started. It meant good business for the horse-breeders who were expert at 'breeding in' the qualities a horse needed.

'Breeding in' began when mares with a good feature, such as a strong back, were mated with stallions with the same feature. Foals born with good backs would be mated with each other. After a few generations the breeder could feel fairly sure that the special feature would appear in all future foals.

Robert Bakewell (1725–1795)

Around 1750 some husbandmen, mostly in the hunting country of the Midlands, began to try in-breeding with farm animals. The best known was Robert Bakewell who was tenant of Dishley Grange Farm near Leicester. Bakewell set out to breed animals which would fetch bigger prices. His first aim was to produce a cow which would give 'not fifty stones divided into thirty stones in coarse boiling and twenty stones in roasting pieces but vice-versa'. He produced a breed of fat Longhorn cattle but he made little profit because many of the cows had dead calves.

New Leicesters

Bakewell had more success when he tried to breed a sheep with lots of fatty meat. The result was the New Leicester breed of round barrel-shaped beasts producing 'coal-heaver's mutton'.

Butchers did not buy this mutton direct from Dishley Grange but from the many husbandmen who began to keep flocks of New Leicesters. They started by hiring a ram from Bakewell to mate with their ewes. It was a profitable business. In 1789 Bakewell's three best New Leicester rams were hired for 400 guineas (a guinea was 21 shillings) each.

Large hiring fees were helped by Bakewell's skill in publicity. He invited writers and painters to Dishley Grange where they were well wined and dined. They repaid him by describing his animals in magazines and painting them in oils. Each year he held viewings, rather like fashion parades, to show off the rams for hire.

Other breeders

Other husbandmen were keen to follow Bakewell's example. Near Darlington two brothers, Robert and Charles Colling, took up cattle breeding. They produced Durham Shorthorns which were good for both beef and milk. In Northumberland, George Culley crossed the local hill sheep with New Leicesters to produce animals which gave wool and mutton. In Sussex John Ellman spent many years changing the local Southdown sheep from long-legged animals into the short, round animals you can still find in the south of England.

Breeding

A

A painting of the New Leicester rams on parade at the hiring show at Dishley Grange, 1809.

1 *Does the picture give any clues that sheep breeding was a profitable business?*
2 *Why are the labourers looking to the right? Might someone not in the picture be standing there? What would his job be?*

Thomas Weaver, *Hiring out Rams at Dishley, Leicestershire,* 1809

B

One of Bakewell's neighbours specialised in pig-breeding. This description appeared in a report on agriculture in Leicestershire.

3 *Why should anyone want to breed such an unpleasant-looking beast?*
4 *What does this tell you about the influence of Robert Bakewell?*

"The improvement of hogs in Leicestershire has been attended to with the same care and success as that of other live-stock. At Dishley . . . I have seen there a hog of small size, when lean, fatted to 20 score weight, or more; his length, height and thickness being nearly equal; belly touching the ground, the legs being enveloped in fat, and the eyes scarcely to be seen for fat, the whole appearing a solid mass of flesh."

William Pitt of Wolverhampton, *A general view of Agriculture of the County of Leicester,* 1809

C

Weight of animals brought to market.

5 *What does this diagram tell you about the importance of improved breeding?*
6 *Which of these animals did most to improve the diet of working people?*

Sources A–C

7 *Was selective breeding the only reason for the changes shown in Source C?*

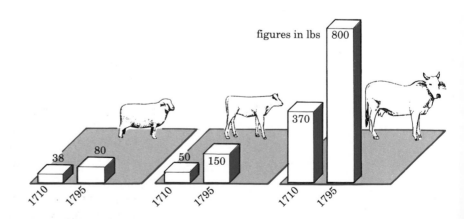

figures in lbs

38 1710
80 1795
50 1710
150 1795
370 1710
800 1795

6
Farm machinery

Improvers did not use much machinery on their farms. Many machines were invented but farmers were only interested in those which were reliable and saved money on wages.

Jethro Tull (1674–1741)

Jethro Tull was the tenant of Mount Prosperous Farm in Berkshire and the odd man out among improvers. He actually thought the crop rotations and marling did no good. For Jethro Tull the secret of good husbandry was to plant crops in rows and keep the soil free of weeds. This was not popular with his farm servants. It meant back-breaking work to put seeds into holes made with a pointed stick and then push-pulling a clumsy wheeled hoe between the rows. It was far easier to use the old way of broadcasting, by scattering the seeds with a sweep of the arm.

To deal with the grumbles Tull invented a seed drill and a hoe which could be drawn by a horse. In 1731 he described these machines in a book, *Horse-hoeing Husbandry*. The book became well known but the machines were not widely used for another hundred years. They broke down too often on heavy soils and it was cheaper to use labourers paid a few pence a day.

Horse ploughing

A more important invention was the Rotherham plough which was made in workshops like the one started by Robert Ransome in Ipswich. They were lighter and easier to steer than village-made ploughs with their clumsy square wooden frame. All the parts were wood, except for the knife, or coulter, at the front. Rotherham ploughs were built on a triangular frame with many iron parts so they could be drawn by horses instead of a team of oxen. Horses trampled much less soil and a skilled ploughman could turn over a field much more quickly.

Winnowing and threshing

The machines which came to be most widely used were those which caused most unemployment. In Defoe's time labourers worked all winter threshing and winnowing in the barn. The thresher cracked his flail on bundles of corn on the floor to shake out the seeds. The straw was taken away and the thresher then swept up the grain mixed with chaff, which was the dried-up ears and a lot of dust. The winnower then took over. He worked in a draught, throwing shovel-loads of sweepings into the air so the light chaff blew away and the grain fell at his feet.

Imagine all the work and time needed to thresh and winnow wheat from even a small field and you can see how farmers could save money with machinery. Winnowing machines first appeared in the 1770s and the first reliable threshing machine was invented by John Meikle in 1786. By the 1820s they were in wide use and labourers lost an important way of earning some winter wages.

The thresher's work
A

This drawing was published in a book written to explain country life to townspeople.

1 *Why does the barn have its doors in the centre?*

2 *What winnowing equipment can you see?*

3 *Why was threshing so important to agricultural labourers? Does your answer throw any light on Source B in Unit 3?*

Jeffreys Taylor, *The Farm*, 1832

B

About the same time, threshing machines were coming into widespread use, as shown in this article from a magazine which was widely read by the landowning classes.

4 *How does the time of the year help to explain the cause of the riots?*

5 *Which words help you to understand the writer's attitude to the riots? Do you think his readers would share his opinion?*

"Some tumultuous proceedings have recently taken place throughout the county of *Kent*, arising from the outrageous conduct of agricultural mobs of the lower classes going about demolishing the thrashing machines of the farmers. A body of men, amounting to upwards of 200 in number, lately assembled at the respective residences of Sir Henry Oxenden, Sir Henry Tucker Montresor, Mr. Kelcey, Mr. Holtum, and Mr. Sankey, farmers, and violently broke into their barns, where they destroyed the thrashing machines they found in them."

Gentleman's Magazine, October 1830

Two ploughs
C

This hand-built plough was made in the early 1900s by a craftsman using methods dating back before the Rotherham plough.

D

This 'factory'-made plough is an improved plough of the 1780s.

6 *How many differences can you find between the two ploughs?*

7 *What advantages would the improved plough have over the village-made one?*

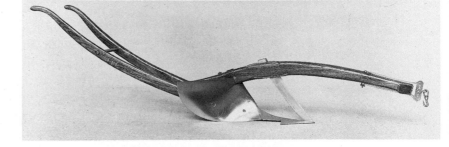

7
Open and enclosed villages

Look first at the two maps of a Lincolnshire village. The map in Source A shows the village before 1769, and it could have been just the same in Defoe's day. Map B shows the village after it was enclosed in 1769. This unit explains what enclosure was and why improvers were in favour of it.

The open-field village

Before 1769 all the husbandmen in Waltham had homes in the village centre. If you look at 'the old enclosures' at the bottom left of Source A you will see a few small fields on each side of the street where their farmhouses would be.

The map should remind you of the plan in the old-fashioned husbandman's head in Unit 4. It has three fields for a three-course rotation and some of the land would have been used for common pasture. Several landowners owned land in these fields between them and rented it to tenant farmers. It did not come in parcels surrounded by hedges but in strips which were divided by a line of grass known as a baulk. You can get some idea of how these strips were laid out from Source C. They run in different directions, which might be up and down the hillside.

Each year the husbandmen would meet to work out what to sow in the fields and how many animals they could keep on the common pasture. There were probably old customs which let the labourers keep pigs and collect firewood on the north furze. A few poor labourers might be squatters in huts there.

Why would an improver in Waltham find it difficult to:

1 Alternate crops and animals on the same land;
2 Rotate them over four to seven years;
3 Breed selectively;
4 Make a water-meadow;
5 Marl or manure;
6 Use a seed drill?

It is easy to see that an improver would prefer the village as it was in Map B where each landowner has a large block. He would then put in hedges and fences to divide it into separate farms.

Enclosed villages

In Defoe's day most villages looked like the one in Map A. The only county with enclosures was Kent, which never had open fields. In other districts there were a few enclosed villages, usually where there was only one landowner who could do as he pleased. In some others all the landowners had agreed among themselves to enclose the whole village. This was known as 'enclosure by consent'. It did not happen often because there were too many objectors.

The objections might have come from a landowner who did not want to have to pay for new fences, farmhouses and roads. Often there were bitter objections from people who feared they would lose the right to use common land after enclosure. Because of the objections, most villages were not enclosed at all or partly enclosed.

By the 1760s more landowners wanted to enclose their estates fully so that they could ask tenants on the new enclosed farms for more rent. When they could not get their neighbours to enclose by consent, they petitioned Parliament for an Act to order the change.

Waltham

A

This map of the village before 1769 was redrawn in 1959 from the original award map of 1771. A chain was 22 yards (about 20 metres).

1 *How far was it to walk from the centre to a strip on the edge of East Field?*
2 *What is furze?*

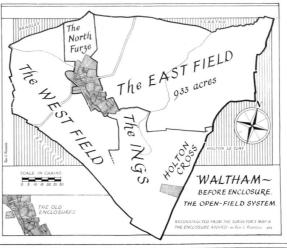

Rex C. Russell, *The Enclosures of Holton-Le-Clay, Waltham and Tetney,* 1959

B

The enclosed village, 1771.

3 *Who are the largest landowners?*
4 *What has happened to the furze?*

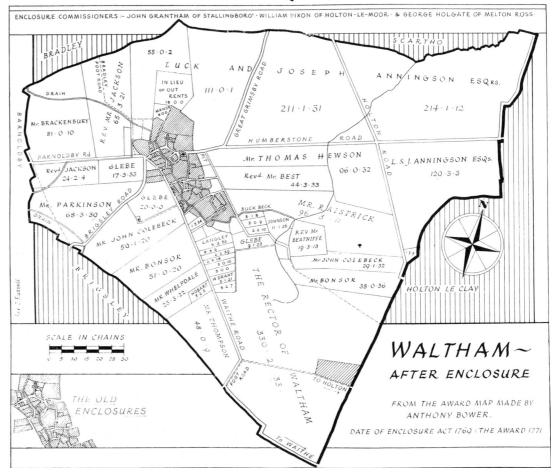

The strip system

C

'Furlong' is an old term for furrow length and became fixed at 220 yards. This 1781 map of Strettington does not show contours.

5 *Suggest reasons for the directions of the strips.*
6 *Where are the farmhouses?*

8
Parliamentary enclosure

This unit is about parliamentary enclosures, how they were carried out and how they changed village life. Refer to the enclosure award map in Unit 7.

Enclosure Acts

The largest group of men in Parliament were landowners. Their favourite coffee-houses buzzed with chat about rents and how they might be improved by enclosures. MPs were almost always willing to pass an Enclosure Act when a petition came in. They made one main condition. The petition had to be signed by the owners of four-fifths of the land. Villagers who only rented land had no say.

Between 1760 and 1820 Parliament passed about 3,500 Enclosure Acts. One-third of these simply finished the process in partly enclosed villages: the other two-thirds dealt with the whole village, open fields and common land together. Most of these full enclosures took place in the English Midlands.

The commissioners

To deal with the details Parliament appointed two to seven commissioners for each enclosure. Their first task was to have the village surveyed. Then they listened to everyone who said he had a claim to land. The biggest problem was sorting out who had rights to use the commons.

The commissioners also dealt with tithes. The vicar, or rector, usually still had the ancient right to collect a tithe, or a fraction, of the food from each farm. It was up to the commissioners to convert, or 'commute', this either into a cash payment to be made each year or into a piece of land or 'glebe' given to the rector.

The Enclosure Award

The work might take two or more years before the commissioners made their award with a map which showed the position of each enclosure. The award was expensive. It often cost the landowners as much as they would get in three years' rent from the new enclosed farms. But they could not put up rents until they had built the new farmhouses, barns, fences and roads.

After enclosure

Wealthy landowners could pay these costs out of savings or a bank loan. Smaller landowners might have to sell their land. Many freeholders, too, sold up to landowners and went on farming as their tenants. On the whole tenant farmers and landowners all earned more after enclosure. Weekly labourers often did well, too. Many were able to move into newly built cottages near their master's new farm.

On the other hand part-time labourers often lost the chance to live on the common or keep animals there. Even if the award had given them an acre or two they could not afford to have it fenced. For a few years after enclosure there was plenty of work on road-making, fencing and building. But the number of extra jobs did not go up as fast as the rise in Britain's population. In the north of England it was possible to find work in nearby mines and factories. In the south there was little industry and many were forced into unemployment for months at a time.

Arthur Young's views on enclosure

A

The best known writer on agriculture of the time was Arthur Young. His books often discussed the pros and cons of enclosure. Here he considers extra profits from sheep.

"About Bendsworth in the Vale of Evesham, the average fleece is 9 lb in the enclosures, but only 3½ lb in the open fields. Can there be a stronger argument for enclosing? . . . By enclosing you have 9 lb of wool instead of three, that is, one sheep yields as much as three did."
Arthur Young, *Northern Tour*, 1770

B

More employment.

1 *List all the ways in which Young says enclosure gave extra employment.*

"not to speak of the great numbers of men that in enclosed countries are constantly employed in winter in hedging and ditching, what comparison can there be between the open-field system of one half or a third of the lands being in fallow, receiving only three ploughings, and the same portion now tilled four, five, or six times by midsummer, then sown with turnips, those hand-hoed twice, and then drawn by hand and carted to stalls for beasts or else hurdled out in portions for fatting sheep! What scarcity of employment in one case, what a variety in the other!"
Arthur Young, *Political Arithmetic*, 1774

C

Part of a survey of thirty-seven villages. Effects on commoners and other poor villagers.

2 *What were the two main causes of the poor being 'injured'?*

"Effects of enclosure on the poor
WESTERN COLVILLE. Cottagers with rights better off, others lost their cows.
CARLETON. Improved.
NORTHWOLD. Suffer. Twenty who kept stock keep it no longer.
HILLBOROUGH. Suffered.
FINCHHAM. Injured in fuel and cows gone.
SHOULDHAM. Much injured in both fuel and livestock.
GARBOISETHORPE. Poor kept twenty cows before, now none.
MARHAM. They have not suffered.
LEXHAM. Cows lessened.

 In 37 cases, not injured only in 12 . . . a mischief that might easily have been avoided and ought most carefully be avoided in future."
Arthur Young, *An Enquiry into the Propriety of Applying Waste to Better Maintenance of the Poor*, 1802

Sources A–C

3 *Summarise Arthur Young's views on the effects of enclosure.*
4 *Suggest reasons why sheep in the open fields produced less wool than those kept on enclosed farms.*

D

The rise in prices of farm produce compared with prices between 1720 and 1740.

5 *Most enclosures took place between 1760 and 1820. What possible reason is suggested by this graph?*

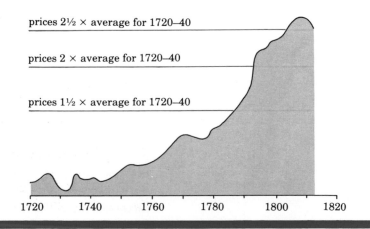

prices 2½ × average for 1720–40

prices 2 × average for 1720–40

prices 1½ × average for 1720–40

1720 1740 1760 1780 1800 1820

9
Spreading the word

This unit looks at four ways of encouraging husbandmen to take up improvements: the influence of their landowners, agricultural shows, writings by men such as William Marshall and Arthur Young, and the Board of Agriculture.

'Turnip Townshend' (1674–1738)

The Townshend estate records show that new rotations were tried there in 1673 and that turnips were grown by 1706. That makes it odd that people used to think that Lord Townshend was the first to experiment with turnips after he left his government position in 1730 and came home to Norfolk to run the estates himself. Still, 'Turnip Townshend' does deserve a place in the history books for making his tenant farmers take up improvements. He would give them a long lease of twenty-one years rather than the usual seven, but only if they agreed to marl their land and use a rotation which gave plenty of turnips and other winter food.

Coke of Holkham (1752–1842)

Thomas Coke was an MP and later Earl of Leicester. But he really wanted to be known as the landowner who gave the greatest encouragement to improving farmers. (His estates are shown in Unit 2.) He used his own 'home farm' for experiments with new crops and machinery such as Jethro Tull's seed drill. He set out to improve on the local sheep which had 'backs like rabbits'. For thirteen years he kept both New Leicesters, bought from Robert Bakewell, and Southdowns, bought from John Ellman. Then he decided that the Southdowns were best for Norfolk and sold off the Leicesters.

Shows at Holkham

Each year Coke held a three- or four-day show at Holkham. There were exhibitions of crops, machinery and animals with prizes for the things Coke approved of. In the evening there were banquets. Coke's tenants rubbed shoulders with famous landowners and leading writers. The tenants were impressed with Coke's friends; and the writers gave him glowing reports.

Shows like Coke's started a fashion for setting up agricultural societies. One of the first was the Dishley Society started by Robert Bakewell for farmers in Leicestershire. Others followed, including the Smithfield Club and the Bath and West Society.

William Marshall

One writer complained that the societies were joined only by the 'superior class' of husbandman. He was William Marshall, who had been an estate agent before he turned to writing. He called for government action to help "the lower classes of husbandman by setting up a board of agriculture for the whole country".

Arthur Young (1741–1820)

Arthur Young was better known than William Marshall. Maybe this was because he was friendly with the most fashionable improvers. He had begun life as a farmer but was too poor to pay for the improvements he wanted. So in 1768 he began writing books on farming (see Unit 8). In 1784 he started a magazine, *The Annals of Agriculture*. Some of the articles were written by 'Ralph Robinson' who was really King George III.

Board of Agriculture

In 1793 the government set up a Board of Agriculture as William Marshall had suggested. The leading civil servant on the Board was its Secretary who had to make surveys of farming in each county. The job went to Arthur Young. Before he died in 1820 he had written surveys of six counties. Two years later the Board ceased to exist. Very few people at the time were really sure that it was the government's job to help agriculture or industry.

The Woburn Show

A

This account describes the show held in 1800 by the Duke of Bedford at his home, Woburn Abbey.

1 *In which ways does this account match the description of Coke's shows given in the narrative?*
2 *Mr Pickford was the head of a famous firm. What was its business?*

B

The engraving below of the Woburn sheep-shearing was done in 1811 from a painting of 1804.

3 *How many different activities can you find in the picture?*
4 *Which different classes of people are mixing together?*
5 *Is there any evidence that this could be the 'New Farm-Yard' mentioned in A?*

"His Grace the Duke of Bedford gave a public breakfast at the Abbey, at nine o'clock.

At about eleven o'clock, His Royal Highness Prince William of Gloucester arrived . . . the company proceeded in a grand cavalcade to the New Farm-Yard, in the park for the purpose of inspecting the sheep-shearing . . .

About three o'clock the company adjourned to dinner; and his Grace entertained near 200 noblemen, gentlemen and yeomen, in the large hall in the ancient part of the Abbey . . .

About six o'clock they left the Abbey and proceeded to the farm-yard again, when a very fine hog, the property of Mr. Pickford, wagon-master, in Market-street, was shown which was supposed to weigh about a hundred stone.

His Grace then conducted the company to a paddock, near the Evergreens, to see some select Devonshire oxen; and from thence they proceeded to the water meadow . . . where there were some very fine Devonshire cows."

Farmers' Magazine, 1800

George Garrard, *Woburn Sheepshearing*, 1811

10
Domestic work in Defoe's time

Look first at the map (Source C) which shows the main manufacturing districts of Defoe's day. Then read about the people who made and sold the goods. Notice that people of the time did not use the word 'industry'. Instead they talked about manufacture (which comes from Latin words meaning making by hand).

Domestic manufacture

Most of the goods shown on the map were made by domestic manufacture. That tells us that the work was done at home, very often by a family team. In most trades men and women worked the same number of hours, and children became part of the team at the age of four or five.

In stocking manufacture the man turned out the flat shape on a knitting frame while his wife and children sewed the seams and sometimes added embroidery. Nail makers worked in small forges next to their homes. The man did the beating and filing while his sons worked the bellows. Potters needed the help of cousins or neighbours because one kiln could keep up to six workers busy.

Specialisation

The map shows that the people of a district usually made one group of goods. But in each district different villages often specialised in one stage of the work. For instance, in woollen manufacture the first stages were carding to straighten out the wool, which was done by children, and spinning which was their mothers' job. The spun yarn was then taken to a larger village or town where it was woven into cloth by men helped by their children. Then it was taken to be washed and dyed.

Employers
Master-craftsmen

Domestic workers almost always worked for a master. The smallest employers were master-craftsmen who made the goods with the help of a few journeymen or daily workers. They were dying out because few had enough money to pay for their raw materials and keep going until they could sell the finished goods.

Merchants

Taking their place as employers were wealthy merchants. They supplied the materials to domestic workers and paid them by piece-rate. In the iron trade the merchants were ironmongers who supplied the iron bars to the forges of the families who made locks, nails or tools. The stocking trade was run by merchant hosiers: domestic knitters collected their thread on Mondays and returned the stockings on Saturdays. In some trades the merchants supplied machines such as knitting frames and charged rent for them.

Workers

Domestic workers had many grievances against employers who paid low piece-rates or charged high machine rents. Some merchants paid wages in 'truck', which meant with food and goods, not cash. Others gave work to unskilled workers so that they could pay them lower wages. There were no permanent trade unions but workers would join together in a 'combination' against the worst masters. When combinations seemed to be getting nowhere the members often rioted to show their strength. At other times the combination asked the local magistrate to fix a fair payment.

Combinations

Middlemen

The biggest merchants had several middlemen working for them. In the woollen trade the middleman was the 'putter-out' or 'bagman'. He went round the villages to hand out wool to the spinners and to collect the yarn they had spun. For selling, merchants used travellers, called 'riders' or 'factors'. The factors sold many of their masters' goods at large trade fairs. The buyers might be stallholders from the towns where there were weekly markets. Or they might be chapmen who were the mobile shopkeepers of their day, taking goods on horseback from one village to the next.

The iron trade of the West Midlands

A

An eighteenth-century nailer's workshop in Dudley.

B

The home an ironmonger built for himself in 1707 in Dudley.

1 *What would working conditions be like inside the workshop?*
2 *What does the ironmonger's house suggest about his business?*

Manufacturing in Defoe's Britain

C

The map shows some of the main centres of manufacture, with Defoe's description of three of them and the fair at Stourbridge. All the extracts come from Defoe's Tour Thro' the whole Island of Great Britain, *1724–6.*

Glasgow

"Here is a manufacture of muslins . . . and they make them so good and so fine, that great quantities of them are sent into England, and sold there at a good price; they are generally striped, and are very much used for aprons by the ladies, and sometimes in head-clothes by the English women of the meaner sort, and many of them are sent to the British plantations."

Sheffield

"the streets narrow, and the houses dark and black, occasioned by the continued smoke of the forges, which are always at work. Here they make all sorts of cutlery-ware, but especially that of edged-tools, knives, razors, axes &c and nails."

Coventry

"The manufacture of tammies [narrow ribbons] is their chief employ, and next to that the weaving of ribbons of the meanest kind, chiefly black."

The fair at Stourbridge

"Here are clothiers from Hallifax, Leeds, Wakefield and Huthersfield in Yorkshire and from Rochdale, Bury &c in Lancashire with vast quantities of Yorkshire cloths, kerseys, pennistons, cotton &c cotton wool; of which the quantity is so great, that they told me there were near a thousand pack-horses of such goods.

I might go on to speak of several other sorts of English manufactures which are brought hither to be sold; as all soughts of wrought iron, and brass from Birmingham; edged tools, knives, &c from Sheffield; glass ware, and stockings from Nottingham and Leicester."

3 *According to Defoe, what is the difference between ladies and women?*

4 *What does Defoe mean by 'plantations'?*

5 *Which of the three towns still produces goods mentioned by Defoe?*

6 *Suggest a possible use for black ribbons made in Coventry.*

7 *Can you suggest reasons why Defoe mentions pack-horses but not carts or wagons in his account of the fair?*

8 *Where would many of the goods bought at Stourbridge Fair go to?*

11
Background to the industrial revolution

List the ways in which modern industry is different from that in Defoe's day. Clearly the twentieth-century person lives in a different world. The first steps towards creating this world took place in the hundred years after Defoe's tour. The changes were so huge that historians have called them the 'industrial revolution'. This unit describes a few of the developments which helped that revolution to take off.

Demand and markets

There were twice as many people in 1830 as in the 1720s, people who needed goods of almost every kind from houses to candles. When more goods are needed we can say that the *demand* has grown or that there is a bigger *market*. Demand and markets can also grow if people have more money. Workers in the 1820s were very poorly paid but many had at least some money wages. So, on average, a family spent two or three times as much on manufactured goods in the 1820s as in the 1720s. Some were quite new products for ordinary people such as soap, bedsteads, curtains, and china ware instead of clay or wooden plates.

Overseas markets

Source B shows the lands where Europeans had colonies across the Atlantic. In 1720 the total population, not counting the American Indian people, was about one million; by 1820 it was about twenty million. The newcomers to those colonies were divided into Europeans, who were farmers, traders, or officials – and Africans, who were slaves. Each year in the eighteenth century about 55,000 slaves were taken there – while about the same number died between capture in Africa and arrival in the colonies.

British people owned many plantations and their ships were the busiest in the slave trade and in supplying settlers. It meant a huge overseas market for British goods. Slaves hoed the ground and cut sugarcane with tools made in the West Midlands. Each year they were handed a new pair of trousers or a petticoat made in Lancashire or around Glasgow. In West Africa, African slave raiders sold prisoners for British-made iron goods, guns and cloth.

Raw materials

Much of the tobacco, sugar, cotton and timber produced by slaves was shipped back to Britain. Tens of thousands of British workers used it to make cloth, furniture or white sugar. Very often these goods were then exported for sale in Europe.

Trade

British merchants were active in other parts of the world, including India and China. Tea came from these countries as well as highly priced goods such as porcelain and wallpaper. At any one time Britain had a fleet of 6,000 merchants ships which gave a great deal of work to sailors and shipbuilders.

Wars

Quarrels over trade caused many wars. Britain and France fought each other every few years over the ownership of colonies in America and India. The wars boosted shipbuilding, the iron industry (for guns) and the textile industry (for uniforms).

Capital

What did merchants do with the money which came from owning an overseas plantation, a merchant company or a shipping business? They spent a good deal on country houses, carriages and luxuries. But they usually had cash left to lend to manufacturers who wanted to buy equipment or open a new work-place. Money which is used to start up industry in this way is called capital.

Banking

The problem in Defoe's day was to get the money from the lender to the borrower. The Bank of England had been set up in 1694. But it did most of its lending to the government, not to private business. So local businessmen started their own banks. Most were outside London and they became known as 'country banks'. One of the first country banks was started in 1759 by Samuel Lloyd, a Birmingham ironmonger. It was then called the Birmingham Bank before it grew into the Lloyds Bank of today.

Slaves and British wealth

A

In 1735 Parliament held an inquiry into overseas trade. This is what one merchant told them. (Guinea is in West Africa; fustians were a mixture of linen and cotton.)

"Mr. John Hardman, merchant, said, that he lives in Liverpool, and trades considerably to Guinea, and the British plantations; and freights the ships, which he sends to those parts, with all sorts of English woollen manufactures . . . and that with these goods, negroes are purchased; and the rest of the freight is of cloths and also iron hoes, etc., and toys fit for the British plantations in the West Indies; for which in return he receives the produce of those islands, and particularly cotton, which is taken in last, and is one-fourth of the loading of most of the ships which come from thence, and is usefully made use of in the manufacturing of fustians."
John Hardman's Evidence to the House of Commons, 15 February 1735

B

America, Africa and Europe, about 1750.

1 *Make a triangular diagram with three points: Britain, West Africa and the West Indies. Show the goods which Mr Hardman's ships carried along the three sides.*
2 *Add a note for each of the three areas saying what Hardman's goods were used for.*

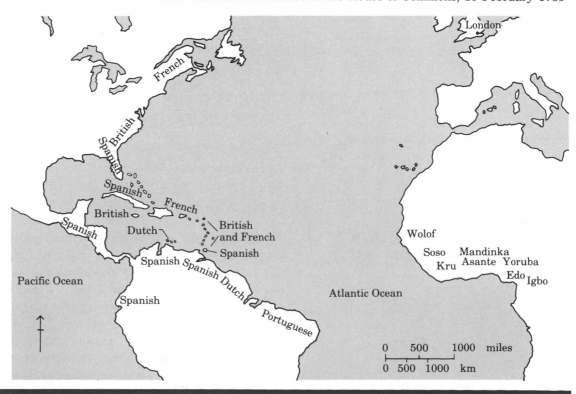

12 Cotton – the new textile

Source A shows four towns important to the textile manufacture of Defoe's time. Eighty years later Exeter and Norwich had grown little; they were centres for the traditional wool industry. Manchester and Nottingham had sprawled into the countryside; they were the centres of new industries based on cotton. The story of 'king cotton' is told in this unit and the next.

Supplies

In the early eighteenth century textile merchants began to import a new raw material which was cheap to produce (by slave labour), light to transport and cleaner than wool. It was cotton. In Lancashire master clothiers used it for the weft (left to right) threads in fustian. Linen was used for the warp threads because cotton snapped too easily. Fustian clothes were cheaper and easier to wash than woollen garments. They also wore out more often which was good for business.

In the East Midlands, around Derby and Nottingham, master hosiers found that cotton could be used instead of silk or wool to make stockings. But it was the silk merchants who had taken the lead in mechanisation.

Thomas Lombe's silk factory

That story had begun with a bit of low cunning when John Lombe went from Derby in 1716 to work in Italy for a man who had a machine for throwing, or making, silk thread. He secretly drew plans and smuggled them home in 1717. Two years later his brother Thomas used them to build a six-storey workshop on the banks of the river Derwent. A water-wheel drove the machinery and three hundred women and children minded the bobbins and tied the threads. The silk yarn was then delivered to merchant hosiers who put it out to their domestic knitters.

Jedediah Strutt (1726–1797)

Silk stockings were bought by men such as David Davies (see Unit 1) but were too expensive for ordinary people. So another Derby man's invention in 1755 turned out to be more important. He was Jedediah Strutt, a merchant hosier, who added a gadget to the stocking-frame so that the knitter could turn out ribbed cotton hose, stronger and warmer than plain. Ribbed stockings made Jedediah Strutt Derby's wealthiest merchant hosier.

John Kay (1704–?1778)

In the Lancashire cloth trade a more humble man took the first step to mechanisation. He was John Kay, a weaver from Bury. In 1733 Kay made a slide for the shuttle to run across the loom with the weft thread. At each end of the slide was a hammer with a cord tied to it. By jerking the cord, the weaver could send the shuttle backwards and forwards. This was John Kay's flying shuttle. It made the weaver's work quicker and less tiring, and meant he could make broadcloth. Other weavers were slow to use the flying shuttle which they feared would mean they had less work. Some raided John Kay's house and he decided to live abroad.

Robert Kay

In 1760 his son, Robert, added a drop-box which could hold several shuttles with different colours. By shifting the drop-box up or down the weaver could change the pattern. After that the flying shuttle became standard. Strutt's knitting frame and Kay's flying shuttle caused a bottleneck in the cotton trade. Knitters and weavers were working so fast that there was a shortage of yarn. Some weavers had to take time off to go round collecting their own. Anyone who invented a machine for spinning would make a fortune.

James Hargreaves (?–1778)

One of the first to try was James Hargreaves, a weaver from Blackburn. About 1764 he made an 'engine', or 'jenny' as the locals called it, by fixing a handle to the spinning wheel. With this, a spinner could turn six or eight spindles at once and still work at home. Jenny makers soon came up with larger machines which used a water-wheel to turn eighty or more spindles.

Domestic spinners were frightened by what the jenny might do to their jobs. In 1768 they wrecked Hargreaves's Lancashire home. To escape trouble he moved to Nottingham and opened a jenny workshop there. But he went bankrupt. The jenny had a weakness. It could only make soft yarn for weft threads in fustian and was quite useless for the knitting frames used in Nottingham.

The growth of four towns 1700–1801
A

The first census was taken in 1801. The other figures were put together from local records made for tax purposes, or death registers.

1 *How does this diagram illustrate the importance of cotton?*

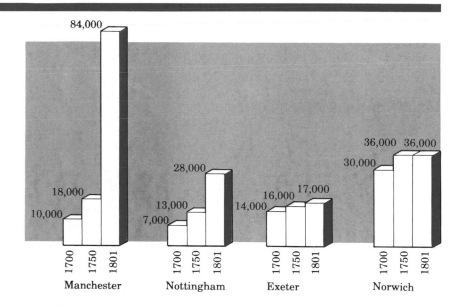

Lombe's silk mill on the River Derwent
B

2 *This has sometimes been called one of the first factories in Britain. What can you see which justifies that label?*
3 *Look closely at the mill to see if you can suggest how power was supplied to the machines inside.*

Engraving from a drawing by J. Nixon, 1798

13
The cotton mills

It is the later 1760s; merchants still cannot find enough strong cotton to hand out to weavers and knitters . . .

Richard Arkwright (1732–1792)

Richard Arkwright began work in Preston as an apprentice barber and wig maker. Afterwards he used his wife's money to set up as a middleman in the wig trade. In the 1760s he was a well-known figure in the market places of Lancashire and Derbyshire as he rode round buying hair from country girls.

Roller spinning

Arkwright must have met many travellers for the fustian and stocking trades and listened to tales about the attempts to make strong yarn by machine. The nearest to success had been Lewis Paul's roller spinning, invented in the 1730s. Try spinning a piece of cotton wool between your thumb and forefinger. The finger moves faster than the thumb. In roller spinning the thread is drawn through pairs of rollers, one going faster than the other.

Lewis Paul never got his machine to work without breakdowns, but Richard Arkwright found two local craftsmen to help him make an improved model in 1768. Arkwright took the plans across the Pennines to Nottingham to Jedediah Strutt who was impressed and paid for a full-sized machine driven by horses. It worked well, so Strutt put up more money for a new mill for his invention in 1771.

Cromford Mill

They chose Cromford, twelve miles away, where there was a good supply of stream water. Local workers soon finished a simple building with four storeys of low rooms. Inside, craftsmen set up rows of rollers linked to one water-wheel. Because it used water power, Arkwright's invention is usually called the water-frame.

New factories

As soon as the first yarn was spun Arkwright sent it to Jedediah Strutt to find out whether it was strong enough for knitting machines. Strutt wrote back that it was. Arkwright had made the big break-through. After three years he had paid off Strutt and was on his way to being the first man to own a chain of factories. He built another mill at Cromford and then eight more in the stocking district. Then he found he could sell his thread to Lancashire for use as warp and he opened mills there too. By the 1790s he had a pot-belly and a knighthood. In 1792 the ex-wigmaker died worth half a million pounds – and a reputation as the founder of the factory system.

By then many had copied him. Jedediah Strutt built his own huge spinning mills in Derby. Many more were built in Lancashire and Scotland. Most looked like Arkwright's box-shaped mills but the machines inside were not usually water-frames: they were mules – the latest invention in spinning.

Samuel Crompton (1753–1827)

It took Samuel Crompton, a Bolton cotton weaver, many months of secret night work to make his first mule in 1779. The mule was a cross between Arkwright's frame and Hargreaves's jenny and it spun a strong but finer thread. It could be driven by the new Boulton and Watt steam-engines just coming onto the market.

The rise of cotton

Strong thread made on power-driven mules put an end to the fustian industry in Lancashire where merchants changed to cloth made entirely of cotton. Around Glasgow the textile industry turned to cotton and gave up its linen speciality. By 1818 there were 337 cotton spinning mills in Britain with an average of 178 workers each. The largest were the New Lanark mills built in Scotland by David Dale. They had 1,600 workers. In England the wealthiest mill-owning family were the Peels. The first Peel sold a small farm to start a mill. By 1800 his son, Sir Robert Peel, owned twenty and a huge fortune which meant he could afford to be an MP. His son, the second Sir Robert, became Prime Minister in the 1840s.

Uses for cotton

At last men and women who could not afford silk or fine linen could wear something else besides heavy woollen clothes. As a magazine said in 1783, 'Every servant girl now has her cotton gown and her cotton stockings.' Just about then John Bell invented a way of using rollers to print coloured patterns on to cotton. So clothes became gayer. There were great benefits for health too. Cotton clothes could be washed and dried easily.

Yorkshire woollens

While cotton boomed, what was happening to wool? The old centres such as Exeter and Norwich went on making cloth but their trade did not grow. It was in Yorkshire that woollen cloth-makers learned two important lessons from the cotton men. One was that bigger profits came from cheaper goods, so they began to specialise in blankets and cloth for everyday wear. They also copied Lancashire inventions. The flying shuttle and drop-box were ideal for patterned wool cloth. Samuel Crompton's mule could be used to spin worsted, the yarn which is used for coats and heavy clothing.

Yorkshire became Britain's leading woollen district making about three-fifths of all the woollen cloth in Britain. In Defoe's time only about a fifth had been made there. Yorkshire wool was an important export. Millions of blankets ended up in America, worn as ponchos or carried on a cowboy's saddle.

Early textile mills

A

An advertisement of 1771.

1 *Who was advertising for these workers?*
2 *Why should he want clock-makers?*
3 *What might attract a weaver from Derby to move with his family to Cromford?*

B

Sir Robert Peel, the Elder, 1786.

4 *Can you suggest reasons why printing by machinery saved colours?*

"Cotton Mill, Cromford, 10th Dec. 1771
WANTED immediately, two Journeymen Clock-Makers, or others that understands Tooth and Pinion well: Also a Smith that can forge and file. – Likewise two Wood Turners that have been accustomed to Wheel-making, Spoke-turning, &c. Weavers residing at the Mill, may have good Work. There is employment at the above Place, for Women, Children &c. and good Wages."
The Derby Mercury, 13 December 1771

"The principal advantage of the English cotton trade arises from our machines, both for spinning and printing; by means of these we can spin both cheaper and better, and we can print not only cheaper and better, but we can save more than half of the colours which before were wasted."
Robert Peel, 1786 (British Museum)

C

This engraving is the earliest surviving picture of Arkwright's first mill at Cromford.

The Mirror, 22 October 1836

D

This engraving of cotton factories in Manchester in 1829 shows how mills changed over fifty years.

Sources C–D

5 *What do the pictures tell you about changes over fifty years in:*
(a) transport, (b) power, (c) the lives of working people?

Lancashire Illustrated from original drawings, . . . 1831

Lancashire and the East Midlands
E

6 *In the 1760s what was the main type of cloth produced in Lancashire? What was it by the 1790s?*

7 *Why did Hargreaves and Arkwright go to the East Midlands?*

8 *What effect did Arkwright's work have on the industry in both districts?*

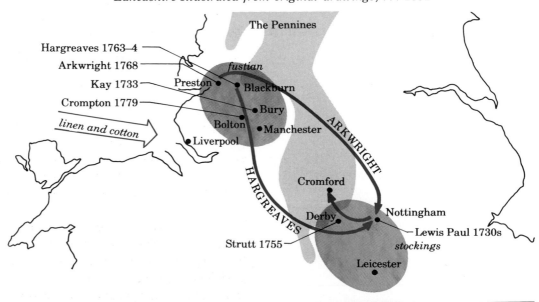

14
In and around the mill

In this unit we look at how the first mills affected working and family life.

Working days

The first textile machines were for spinning. The women and children who had done the job in the domestic industry now had to leave their homes and work in the new mills. Some men worked there too as spinners, or millwrights in charge of machinery. More went on with the work of knitting or weaving in attics and cellars. Women spinners took their own children to the mills. Some were piecers who tied the threads of yarn when they broke; others were scavengers who swept up waste under the machines. So the mills did not break up families but they certainly altered their lives.

For the first time in history time-keeping became important. From Monday to Saturday the factory bell rang out the starting time at 6 or 7 in the morning. The water-wheels and steam engines went on turning for six hours before the one meal break and for six hours after. It was not possible to choose to start later on a dark morning; no longer could families work extra hard from Tuesday to Saturday and give themselves a rest on 'Saint Monday'.

Workers' lives

Some mill-owners like Richard Arkwright built houses for workers, often with a large-windowed room at the top where the father could work at his loom. But in the new factory towns on the coalfields there was little choice. Families rented one or two rooms in a large old house or moved into one of the cheap houses with thin walls and damp floors put up by jerry builders.

The new way of life troubled many mill-owners and their friends who were businessmen, lawyers and clergymen. After all, they thought, these people had come from villages where the JP had dealt firmly with crime and the parson kept an eye out for sin. Older people had been around to watch the behaviour of children and look out for 'immorality' between young men and women. Now the same people lived in their own districts, they had money for drink, few went to church and children roamed about on Sundays.

Factory rules

Most mill-owners believed that harsh rules were needed to tame their workers. They fined them for lateness, swearing, being unwashed or disorderly. A very few believed they had a duty to encourage them to live a decent home life. Richard Arkwright let allotments at cheap rents and gave milk cows as a bonus to his best workers. He and the Strutts started Sunday schools but most mill-owners in large towns took much less trouble.

'Apprentices'

For a few years some mill-owners used child 'apprentices' as cheap labour. They were orphans and other children being cared for by parish overseers of the poor, mostly in the south of England. The parish saved money by handing them over for factory work. In the worst cases apprentices suffered from cruel punishment, dreadful food and overwork. They lived together in crowded 'apprentice houses' and often children on different shifts took turns in the same bed. The best mill-owners never used them and others gave up when they found it cheaper to use the children of local workers. In 1802 Parliament passed an Act limiting apprentices' hours to twelve a day and laying down that boys and girls should have separate dormitories.

The Strutts and their workers

A

Jedediah Strutt's family kept back a sixth of each worker's wages. They called it gift money and paid it at the end of each quarter. Workers who left before then did not get it and those who had broken factory rules had fines or 'forfeits' deducted.

1 *Using these entries, work out some of the rules in the Strutt factory.*

	Forfeit		Gift Money		
	s	d	s	d	
John Sandom *Spinner*	18	6	18	6	For throwing roving bobbins through window into Cut
Mary Pym *Carder*	2	4½	2	4½	Left [5 weeks before end of quarter]
Mary Hall *Picker*	2	3	5	10½	Refusing to spin
Joseph Lievers *Workman*	2	6	31	5	Off 1 day without leave
William Porter *Workman*	4	9½	4	9½	To go towards paying off his debts to Messrs Strut
Hannah Seal *Roller Coverer*	9	11½	14	3	Bad conduct
Frank Orme *Reeler*	5	0	12	11	For Counting hanks wrong
Sarah Philips *Picker*	3	0	7	10½	Ill behaviour
Charles White *Carder*	1	8	19	3½	Forfeited for not giving Notice when he left during Dinner hours
William Bailey *Carder*	2	0	5	8½	For letting the grinding stick go between the Cylinders
Thomas Ball *Workman*	2	6	30	6	Off 1 Day Drinking

Quarterly Wages Books, 1801–5

B

2 *Why was it necessary to hold this school on Sundays?*

3 *What might lie behind the view that the young workers were living in an age of luxury, vice and immorality?*

Sources A–B

4 *What would be a fair description of the Strutts as employers of the 1780s?*

"Mr. Strutt has, (with a Liberality which does Honour to the human Heart) entirely at his own expense, instituted a SUNDAY SCHOOL for the benefit of ALL the Youth of both Sexes employed in his Cotton Mill …; and provides them with all necessary Books, &c for learning to read and write … it becomes the Duty of every thinking Person, in the Age of Refinement, Luxury and Vice, to hold forth an assisting hand, to stop the tide of Immorality."
The Derby Mercury, 25 August 1785

'Apprentices'

C

The man who drew up the 1802 Apprentices Act was the first Sir Robert Peel, of the family described in Unit 13. Here he explains to a committee of MPs that his firm once used apprentices.

5 *List the main evils of the apprentice system described in Sir Robert Peel's statement. What others do you know of?*

6 *What explanation does Peel give for excessive hours?*

"I was struck with the uniform appearance of bad health, and in many cases stinted growth of the children; the hours of labour were regulated by the interest of the overseer, whose remuneration depending on the quantity of the work done, he was often induced to make the poor children work excessive hours, and to stop their complaints by trifling bribes. Finding our own factories under such management … I brought in a Bill … for the regulation of factories containing such apprentices."
Evidence to the Select Committee on the state of children employed in the manufactories, 1816

15 Making iron in Defoe's day

If you took some common iron objects of the 1720s it would be possible to divide them into three groups according to the way they were made:

gun barrels	gun-carriages	swords
fire-back plates	horseshoes	knives
cooking-pots	bolts, locks, chains	files

Cast iron

Objects in the first column needed to be of hard iron which did not wear down. The way to make them was by casting. Iron ore was heated by burning charcoal in a blast furnace (made red-hot with air blasted in by bellows). When it was liquid the workers unplugged the taphole and let the iron run out into moulds made from sand. Some were in the shape of the goods to be sold. Other moulds made blocks of pig iron.

Wrought iron

Pig iron was the raw material for goods in the middle column. If they were made by casting they would be brittle and shatter. That was because the charcoal transferred some traces of carbon to the iron. To take out the carbon, the pig iron had to be reheated into a ball of spongy metal and then beaten or 'wrought' (the old word for 'worked') in a forge.

The forge-worker turned out his wrought iron in bars. This bar iron was passed on to smiths, toolmakers and nailers who heated it again and beat it into the shape they needed.

Steel

Goods in the third column needed to be shatter-proof but very hard. This meant putting back a tiny amount of carbon. Pieces of bar iron were covered with charcoal and heated for several days. Then they were dropped into water to cool. The result was blister steel.

All workers in the iron trades used charcoal. In 1700 charcoal burners were using 300,000 cartloads of wood a year. They stacked it in heaps and burned it slowly until it turned into brittle sticks. Centuries of charcoal burning had turned the Weald in Kent from a forest into an area of open heath. That was why the busiest charcoal districts in Defoe's time were the woods along the River Severn, where most of the pig iron was made.

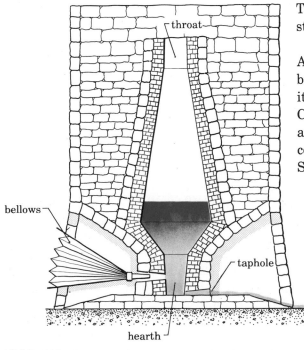

A blast furnace

16
The Darbys and Wilkinson

Cast iron was the first part of the industry to change to large-scale production. The Darby family were the pioneers at the Coalbrookdale works. Later there were other iron-makers such as John Wilkinson.

Abraham Darby I (1677–1717)

Abraham Darby began business life in Bristol as a partner in a firm which made brass goods. In 1707 he patented a new way of casting iron into awkward shapes, such as cooking-pots. In the same year he left Bristol for Shropshire where he rented his own blast furnace at Coalbrookdale near the River Severn.

Coke smelting

At first Darby used charcoal for his blast furnace. Then he experimented with coal. The tar in the coal made it clog so he treated it in the same way as charcoal. Heaps of coal were cooked slowly until they became piles of hard cinders. It was this 'coke' which went into the blast furnace, along with iron ore and limestone.

Coke did not crumble in the same way as charcoal, so heavier weights of ore could be tipped into the furnace, which Darby could build bigger with a stronger blast of air. This gave extra heat so the iron ran out more like liquid than glue. Darby could then cast the liquid into delicate shapes. Coalbrookdale pots, smoothing-irons, and back plates for fires became everyday goods. Many were sent down the River Severn to Bristol for export, especially to Africa.

Richard Ford

Abraham Darby I died in 1717 and the firm was run by his son-in-law, Richard Ford. He improved iron casting so that it could be used for cylinders and pistons in Newcomen steam engines (see Unit 19). Before, these had been made of expensive brass.

Abraham Darby II (1711–1763)

After Richard Ford, Abraham Darby II, the first Abraham's son, became manager. He bought a Newcomen engine to pump water into a mill pond above the wheel which worked the furnace bellows. This made sure of a steady air blast even when the streams were dry. With the improved blast he made pig iron suitable for use by wrought-iron tool-makers in the West Midlands.

Abraham Darby III (1750–1791)

Abraham Darby II's son was manager from 1768 to 1789 and took charge of casting the parts for the world's first bridge made entirely of iron. By 1779 the parts had been joined and bolted together to span the river Severn at Ironbridge.

John Wilkinson (1728–1808)

In 1763 John Wilkinson took over two casting works in Shropshire and one at Bilston, near Wolverhampton. In 1774 he invented a new cannon-lathe which could bore a barrel down the centre of a block of cast iron. Next year war broke out between Britain and her colonies in America creating a good market for cannon. Boulton and Watt made their first steam engine in the same year, 1775. They found that only Wilkinson's cannon-lathe could make cylinders for the engine which did not let steam leak away. In the next twenty-five years they made five hundred engines and nearly every one had cylinders from Wilkinson's foundry.

Iron-mad Wilkinson

Wilkinson himself bought the third engine ever made, to drive the bellows at his Bilston blast furnace. By 1780 he had four steam blast furnaces at work to help him build a huge export business selling guns and engine parts to Europe. In 1788 he supplied 40 miles of cast-iron pipes for Paris's water supply. At home he became known as 'iron-mad Wilkinson' as he dreamed up even more uses for his metal. He was one of the first to see that iron beams could replace wood for building. He tried to make an iron boat. Iron tokens with his head printed on them were used alongside coins in the Midlands. When he died in 1805 he was buried in an iron coffin.

Coalbrookdale

A

Coalbrookdale in Abraham Darby II's time.

1 *Which two raw materials came from the mines?*
2 *Why was it essential for the furnaces at Coalbrookdale to be on the banks of a stream?*
3 *What did Abraham Darby II do to improve the water supply?*
4 *What does the map suggest about the size of the local mines?*
5 *What was the value of the River Severn to the Darbys?*

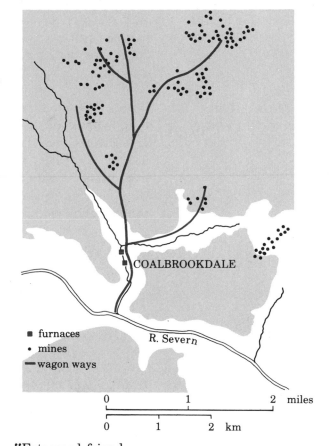

COALBROOKDALE

■ furnaces
• mines
— wagon ways

R. Severn

```
0          1          2   miles
0     1      2   km
```

B

Abiah Darby was the wife of Abraham Darby II. In 1755 she wrote to a friend telling what she knew about the history of her husband's firm. Here she describes the work of Abraham Darby I.

6 *What date does Abiah Darby give which is different from the story told in the narrative?*
7 *Where does she suggest that Abraham Darby got the idea of drying coal from?*
8 *Does the passage give any clue how 'coke' got its name?*

"Esteemed friend,

About the year 1709 he came into Shropshire to Coalbrookdale, and with other partners took a lease of the works, which only consisted of an old Blast Furnace and some Forges. He here cast Iron Goods in sand out of the Blast Furnace that he blow'd with wood charcoal; for it was not yet thought of to blow with Pit Coal. Sometime after he suggested the thought that it might be practable to smelt the Iron from the ore in the blast furnace with Pit Coal: Upon this he first try'd with raw coal as it came out of the Mines, but it did not answer. He not discouraged, had the coal cook'd into Cynder, as is done for drying Malt, and it then succeeded ..."

Abiah Darby, 1755, in T.S. Ashton, *Iron and Steel in the Industrial Revolution,* 1924

17
Wrought iron

The story moves from cast iron to wrought iron. Until the 1780s forge workers still made wrought iron bars by hand-beating or hammering (see Unit 15). Most were sold to workers who made small objects such as nails or locks. But new machines had been invented which needed large pieces of wrought iron and this unit tells how they were first made and used.

The Cranage brothers

Before pig iron could be hammered into bars it had to be softened by heat. Until 1766 this was done by charcoal. Coke added too much carbon and made the iron brittle. Then two brothers, Thomas and George Cranage, found a way with their 'reverberatory furnace'. It was a huge fire-grate with two compartments. Iron was put in one and coke was burned in the other. The heat and flames were bounced, or reverberated, from the roof down on to the iron.

Henry Cort (1740–1800)

With a Cranage furnace, workers could make large balls of spongy iron faster than the hammers could beat them into bars. No one was able to solve the problem of how to shape wrought iron more quickly for twenty years. Then Henry Cort, a middleman buying iron goods for sale to the navy, started making them himself in 1775. In 1784 he opened a new production line using a method he called 'puddling and rolling'.

He had created the worst job in British industry. Even as late as 1861 a puddler's average life was only thirty-one years. He had to stand in the blazing heat in front of a huge reverberatory furnace and every few minutes he puddled, or stirred, the metal with a long spoon-shaped rod (or rabble). Then he twisted the iron into a ball and lifted it out with a pair of giant tongs. The balls were knocked into square blocks and, still hot, were passed through rollers which squeezed the iron into long bars.

New iron works

Puddling and rolling soon put the small charcoal forges out of business. In their place came a few vast ironworks which were always on a coalfield. All the stages of wrought iron making were integrated. Pig iron was smelted in blast furnaces and taken straight to the puddling furnace and then to the rolling mills. By the 1790s the rollers could squeeze the iron into the shapes a customer wanted. Coalmine owners bought rails to run trolleys along. When steam railways came in the 1830s, the ironworks' biggest customers were railway companies, followed by bridge builders.

Merthyr Tydfil

Up to the 1770s the villages at the tops of the valleys in South Wales had been quiet. The only people there were farmers and a few gangs of coalminers digging in tiny pits. Then Englishmen moved in to build ironworks. Two were in the tiny village of Merthyr Tydfil, the Dowlais Works and the Cyfarthfa Works.

Richard Crawshay

The man who started the Cyfarthfa Works was Richard Crawshay. In 1787 his workers made only 500 tons of iron. But that was the year he visited Henry Cort and came back with plans for puddling and rolling. By 1812 Cyfarthfa was making 10,000 tons a year and Richard Crawshay had 2,000 men and boys on the payroll. The Dowlais Works had grown just as fast and Merthyr Tydfil had become a sprawling smoke-covered town. By the 1830s the valleys had a total of 191 blast furnaces making iron for rolling mills.

The Black Country

In the eighteenth century the countryside of the West Midlands had been dotted with small forges where domestic workers made nails, locks and small tools. By the 1830s this district had become the 'Black Country' where the air was 'black by day and red at night' with the smoke and flames of 129 blast furnaces. Many specialist trades grew up there. Chains were made for underground haulage and for ships. One firm found a way to make the miles of gas pipe laid each year in the 1820s and 1830s.

James Neilson

Scotland had a smaller wrought iron industry but one that produced two important later inventions. In 1829 James Neilson hit on the idea of using a massive stove to heat the air which was blown into the blast furnace. His hot blast could get the temperature inside up to 600°F and that meant three times as much iron could be smelted with the same amount of coke.

James Nasmyth (1808–1890)

By the 1830s wrought iron was needed for making parts of railway engines and other machines. These complicated parts could not be made by rollers so they had to be beaten into shape by heavy tilt hammers. Even a skilled man could not work to a very accurate measurement. In 1840 James Nasmyth invented a new form of steam hammer which lifted the head up and down directly over the metal. The operator could set the controls so that he could crack an egg or shape an engine part weighing many tons.

A

A painting of the rolling mills at Dowlais.

1 *What product is being turned out?*
2 *The picture shows four separate stages in production (roughly from left to right in the picture). Write notes describing each stage.*
3 *Suggest a use for the gadgets on top of the blocks which hold the rollers.*
4 *What does the picture tell you about the general working conditions in the mill?*

18
Power in Defoe's time

This unit describes the main forms of power before the invention of the steam engine – one of the greatest achievements of the eighteenth century.

Human and animal strength provided the power for many machines. Wheels were often used to convert their energy into power.

For heavier jobs, the wheels were turned by water. Nearly every village had a water mill for grinding corn. As this was a winter job water shortage was not usually a problem. Owners of forges and furnaces would use water power for jobs such as working bellows. To be sure of a regular supply they usually stored water in a mill pond.

Wind was the least reliable form of power. Windmills were used mostly to work pumps which lifted water out of swampy ground in the Fens in East Anglia.

Today most of our power comes from fossil fuels such as coal and oil. In Defoe's day people used coal for heating homes, especially in London, and other large towns where wood was scarce. Some industries needed it for boiling especially for making salt and brewing ale. Only a handful of engines in the country used coal to create power.

Animal strength: a mid-eighteenth-century painting of a village inn, showing the spit being turned by a dog.

Water power: the design of the wheel depended on the water supply.

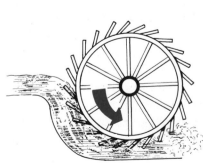

breast shot

over shot

under shot

19
Savery, Newcomen and Watt

Steam power was first used for pumping water from mines. Thomas Savery made the first fire-engine to do this in 1698 and Thomas Newcomen improved on it with his atmospheric engine in 1712. Fifty years later James Watt found a way of halving the fuel costs.

All over early eighteenth-century Britain gangs of men were digging underground for iron, lead, tin and coal. As they went deeper they found their pits filled with water. They could only lift this out in buckets which were hauled up by horse or water power.

Thomas Savery (c.1650–1715)

Thomas Savery was a Cornishman who became a captain on merchant ships. He had also trained to be an engineer and set out to find a way of pumping water out of Cornish tin mines. He knew that Frenchmen had tried to do this with the help of steam power and he used their ideas to make his first 'engine to raise water by fire' in 1698. Savery called it the 'miner's friend' but it was hardly that. The hot steam sometimes melted the joints in the boiler and caused an explosion. Even when it worked safely it could raise water only forty feet.

Thomas Newcomen (1663–1729)

Thomas Newcomen was a blacksmith who sold iron tools to Cornish miners. He called in a plumber to help him make a safer and more powerful fire-engine in 1712. Because of the way it worked it was called an 'atmospheric engine'.

Atmospheric engines

The Newcomen engine could pump water from a greater depth than Savery's but tin miners had to import their coal by sea which meant it was very expensive. So the first atmospheric engine was used not in Cornwall but in a coalfield in Dudley in the Midlands. Other mine-owners bought them, especially after Abraham Darby began to make his cylinders from iron instead of brass (see Unit 16). These could now be up to 6 feet in diameter which meant the pumps could be even more powerful. By 1769 there were ninety-nine Newcomen engines pumping water out of coal-mines.

James Watt (1736–1819)

James Watt was a mathematical instrument maker in Glasgow. In 1763 or 1764 he repaired a model of a Newcomen engine and realised that it used nearly twice as much coal as necessary. After each piston stroke the cylinder had to be cooled and then reheated. In 1766 Watt proved that he had a solution when he made a model where the steam was drawn into a separate condenser. To build a full-sized engine he went into partnership with John Roebuck who owned the ironworks at Carron. Their first machine worked but not too well because steam escaped where the piston did not exactly fit the cylinder. Roebuck had no money for more trials and Watt wanted to leave him and go into partnership with Matthew Boulton in Birmingham. But Roebuck refused to give up his share in the steam-engine. So James Watt had to forget his great idea for seven years while he earned his living as a canal surveyor.

The Newcomen engine
A

A drawing made in 1717.
The boiler is inside the dome. Steam was let out to push the piston inside the cylinder (c) above the boiler. When it reached the top cold water was let into the cylinder from the tank on the top horizontal bar. The cold water cooled the steam below the piston which left a vacuum. The pressure of the atmosphere then forced the piston back down.

1 *Why did this fire-engine get the name 'atmospheric' engine?*
2 *What was the purpose of the chains leading into the ground on the left?*
3 *What was the main advantage of this engine over Savery's?*

Watt's separate condenser
B

A modern copy, with added labels, of a drawing made in 1775.

4 *Use this drawing to explain how Watt had improved on Newcomen's engine.*
5 *What would be the main advantage to someone who might want to buy an engine with the separate condenser?*

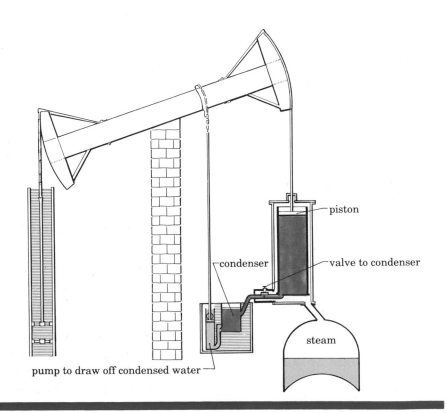

20 Making for the whole world

In 1774 James Watt left Scotland to join Matthew Boulton in Birmingham and the two men were partners in making and selling steam-engines for the next twenty-five years. In 1781 came Watt's greatest invention, a way to make steam-engines drive wheels. The modern machine age had begun.

Matthew Boulton (1728–1809)

James Watt's dream of the ideal man to produce his steam-engine could easily have been Matthew Boulton. Boulton had started with his father's buckle-making workshops and become Birmingham's leading maker of metal goods. In 1764 he opened a new works, the Soho Manufactory, to put all his workers into one purpose-built building. It was divided into workrooms for different products: buttons, buckles, jewellery, silver ware, coins and iron tokens for John Wilkinson, a friend of Matthew Boulton's. Boulton and his craftsmen designed many machines to speed up the work but without spoiling its quality. Matthew Boulton also had the business sense to see the possibilities in Watt's engine but he could do nothing while John Roebuck refused to sell his share in it.

In 1773 John Roebuck went bankrupt and finally sold his share to Matthew Boulton. At last the two men could work together and Watt moved south to the Soho works in Birmingham in 1774. Within months they found they could stop the leaking steam by using cylinders bored on John Wilkinson's cannon-lathe (see Unit 16). In 1775 the partners now made sure that the engine could not be copied for twenty-five years by taking out a patent.

Boulton and Watt engines

The engine's strongest selling point was that it saved on fuel. Most orders at first came from Cornish tin mines. There was so much work in Cornwall that the partners sent William Murdoch to take charge of building the engines on the spot with the working parts sent down from Soho. Boulton and Watt did not charge a lump sum per engine. They asked for a third of the cost of the fuel saved by using their engine instead of a Newcomen.

Rotary power

Up to 1781 Boulton and Watt supplied engines only for pumping or working bellows. In 1781 Watt worked out the sun-and-planet motion which meant the engine could turn a wheel. This was rotary power, one of history's greatest inventions after the wheel itself. A driving belt from the wheel could work a machine without muscle, wind or water power. Afterwards came three other improvements to make the engine work more powerfully and smoothly.

Horsepower

Boulton and Watt charged for a rotary engine by the amount of power it would give. James Watt found that a horse could lift 33,000 pounds one foot in one minute and called that 1 horsepower (hp). The first rotary engine was sold to John Wilkinson to drive a tilt hammer. Cotton-mill owners bought them to drive Compton's mule. Rotary engines soon appeared in waterworks and breweries. In 1796 Boulton and Watt opened a second factory, the Soho Foundry, just to make engines. Four years later the two men retired and handed the business over to their sons.

The Boulton and Watt story

A

Boulton wrote this letter to Watt in 1769, saying he would like to make steam-engines in Birmingham. John Roebuck had suggested a limit of three counties so that he himself could sell the engines everywhere else.

1 *Explain why Boulton believed he could make better engines than other firms.*
2 *What were the industries in which Boulton could see a use for steam-engines?*
3 *Why did Boulton think it worth while only if he could 'make for the whole world'?*

B

A diagram of the Boulton and Watt steam engine based on plans of the model they sold between 1787 and 1800. By 1787 Watt had made four major improvements to the engine he and Boulton first built in 1775.

4 *What do you think was the importance of the sun-and-planet motion in world history?*
5 *Which of the developments shown in the diagram would most increase the power of the engine?*
6 *Why would factory owners be keen to buy an engine fitted with a governor?*

C

An enthusiastic writer summed up the benefits of Boulton and Watt engines in 1835.

7 *Put the writer's list of benefits under these headings: reliability, cost, employment, transport, trade.*
8 *Give some examples of what you think the writer meant by 'necessaries and comforts of life produced in foreign lands'.*

"my idea was to settle a manufactory near to my own by the side of our canal where I would erect all the conveniences necessary for the completion of the engines and from which manufactory we would serve all the world with engines of all sizes. By these means and your assistance we could engage and instruct some excellent workmen (with more excellent tools than would be worth any man's while to procure for one single engine) and could execute the invention 20 per cent cheaper than it would otherwise be executed and with as great a difference of accuracy as there is between the blacksmith and the mathematical instrument maker. It would not be worth my while to make for three counties only: but I find it well worth my while to make for the whole world."
Matthew Boulton, 1769 (City of Birmingham Museum)

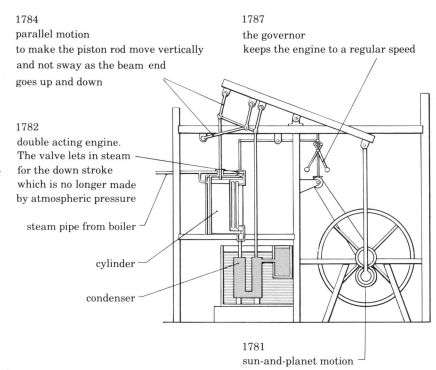

1784
parallel motion
to make the piston rod move vertically and not sway as the beam end goes up and down

1787
the governor
keeps the engine to a regular speed

1782
double acting engine.
The valve lets in steam for the down stroke which is no longer made by atmospheric pressure

steam pipe from boiler

cylinder

condenser

1781
sun-and-planet motion

"There are many engines made by Boulton and Watt, forty years ago, which have continued in constant work all that time with very slight repairs. What a multitude of valuable horses would have been worn out in doing the service of these machines! and what a vast quantity of grain would they have consumed!

Steam-engines . . . create a vast demand for fuel; and, while they lend their powerful arms to drain the pits and to raise the coals, they call into employment multitudes of miners, engineers, ship-builders and sailors, and cause the construction of canals and rail-ways. . . . Steam-engines, moreover, by the cheapness and steadiness of their action, fabricate cheap goods, and procure in their exchange a liberal supply of the necessaries and comforts of life, produced in foreign lands."
Andrew Ure, *The Philosophy of Manufactures*, 1835

21
Coal in Defoe's time

This unit describes how coal was mined and used in the early eighteenth century.

Mining coal

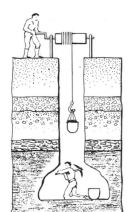

The smallest mines needed only two or three miners with their wives and children to carry the coal away. These miners dug out a bell-shaped pit or they made a tunnel or 'drift' into the hillside.

Larger mines had twenty or thirty workers who dug a shaft through the earth and rock to a coal seam. In most districts they dug the coal in teams of three, using the long wall system. The first man had a pick to prise the coal from the bottom of the seam. The next hammered wedges into the coal above the space the first man had left. This brought it down in large lumps which were broken up by the third man. After it was cleared away, another line of men packed the space with rocks leaving some roads.

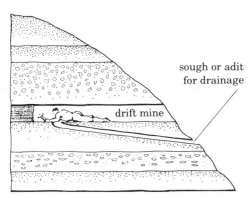

sough or adit for drainage

drift mine

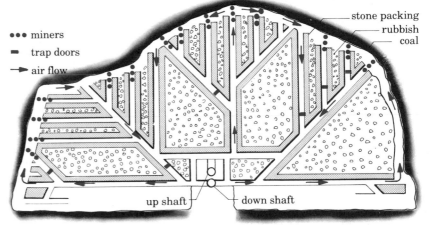

••• miners
━ trap doors
→ air flow

stone packing
rubbish
coal

up shaft down shaft

(Above) Drift mine
(Right) Long wall mine

The biggest coalfield was in Northumberland and Durham. Here each coal-face worker had his own tunnel or stall. He had to do his own undercutting, splitting and breaking. Between him and the next stall there was a pillar of coal to hold the roof.

Women and children

In both sorts of mine it was women and children who dragged the coal to the shaft in baskets, known as corves. Sometimes they put the corves on sledges pulled by harnesses round their waists. In the most primitive pits they had to carry the corves up the shaft using ladders. The more usual way was to use horses who walked round a pulley, or whim-gin, which hauled a rope up the shaft. Many women and children died or were terribly injured in falls.

Uses of coal

Most of the coal was sold for heating houses, especially in London. The rest went to trades which needed fuel for boiling, such as making salt from brine, candles and soap from sheep fat, or sugar from muscovados. Coal was hardly ever used in heavy industry.

Half of all coal was carried to London from Northumberland and Durham by sea. This sea-coal trade needed a thousand ships known as colliers. The coal was taken out to them in narrow boats called keels. In London the colliers were met by lightermen who unloaded the coal into barges which took it ashore. Inland mines used rivers for transport. Before proper roads were made it was too expensive to use carts to take coal more than about ten miles.

22
Coal in the 1820s

By the 1820s miners brought up ten times the amount of coal dug in Defoe's time, helped by new methods and machinery. This led to terrible working conditions and dangers.

Use of coal

A hundred years after Defoe most coal was used for industry, not for house-heating. The biggest users were the giant ironworks, followed by the textile industry. Gasworks were beginning to burn thousands of tons a year (see Unit 23).

Deeper mines

The only way to produce more coal was to work further underground. Many shafts went so far that horses on the surface had not the strength to turn the whim-gin to pull men or coal to the top. From the 1780s most very deep mines had steam-powered winding gear at the pithead. This was expensive and so was paying for a deep shaft to be dug, so mine-owners wanted to use them for as long as possible. Miners were sent to work, by candlelight, at seams which got further from the shaft. This meant longer distances for women and children to haul the corves. From the 1750s their sledges were often replaced by trolleys which ran on rails. At first most rails were wooden, until iron was used after puddling and rolling was invented (see Unit 17). Women and children still had to load the trolleys and in some pits young children were used to guide them or lead the ponies which pulled them.

The deep mines quickly filled up with water. Miners had to make drains to run this into another pit, or sump, so that it could be pumped out, usually by Newcomen engines (see Unit 19).

Gas

Everyone in a deep mine was in greater danger from gas. There were two kinds. One was 'coal damp', a mixture of carbon dioxide and nitrogen – and no oxygen. To be trapped in a pocket of coal damp meant death, so miners sent a dog or canary in first to try the air. Firedamp was even more dangerous. This was methane gas made by vegetation rotting underground for thousands of years. If the mixture of gas and air was right (or wrong!) one spark would lead to an explosion. And that was all too easy when miners worked by candlelight.

In many pits one miner was the 'fireman'. Soaked with water he lay in a hollow under a plank. Then he pulled a string to draw a candle along a wire until it reached a pocket of gas which exploded and burnt itself out. But that only worked if miners knew the gas was there. Accidental explosions killed many. In just two years in the 1800s, six hundred miners were killed in the Northumberland and Durham coalfield. Then in 1815 came the Felling Colliery disaster when ninety-two men and boys died. A group of local coal-owners and clergymen asked the well-known scientist, Humphry Davy, to recommend a safe way of lighting mines.

Safety lamps

In his laboratory Davy found gas would not explode if it passed through narrow holes. So he made a safety lamp which was simply an oil lamp with a wire gauze round the flame. At the same time George Stephenson, a mine engineer, was risking his life to try out his own safety lamp in dangerous places underground. His 'Geordie lamp' had the flame surrounded by a sheet of metal with holes punched in it. So by the end of 1815 there were two almost identical safety lamps. Humphry Davy got £2,000 and fame for his invention. George Stephenson got only 100 guineas at first and many books have ignored his Geordie lamp which worked just as well as Davy's lamp.

Ventilation

Safety lamps saved lives but they often meant that miners were sent into deeper and more dangerous places where an accidental spark from a pick could cause an explosion. The only complete answer was to ventilate the mines thoroughly and get rid of the gas before miners set to work. The best mines had two shafts, partly to help rescue work if one became blocked, and partly for ventilation. The down-shaft brought in fresh air and the up-shaft took away stale air and gas.

To make this happen every passage had to be blocked off with doors which let the air flow only one way towards the up-shaft. Here was another use for very young children. They worked as trappers who sat underground for twelve hours or more, pulling a string to open and close a trapdoor to let trolleys through.

Pit scenes

A

A drawing of a pit-head in the 1840s.

1 *Use the drawing to explain the importance of rotary steam-engines to coal-mining.*
2 *What difference did they make to the work of the miner?*

Coal-winding steam engine, from C. Tomlinson, *Cyclopaedia of Useful Arts*, 1852

B

A Durham miner, George Parkinson, who started work aged 9 in 1837, wrote this account of his first day underground.

3 *How old was George Parkinson when he wrote this? Are there any reasons why this might not be a fully accurate source for children's underground work in the 1830s?*
4 *What would be the worst part of this work for a 9-year-old?*

"Everything was new and strange to me; and as we passed along the narrow waggon-way, with its wall of coal on either side and its stone roof so near, it seemed to me a little world to live in. A few hundred yards brought us to a large trap door about six feet square, closing the whole avenue. This was to be my abiding place for the next twelve or thirteen hours, and my father set to work to make a trapper's hole behind the props, in which I might sit safely and comfortably. After hewing out a good shelter for me he put a nail in the door, to which he fastened my door-string, attaching the other end of it to a nail in a prop where I sat, so that I could pull the door open . . ."
G. Parkinson, *True Stories of Durham Pit Life*, 1911

23
Gas

The story of Britain's gas industry begins with William Murdoch who was Boulton and Watt's foreman in Cornwall.

The first gas light

William Murdoch's home was in Redruth in Cornwall. In 1792 he rigged up a line of metal pipes round the house. At one end he roasted coal in a closed iron pot, or retort. He let the smoke out into a flask of water which trapped the tar and chemicals such as ammonia. The purified gas bubbled through into the piping. At the other end of the piping he had punched tiny holes. When he put a flame to them he had a light much brighter than candlelight.

In 1798 Murdoch moved back to the Soho works and built equipment to light the rooms there. Boulton and Watt then opened a workshop to make retorts, pipes and gasholders. In 1808 they sold equipment to Philip and Lee's cotton mill in Manchester. The firm was spending £3,000 a year on 2,500 candles for early morning and evening. Gaslight brought the cost down to £650.

Public lighting

In 1812 a group of Londoners started the Gas Lighting and Coke Company. By the end of the year there were 26 miles of main pipes in the city streets. After that gas-making became a boom industry and by 1830 there were two hundred companies. Nearly all the gas was used for lighting and hardly any for heating or cooking. But it was a major industry giving work to thousands.

Most gasworks were large-scale versions of William Murdoch's simple equipment except that they purified the gas with lime, not water. They soon found uses for their waste material. Coke, left over from roasting the coal, was sold to ironworks and chemical companies bought the ammonia to use in making bleaches.

In 1819 the Glasgow Gas Works sold all its chemical waste to Charles Macintosh who owned a dye-making factory. After he had used the ammonia he still had another chemical, naphtha. He discovered this would dissolve rubber and hit on the idea of soaking cotton cloth in the rubber solution to make a waterproof material. Shortly afterwards he opened another factory in Manchester to make raincoats.

Gas light
A
An account of the benefits of gas lighting was written in 1827.

1 *What two reasons can you find for the popularity of gas light?*

"We all remember the dismal appearance of our most public streets previous to the year 1810; before that time, the light afforded by the street lamps hardly enabled the passenger to distinguish a watchman from a thief or the pavement from the gutter. The case is now different, for the gas-lamps afford a light little inferior to daylight . . ."
W. Matthews, *An historical sketch of the origin and process of gas lighting,* 1827

24 Chemicals – a new industry

Industrialisation does not mean only factory production of textiles, metals and machines. It includes another major industry – making chemicals out of common materials from the ground, such as salt and coal and, nowadays, oil. This unit describes some of the first steps in industrial chemistry.

Alkali and acid

Wool has to be washed to remove the grease from the animal's body. Cotton needs to be bleached. Up to the 1780s wool was washed with soap made from boiling together tallow (from mutton fat) and potash – which came from the ashes of burnt plants or seaweed. To the chemist, potash is an alkali substance.

Cotton was bleached by hooking the greyish cloth on to frames known as tenters which stood in the fields around weavers' cottages. For up to six months the cloth was wetted every now and then with buttermilk, which is an acid.

Shortages

By the 1780s there was not enough buttermilk and potash to cope with the huge amounts of cloth being made. Glassmakers were also short of potash. Clearly there was a need to make alkalis and acids out of something more common than buttermilk and potash. It was not likely that an Englishman would lead this search because to study chemistry you needed to go to a university in Scotland, Germany or France.

John Roebuck (1718–1794)

This is what John Roebuck did. He was born in Sheffield but he studied medicine and chemistry in Edinburgh and Germany. He later started the Carron Iron Works (and then held up Watt's steam engine; see Unit 19) but his first contribution to industry came in 1746.

Lead chamber acid

Before then chemists made sulphuric acid by burning saltpetre and sulphur in one glass jar and capturing the gas which came off in another jar, where it was mixed with water. The result was expensive acid costing up to 2s 6d for half a pound. In 1746 Roebuck invented the lead chamber process. He made chambers, or boxes, out of lead and put a few inches of water in the bottom. Then he put ladles with burning sulphur and saltpetre into each chamber. The gases cooled on the sides of the chamber and trickled into the water. Three years later Roebuck opened the Prestonpans Vitriol Company, the first ever large-scale chemical works. The factory floor was covered with rows of lead chambers producing sulphuric acid at 1¾d for half a pound.

Bleaching powder

With the help of cheap sulphuric acid chemists could make acid and alkali products on a large scale. The pioneer was Charles Tennant who opened a works in Glasgow in the 1790s. There he mixed salt and sulphuric acid to make chlorine. The chlorine was then soaked in burnt limestone to produce bleaching powder in bulk which was far cheaper than buttermilk.

Soda

Sulphuric acid was also the first step to making soda, an alkali to replace potash for washing. Again, the main raw material was salt. The method was invented by a French scientist, Nicolas Leblanc. In the Leblanc process, sulphuric acid and salt water were heated to make salt cake. This was heated with coal and lime to make 'black ash'. The soda was then washed out of the black ash.

Leblanc factories were opened in Newcastle, Glasgow and Merseyside in the early 1800s. These three districts are still main centres of the chemical industry. Leblanc soda soon found uses outside the textile industry. It became a main material in making glass as well as hard soap for washing human bodies. Both these industries had their main centres near the Mersey where there were coal and salt mines.

Bleaching

A

The traditional method continued into the 1840s as shown in this drawing of a bleach field near Glasgow.

Penny Magazine, 29 July 1843

B

By the 1840s it was more usual to bleach cloth with powder in large tumbling machines, as shown in this drawing of a factory near Manchester.

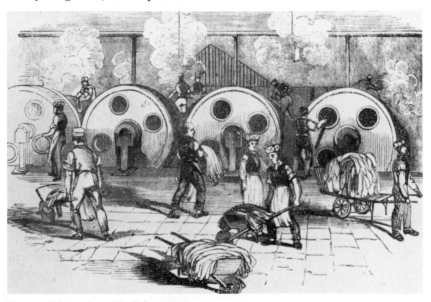

Penny Magazine, 27 July 1844

Sources A–B

1 (a) *List all the differences you can see between the two pictures.*
  (b) *What do the differences tell you about changes taking place in the chemical industry?*
  (c) *Do they suggest that it developed in similar ways to industries such as textiles and iron-making?*
2 *What do the pictures tell you about the connections between the textile, engineering and chemical industries?*

25 Pottery

Josiah Wedgwood and other potters turned the domestic industry of the Staffordshire potteries into a leading world centre for useful and ornamental 'china'.

Earthenware

In most homes of Defoe's day there were a few jugs and pots made of earthenware, usually with a shiny red or brown glazing. (Plates were mostly made of wood, unless you could afford silver or pewter.) Most of the earthenware was made from local clay in one of forty family potteries in Tunstall or Burslem in Staffordshire.

China

A few potters saw that there were good markets for finer goods. Tea, made with leaves imported from China, was becoming popular. At the same time, traders were importing fine Chinese porcelain. So the leading potters set out to make their own 'china'. One was Thomas Whieldon who made tea services in the shape of cauliflowers and pineapples.

Josiah Wedgwood (1730–1795)

Josiah Wedgwood was born into a family of potters. He became a skilful potter but could not do much heavy work because of an attack of smallpox. The after-effects meant he later had one leg amputated. When he could do light work he experimented with new designs and colourings. Thomas Whieldon took him on as a partner and Wedgwood invented a new glaze for the cauliflower service.

Useful ware

In 1759 Wedgwood opened his own works. Here he made cream-coloured china decorated with paintings of flowers or buildings. He called it Queensware after he sold some to Queen Charlotte. But he also thought of it as 'useful ware' to be sold to as many people as possible. To make large quantities he divided workers into specialists for each stage. When there was a shortage of skilled painters Wedgwood found a Liverpool firm to supply him with paper transfers so that the job could be done by semi-skilled labour.

Running the business

For some of the heavier jobs, such as mixing clay or grinding stone into powder, Wedgwood used steam power. The machinery was set up by a local engineer, James Brindley. In 1766 Brindley began work on building the Trent and Mersey Canal after Wedgwood had taken the lead in collecting funds for it. The canal linked the potteries to Liverpool and solved his firm's transport problems. The fine white clay he needed from Cornwall was sent by ship round the coast to Liverpool and then down the canal to Staffordshire. China could be carried without breakages on barges to Liverpool for shipping overseas.

Salesmanship was another reason for Wedgwood's success. He started showrooms in Bristol and London. He gave samples of his best china to the British ambassador in Russia who showed them to wealthy Russians. This brought many orders including one from the Empress of Russia. To make her dinner service he had to find 1,282 pictures of different country houses to paint on to the pieces.

Etruria works

As well as useful ware, Wedgwood also made ornamental ware with a Liverpool merchant, Thomas Bentley, as a partner. In 1769 the two men opened a new factory, the Etruria works. Etruria was a district in ancient Italy which specialised in red pottery with black figures. Wedgwood and Bentley copied these designs, then they went on to make Jaspar Ware with white figures on a blue, green or black background. This is still sold under the name of 'Wedgwood'.

The Wedgwood business

A

The London showroom, in 1809.

1 *What does the picture tell you about Wedgwood's business methods?*

Illustration in Ackermann's Repository of Arts, February 1809

B

The Etruria works on the banks of the Trent and Mersey Canal, based on an early nineteenth-century woodcut.

2 *What part did Wedgwood play in building this canal?*
3 *In what ways did it help his business?*

Sources A–B
4 *Using these pictures as evidence, explain how Wedgwood turned pottery from a craft into an industry.*

C

Wedgwood made many thousands of these medallions to distribute free in support of the anti-slavery movement.

5 *Explain in your own words the message of the medallion.*

Medallion modelled by
William Hackwood, 1787

26
The roads that Defoe knew

Daniel Defoe added an appendix in his *Tour* to complain about the country's roads. Part of it is in Source A and this unit will help you understand what he was grumbling about.

Legs and wheels

Daniel Defoe did all his travelling in the usual way for a gentleman, on horseback. Women were usually not taught to ride so many never went more than a mile or two from home. Few people owned carriages and there was not one coach service from London to the north or Scotland. For ordinary men and women their own two feet provided the only means of getting about.

Mail

The government-run Post Office delivered mail but it was hardly an express service. Riders carried the letters in pouches and changed horses at post-houses, which were inns where the keeper was paid a fee by the Post Office. Letters did not move at much more than thirty miles a day. That tells a lot about road conditions.

Packages

No one tried to move very heavy goods by road but there was a big traffic in lighter packages. In hilly districts trains of pack-horses picked their way, nose to tail, over narrow tracks and hump-backed bridges. Elsewhere packages were moved by carriers who ran stage-wagon services. The country was crisscrossed with stage-wagon routes which met at inns where packages could be loaded or transferred to another wagon. But foot travellers and horsemen cursed these lumbering wagons with their eight heavy horses in front. They churned up the mud leaving deep ruts.

The highways

According to Defoe the worst highways went across clay soils. But the real problem was that a highway was not a properly made road but simply a way over the land. As Defoe pointed out, the Romans had been the last people to build roads with layers of stone. In Defoe's time the law said that each parish had to repair the stretches of highway that ran through it. The local magistrates did their best to see the law was obeyed by choosing one man to be Surveyor of Highways. He could call on every household in the parish to give six days' work a year. Usually they did little but dump rubbish in the deepest holes. That was good enough for local carts, but not for the juggernauts of the day, the eight-horse stage-wagon.

Turnpikes

Defoe thought that the new turnpike trusts gave the best hope for improvement, even though there were only about thirty at the time he made his tour. The starting-point for a turnpike trust was a meeting of local people who thought their industry or trade would be helped by a better road. They needed Parliament to pass a Turnpike Act for their district to give them the power to charge tolls. Then they put up a gate at each entrance to the road, where the cash was collected. The tolls were fixed in the Act and the highest were paid by the traffic which did the most damage. All the money was to be used for repairing the road and any bridges.

Turnpike trusts were never popular with locals who resented having to pay tolls just to get to market or move sheep from one farm to the next. The eighteenth-century way of protesting was to riot and hundreds of turnpike gates were torn down. But there were too many advantages and too much profit for the trusts to be stopped. Their numbers grew with a spurt in the 1750s and 1760s.

Parliament backed the turnpikes with laws to cut down damage. In 1741 they put a weight limit of three tons on wagon loads and in 1753 they said that heavy vehicles should have 9-inch metal tyres, which would roll the roads rather than cutting ruts. All the laws were put together in 1772 in the General Turnpike Act.

Defoe's complaint about the roads
A

1 What does Defoe mean by 'causeway'?
2 What difference does he say the turnpikes brought to the roads?
3 Why were carts, coaches and wagons charged differently?
4 What evidence is there that the way of getting meat to market described in Unit 2 was common in Defoe's time?

"the soil of all the Midland part of England, even from sea to sea, is of a deep stiff clay; ... the great number of horses every year killed by the excess of labour in these heavy ways, has been such a charge to the country, that new building of causeways, as the Romans did of old, seem to me to be a much easier expense....

... from London through this whole country towards Ipswich and Harrow.... roads were formerly deep, in times of flood dangerous and at other times, in winter, scarce passable; they are now so firm, so safe, so easy to travellers and carriages as well as cattle, that no road in England can yet be said to equal them; this was first done by the help of a turnpike, set up by Act of Parliament, about the year 1697 ... they take 8d for every cart, 6d for every coach and 12d for every waggon; and in proportion for droves of cattle."

Daniel Defoe, *A Tour Thro' the whole Island of Great Britain*, 1724–6

Road repairs
B

An extract from the minutes of a magistrates' meeting in Kent. (To distrain means to have the power to take what is owing.)

5 Can you explain the difference between a team defaulter and a labourer defaulter?
6 Suggest how Margaret Fairman came to be on the list.

"A warrant was this day signed, upon the complaint of William Lee one of the surveyors of the highways for the parish of West Peckham, to distrain the several persons hereunder named for makeing default in their days labour towards repairing the highway in the said parish."

Team Defaulters		£	s	d
Richard Fairman	two days		10	0
Thomas West	one day		5	0
Robert May	two days		10	0
Labourers Defaulters				
Benjamin Streaton	two days		3	0
Margaret Fairman	six days		9	0
George Luck	three days		4	6"

Minutes of the Petty Sessions, Malling, Kent, 4 November 1752

27
Britain on wheels

By the 1760s most larger towns of the time were connected by turnpike roads. Long-distance travellers and goods carriers gave up horseback and took to wheels.

Stage-coaches

Stage-coaches got their name because they ran from stage to stage at regular times. Each stage was an inn. Horses were changed while passengers rested and ate or waited for a connection. Stage-coach operators were in cut-throat competition to attract passengers with faster and more frequent services. The rivalry became fiercer after the mail-coach service was launched in 1784.

Mail coaches

The mail coach was the idea of a theatre manager in Bath, John Palmer. He wrote to the Post Office (in charge of letter delivery since 1686) to complain that letters sent on Monday did not reach London until Wednesday morning. The stage-coach delivered its passengers by Tuesday morning. He asked if he could set up a mail service using short stages for the horses to be changed often. The Post Office agreed and John Palmer's first mail coach beat the passenger stage by an hour.

The Post Office saw the point and opened up a new mail service. For each route they allowed one coach operator to carry the mail (for a fee) as well as passengers. All operators had to use a standard coach built by a London firm. By 1792 there were 150 on the roads. Passengers preferred them because they were faster and more reliable than ordinary stage-coaches. Mail guards were sacked if they let drivers stop at any place apart from the stages.

Coaches gave a rough ride. Four passengers paid extra for the privilege of sitting inside, knee to knee, in a stifling box. They could see little through the tiny windows except flying dust or mud. It cost less to be one of the four outside passengers and have your bones shaken on a perch above the axle.

Passengers had good reason to praise the name of Obadiah Elliott who invented the metal coach spring in 1805. The ride was more comfortable and the new sprung coaches could be large enough to fit benches on top for ten or twelve outside passengers.

Private travel

Wealthy families bought carriages for their own use. A new carriage could change their way of life, especially that of the women. They now had the chance to go with their husband, maid and servants to one of the new resorts that grew up to serve the carriage trade. You could choose a seaside town, such as Brighton or Scarborough, or you might prefer a spa. The nasty-tasting spa waters were said to be good for gout but the real attraction was the company of other rich people at the concerts and balls.

Inns

The new traffic created a lot of new jobs: for horse-breeders, workers in glass, metal and leather, and for everyone connected with coaching inns. Many new inns were built, large rambling buildings with a wide arch which led to the coach-yard and stables. Exeter's main coaching inn, 'The New London', needed stabling for 300 horses. When a coach dashed into a yard, kitchen workers served a quick meal while the stable-hands changed the team.

Stage-wagons

The goods carriers copied the coaches by running timetabled services. As well as goods they carried 'poor riders' who paid a small sum to perch among the packages. Competition was fierce and the firms which did best were those with the fastest and most frequent services.

Pickfords

In the record books of the modern firm of Pickfords the first name is James Pickford. He had a farm just south of Manchester used for resting and feeding fifty horses which pulled his wagons. They were used for two services a week from Manchester to London. The journey took nine days. In 1776 a rival cut the journey to six days. James Pickford's son, Matthew, replied with a five-day travel time and a three-day-a-week service. In 1780 he put this up to a four-day service and in 1788 he began a daily run.

In 1814 Pickfords were the first carriers to use the metal spring. They started a service with 'flying vans', built like coaches, which needed only four horses to pull three tons at six miles an hour.

Coach travel

A *(centre)*

The fastest travel times from London, 1740–1820.

1 *In which twenty-year period were the greatest improvements made?*
2 *What would be the main reasons for these improvements?*
3 *Why were improvements after 1800 smaller?*

B *(right)*

A coaching advertisement.

4 *What is the object by the feet of the front horses?*
5 *Why do you think they advertise 'only four inside'?*
6 *What times are allowed for meals on the journey?*
7 *What did the coachmen and guards lose if the coach was late?*

To Edinburgh

1740	170 hours
1760	160 hours
1780	80 hours
1800	65 hours
1820	55 hours

To Manchester

1740	72 hours
1760	58 hours
1780	31 hours
1800	28 hours
1820	28 hours

To Bath

1740	35 hours
1760	29 hours
1780	15 hours
1800	14 hours
1820	12 hours

Crown Inn, Redcross-street, Liverpool.

NEW POST COACH,
(Only Four Inside,)
TO LONDON,
CALLED PRINCE SAXE COBOURG,

LEAVES the above Inn every Morning at Seven p'clock, and arrives at the SWAN-ITH-TWO-NECKS, Lad-lane, LONDON, the following day, at Three o'clock precisely.
Performed by SAMUEL HENSHAW & Co.
Liverpool;
Who are happy to announce, they have succeeded in establishing this Coach on the most respectable system. It performs its Journey in less time than others, not by excessive driving, but by its taking the shortest rout, and strict attention paid that no time is unnecessarily lost. Steady Coachmen and Guards are selected; and the Public are respectfully informed, that every exertion has been used to complete it a respectable, safe, pleasant, and expeditious conveyance, well guarded and lighted, and only four Coachmen.

TIME BILL,
FROM LIVERPOOL TO LONDON,
Off at Seven o'Clock.

Miles.	Time allowed. H. M.		Towns.	Time to arrive H. M.	
18	2	30	At Warrington	9	30
12	1	35	Knutsford	11	5
14	2	5	Congleton	1	10
11	1	30	Burslem	2	40
		50	Dinner, and off	3	10
11	1	30	At Stone	4	40
22	3	20	Lichfield	8	0
		30	Supper, and off	8	30
15	2	10	At Coleshill	10	40
12	1	50	Coventry	12	30
11	1	30	Dunchurch	2	0
8	1	10	Daventry	3	10
12	1	50	Towcester	5	0
8	1	10	Stratford	6	10
		30	Breakfast, and off	6	40
27½	4	25	At Redburn	11	5
11½	1	35	Mims	12	40
17	2	20	London	3	0
	32	0			

To arrive in London at three o'clock precisely.
NOTE—If the above Time be not strictly kept, (accidents excepted) the Passengers are particularly requested not to give the Coachman or Guard their usual perquisite.

☞ FROM THE ABOVE INN, COACHES PROCEED TO EVERY PART OF THE KINGDOM.

The Liverpool Mercury, 23 May 1817

28
Three road engineers

The first turnpike trusts did little more than mend the roads regularly. But as wheeled traffic increased there was a need for skilled road and bridge makers who became known as civil engineers.* This unit tells the story of three pioneers in this new profession.

John Metcalfe (1717–1810)

John Metcalfe was blind from the age of six but this did not stop him running his own carrier business from Knaresborough in the Pennines. 'Blind Jack' began with pack-horses which he led over the hills himself, testing the ground with a long staff and judging how steep it was with his legs. Then he bought a coach and became interested in road building. Between 1765 and 1792 he built 192 miles of road, mostly to replace trails in the Pennines.

Blind Jack's labourers began building with a foundation of large stones. On top they laid a layer of small jagged stones which made a solid surface when they were crushed by wagon and coach wheels. Smooth pebbles would have been rolled aside. Metcalfe's method meant that now there could be a curved surface which let rain water run off into drains dug on each side of the road.

Thomas Telford (1757–1834)

Thomas Telford was born in Scotland. When he was twenty-five he rode to London, carrying a letter from a wealthy woman in his village. The letter got him a job with one of the country's leading architects. From there he went on to build a new prison and several bridges in Shropshire.

Next, Telford was asked to design and oversee the building of a network of canals in Shropshire and Cheshire. Then he moved to the Scottish Highlands where the government planned to build the Caledonian canal and new roads in an effort to bring more work. Telford was put in charge of both schemes. In twenty-two years he supervised the canal as well as 920 miles of roads with 1,117 bridges. He won a name for being able to keep an eye on dozens of different contractors and their gangs. He was the leading figure in the new profession of civil engineers and became the first president of their new Society in 1818. Clearly Telford was the ideal man to build the 250-mile road from London to Holyhead.

London to Holyhead

The road was needed for political reasons. In 1801 England and Ireland were united (in a shot-gun wedding from the point of view of many Irish). MPs from Ireland complained about the poor coach and mail service from London to Holyhead where boats left for Dublin.

The road ran through many turnpike areas but Parliament forced each trust to let Telford make the road to his own high standards. At the base there was a 7-inch layer of large stones, placed on edge by hand. After that came two layers of broken stones which had to be able to pass through a 2½-inch ring. After these

---

* Before the 1700s most roads and bridges were built to make it easier for armies to move about. The men who built them were 'military engineers'.

were crushed by traffic, a top 1 inch of gravel was added. To cross from Wales to Anglesey, Telford built the Menai Bridge which still carries road traffic today.

John Loudon McAdam (1756–1836)

If Telford was still alive he would be a motorway builder ripping up land for new roads. But just as important as building roads is the work of re-surfacing them so that holes do not appear. Today this is done with a mixture of tar and small stones called 'tarmac' or tarmacadam. The method goes back to John Loudon McAdam.

He was another Scot, born in 1756. He left his poor family farm and emigrated to the USA. Later he decided to come back and was given the job of surveyor to the Bristol Turnpike Trust. Bristol was already a busy centre for coach traffic and had enough new roads. What the Trust wanted was a cheap way of repairing them.

McAdam's system

McAdam's methods were ideal. Most of his workers were unskilled labourers on low piece-work rates divided into gangs with a simple job each. Some brought up the stones for the road and others broke them into pieces. There was a gang to rake them level and ram them flat with wooden pounders. There was no need to fill the tiny spaces with gravel as coach and wagon wheels would crush the small stones into a solid mass. (Later, rubber tyres sucked up the small stones so tar was added to them.)

McAdam showed that foundations made of large stones could shift apart and cause pot-holes (unless they had been carefully hand-laid). So many trusts took up their first turnpike roads and replaced them with macadamised surfaces. This made the McAdam family fortune. At one time McAdam and his three sons worked for 107 trusts with 2,000 miles of roads. John McAdam himself was surveyor to all the London Trusts and between 1827 and 1836 he was Surveyor-general advising trusts throughout the country.

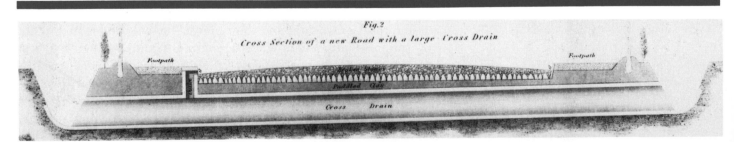

Fig. 2

Cross Section of a new Road with a large Cross Drain

Footpath   *Footpath*

Puddled Clay

Cross Drain

Thomas Telford

A

Telford's plan for a new Scottish road.

B

Telford's plan for Waterloo Bridge on the London–Holyhead Road.

3 *What materials were used in building Waterloo Bridge?*

1 *What materials were used in making the road?*
2 *What are the arrangements for drainage?*

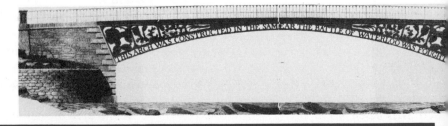

C

Telford's plan for a toll-house on the London–Holyhead Road.

4 *How would the toll-house compare with other working-class housing of the time?*

5 *What do the plans A–C tell you about the care Telford took over the appearance of his roads?*

John McAdam

D

His directions for repairing a road.

6 *What does this tell you about the workers used by McAdam?*

7 *Why were McAdam's methods cheaper than Telford's?*

"Materials to be broken.

The stone in the road is to be loosed up to the depth of a foot, and broken so as to pass through a screen or harp of an inch in the opening, by which no stone above an inch in any of its dimensions can be admitted.

Road to be quite flat.

The road is then laid as flat as possible, if it is not hollow in the middle it is sufficient; the less it is rounded the better; water cannot stand upon a level surface.

The broken stone to be laid on: better half at a time.

The broken stone is then to be laid evenly on it, but if half or six inches is exposed a short time to the pressure of carriages, and then a second coat of six inches laid on, it has been found advantageous in consolidating the materials.

Small hammers.

... stone is to be broken by persons sitting, with a hammer about 15 inches in length in the handle, and about an inch broad in the face, calculated as to weight to the strength of a woman's single hand; should any stone, such as whinstone, be found too hard for women or old men to break, stronger men must be employed, but in either case they must be made to sit down: a woman *sitting* will break more limestone for a road than two strong labourers on their feet with long hammers, in a given time."

John McAdam, *Observations on the Highways of the Kingdom*, 1810

E

A newspaper announcement.

8 *What did* The Times *mean by Macadamizing?*

Sources D–E

9 *How do Sources D and E agree in describing McAdam's methods?*

10 *Was John McAdam a road-builder?*

"Yesterday the workmen began to Macadamize the wide roadway from Charing Cross to Parliament Street. Temporary fencing is raised half way over the street from the Admiralty to the Horse Guards, thus preventing any interruption of this great thoroughfare. The great granite stones are broken into small pieces as soon as they are taken up, and thus, as rapidly as the way is cleared the materials are ready for the commencement of the Macadamizing system."

The Times, 8 October 1824

29
Inland navigation

Imagine four transport problems for traders of Defoe's time. How would they get: lead from a Derbyshire mine to a house-builder in Cambridge, wine from France to Leeds, iron manacles from Wolverhampton to the West Indies, or cheese from Gloucestershire to London. Unit 26 explained why they would use as little highway as possible. This unit shows how they would use water transport or 'navigation'.

Navigable rivers

In Defoe's day there were 1,200 miles of river which were navigable for boats, far more than there would be today. By the 1720s it had taken more than fifty years of improvement works. Where there was a sandbank or difficult bend a 'cut' had been dug to by-pass it. Where the water was shallow you would find a flash lock. This was a gate which dammed up the river until there was enough water to float a barge through when the gate was opened.

The improvements were not popular with landlubbers. Husbandmen did not want cuts going through their pastures. Mill-owners feared that flash gates would stop water getting to their water-wheels. So each improvement had to be backed by an Act of Parliament which gave a Navigation Company the power to do the work and collect a toll from each boat.

The maps show two of the main navigation networks. One led to the port of King's Lynn and the other to Bristol. Three other networks ended up at Hull, Liverpool and London. The best way of getting goods from one network to another was to take them between these ports by sea.

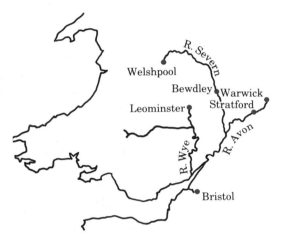

Defoe's tour of Wales and the West Country.

Defoe's tour of East Anglia and Kent.

"Leominster, a large and good trading town on the river Lug. This river is lately made navigable to the very great profit of the trading part of this country who now have a very great trade for their corn, wool, and other products of this place, into the river Wye, and from the Wye, into the Severn and so to Bristol.

The navigation of the river Avon in an exceeding advantage to the city of Bristol . . . they drive a very great trade for sugar, oil, wine, tobacco, lead, and, in a word, all heavy goods which are carried by water almost as far as Warwick; and in return the corn and especially the cheese is brought back from Gloucestershire and Warwickshire, to Bristol."
Daniel Defoe, *A Tour Thro' the whole Island of Great Britain*, 1724–6

"Here is also a great corn market, and great quantities of corn are bought here, and carried down by barges and other boats to Lynn. . . . By these navigable rivers the merchants of Lynn supply about six counties wholly and three counties in part, with their goods, specially wine and coal. . . .

All heavy goods are brought . . . by water carriage from London, and other parts; first to the port of Lynn, and then in barges up the Ouse, from the Ouse into the Cam."
Daniel Defoe, *A Tour Thro' the whole Island of Great Britain*, 1724–6

30
The canals

Between the 1760s and 1820s about 2,000 miles of canal were built. The story begins with a young man who found work more fun than love.

The Duke of Bridgewater (1736–1803)

Between the ages of 17 and 22 the third Duke of Bridgewater toured Europe and whirled around London, in love with a Duchess. He left her to run the family estates at Worsley in Lancashire.

The biggest part of the estate's profits came from selling coal from mines at Worsley to salt refiners on Merseyside. It was sent along the river Irwell, after paying tolls to the Irwell Navigation Company. But in 1757 the refiners stopped buying the Duke's coal. They had formed a company to improve the Sankey Brook which ran to a nearer part of the coalfield.

The Duke decided to sell his coal in Manchester instead. But he would not use the Irwell. Even with the improvements by the Navigation Company the water was so rough that gangs of men were needed to guide the barges. Instead, he would build his own canal. He raised the money by selling his London home and borrowing from banks. Then he needed an Act of Parliament. The owners of the Irwell Navigation objected but he got his Act with backing from rich Manchester mill-owners who wanted cheap coal.

James Brindley (1716–1772)

He chose James Brindley as engineer. Brindley could hardly read or write but he was well known as a practical engineer. For this new job he had to solve three problems. The first is clear from the map (Source A): how was the Duke's canal to cross the Irwell? Brindley's solution was to carry it across the valley on an aqueduct. Second, how could water be stopped from soaking through the canal bed? Brindley taught workmen to mix clay with sand and water and puddle it into a sticky lining by digging it in with their heels. Third, how were barges to be loaded and unloaded? At the Worsley end Brindley linked the canal with tunnels which ran into the mines. At the Manchester end he built a crane to lift the coal to street level.

The canal network

The Bridgewater Canal opened in 1761 and the price of coal in Manchester dropped from 7d to 3½d per hundredweight. The Duke was so sure he would get his money back from his first 10½ miles of canal that he asked Brindley to begin work on a longer length to join up with the Mersey. It was the start of an age of canal building which went on until the coming of the railways. Until he died in 1772 Brindley was adviser to nearly a dozen canal companies. His dream was a 'silver cross' of water to link the four largest networks of navigable rivers. The first arm of the cross was the Trent and Mersey canal which Josiah Wedgwood and other potters wanted. The next arm was the Staffordshire–Worcestershire canal. Brindley chose the busy river port of Bewdley to join the canal with the river Severn but its traders told him they did not want his 'stinking ditch'. So he looked further south and found a piece of open country with just one inn. He built docks, canal basins, offices and warehouses. The place became the busy town of Stourport. Bewdley became a sleepy backwater with almost no river traffic.

Brindley made his canals narrow and kept them at the same level for as long as possible, even if it meant going almost in a circle round a hill. If this was not possible he built locks, although he had never seen one. Later canal builders had to take their canals over more difficult countryside. The new more powerful steam-engines could help with pumping water and lifting earth. So their canals were wider and straighter with taller aqueducts, longer tunnels and more locks. When Thomas Telford built the Ellesmere Canal he made a cast-iron aqueduct 127 feet above the river Dee at Pont-Cysyllte. At Bingley in Yorkshire the Leeds–Liverpool canal is lifted 60 feet up a stairway of locks.

Canal companies

After the Duke of Bridgewater no one ever paid for a canal himself, because of the huge sums needed to make the cutting, the bridges and the reservoirs before any money was earned. Yet canal companies were set up all over the country, usually by groups of landowners, mine-owners and manufacturers who could see the benefits of smooth water to move ever larger amounts of coal, food and industrial goods. They had no difficulty in selling shares.

In 1767 the Birmingham Canal Company issued its first shares at £140 each. Two years later the canal had reached the South Staffordshire coalfield. The price of coal in Birmingham dropped from 15/- to 4/- a ton. It was just the shot in the arm for Midlands industry that the investors had hoped for. Mine-owners sank new pits and took on more miners. The metal trades got plentiful cheap fuel. The Canal Company made so much money from tolls that its shares were worth £370 in 1782. In 1792 they were worth £1,170. The 'canal mania' of the early 1790s was in full swing. In just five years fifty-one new companies were set up. Canal mania was partly the cause and partly the result of a surge in industry which was boosted by the war against France which began in 1793.

Brindley's first three canals

A

1 *How did the first canal cross the River Irwell?*
2 *Who had paid for the Sankey Brook Navigation?*
3 *Name canals 2 and 3.*
4 *Who benefited most from canals?*
5 *Suggest why the Weaver had been made navigable.*

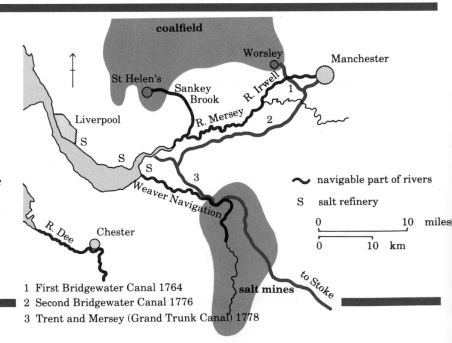

1 First Bridgewater Canal 1764
2 Second Bridgewater Canal 1776
3 Trent and Mersey (Grand Trunk Canal) 1778

Important canals in 1820
B

6 *Do you think that Brindley's 'silver cross' had come about? Which town might be said to be at its centre?*

7 *Use the map to explain the importance of canals to Britain's export trade.*

8 *Were the main navigable rivers any less important in 1820 than 1720?*

1 Bridgewater
2 Trent & Mersey
3 Oxford
4 Thames & Severn
5 Staffordshire & Worcester
6 Coventry
7 Forth & Clyde
8 Leeds & Liverpool
9 Lancaster
10 Huddersfield
11 Grand Junction
12 Kennet & Avon

—— navigable rivers
—— canals

A traveller's view of the benefits canals brought to Cheshire
C

9 *Use the maps to suggest how slate reached Cheshire.*

10 *How did farmers benefit?*

11 *In the last sentence Pennant is writing about the canals' effects on coal and corn prices. What does he suggest corn merchants did before the canal was built?*

"The cottage, instead of being covered with miserable thatch, is now secured with a substantial covering of tiles or slates, brought from the distant hills of Wales or Cumberland. The fields, which before were barren, are now drained, and, by the assistance of manure, conveyed on the canal toll-free, are clothed with a beautiful verdure. Places which rarely knew the use of coal, are plentifully supplied with that essential article upon reasonable terms: and, what is still of greater public utility, the monopolisers of corn are prevented from exercising their infamous trade."
Thomas Pennant, *A journey from London to Chester*, 1789

31
Canal workers and users

The man who did the heavy work in building a canal navigation was called a navigator. About 1830 the word was shortened to 'navvy' – just in time for it to mean a labourer on railway work as well as canal building. This unit first describes a navigator's work and then some of the other men who kept the boats moving.

Navigators

If you went outside and dug a trench thirty-five metres long, a metre deep and a metre wide (on a rainy day with clay soil), you would have done a standard day's work for a navigator – but only when you had shifted the earth. The navigator did that with the help of his wheelbarrow. He slipped a rope round it. A horse at the other end pulled and the navigator steered the wheelbarrow up a greasy plank.

Contractors

Navigators worked for contractors who were paid a fixed sum to do all the work on part of a canal. Some contractors specialised in digging a length of canal bed and most of their navigators were unskilled barrow men. Others specialised in bridges, locks or aqueducts and they would need masons, bricklayers and carpenters.

Most of the unskilled navigators were the same men who did seasonal work at busy times on farms. There was a great number of Scots and Irish among them. They stayed in one place for a few months, living in overcrowded huts or tents and being heavily overcharged by the people who sold them food and drink after a hard day's work. It is hardly surprising that they got a name for drunkenness and rowdy behaviour.

Boatmen

Most canal boatmen worked for a carrying company or for a factory or mine which had its own fleet of barges. Canal companies did not own their own boats. Their income came from tolls charged for using the canal. Charges were made for each ton moved per mile. All canal barges had lines painted on the side and the weight could be checked by noting which line was at water level.

Wharfmen

After the boatmen, the next biggest group of canal workers were the men who loaded and unloaded at the wharves. These wharves were lined with warehouses used by carrier companies to store goods waiting to finish their journey by road. Many factories and gasworks had private wharves for their own use and canal banks became favourite places for new factory building.

Passengers

Road carriers often went into the canal business. Pickfords ran regular barges to connect with their stage-wagons on some routes. A single horse pulling a canal barge could generally manage a steady walking pace of 4 mph. Some companies ran faster services with two horses. Then came the fly-boat which gave a very fast trip like the fly-wagon on land. With a specially built boat and two horses which were changed every few miles they could travel up to 10 miles an hour!

Navigators
A

The problem described here was a common one.

1 *What problem was the Committee discussing?*
2 *Why would innkeepers be able to make 'extravigant' charges?*
3 *What is meant by 'meat' here?*

"The Labourers for cutting the canal are much imposed on by extravigant charges of the Inn keepers and the Committee are desired to consider if any scheme can be come into for the convenience of such Labourers by erecting Tents, Booths, &c &c providing them with meat & drink in a more easy expence."
Leeds and Liverpool Canal Company, *Minute Books*, 3 January 1771

Carriers
B

An advertisement for the light goods trade.

4 *What would be most likely to happen to goods which reached Stourport on a 'stage boat'?*
5 *Why would lock-up boats be needed for wines and spirits?*

"Crowley, Hicklin & Co. run fly-boats to London and stage boats to Kidderminster and Stourport every Thursday, loading there on Mondays to return. They provide lock-up boats for wine and spirits, and if required send goods by land (at the higher land rates) when the canals are stopped by frost."
Aris's Birmingham Gazette, 25 March 1811

C

An advertisement for heavy goods carriage.

6 *Use the map in Unit 30, Source B, to suggest a route for the goods Thomas Coleman took to London. Which waterways would he use to take goods to Hull?*
7 *What does this advertisement tell you about the importance of sea shipping?*

"Thomas Coleman loads daily for Liverpool, Manchester & Chester. From Liverpool goods can be shipped to Lancashire and Cumberland ports, Glasgow, Ireland or North Wales. Boats also load for Gainsborough and Hull for Sheffield, Lincolnshire, the East and West Ridings, Newcastle, Edinburgh and eastern Scotland."
Aris's Birmingham Gazette, 12 September 1811

Canals and industry
D

A painting of the Birmingham Canal in 1772, where it passed W. Millington's ironworks.

8 *What evidence is there that W. Millington's owned their own fleet of canal boats?*
9 *Suggest two products that were brought to the works by canal.*
10 *What does the picture suggest about the links between canals and industry?*

32
Counting heads

Look first at the population table at the back of the book, which shows Britain's population since 1720. For the years up to 1801 it is only an estimate and this section explains why it is impossible to be absolutely sure of Britain's population before 1841.

Gregory King (1648–1712)

Gregory King dabbled in many things: family trees for noblemen, architecture and insurance. In 1696 he completed a report for the government on the numbers and wealth of the people in England and Wales (but not Scotland). The government wanted to know how much tax could be collected to pay for a war with France.

Every household in the country had to pay a hearth tax so Gregory King started with the tax collectors' lists which should have shown every home. He could only estimate how many lived in each. He thought the average in a lord's household would be 40

The first census
A

An enumerator's form for the census of 1801.

1 *Imagine you were a parish overseer with six people to help you with this form. What instructions would you give them?*

2 *Would the answers be most accurate for a city or country parish?*

3 *Which part of 'question 1st' would be most difficult to answer accurately?*

An Act for taking an Account of the Population of Great Britain, 1800

FORM of ANSWERS by the OVERSEERS, &c. in

To the Queſtions contained in the Schedule to an Act, intituled, *An Act for taking an Account of the Populati*

County, &c.	Hundred, &c.	City, Town, &c.	Parish, &c.	QUESTION 1ſt. HOUSES.			QUESTION 2d. PERSONS, including Children of whatever Age.		Total of PERSONS in Anſwer to Queſtion 2d.	Perſons emplo Agricu
				Inhabited.	By how many Fa- milies oc- cupied.	Uninha- bited.	Males.	Females.		

N. B. *If any Family occupies Two or more Houſes in different Pariſhes, Townſhips, or Places, the Individuals belonging to Places where they ſeverally happen to be at the Time of tak*

ıſt Queſtion.
2d Queſtion..
3d Queſtion.

REMARKS, in Explanation of the Matters ſtated in Anſwer to

ATTESTATION on Oath (*or* Affirmation) by the OVERSEERS *or* ſubſtan

I, *A. B.* One of the Overſeers (*or* a ſubſtantial Houſeholder) of the Pariſh, Townſhip, &c. of . iı above Return contains, to the beſt of my Knowledge and Belief, a full and true Anſwer to the Queſtions con *Account of the Population of* Great Britain, *and of the Increaſe or Diminution thereof.*

The above-mentioned *A. B.* was ſworn (*or* affirmed) before us the Juſtices of the Peace in and for the because of the number of servants. Farmers, who had a few living-in labourers, he worked out at 5 and for the poorest cottages he gave an average of $3\frac{1}{4}$ people. He reckoned there were just over $5\frac{1}{2}$ million people in the kingdom. Modern historians who have done his sums over again think it was probably nearer $5\frac{1}{4}$ million.

The Census

No one tried to count the whole population until England was again at war with France in the 1790s. The government needed more taxes and a civil servant, John Rickman, suggested they made a 'general enumeration of the people'. The Census Office was set up to make the first enumeration in 1801. One has been taken every ten years (except 1941) since then. John Rickman was in charge of the first four.

Enumerators

The enumerators for the first three censuses were the overseers of the poor in each parish (see Unit 52). They visited each house, counted the people and sent the totals to the Census Office. The results were probably on the low side because enumerators did not try too hard to get the truth from awkward householders. So, in 1841, they were given forms to write down details of each person's age, place of birth, occupation etc. This is still how the census is taken. Because of the personal information, enumerator's forms are locked away for a hundred years before they can be read.

Parish registers

Gregory King's estimate was on the high side and the first censuses on the low side. What about the years between? Rickman tried to work out figures from the parish registers where clergymen were supposed to record all baptisms, marriages and deaths. He sent each clergyman a form to fill in from their registers and used their answers to show that the population seemed to have grown more quickly from the 1740s onwards. But parish registers were not terribly accurate. Some had ended up as firelighters or wrapping paper. People such as Quakers, who were not married in church, were not on the registers.

Yet the registers can still be useful. Recent historians have used them to show that the population was growing faster in some parts of the country than in others. If they study the registers over a period of years they can sometimes see changes in the average age of death or marriage. Registers can also give information about social life and work such as when men and women were no longer put down as agricultural labourers but had an industrial trade.

Comparing the figures from Gregory King, the parish registers and the first censuses, we can be fairly sure of two important things about Britain's population. First, it began to grow quickly from the 1740s. Second, it grew more in some parts of the country than others.

'D,

ritain, *and of the Increase or Diminution thereof.*

TION 3d. PATIONS.			TOTAL of PERSONS.
chiefly em-d in Trade, actures, or ndicraft.	All other Persons not comprised in the Two preceding Classes.		N. B. This Column must correspond with the Total of Persons in Answer to Question 2d.

e to be numbered only in those Parishes, Townships, or

ng Questions.

ders in ENGLAND.
f   do swear (or affirm), That the
Schedule to an Act, intituled, An Act for taking an

       this   Day of
                       C. D. and E. F.

Gregory King
B

Gregory King's estimate of the population of England and Wales, 1696.

4 *Explain: temporal lord, spiritual lord, vagrant, gentleman, freeholder.*

5 *What are the out-servants? Where would in-servants be included in this table?*

6 *Who were the people who were 'Decreasing the Wealth of the Kingdom'? What reason had Gregory King for describing them in this way?*

7 *In what ways does the table describe a different society from that of the time of Richard Arkwright and James Watt?*

Sources A–B

8 *List the advantages and disadvantages of using (a) the methods of Gregory King and (b) the 1801 census to get an accurate estimate of population.*

Number of families	Ranks, degrees, titles and qualifications	Heads per family	Number of persons	Yearly income per family	
160	Temporal Lords	40	6,400	2,800	
26	Spiritual Lords	20	520	1,300	
800	Baronets	16	12,800	800	
600	Knights	13	7,800	650	
3,000	Esquires	10	30,000	450	
12,000	Gentlemen	8	96,000	280	
5,000	Persons in Office	8	40,000	240	
5,000	Persons in Office	6	30,000	120	
2,000	Merchants and Traders by Sea	8	16,000	400	
8,000	Merchants and traders by Land	6	48,000	200	
10,000	Persons in the Law	7	70,000	140	
2,000	Clergymen	6	12,000	60	
8,000	Clergymen	5	40,000	45	
40,000	Freeholders	7	280,000	84	
140,000	Freeholders	5	700,000	50	
150,000	Farmers	5	750,000	44	
16,000	Persons in Sciences and Liberal Arts	5	80,000	60	
40,000	Shopkeepers and Tradesmen	4½	180,000	45	
60,000	Artizans and Handicrafts	4	240,000	40	
5,000	Naval Officers	4	20,000	80	
4,000	Military Officers	4	16,000	60	
511,586		**5¼**	**2,675,520**	**67**	
50,000	Common Seamen	3	150,000	20	
364,000	Labouring People and Out Servants	3½	1,275,000	15	
400,000	Cottagers and Paupers	3¼	1,300,000	6	10
35,000	Common Soldiers	2	70,000	14	
849,000		**3¼**	**2,795,000**	**10**	**10**
	Vagrants		30,000		
849,000		**3¼**	**2,825,000**	**10**	**10**

SO THE GENERAL ACCOUNT IS

Number of families	Ranks, degrees, titles and qualifications	Heads per family	Number of persons	Yearly income per family	
511,586 Families	Increasing the Wealth of the Kingdom	5¼	2,675,520	67	
849,000 Families	Decreasing the Wealth of the Kingdom	3¼	2,825,000	10	10
1,360,586	Nett Totals	4$\frac{1}{20}$	5,550,520	32	

Gregory King, *National and Political Observations upon the state and Condition of England,* 1696

33 Death

The death-rate went down in the eighteenth century, but few people lived to be very old. The important change was that fewer children and young people were wiped out by disease than in earlier times. Some possible reasons are given in this section, beginning with the decline of the three great killer epidemics; the plague, typhus and smallpox.

The plague

The plague began as a disease among black rats. When they died fleas left them for humans whom they bit and infected with the plague. It came in great epidemics which could kill tens of thousands, mostly the poor who shared their homes with rats. But it did not come back to Britain after 1665. No one knows why, except that it had nothing to do with doctors. Brown rats may have killed off black rats or their fleas may have chosen a new home.

Typhus

Typhus was also a poor person's disease. It was carried by lice and there were more of them in winter when clothes and bodies were washed less and doors were kept closed. Then people who were already weak from poor food and damp housing caught typhus easily. So the reason why typhus became less of a killer is probably to do with the coming of cotton and soap as everyday articles.

Smallpox

Smallpox was different. Poor and rich caught it. Some survived and their faces could look like the moon's surface in miniature.

The Turks were way ahead of the British in treating smallpox. The wife of the British ambassador to Turkey saw people being inoculated in 1717. Her letter, Source B, explains how inoculation was done. It was read at court and the king's children and grandchildren were inoculated – but not until it had been tried on criminals and orphanage children! After that, inoculation (which means 'making harmless') became the first example of public health treatment. Many parishes decided it was cheaper to pay for mass inoculation than to help widows and orphans of smallpox victims.

Edward Jenner (1749–1823)

Yet inoculation could go wrong because it was difficult to be totally sure that the matter scratched into people's arms would not give them the disease. A safer method altogether was developed by Edward Jenner, a country doctor in a village near Bath. He treated many milkmaids who had caught cowpox from sick cows. The arms came out in spots filled with pus but the fever lasted only two or three days. Jenner wanted to test the local belief that the milkmaids would never catch smallpox.

Vaccination

It was easy for Dr Jenner not to worry when he scratched cowpox pus into the arm of eight-year-old James Phipps. He knew the lad would soon recover. But imagine his thoughts when he scratched him with smallpox pus a month later; and the relief when he stayed healthy. He repeated the experiments on twenty-eight others. By 1798 Jenner was sure enough to write about his discovery of a safer method of preventing smallpox.

He called it vaccination, from the Latin word, *vacca*, meaning cow. Other doctors became rich from vaccinating wealthy people but Jenner himself stayed on as a village doctor. In other parts of the country it was many years before the poor were given vaccinations instead of the less safe inoculations.

Living conditions

By our standards, housing and diet were appalling in the 1820s. But there are two views about whether they were better than in the 1720s. Improved farming and easier transport of food probably meant that fewer people went hungry. Tea drinking was widespread which meant that water was boiled before drinking. In the 1720s gin had been a popular way for the really poor to drink themselves to death. In 1716 the government put a high tax on spirits and it was no longer possible to be 'drunk for a penny and dead drunk for tuppence'. On the other hand food in town shops was often adulterated. Alum (a powder made from slate) was added to flour, water to milk and all manner of sweepings to tea leaves. Some shopkeepers gave their poorest customers lifelong stomach pains if not an early death.

Houses built for industrial workers from the 1770s were cramped and tiny yet they were built of bricks and tiles. It is possible that bugs and germs found it harder to live there than in the ruined timber and soggy thatch of country cottages. Iron bedsteads were mass produced so that most people began to sleep off the floor. On the other hand, heaps of sewage polluted the wells and rivers which supplied water and there was a new health hazard in the smoke and chemicals belched from factory chimneys.

The best we can say is that some of these improvements must have been enough to save some lives and to give some extra children the chance to live long enough to become parents themselves. Very few people were healthier than in the 1720s, and it was another hundred years before diphtheria, scarlet fever and tuberculosis were beaten. But more people lived on for a few extra years which meant a strongly growing population from the 1740s.

Hospitals

In many towns rich people gave money to pay for medical care for the poor. Sometimes a hospital was built but it often caused more deaths than it saved. Doctors did not know about bacteria which carried infections from patient to patient. Surgeons operated (with no anaesthetics) without sterilising their knives, in front of a group of germ-breathing spectators. Mothers and babies died in their thousands from an infection called puerperal fever in lying-in (maternity) hospitals. One hospital which did save lives was the London Foundling Hospital started by Thomas Coram to take in abandoned babies. Two out of three lived to the age of ten!

Dispensaries

Usually the charity money did more good if it paid for a dispensary where an apothecary, a sort of doctor-chemist, supplied medicines to the sick and injured. Without the dispensary most people would have had no medical help at all.

Bleeding
A

A Liverpool surgeon recommended bleeding as a way of curing sick babies. ('Startings' are fits; leeches are small blood-sucking worms.)

1 *Why were leeches used instead of a knife to bleed babies?*

"Bleeding is a remedy much to be depended on when the symptoms of heat, fever, drowsiness and startings are urgent: it is commonly done to children by means of leeches, which may be applied to the foot or heel, and may be repeated every other day ... Two leeches may be applied at one time to a child about three months old and three to one of five or six months."

William Moss, *Essay on the Management and Nursing of Children in the Earlier Periods of Infancy*, 1781

Inoculation
B

Lady Mary Wortley-Montagu's letter from Turkey, 1 April 1717.

2 *Can you give an explanation of why this method of inoculation was successful?*

3 *How important was this letter to the story of inoculation in England? Give reasons for your judgement.*

"There is a set of old women who make it their business to perform the operation every autumn, in the month of September, when the great heat is abated. People send to one another to know if any of their family has a mind to have the smallpox; they make parties for this purpose and when they are met (commonly fifteen or sixteen together), the old woman comes with a nutshell of the matter of the best sort of smallpox, and asks what veins you please to have opened. She immediately rips open that you offer to her with a large needle (which gives you no more pain than a common scratch), and puts into the vein as much venom as can lie upon the head of her needle, and after binds up the little wound with a hollow bit of shell; and in this manner opens four or five veins. The children or young patients play together all the rest of the day, and are in perfect health to the eighth. Then the fever begins to seize them, and they keep their beds two days, very seldom three .... There is no example of anyone that had died in it, and you may well believe that I am well satisfied of the safety of the experiment, since I intend to try it on my dear little son ..."

Treating the sick poor
C

John Heysham was the apothecary for the dispensary at Carlisle. This is his statement of the number of people treated in 1784–5. In that year the dispensary took in £148 in subscriptions to pay for medicines and John Heysham's wages.

4 *Can you see any diseases which would probably be caused by:*
(a) bad living conditions,
(b) poor food?

5 *What example of preventive medicine can you find in this list?*

6 *List five entries in this table which describe symptoms and not actual diseases. What do they tell you about medical knowledge in the 1780s?*

The STATE of the DISPENSARY for adminiſtering medical Relief to the Sick Poor of Carliſle, from July 1ſt, 1784, to July the 1ſt, 1785.

DISEASES.

Disease	No.	Disease	No.
Ague	20	Jaundice	8
Inflammatory Fever	7	King's Evil	3
Putrid or Jail Fever	43	Herpes	46
St. Anthony's Fire	2	Scald Head	7
Pleuriſy	14	Venéral Diſeaſe	14
Rheumatiſm Chronic	25	Whites	2
Sore Throats	4	Prolapſus Ani	1
Natural Small Pox	60	Cancer	1
Inoculated	91	Itch	40
Coughs and Colds	36	Fractures	8
Inflammation of the Eyes	16	Sprains	5
Spitting of Blood	3	Ulcers and Abceſſes	45
Flooding	5	Tumours	11
Piles	7	Wounds, Bruiſes, and Burns	28
Conſumptions	6	Bite of a Dog	2
Palſy	3	Worms	18
Aſthma	3	Tooth Ach	2
Convulſions	1	Painful Affection of the Face	1
Epileptic Fits	1	Stone and Gravel	1
Hyſteric Fits	5	Suppreſſion of Urine	4
Fainting Fits	1	Deafneſs	1
Stomach Complaints	69	Abortions	1
Water Braſh	1	After Pains	9

The Carlisle Dispensary Record, 1784–5

34
Marriage and birth

The extra numbers in the 1820s could not have been due only to the fall in the death-rate. The birth-rate also went up.

More parents

The falling death-rate meant that more babies were born. As fewer people were killed by disease in their twenties and thirties so more were around to have children. If more infants survived to be adults they too would have children.

Earlier marriage

But that was not the only cause of more births. On average men and women got married a few years earlier in 1800 than in 1700. There were many possible reasons. Farmers began to use fewer living-in servants and more day labourers so a milkmaid and a ploughman, for example, could begin life together in their own cottage in their early twenties. In industrial trades unskilled workers were replacing craftsmen who had to complete a seven-year apprenticeship living in with their master's family.

Young people lived freer lives if they moved from tiny villages to work in nearby towns. That might mean the difference between being a servant in your second cousin's farmhouse where everyone (including the parson) knew you, and being in a workshop, factory or mine with people of your own age. It was easier to set up home when shopkeepers were keen to sell you factory-made goods and landlords were eager to rent you a room or a tiny house.

This greater freedom also pushed up both the birth-rate and the marriage-rate. There was a sharp rise in pregnancy before the mothers and fathers married – as they usually did. Women who married early usually had larger families than their mothers.

*Rising
birth-rate*

The birth-rate went up everywhere but much more in the industrial areas. By looking at parish registers we know that the extra people in the iron, coal and textile areas were not just the result of people moving there from long distances away.

The earlier marriages and larger families led to sharp arguments. Factory owners, traders and food growers saw them as a sign of booming times. There were more people to buy their goods and more labour (including child workers) for their factories and mines. Others took a sourer view. They believed that early marriages were encouraged by handouts from the Parish Poor Law funds to make up wages.

*Thomas Malthus
(1766–1834)*

A clergyman, Thomas Malthus, gave these critics more ammunition when he wrote *An Essay on the Principles of Population* in 1798. He claimed he had discovered a law by which population grew in geometric stages (2, 4, 8, 16) while food supply could increase only arithmetically (1, 2, 3, 4). In the past, population had been brought back into line with food supply by 'checks' such as plagues and wars. In the England of his day, so he said, Poor Law handouts were stopping the natural checks from keeping numbers down. More people would have to live all their lives in poverty and the wealthy would have to dig deeper into their pockets to help them. If the poor could not be thinned out by disaster, he believed they should be forced to practise 'moral restraint'.

Moral restraint was his delicate way of saying that young men and women should stay apart until they had enough savings to set up home — and would be too old to have very large families.

A reply to Malthus
A
William Cobbett was a political journalist who always took the side of the poor. In his play Surplus Population *a landowner wants all his villagers to practise moral restraint. In this scene he sends his agent, Thimble, to persuade a pretty village girl not to marry.*

1 *Why does Thimble say that 'the country is ruined'?*
2 *What other parts of this scene show that Thimble was a believer in Malthus's ideas?*
3 *The play was banned by magistrates in one town in 1835. Suggest reasons.*

"THIMBLE: So, young woman, you are going to be married, I understand?
BETSY: Yes, sir.
THIMBLE: How old are you?
BETSY: I'm nineteen, Sir, come next Valentine's Eve.
THIMBLE: That is to say, you are *eighteen*! [*Aside*] No wonder the country is ruined! And your mother, now; how old is she?
BETSY: I can't justly say, Sir; but I heard her say she was forty some time back.
THIMBLE: And how many of you has she brought into the world?
BETSY: Only seventeen, Sir.
THIMBLE: Seventeen! *Only* seventeen!
BETSY: Seventeen now alive, Sir; she lost two and had two still-born, and –
THIMBLE: Hold your tongue! Hold your tongue! [*Aside*] It is quite monstrous! Nothing can save the country but plague, pestilence, famine, and sudden death. Government ought to import a ship-load of arsenic. [*To her*]: But, young woman, cannot you impose on yourself '*moral restraint*' for ten or a dozen years?
BETSY: Pray, what is that, Sir?
THIMBLE: Cannot you keep single till you are about thirty years old?
BETSY: Thirty years old, Sir! [*Stifling a laugh.*]"
William Cobbett, *Surplus Population*, in the *Political Register*, 1831

B
A summary of the birth-rate and death-rate, England and Wales, 1740–1820.
4 *Use the graph to say what were the main changes in the birth-rate and death-rate between 1740 and 1820.*
5 *Do you think these changes were due mainly to medical causes or to differences in living conditions? Give examples to support your answer.*

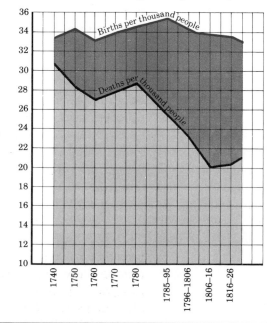

35
Coal – the basis of wealth

This is the first unit on the major industries in Britain between the 1830s and 1913, the year before the First World War. Coal led the field in these years, which have been called 'the age of steam'. The sources give some reasons why mining was so important to other industries.

The hewer

In 1913 one out of every fourteen British workers was employed at a coal-mine. They dug 187 million tons, far more than any other country apart from America. The hewer still lay on his side to cut under the seam with a short-handled pick. But now he brought down the coal above the cut by drilling a hole and plugging it with dynamite which was set off by the specialist shot-firer. Mechanical coal-cutters had been invented but they were used to dig less than a tenth of Britain's coal. It was behind the hewer that machinery had become important.

Machinery

In 1830 steam engine-power could wind men and coal up and down a few hundred feet. By the 1860s there were pit-head engines of 1,500 hp. Shaft diggers took up to three years to make the shaft and line it with two or three million bricks. An owner who had paid for so much labour and materials would want as much as possible from the mine so the coal-face was often a mile or more from the pit bottom. Some miners would walk a quarter of a mile from their cottage to the pit-head and then travel more than that distance into the earth. A steam-engine hauled wagons by rope or wire along the main road. Then they were pushed into a cage which went up the shaft while another came down with the returned empties. At the surface the coal was washed and graded into different sizes, often by women, and hauled to towns by rail.

South Wales

For a hundred years after 1850 coal made up half the railways' freight business. The coming of railways (see Units 40 and 41) had a dramatic effect on the valleys of South Wales. In the 1840s they produced small amounts of coking coal from pits near to canals.

The Taff Valley

Then the Taff Valley Railway (TVR) planned lines into the two Rhondda valleys. They offered a prize to the first person to sink a mine there. In 1855 the first 38 tons of coal were brought down to Cardiff by the TVR. It was steam coal which was ideal for railways and steamships because it burned with little smoke and did not leave hard cinders in the furnace.

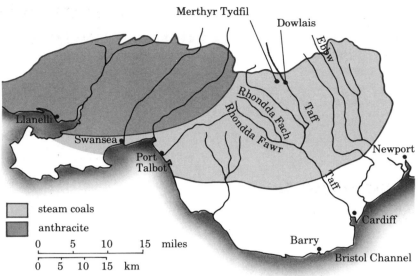

The mining valleys of South Wales.

Exports

By 1913 the TVR was carrying ten million tons a year to new docks in Cardiff, Barry and Newport. Coal-carrying ships were then as important as oil tankers today. Sometimes they carried fuel for overseas railways which had often been built by British engineers. Many tons went to foreign ports and were loaded into bunkers where ships stopped to re-fuel. Several Rhondda companies owned their own bunkering stations around the world.

The importance of coal
A

You can see evidence of coal's value to industry and trade in these tables based on information from a number of sources.

1 *By how many times did the amount of coal mined increase between 1830 and 1910?*
2 *What fraction (roughly) of coal was exported in 1830 and in 1910?*
3 *What is meant by horsepower (see Unit 20)? What does the table showing horsepower tell you about the importance of coal?*
4 *Which of the users in the second table used coal mainly (a) to drive machinery, (b) for heating, (c) as a raw material to make another product?*

Coal output in million tons		Coal exports in million tons		Horsepower in British industry	
1830	22.5	1830	0.4	1800	7,500
1850	49.4	1850	3.2	1850	300,000
1870	121.3	1870	12.3	1870	977,000
1890	180.3	1890	29.3	1901	9,700,000
1910	270.0	1910	64.7		

Uses of coal in million tons, 1913

Factories	60.00
Domestic	35.00
Iron and steel	31.00
Mines	20.50
Gasworks	18.00
Railways	15.00
Brickworks, potteries, glass and chemical works	5.75
Coastal steamers	2.25
Other	1.25

H.S. Jevons, *The British Coal Trade*, 1915

36
Coal – the human cost

Work in the mines was hard and dangerous. Between 1842 and 1913 Parliament passed at least thirteen laws to make the work of miners safer and healthier.

Women and children

In 1840 about one in ten of all people working underground was a boy or girl under 13. We know a great deal about them because an MP, Anthony Ashley Cooper (later Lord Shaftesbury), persuaded Parliament to set up a Royal Commission of four men to inquire into their work and conditions. Their report came to three books of evidence collected by twenty sub-commissioners who interviewed mine-owners and workers. It told stories of infant trappers and children who worked as hurriers, or half-naked men and young women working together in the gloom.

The Mines Act, 1842

Public disgust was too great for MPs to agree with mine-owners who told them that pits would close if they could not use women or children. So Parliament passed the Mines Act in 1842. No women or girls were to work underground, nor any boy under 10 An inspector (but only one!) was to check that the law was obeyed.

Accidents

The Act said one thing about safety. No boy under 15 could be in charge of the engine which let miners down the shaft. You can imagine what led to that rule! But nothing was said about the other accidents which killed five out of every thousand underground workers each year. To prevent explosions the best mines had two shafts a good way apart from each other (see Unit 22). In the 1880s extractor fans were used to suck air up the second shaft. But explosions still happened when safety lamps were broken, or uncovered by miners. Shot-firing was dangerous when it was done with ordinary gunpowder and paper fuses lit with matches. Mines became safer when special dynamite was used and one man had the job of setting it off, sometimes by electricity.

Later Mines Acts

Miners and trade union leaders campaigned for laws to see that all mines used the safest methods. The 1850 Mines Act said that there should be six inspectors to check on ventilation. The 1860 Mines Act raised the age limit for underground workers to 12, and for machine-minders to 18. It said that safety lamps were to be checked and locked before miners took them underground.

In 1862 a pumping engine fell and blocked the single shaft at Hartley Colliery in Northumberland, and 204 men and boys died from slow suffocation. Public anger led to another Mines Act in the same year. All mines were to have two shafts to give an escape route. Later Acts said there were to be 'firemen' to watch for gas. Miners could elect their own deputies to double check for safety. The age limit for boys working underground was raised to 13 in 1900.

Safety in 1913

In 1913 there were sixty-two inspectors for the 3,289 pits. But Source B will show you how dangerous mines still were. In one explosion in Wales 439 workers lost their lives. Many could have been saved if the mines had had proper equipment. The manager was fined £22. As the local paper said: 'Miners' lives at 1s 1¼ each!'

The cost of coal

A

Part of the 1840 Report used the evidence of J.L. Kennedy, sub-commissioner for Lancashire and Cheshire.

1 *What was the job of a trapper?*
2 *How would the pictures help the aims of people such as Anthony Ashley Cooper?*
3 *Using this source, work out how a mineowner could justify using women and children underground.*

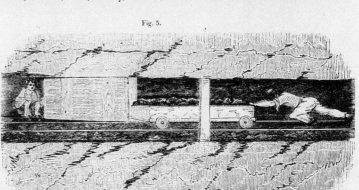

EMPLOYMENT OF CHILDREN.   81

COAL MINES.
———
Nature of Employment.

Lancashire and Cheshire.

are naked; I would rather work in mill than in coal-pit.—[Sub-Commissioner: " This girl is an ignorant, filthy, ragged, and deplorable-looking object, and such a one as the uncivilised natives of the prairies would be shocked to look upon.]" (Ibid. No. 26: p. 108, l. 8, 17).

328. LANCASHIRE AND CHESHIRE.—The Sub-Commissioner accompanies his account of the occupation of the trappers in this district with the sketch " of an air-door tender in a thin mine in the act of opening an air-door to allow a waggon to pass through." The Child is represented "as sitting on his heels, as is the universal custom of all colliers, young and old, in this district." (See Fig. 5.)

329. " This occupation is one of the most pitiable in a coal-pit, from its extreme monotony. Exertion there is none, nor labour, further than is requisite to open and shut a door. As these little fellows are always the youngest in the pits, I have generally found them very shy, and they have never anything to say for themselves. Their whole time is spent in sitting in the dark for twelve hours, and opening and shutting a door to allow the waggons to pass. Were it not for the passing and repassing of the waggons it would be equal to solitary confinement of the worst order" (J. L. Kennedy, Esq., Report, § 122: App. Pt. II., p. 166).

330. " But by far the greater number of Children and persons employed in coal-mines are engaged in propelling and drawing tubs laden with coal, from the face to the pit-eye, or the main-levels in those pits where they have horses. This is done by placing the hands on the back of the waggon, and propelling it forward with as great velocity as the inclination of the mine, the state of the road, and the strength of the waggoner admit of. The mines in this district are for the most part laid with rails, and the waggon runs on wheels of various diameters from four to six inches. There are, however, mines throughout the district—namely, Clifton, Bolton, Outwood, Lever, Worsley, Blackrod, and St. Helen's—where the old mode

Fig. 5.

Report of the Commissioners on the Employment of Children, 1840

B

Part of a table from a book written in 1915, showing mining deaths and injuries in 1913.

4 *Which big disaster caused most of the deaths from explosion in 1913?*
5 *List, in order, the six main causes of death. Do the same for injuries. Can you explain the differences?*
6 *Which cause of death could not have happened in 1830?*
7 *Which small cause of death in 1913 would have been much greater in 1830?*
8 *If you were looking into mining accidents in 1913, what steps might you have recommended to cut them?*

	Killed	*Injured*
Explosions	462	131
Falls of ground		
At working face	401	49,311
On roads	215	12,707
In shafts	4	76
Shaft accidents	98	825
Other causes		
Explosives	30	263
Suffocation by gas	5	11
Fires	25	10
Drowning	9	5
Haulage ropes or chains breaking	8	191
Crushing by trams or tubs	214	25,682

H.S. Jevons, *The British Coal Trade*, 1915

37
Steel

Unit 17 explained why there were so many large wrought iron works after Henry Cort invented puddling and rolling. Wrought iron kept its lead as the biggest metal industry until ways of mass-producing steel were discovered. This unit explains the most important inventions in steelmaking.

Wrought iron

In 1853 the engineer Isambard Kingdom Brunel wrote a contract for the men who would make the world's largest ship, the *Great Eastern*. It said "No cast iron to be used anywhere except for slide valves and cocks without the special permission of the engineer." Brunel insisted on wrought iron because cast iron parts would have shattered as the huge ship, with six steam-engines throbbing inside, rode the Atlantic. For the same reason locomotives, railway tracks and bridges had to be built of wrought iron.

Wrought iron was made in the huge combined steelworks of the Black Country, Wales and Scotland. But, no matter how hard he worked, the puddler could only make a hundredweight of wrought iron each hour to pass on to the rolling mills.

Henry Bessemer (1813–1898)

Henry Bessemer found a way to do without puddling. He spent his life inventing machinery, including a machine for squeezing the juice out of sugar-cane in Jamaica. In 1856 he built a converter to hold liquid iron taken straight from the blast furnace. Cold air was blown through it so the oxygen burned off the carbon and left iron that could be rolled in the same way as wrought iron.

Steel

Bessemer called this material 'steel'* because it was much harder than ordinary wrought iron. The Midland Railway Company laid steel rails on a crossing used by five hundred trains a day. They were still sound ten years later. Before that the Company had needed to change the wrought iron rails every six months. Three-quarters of all steel made in Bessemer converters was used for railway lines. But it was not strong enough for ships and bridges.

Siemens-Martin

A German scientist, Friedrich Siemens, took the first step to stronger steel. He invented an open-hearth furnace which saved fuel by storing waste hot gases in a huge pile of bricks. Two Frenchmen, Émile and Pierre Martin, found the furnace could be used to make steel by heating pig iron and scrap iron in the right proportions.

Ships and bridges

The biggest use for open-hearth steel was in shipbuilding. In 1877 90 per cent of all ships made on the river Clyde were wooden. Ten years later, 90 per cent were steel. By 1913 British shipyards made half of the world's steel ships. Most were built on the Clyde or on the rivers Tyne, Wear and Tees in north-eastern England. They were deep enough to take the new huge vessels.

* 'Steel' had been used for centuries to describe the sort of very hard iron used for objects such as sword blades.

Open-hearth steel was also used for building. When the Forth Bridge opened in 1890 it was the world's longest. Its engineer said: "with iron it would have been twice the weight in consequence of the less strength of the material, and more than twice the cost".

New manufacturing districts

Steel-makers found one big problem with converters and open-hearth furnaces. If they used ore which contained phosphorus the steel was shot through with cracks. The only non-phosphoric iron ore in Britain was in Cumberland. The rest had to be imported from Spain and Sweden. So most new steelworks were built on the coast. The first was at Barrow-in-Furness in Cumberland. The town also became a busy port sending ore to other districts. Most went to Middlesbrough which had only 7,000 people in the 1851 census. In 1901 the town was importing 100 million tons of ore each year and its population had grown to 91,000. Spanish ore changed South Wales. The ironworks at the tops of the valleys lost business while new steel and tin-plate works opened on the coast.

The only really important inland steel town was Sheffield which became a centre for more specialised types of steel. A Sheffield man, Harry Brearley, first added chromium to make stainless steel in 1913. A Sheffield firm, Vickers, was the first to use steel for guns and shells. In the 1890s they bought shipyards to build warships armed with their own weapons. Between 1900 and 1910 Vickers supplied the Navy with a hundred warships.

Basic steel

In the late 1870s a young clerk, Sidney Gilchrist Thomas, heard a night-school teacher say 'the man who eliminates phosphorus from the Bessemer converter will one day make a fortune'. Sidney decided to be that man with the help of his cousin, P.C. Gilchrist, a chemist in a Welsh ironworks. They found a way of lining blast furnaces with dolomite, a kind of limestone. The dolomite joined with the phosphorus to make a slag, which could be skimmed off the iron. Iron made in this way could be used in a converter or an open-hearth furnace to make 'basic' steel.

British firms were slow to take up basic steel. They did not want the expense of changing their converters and furnaces and they had got used to using ore from abroad. The British steel industry began to lose its leading position in world trade.

A

Britain's share in world steel production, 1875–1914

1 *What reasons can you suggest for the changes shown here?*

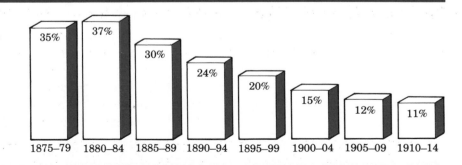

1875–79	1880–84	1885–89	1890–94	1895–99	1900–04	1905–09	1910–14
35%	37%	30%	24%	20%	15%	12%	11%

The Bessemer converter
B

Diagrams from Henry Bessemer's An
Autobiography, *1905.*

A *the converter at rest*
B *the converter tilted and molten iron
    poured in*
C *the converter blowing – with cold air
    through the tubes*
D *steel is poured into the ladle*

2 *What was burned off when the converter
   'blew'?*
3 *What was the advantage of this method
   over puddling iron?*

C

*An account of Bessemer's first trials with
the converter.*

4 *Explain what was happening to the
   metal when the white flame could be
   seen.*
5 *What two advantages over puddling does
   Bessemer write about?*

The open-hearth furnace
D

6 *In what way did this do the same job as
   a converter?*
7 *What were the advantages over the
   converter method?*

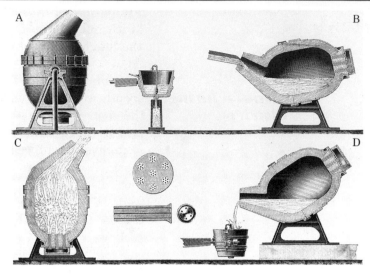

H. Bessemer, *An Autobiography*, 1905

"After an interval of ten or twelve minutes, when the carbon contained in pig iron . . . is seized on by the oxygen a white flame is produced which brilliantly illuminates the whole space around. I watched with some anxiety for the expected cessation of the flame as the carbon gradually burnt out. It took place almost suddenly. . . . The furnace was then tapped, when out rushed a . . . stream of iron, almost too brilliant for the eye to rest upon; it was allowed to flow vertically into the ingot mould. . . . we had as much metal as could be produced by two puddlers and two assistants working for hours with an expenditure of much fuel."
H. Bessemer, *An Autobiography*, 1905

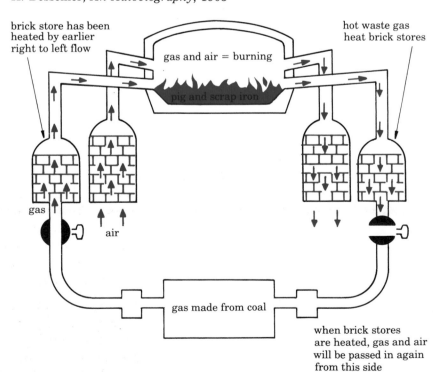

brick store has been
heated by earlier
right to left flow

hot waste gas
heat brick stores

gas and air = burning

pig and scrap iron

gas

air

gas made from coal

when brick stores
are heated, gas and air
will be passed in again
from this side

38 Chemicals

The chemical industry was divided into several branches. The oldest made soda (or alkali) products. Others then started making dyes, fertilisers, soap and explosives. As in steel, Britain lost her lead over the rest of the world.

Alkali

Up to the 1870s soda was still made in alkali works by the Leblanc process (see Unit 24) which meant mixing salt with sulphuric acid and heating it. Most alkali works were in Tyneside or South Lancashire where there was plenty of coal and salt.

Health hazards

Alkali work was dangerous to health. The men (and some women) who raked the saltcake mixture had the worst job. It gave off gusts of hydrochloric acid which rotted teeth so they could always be recognised by their toothless mouths.

Families near a Leblanc works had to get used to the sulphur smell. Every few hours the air would be darkened as the factory belched out waves of hydrochloric acid. At first the only way to limit this was to spread it over a wide area by using very tall chimneys. Then some factory owners realised how wasteful this was and turned the gas back into a liquid making other chemicals. In 1863, Parliament passed the Alkali Act to make this compulsory.

The Solvay process

Soon afterwards the Leblanc process had a rival. A Belgian chemist, Ernest Solvay, made soda by using ammonia and brine. That interested Ludwig Mond who was born in Germany and set up as a chemical engineer in Britain. He visited Solvay and came back with a licence to use his system here. With his partner, John Brunner, Ludwig Mond chose a site in Cheshire where salt could be pumped from the ground in water. Soon they were making soda which was much cheaper than that produced by the Leblanc factories.

Brunner-Mond

Their success gave Brunner and Mond the funds to branch out into other chemicals, such as making ammonia from coal. It also meant a fall in business for the Leblanc companies. To save their industry they formed one United Alkali Company in 1891. In 1926 this joined the still growing Brunner-Mond to form ICI.

Coal products

Each year gasworks turned out thousands of tons of waste tar. It was turned into creosote used especially for weatherproofing the millions of railway-line sleepers. As naphtha it was used for flares to light up public buildings before electric arc lights. It could be thinned in other liquids to become benzine. Charles Macintosh dissolved rubber in it to make waterproof material. Benzine was also the starting-point for a new service industry, dry cleaning.

Dyes

Out of benzine came aniline. In 1856 an 18-year-old chemistry student, W.H. Perkin, was experimenting with aniline and accidentally made purple dye. Up to that point all dyes were made from plants, animals or soils. Perkin and his father and brother opened a factory to make the dye, which they called 'mauve'.

Other synthetic dyes made from aniline were discovered in England, but they were mostly mass-produced in Germany. The Germans were better than the British at building the complicated works needed for synthetic products. In 1879 Perkin pointed out that Britain had five colour-works making £450,000 worth of goods a year while Germany had seventeen turning out £2,500,000. Often the coal tar they used came from Britain.

Fertilisers

High farmers (see Unit 67) were the biggest customers for fertilisers. Some were waste products from other industries. Sulphate of ammonia (which helps plants go green) came from coke works. Gilchrist-Thomas steelworks sold basic slag as a phosphate (essential for root growth). Some factories began to make 'superphosphates' by grinding rock or bone and treating it with sulphuric acid. There were also many small-scale works which made phosphates out of old bones, woollen waste and other rubbish. This trade grew especially in the middle of towns and was a health hazard.

Soap

Soap was made by boiling alkali, salt and fat in water. At first it was a small-scale trade. In the 1860s the new director of a London firm pushed up the advertising bill from £80 a year to £130,000. He spent the money on posters and slogans such as 'How do you spell soap? – Why P-E-A-R-S, of course'!! He should be remembered as a pioneer of one of today's biggest industries – advertising.

In any case, London was not the place for mass-producing soap. That was in the north-west where you could buy alkali from nearby factories, salt from Cheshire and plenty of coal for boiling. You could also import fats through Liverpool. At first soap-makers mostly bought fish-oil and whale-oil. Then palm-oil was added after European countries 'opened up' Africa and started plantations.

W.H. Lever

W.H. Lever began making Sunlight soap with palm-oil in the 1880s. In 1888 he opened his Port Sunlight factory near Liverpool. It was the basis for a huge business which owned palm plantations, whale fishing boats and steadily bought up rivals, such as Pears, Gibbs and Erasmic. In 1929 the Lever empire merged with a Dutch firm which controlled most of the supplies of oil for margarine – and Unilever was born.

Explosives

After boiling soap, glycerol is left. Up to 1871 soap-makers let it go to waste. In that year a Swedish industrialist, Alfred Nobel, opened a branch of his firm at Ardeer in Scotland to make a new explosive. It needed glycerol and nitrate (imported from Chile) and the result was nitro-glycerine which was far more powerful than gunpowder. Nobel gave it the name 'dynamite'. Shortly afterwards Nobel invented a 'gelatine' explosive which was a great help in blasting rock because an expert could control the amount used.

Ardeer was just one of many factories around Europe which made Alfred Nobel immensely rich. He left his wealth for prizes to scientists and writers as well as the Nobel Peace Prize – a curious gift from the man who made the material which shatters lives.

Chemicals and health

A

In 1848 James Muspratt moved his alkali factory to St Helens from Liverpool. This account describes St Helens in that year.

"a very prettily situated, nice little country town. It was the residence of several well-to-do families, who lived in substantial comfortable homes attached to their shops or close to their business. Gardens and well-stocked orchards ran from street to street, the roads that led out from the town were lined with avenues of trees, and on all sides were rich farm lands."
Chemical Trades Journal, 1889

B

An account of St Helens written in 1900.

"A great cloud of smoke hangs continuously over the town, and choking fumes assail the nose from various works. In the face of such atmosphere it is not to be wondered at that trees and other green things refuse to grow."
Victoria County History, 1900

Sources A–B

1 *Explain what the first writer meant by calling St Helens a 'nice little country town'.*
2 *What does the second account suggest about the effect of the 1863 Alkali Act?*

A new branch of the industry

C

The Ardeer works photographed just after they were opened in 1871.

3 *What was made here?*
4 *Explain the layout of the works.*
5 *The building on the top is a look-out. Why was it needed?*

Chemicals and science

D

A chemical engineer born in Germany, who owned a dye-works in Britain, wrote this in 1886.

6 *What is Ivan Lewinstein complaining about in the first paragraph?*
7 *What explanation does he give in the second paragraph?*

"we still supply Germany with three-fourths of the hydrocarbons which she requires; and we still allow Germany to supply us with at least three-fourths of the colouring matter which we use. . . .

What are the reasons why far greater progress has not been made in this country in the manufacture of these products? The development of industrial enterprise in this country has for the last thirty years been practically confined to cotton, wool, iron and coal, while the chemical industries have been left in the hands of a few, whose names have a world-wide reputation but we do not possess what may be termed chemical engineers."
Ivan Lewinstein, *Journal of the Society of the Chemical Industry*, 1886

39
Electricity

A new industry was started when Joseph Swan invented the electric light bulb and engineers made electric motors for use in industry and transport. Powerhouses were built to make electricity. They produced so many different currents and voltages that it was difficult to use and the Americans and Germans took the lead in this vital new industry.

Electric lights

By the late 1870s many people had seen arc lights blazing in factories, at the Blackpool illuminations or even floodlit football matches. The arc was made when an electric current jumped between two carbon rods and burnt in the air, which made it too bright and smelly for home use. In 1878, in Gateshead, Joseph Swan used a pump to draw all the air from a glass bulb and then got a piece of carbon wire to glow, instead of burning, so it gave a steady light. Thomas Edison did the same in America in 1879 and the two made Ediswan light bulbs together in Gateshead for a time.

A new form of power

Electric lighting was soon popular with shops, theatres and better-off families. Engineers were also working on electric motors. They could be used to drive machinery, lifts, trams and do away with heavy, dirty steam-engines and horses. The electricity was made in a powerhouse by turning a generator using one of Charles Parsons's steam turbines – another Gateshead invention of 1884.

Power-stations

In the late 1880s and 1890s powerhouses appeared in most towns and very often more than one. Some were private companies supplying power for just a few thousand lamps, others were built by local councils to run their trams. There were two different kinds of current (AC and DC) and many different voltages. The small power-stations and the different currents made life difficult for the customer and made electricity expensive. The answer was to have large power-stations supplying a wide area with the same current. But jealousy between the different companies meant this did not happen, except from Europe's largest power-station which was run by NESCo, the Newcastle-on-Tyne Power Company. Its manager, Charles Merz, made agreements with local councils, factories and mines over a wide area. This meant he could make the best use of his generators by switching the load from daytime factories to the evening rush on the trams, and then to night-time lighting.

Germany and the USA

Between 1902 and 1913 NESCo's sales went up thirty-two times while the rest of the country's power-stations made only four times as much electricity. Germany and America both had larger electric supply services and more factories using electric power instead of steam. That had a knock-on effect; they led the field in the newest twentieth-century industry, making electric motors and parts for machinery, lifts, trams and so on. By 1913 Americans owned three of the four leading electrical goods firms in Britain. They also supplied the electrical equipment for the London underground Central Line and for three-quarters of all the trams in Britain.

The electricity revolution

A

In the 1960s a woman remembered the early days of electricity.

Some early uses of electricity

B *(below left)*

One of the first Hoovers, invented in 1908 by Charles Spangler. Spangler was caretaker in the home of W.H. Hoover who owned a saddle-making factory in America. Hoover turned to making vacuum-cleaners. The first models cost £25 – more than a maid's yearly wages.

C *(far right)*

A hotel sign of the 1890s.

D *(centre)*

The first trials of an electric tram in Bradford in 1892. Trams were in regular use in the town by 1898.

E *(bottom)*

Seaside towns often set up power stations to light their sea fronts. Here, the mains are being laid in Torquay in 1898.

Sources A–E

1 *Suggest why the use of electricity for trams and street lighting went ahead faster than its use in the home.*
2 *In the home, why did lighting spread faster than household aids?*
3 *What evidence is there in these sources that electricity was once thought a strange and wonderful invention?*
4 *What do you think the main changes would have been when a household had electricity? What else would you have liked to ask the woman in Source A if you had met her in the 1960s?*

"In 1889 we stayed at an hotel in Southampton, that had electricity installed, and our mother (who wasn't sure how to switch on the light) had to ring for a maid, to ask her how to do it. In 1890 we were living in a small town in Yorkshire (Harrogate), and ours was the first home in the town to be lighted with electricity. We generated our own power. People living in the town used to drive up to our gates in carriages and also bring their visitors, to see 'the house with the lights'. As young children when we heard the sound of horses' hooves at dusk in our quiet road, we rushed around the house switching the lights on and off so that the spectators outside would not be disappointed."
Quoted in R.A.S. Hennessy, *The Electric Revolution*, 1972

This Room Is Equipped With **Edison Electric Light.** Do not attempt to light with match. Simply turn key on wall by the door.

The use of Electricity for lighting is in no way harmful to health, nor does it affect the soundness of sleep.

Photograph supplied by the Electricity Council

Photograph supplied by the Electricity Council

Electrical Review, 1898

40
The Stephensons

Before the Stockton and Darlington Railway was opened in 1825, all railways were privately owned. George Stephenson built the Stockton and Darlington for a company which let others run their trucks on its rails for a fee. In 1830 he finished the Liverpool and Manchester Railway – the first to run its own services instead of charging tolls to others.

George Stephenson (1781–1848)

In 1810 businessmen met in Stockton to discuss carrying coal from mines twenty miles away. Some wanted a canal, dug over the shortest route. Edward Pease, a banker from Darlington, wanted a railway which could meander about to connect with other towns. Nine years later the railway side won and set up the Stockton and Darlington Company which asked Parliament for the right to build the line. Edward Pease asked George Stephenson to take charge.

Stephenson agreed to do the job part-time as he was already engineer at Killingworth Colliery and was also helping to build private railways for other mines. Tracks of rails made it much easier for a horse to pull cart-loads of coal to the nearest river or canal. The first rails had been put down a hundred years before. Until Darby made cast iron ones, the rails were made of wood.

Stephenson still recommended horses for pulling wagons on level stretches. But he used steam-engines to haul them up steep slopes. For long distances and heavy loads, Stephenson preferred the latest idea, a steam-engine on wheels. He had already built five himself, starting with *Blucher*.

Early locomotives

The first locomotive had been made by Richard Trevithick, a Cornish mining engineer. He began by building a steam-engine, light enough to fit on a road carriage. Other steam carriages were made up to the 1830s but Trevithick himself turned to making locomotives to run on rails. His first in 1804 was for hauling wagons at an ironworks in Merthyr Tydfil.

The idea was copied by engineers in the north of England. In 1812 John Blenkinsop and Matthew Murray built a $3\frac{1}{2}$-mile railway from Middleton Colliery to Leeds. In 1813 William Hedley built the *Wylam Dilly* for Wylam Colliery. In 1814 Stephenson made *Blucher*, with ideas taken from all the earlier inventors.

The Stockton and Darlington

Stephenson had the Stockton and Darlington line finished by 1825. He used rails made of wrought iron for $25\frac{1}{2}$ miles of single track with a few loops where wagons could pass.

At the western end there were two hills and Stephenson put

The Stockton and Darlington Railway

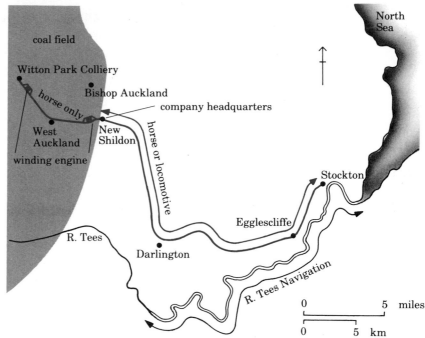

winding engines on top. The short stretch of level track between was meant for horses only. The rest of the way he made for horses or locomotives. On the opening day there was only one of these, *Locomotion*, built by Stephenson's son, Robert. It pulled 24 trucks for 300 ticket-holders. It travelled at 8 miles an hour and only broke down once. For several years most pulling was done by horses, until it became clear they cost more than locomotives.

The Company copied the canal owners' way of doing business. They charged a toll to carriers for using the track. Nearly all the traffic was coal with one passenger coach each day.

The Liverpool and Manchester

While he was still working on the Stockton and Darlington, George Stephenson was asked by businessmen in Liverpool and Manchester to build a railway between their towns. They hoped it would undercut the canal charges. The canal-owners' first reply was to stop surveyors going on to lands which they owned. So the survey started in 1824 had to be done again in 1828.

People told George Stephenson that no one could build a track across the huge peaty bog called Chat Moss. He proved them wrong by sinking piles of brushwood to hold up an embankment made with millions of barrow-loads of earth. He made most of the 30-mile length fairly level with just one steep slope for the last 1½ miles into Liverpool. Here there would be a fixed winding-engine to pull the carriages. For the rest of the route Stephenson planned to run locomotives. But many of the Company directors wanted fixed engines to pull trains the whole way, section by section.

To settle the question they held the Rainhill trials in 1829. Six locomotives were entered but only one completed the trial. It was Robert Stephenson's *Rocket*, built in a new way with pistons at the side inside of on top. Still more important was the boiler. Instead of being heated like a kettle on a fire, the heat was taken through the water by a concertina of pipes. With these two improvements *Rocket* reached 19 mph.

The opening

The company bought seven more engines for the day in 1830 when the Prime Minister, the Duke of Wellington, was to open the railway. He was hated by unemployed weavers and people who wanted reforms in the electoral system. Every yard of track was guarded. The Duke got away with an angry demonstration but William Huskisson, MP for Liverpool, got off the VIP train and was struck by the *Rocket* pulling another train. Confusion followed until George Stephenson took the controls of the *Northumbrian* and drove Huskisson to Eccles. The poor man died there but his last journey was the fastest in history so far: 36 mph.

Running the railway

The Liverpool and Manchester was the first railway to use only locomotives and no horses. There would have been dangerous chaos if the company had let out the track to private carriers to run their own locomotives. So they ran all the trains themselves with their own drivers and signalmen who had to obey strict rules on safety.

At first the railway attracted more passengers than freight. In the first three years, the trains carried an average of a thousand people a day, at half the cost and twice the speed of stage-coaches.

Early railways
A

A railway on the Northumberland and Durham coalfield in 1773. The truck ran downhill by gravity and the driver has a brake to slow it. In the background there is a 'keel' boat which would take the coal out to sea-going coal ships.

1 *What was the horse used for?*
2 *How do the wheels and tracks differ from later ones?*

Liverpool and Manchester Railway
B

Stephenson wrote this letter to Edward Pease. (Derby, Sefton and Bradshaw owned shares in the Bridgewater Canal and land on the route of the railway.)

3 *Why did Stephenson and his men want to go on these lands?*
4 *Why did the landowners try to stop them?*
5 *Why did the Company think the landowners had no right to stop the survey?*

"We have sad work with Lord Derby, Lord Sefton and Bradshaw the great Canal Proprietor whose ground we go through with the projected railway. Their ground is blockaded on every side to prevent us getting on with the survey. Bradshaw fires guns through his ground in the course of the night to prevent the surveyors coming in the dark. We are to have a grand field day next week. The Liverpool Rly Co. are determined to force a survey through if possible. Lord Sefton says he will have 100 men to stop us. The Company thinks those great men have no right to stop our survey. It is the farmers only who have a right to complain and by charging damages for trespass is all they can do."
George Stephenson, 1824, in L.T.C. Rolt, *George and Robert Stephenson*, 1960

41
A railway network

Railway building boomed in the 1830s and 1840s and went on through the nineteenth century. This unit looks at some of the difficulties: in engineering, paying for the railways and standardising the tracks and services.

Lines of the 1830s

After the success of the Liverpool and Manchester Railway other Companies asked for Acts of Parliament to build railways between towns even further apart. The first was the Grand Junction which connected the Liverpool and Manchester to Birmingham. Soon after came the 112-mile London–Birmingham line built by Robert Stephenson. He had huge problems, most of all at the 2,000-yard Kilsby tunnel near Northampton where they hit a layer of water-logged sand. It needed thirteen pumps drawing up 1,800 gallons a minute for nineteen months before work could begin.

The government and the railways

The government welcomed the railways. It used them for mail from the earliest days and started the penny post in 1840. In 1842 it sent troops by rail to Chartist trouble-spots (see Unit 72). Yet ministers refused to have anything to do with the idea of the French and Belgians that the state should own the railways. Even so, they had to take steps to see that they were safe and the Companies were honest. To deal with these questions, an Act of 1840 gave Board of Trade inspectors the job of holding enquiries into accidents. The Railway Act, 1844, laid down that all railways must run one train a day which stopped at every station and charged only 1d a mile. If they saved, ordinary working people could now take journeys on one of these 'parliamentary trains'.

Railway mania

Between 1844 and 1848 Parliament agreed to 12,000 miles of new railway. These were the years of the 'railway mania', when people with money to invest believed they would get the best interest from railway shares. The mania stopped when it was realised that many schemes were foolish and some were plain dishonest. But it still gave the spurt to building up the system of 1852.

George Hudson

By 1852 the best known figure of the mania had risen and fallen. He was George Hudson, a draper in York. Someone left him £30,000 which he used to buy shares in a railway to link York to the Leeds–Derby line. It put York on the railway route to London and George Hudson's plan then was to make it the centre of a web of lines under his control. He built up his own Midland Railway by buying smaller companies. This was when a newspaper first called him 'the Railway King'.

Hudson was also a rogue. He made false statements about likely profits to get people to invest and bribed others to give false evidence to Parliament. But he got away with it and even became an MP himself in 1846. In 1848 Hudson's shareholders began to ask awkward questions. Banks demanded their money back. MPs could not be arrested for debt while Parliament was sitting so on the last day of each session he took a boat to France. In the end he was arrested during an election and spent a short time in prison.

Amalgamation

Hudson was right about one thing. There were too many railway companies which meant awkward connections and separate bookings for passengers and goods. One answer was amalgamation. By 1852 four companies were shaping up to be the giants who owned over half the lines in 1913. One was Hudson's old company, the Midland. The others were the North Eastern, the London and North Western and the Great Western. The other half of the lines were owned by a hundred separate companies.

Even after amalgamation, the companies still needed to make pooling arrangements so that trains could run over each other's lines after a booking had been made with one of them.

The railway system in 1852

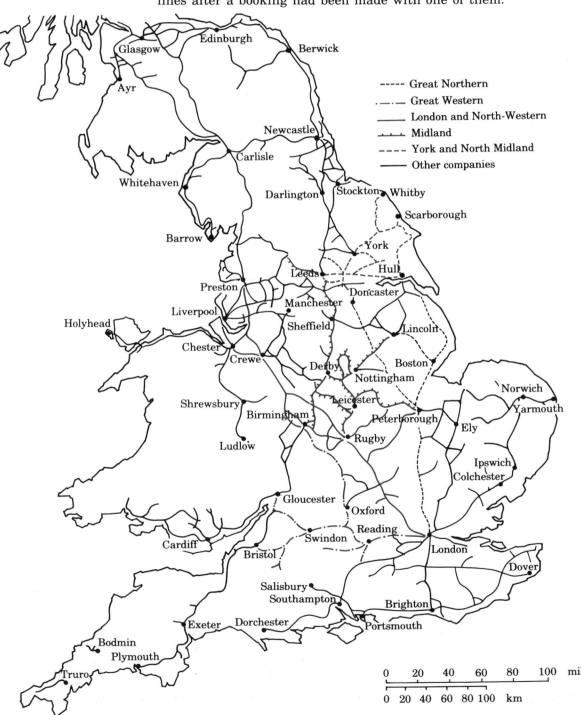

Brunel and the Great Western

For many years the Great Western Railway stood out from the others. That was because their engineer, Isambard Kingdom Brunel, wanted his trains to be more stylish than the others which were all built by the Stephensons or men who had once worked with them. Their tracks were 4'8½" wide, the usual distance between wagon wheels around Stockton and Darlington. Brunel mocked at this 'coal wagon gauge' and built his tracks 7 feet wide to give a more comfortable ride. The idea was sound and the Great Western was the first to run regular express services.

The battle of the gauges

But, by the 1870s, there were thirty places where the Great Western's broad gauge met up with narrow tracks. In some places passengers were forced to change trains. In others a third inside line had to be laid to make the track suitable for both kinds of engines. In the end the Great Western stopped fighting the 'battle of the gauges' and laid new 4'8½"-wide lines.

Hudson, the 'Railway King'
A

This cartoon appeared in Punch *in 1845. A levée is a reception at a royal court.*

1 *What is the occupation of King Hudson's attendant?*
2 *Who are the people kneeling?*
3 *What might have been the interest in railways of the woman at the right?*
4 *Is this a friendly or hostile cartoon?*
5 *Does this cartoon help to explain what is meant by 'railway mania'?*

KING HUDSON'S LEVEE.

Punch, 29 November 1845

The work of Brunel
B

Brunel built the Saltash bridge over the 300-yard-wide River Tamar to carry the Great Western Railway into Cornwall. The central column goes 90 feet below the surface.

6 *Suggest reasons why the bridge was built so high.*
7 *What material is it made of?*

A drawing by C. A. Scott, 1854.

42
Working and
travelling

Constructing the railways was the biggest building and earth-shifting job in British history up to that time. In 1845 alone about 3,000 miles were being laid – compared with about 2,000 miles of canal in eighty years. This unit begins by describing the work of navvies and then goes on to look at travelling by rail.

Navvies

In 1845 there were about 200,000 navvies. Most of them worked only with shovels and wheelbarrows but navvying was still a skill. It took a newcomer a year to become speedy enough and strong enough to keep up with his mates. That was important because navvies worked in gangs. Their leader, the ganger, agreed to get so much done in a certain time. He made this arrangement with a subcontractor who was paid a fixed price for building a stretch of track, a bridge or a tunnel.

When one job was finished navvy gangs would tramp to another. Near the new job the subcontractor put up bare wooden sleeping huts, called 'shanties'. Several thousand navvies might camp together for a year or two. Some subcontractors made a fortune by paying them in tickets for food and beer from their own 'tommy shops'. Local villagers were often said to be terrified by the navvies' drunken ways. Other people admired them when they saw them at work.

Travelling classes

From the start travellers thought railways were an improvement over road transport. The wealthy could travel in a first-class coach which looked like a stage-coach but was roomier inside with six seats and elbow rests. A second-class carriage was plainer and bumpier but better than being outside on a stage-coach. To begin with, third-class passengers had only wooden benches in an open carriage with low sides. Even that was better and faster than walking or taking a ride on a stage-wagon. In 1844 the Railway Act said that trucks on parliamentary trains must have covered tops.

The three classes lasted to the 1870s. Then the Midland Railway put third-class carriages on all trains and made them more comfortable. Afterwards it abolished the second class. Other companies did the same and up to the 1940s the two classes were known as first and third. In the 1880s came compartments with lighting and heating and the first corridor trains with lavatories.

Safety

As trains became longer and faster, accidents became more serious. To prevent them, improved signals and brakes were needed. The first signalling was done by railway policemen with flags. They were replaced by signalmen who worked long-armed signals on tall poles. There were still crashes and block signalling was started in the 1860s. No train was allowed into one block if another was already there. This kind of signalling meant that 'line clear' messages had to be sent from one signal box to the next along electric telegraph wires.

Even with block signals, trains needed a better way of stopping than one guard's van at the back with hand-worked brakes to halt hundreds of tons of metal. The railway inspectors said the only safe way was continuous brakes which ran throughout each carriage. The companies dragged their feet on this improvement because of the cost. In 1899 they were made to fit continuous brakes by law, but only after an accident in which eighty people had died.

Navvies

A

The Rev. William Young's views given at an enquiry, 1846.

"comparing them with others of the lowest class of society ... I think they are the most neglected and spiritually destitute people I have ever met. Yes, most vile and immoral characters ... they are ignorant of Bible religion and gospel truth ..."

Report of the Select Committee on Railway Labourers, 1846

B

Samuel Peto MP, one of the two biggest railway contractors, spoke in Parliament about navvies on Irish railways in 1851.

"I know from personal experience that if you pay him well, and show you care for him, he is the most faithful and hardworking creature in existence; but if you find him working for fourpence a day, and that paid in potatoes and meal, can we wonder that the results are as we find them. But give him ... remuneration for his services, show him you appreciate those services, and you may be sure you put an end to all agitation. He will be your faithful servant."

H. Peto, *Sir Samuel Peto, A Memorial Sketch*, 1893

Sources A–B

1 *How many points of disagreement can you find between Sources A and B?*
2 *Can you explain why you might expect the clergyman and Samuel Peto to disagree?*

C

Building the Tring cutting on the London and Birmingham line.

3 *What do you learn from the painting about the way that navvy work was organised?*

Drawings of the London and Birmingham Railway, J. C. Bourne, 1839

Railwaymen

D

A booking clerk, writing in 1870.

4 *Why did the writer of this letter not put his name to it?*
5 *Suggest reasons why men still wanted to be booking clerks, despite the hours.*

"One of your correspondents asks what hours a clerk is expected to work for his 15s., 18s. or 20s. a week. I will give you my experience. At our station (which shall be nameless) we are obliged to work ten, twelve, and sometimes fourteen hours a day, and when asked for extra pay our managers coolly refer us to rule one of our *Rules and Regulations*: 'Every servant must devote himself exclusively to the service of the company, attend during the appointed hours, reside and do duty *where and when required, Sundays included'*."

NIL DESPERANDUM"

Railway Services Gazette, 9 March 1872

43
The Railway Age

Railways put stage-coaches and many canals out of business. They also affected everyday life: food, housing, leisure and even time-keeping. .

Effects on other transport

The mail-coach and stage-coach network quickly became a thing of the past. Turnpike Trusts collected less toll money and had to be disbanded. Laws of the 1880s and 1890s gave the job of road repair to county councils and local councils. Goods carriers, such as Pickfords, did not suffer like the coach firms because they found work carrying goods from homes or factories to railway stations.

Railways could not take the business from canals until they had built sidings where they could collect goods. Then it was possible to make up a freight train with only three men in charge. Barges needed one man and horse each and travelled far more slowly. The only canals which continued to be heavily used were the short ones which linked factories and mines in one district.

Food supplies

As soon as refrigerated trucks were built, animals and poultry were killed in slaughterhouses in country towns and carried to market as meat. Many people tasted their first fresh fish. Fleets unloaded their catch at dockside railway lines where it was packed in ice for the journey. Large towns built new early-morning markets where greengrocers and fishmongers could buy fruit, vegetables and fish which came in by overnight train.

Goods in the shops began to be standardised. Jesse Boot's new firm packaged medicines which could be sent by rail to chemists' shops. The railways made it possible to set up the first chain stores, such as the Army and Navy or Lipton's grocers.

Standard time

Before railways the time depended on how far you lived east or west of Greenwich. London was eleven minutes ahead of Bristol. Railway clocks used London or 'railway time', which was checked by telegraph. Gradually other public clocks gave up showing local time. In 1872 the Post Office used London time in all its offices. In 1880 time was standardised by law as 'Greenwich Mean Time'.

Railway towns

Some places became towns simply because of the railway. In 1847 Crewe was nothing more than a farmhouse. Then the Grand Junction and London and North Western Railway (LNWR) Companies made it a junction for railways, linking the Midlands, north-west England and Scotland. The LNWR also opened a works for building locomotives. Crewe became a large town with company-built churches, schools and railway workers' cottages. The market village of Swindon was overshadowed by New Swindon, the junction and workshop town for the Great Western Railway.

Seaside resorts

A second type of new town was the seaside resort. Before the railway, places such as Brighton, Weston-super-Mare or Scarborough saw only wealthy families who arrived by coach and took rooms for themselves and their servants. In the 1840s trippers came on cheap excursions which gave them the thrill of a train ride and many people's first-ever sight of the sea. Soon holiday-makers came to spend the week in boarding-houses near to the newly built promenades and piers. The wealthy moved to the new hotels with names like 'Grand' and 'Esplanade'. Some of today's seaside towns such as Rhyl, Bournemouth, Skegness, and Morecambe only began as resorts when the railways reached them.

In older towns the railways bought up whole streets to clear for new stations and railways. The landlords who owned the buildings were paid well but their tenants got no compensation and had to move to rooms in other already overcrowded districts. In London Parliament protected the public buildings and town houses of the wealthy by making the railways stop outside the central areas.

New suburbs

Railways also led to the growth of new leafy suburbs on the edge of most large towns. Middle-class men rode by train each day to work in the town centre. You can still often see their villa homes dotted in the streets near suburban railway stations.

At first fares were too high for working people to follow the managers and senior clerks. The Railway Companies did not offer cheap tickets for fear they would attract too many of the poorer classes and lose trade from the better off. They also did not want to provide rush-hour trains with drivers working for two short shifts. In the 1880s Parliament said that cheap 'workmen's fares' must be sold in London. By then, anyway, the horse-drawn tram was taking workers out to the first ring of new suburbs. So the railways extended their lines to new housing.

The underground

The first London underground service was planned to connect with the overground railways. Fourteen railway companies had terminuses around the edge of central London but no lines crossed the city to link them up. In 1863 work started on the Circle Line to help passengers change stations. To avoid taking housing and street space it was built underground. As the trains were pulled by steam-engines passengers must have suffered from dirt and smoke. In the 1890s the electric underground was started.

Railways and towns
A

An advertisement, 1850.

1 *Why were the excursions on Sundays?*
2 *Who would you expect to use these trains?*

Railways and freight
B

A journalist's description of the scene at Camden Goods Station in 1864.

3 *What evidence is there here that the canals had lost some of their most valuable cargoes?*

"In the grey mists of the morning, in the atmosphere of a hundred conflicting smells, and by the light of faintly burning gas, we see a large portion of the supply of the great London markets rapidly disgorged by these night trains: Fish, flesh and food, Aylesbury butter and dairy-fed pork, apples, cabbages, and cucumbers, alarming supplies of cats' meat, cart loads of water cresses, and we know not what else, for the daily consumption of the metropolis. No sooner do these disappear than at ten minutes' interval arrive other trains with Manchester packs and bales, Liverpool cotton, American provisions, Worcester gloves, Kidderminster carpets, Birmingham and Staffordshire hardware, crates of pottery from North Staffordshire and cloth from Huddersfield, Leeds, Bradford, and other Yorkshire towns, which have to be delivered in the City before the hour for the general commencement of business. At a later hour of the morning these are followed by other trains with the heaviest class of traffic: stones, bricks, iron girders, iron pipes, ale (which comes in great quantities, especially from Allsopps', and the world-famous Burton breweries), coal, hay, straw, grain, flour . . ."
Railway News, December 1864

The railway victorious
C

An inn and coach owner, Edward Sherman, gave evidence to an enquiry into turnpike trusts in 1839.

"(I) Would you state to the Committee whether or not of later years, say within the last two or three years, you have experienced any result from the formation of railroads? – I have a reduction on the North road, since the opening of the railroad, of 15 coaches daily.

From what period? – From the opening of the railroads . . .

You are now working two coaches? – Yes, between London and Birmingham.

How many did you work before the railroad opened? – Nine, which I had for the whole year previously."
Parliamentary Select Committee on Turnpike Trusts, 1839

D

The fastest service from London to some other towns, 1844–1914.

Town	By coach 1836		By train 1844		1854		1876		1900		1914	
Birmingham	11hr	00m	8hr	55m	8hr	00m	2hr	45m	2hr	15m	2hr	00m
Brighton	5	15	1	80	1	15	1	10	1	05	1	00
Bristol	12	14	4	20	3	00	2	86	2	25	2	00
Cardiff	17	22	–		4	81	4	58	3	17	2	50
Hull	18	00	11	05	5	50	5	20	4	10	3	52
Leeds	21	21	8	45	4	50	4	35	3	49	3	25
Liverpool	21	15	8	15	5	45	5	00	4	15	3	35
Manchester	18	80	7	45	5	30	4	45	4	15	3	30
Newcastle	30	20	12	15	7	25	6	05	5	82	5	20

J. Simmons, *The Railway in England and Wales, 1830–1914*, 1978

4 *Which railway line affected Edward Sherman's business? Roughly when was it built?*

5 *How many reasons can you think of for the steady improvement in journey times between 1854 and 1914?*

Sources A–D
6 *Use Sources A to D to explain the impact of the railways (for better or worse) on life in the nineteenth century.*

44
Steam and sail

Steamships were built before steam locomotives but for many years they were used mostly for mail and wealthy passengers. Poor emigrants and bulky cargo were carried by sailing ships up to the end of the 1860s.

Steam on the Clyde

Two years before Richard Trevithick put a steam-engine on wheels in 1804, William Symington built a paddle-steamer, the *Charlotte Dundas*, to pull barges on the river Clyde. In 1812, thirteen years before the first public railway, Henry Bell's *Comet* ran the first paddle-steamer service up and down the Clyde.

The mail service

By the 1820s steam-driven paddles were fitted to sea-going boats to use when the wind was not behind them. William Anderson cut the time for the round trip to Gibraltar from three weeks to six days. That was far faster than the government's packet service which carried mail and passengers. The government announced that it would pay private owners to take over the service if they could prove they would be reliable. In 1837 William Anderson won the contract to carry mail to the Spanish Peninsula. In 1840 he was allowed to add the Orient (or eastern countries). This was the start of the Peninsular and Oriental, or P & O, shipping line.

The Great Western

The most wanted contract was the one to carry mail across the Atlantic. (The trip had been done by a paddle-steamer, the *Savannah*, in 1819 but she had used sails for most of the way.) Isambard Kingdom Brunel decided to try by building the largest ship ever, the *Great Western*. She had to be huge to carry enough coal for a steam-only crossing. This was proved on her first voyage in 1838. A rival company sent out an Irish Sea steamer, *Sirius*, three days before the *Great Western*. *Sirius* got to New York only a couple of hours ahead of the *Great Western* and only after burning part of her cargo when the coal ran out. The *Great Western* had 200 tons left.

Brunel did not win the contract. The *Great Western* was his only ship and its port, Bristol, was at the end of his wide-gauge railway. The contract went to a Canadian, Samuel Cunard, who built four new steamships to run a twice-monthly service from Liverpool, which had better rail connections.

The Great Britain

The first Cunarders had to carry three-quarters of their cargo as coal. They offered a fast mail and passenger service but could not make a profit from carrying goods. So Brunel was on the right lines with his second ship, the *Great Britain*. He built her out of iron plates instead of the usual wooden planks over an iron frame. That way she was twice the size of a Cunard liner. She was also narrower and faster because Brunel was the first to fit a propeller to a sea-going ship. Not long after her first voyage the *Great Britain* ran aground. A wooden ship would have splintered into a wreck. All the *Great Britain* had was a hole which could be mended.

Emigrants

Brunel had built a fast, safe, luxury passenger ship but she was still too expensive in fuel for large cargoes. Yet this was a time when British trade was growing in all parts of the world so the next twenty years were good for sailing-ships. Across the Atlantic food, timber and cotton came into Britain but the 'cargo' the other way was usually human. By 1850, 100,000 people emigrated each year from Europe to the USA. Many of them made their way first to Liverpool, especially the Irish who were fleeing after the potato famine of the 1840s. All they could afford was a few feet of space in the steerage between the decks for a journey which could take six weeks. In that time many might die from exhaustion or one of the fevers which swept through emigrant ships. Later there was a good trade in carrying emigrants on the longer trip to Australia.

Clippers

Sailing-ships were also busy bringing food and raw materials from China, India and Australia. The flashiest boats were the clippers. They were crammed with huge sails to race from China with the first crops of newly picked tea. One of the most splendid was the *Cutty Sark*. She was built in 1869, the year the Suez Canal opened. That gave steamships a shorter route to eastern countries and clippers no longer had the advantage of speed. A few sailed on to the early 1900s, mostly carrying wool from Australia, but the age of the sailing ship was over.

Emigrants

A

An account written in 1855 by William John Adams who emigrated with his wife to Australia.

1 *What might make a man such as William Adams leave England for Australia?*
2 *Why would he take a jar of red cabbage?*

B

An advertisement for a Cunard Line service in the early 1860s.

3 *What does the illustration tell you about how much steam-engines were trusted in 1850?*
4 *How can you tell that the advertisement is aimed at well-to-do passengers?*
5 *Apart from passengers what would the* Sidon *carry?*

"The wind Blew and the Sails tore and Chains and Ropes Rattled and the Seaman and Captain Run and hollwed about and the Women Cried and Prayed and men Run about onley with their Shirts on and the warter Came in two hatchways By Streams and Sometimes the lamp was out and it Seems Verrey miserable and the Ship Roald heaved and Groand From one Side to the Oather and now and then a Rat Squik and Run Oaver Some Boday and then they would Sing out and then the Tables and all the Temprey Fixtures would Rattle and the tins Fall From the Shelves and Tables Sometimes on Your head as you lie in your Bed and the Jars and Books i had to hold in my Bed and Jar of Red Cabbage Fell over and Wetted the Bed."
William John Adams, 1855 (Mitchell Library, Sydney)

45
Steam and trade

From the 1870s ships were built of steel and driven by compound steam-engines. Britain became the world's leading shipbuilder and owned the largest merchant navy, with tramp steamers and passenger 'liners'. In the early 1900s the liners began to be fitted with turbines.

Steam replaces sail

There were many reasons why steam replaced sail. From the 1870s shipbuilders could use steel which was lighter and stronger than iron. They fitted the new compound engines which had two or three pistons and cylinders, not just one. This meant greater speed and saving on fuel which left more space for cargo. Ships' captains could call in at the dozens of coaling stations around the world.

Shipbuilding

By 1914 three-quarters of the world's ships were built in Britain. The biggest yards were on the rivers Tyne and Clyde which had deep water and nearby iron and coal. Other yards on shallow rivers had to close down.

Ports changed in the same way. Britain's coast was dotted with small harbours which lost work as ships became larger. Even the river Avon at Bristol was too narrow to take them. In their place ships used the miles of new docks which were built in London and Liverpool. Behind them were huge warehouses where goods were stored before being sent inland by rail. Southampton grew into another huge port which specialised in passengers.

Tramp steamers

Britain had the largest merchant navy with nearly half the world's tonnage of ships in 1910. Most important were the tramp steamers which left Britain carrying coal or manufactured goods. After these were unloaded they tramped from port to port carrying cargoes which their owners in Britain arranged by cable. They came home with their holds full of food or a raw material such as cotton.

Imports

In Britain people became used to cheap food such as rice, sugar and wheat as well as new fruits, vegetable oil which was made into margarine, and cocoa, for making chocolate. These led to changes in working lives in other parts of the world. Africans left their villages to work on palm-oil plantations. The Liverpool line, Elder–Dempster, opened plantations for bananas and tomatoes in the Canary Islands and later it got a government contract to ship bananas from Jamaica. For farmers in Australia and New Zealand the coming of refrigerated ships in the 1880s meant new markets for their meat.

Liners

Tramp steamers earned most money but passenger liners got more attention because their owners tried to attract passengers by advertising luxury and speed. The Blue Riband was awarded to the fastest boat to cross the Atlantic. In 1907 this was won by a Cunarder, the *Mauretania*. What made the *Mauretania* special was her steam turbine engine built by Charles Parsons.

Charles Parsons (1854–1931)

The idea began when the engineer, Charles Parsons, was asked to design an engine to drive a generator to make electricity. A generator needed a spinning movement. Parsons' solution was the turbine, where steam spins blades on the main engine shaft.

The turbine

In 1896 Charles Parsons built the *Turbinia*, a tiny boat with great power packed into the three turbines which drove her propellers. He ran her round the ships at the Royal Navy's review at Spithead in 1897. Angry admirals ordered their fastest destroyers to drive her away but the *Turbinia* could do 34½ knots to their 25. The Navy was impressed and in 1906 put turbines into HMS *Dreadnought*, the greatest battleship afloat.

A

Average imports from the Canary Islands to the United Kingdom (not all carried by Elder–Dempster's ships).

1 *In what years were records kept separately for bananas and tomatoes? Does that mean that none were imported into the UK before?*
2 *Which other islands did Elder–Dempster import bananas from?*

	Cochineal	Bananas	Tomatoes	Total
	£	£	£	£
1885–89	64,579	–	–	99,179
1890–94	36,184	–	–	255,757
1895–99	29,805	–	–	612,307
1900–04	14,186	785,559	312,849	1,246,361
1905–09	19,147	863,120	440,675	1,542,217
1910–14	13,388	727,396	546,254	1,494,108

Annual Statements of Figures from the Board of Trade

Sir Alfred Jones and the Canary Isles
B

Alfred Jones, the owner of the Elder–Dempster line, visited the Canary Islands in 1892. As he explains, it turned out to be the start of an important new trade.

3 *Why would Alfred Jones need a coaling station in the Canaries?*
4 *Check with Unit 38 to explain why the islanders were being ruined.*

"I visited the Islands for the purpose of deciding on the feasibility or otherwise of establishing a coaling station for our African steamers. I was much struck by the poverty of the Old Spaniards who form the bulk of the population. They formerly existed by producing cochineal, and on the substitution of the aniline dyes the community was practically ruined. The cochineal had fallen from 10s to 2s a pound; the land was laying waste and the people sunk in an apathy of despair. Well observing the prolific character of the soil, I bought up what land I could and grew fruit on it. Then, as I knew that that was not nearly enough for the trade I could foresee, I went round to the farms and offered so much for all the fruit they could grow."
Alfred Jones, writing in *Great Thoughts*, 18 June 1898

C

Back in England he had difficulties which were described by The Times *in 1909.*

5 *Why would it have been hard at first to sell bananas in the north of England?*

"When Jones first began to import Canary bananas in his African ships he encountered great difficulties in obtaining a market for them – difficulties of transport and difficulties of retail sale. But he was not to be beaten. Finding that the retailers would not help him, and that even the carters put difficulties in his way, he engaged a number of coster-mongers, bringing some of them, it is said, from London and loading up their barrows from one of his ships, he told the carters to go and sell them in the streets of Liverpool for what they would fetch, and that he did not want to be paid for them. By this means he popularised the consumption of the banana first in Liverpool and afterwards throughout Lancashire and the North of England."

The Times, 12 December 1909

A new dock

D

A drawing of 1886 showing the new docks opened that spring at Tilbury, 20 miles downstream from London.

6 *Explain the advantages of docks such as these from the point of view of*
 (a) a company in the import-export business,
 (b) a ship's captain.

Published in *The Graphic*, 24 April 1886

7 *Suggest reasons why these docks were built nearly twenty miles downstream from the older London docks (shown in Unit 80).*

8 *How were goods taken to the rest of Britain?*

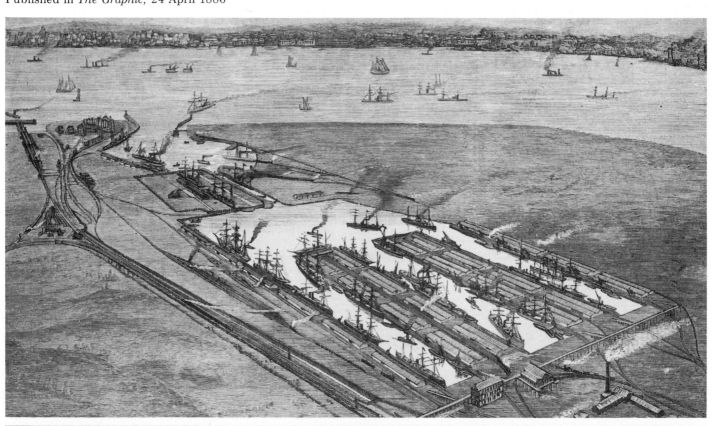

46 'Workshop of the world'

Machine tools are used for making standardised metal parts, to exactly the right size, which are put together to make other machines and engines. This unit describes the work of important pioneers of the machine-tool industry. By the 1850s this work had led to machine tools being used in engineering workshops throughout the country. The machines and engines they made were the reason for the boast of the time that Britain was the 'workshop of the world'.

Henry Maudslay (1771–1831)

Henry Maudslay began work as a blacksmith in a government arms factory. Later he was an assistant to Joseph Bramah who made many important inventions. There was the first workable water-closet and the first hydraulic lift for jacking up heavy objects by water pressure. All these needed accurate parts and Henry Maudslay's job was to find ways of making them.

This set him on the road to being the 'father of the machine-tool industry'. In 1798 he had the money to open his own workshop. He began with lathes – the machines which turn a piece of wood or metal while it is being shaped with a cutter. Maudslay made the first all-metal lathe and fitted it with a slide rest which held the cutting tool in position. On all earlier lathes the operator had held the cutter and could never make two objects exactly the same.

Maudslay's next machine planed pieces of metal so that they were absolutely flat and would slide against each other. That brought up the problem of measuring thickness, which had always been done with calipers. Henry Maudslay's new micrometer, could measure down to a ten-thousandth of an inch by using a screw. To make such accurate screws needed another invention, Maudslay's screw lathe.

Joseph Whitworth (1803–1887)

Joseph Whitworth worked for seven years with Henry Maudslay. Then he set up on his own in Manchester and took everything he had learned one step further. Whitworth's self-acting planing machine cut metal in both directions. His micrometer could measure down to a hundred-thousandth of an inch.

Whitworth knew that engineers needed to use the same sizes of screws and bolts. In 1841 he worked out a standard so that there was the same number of threads to each diameter of screw. By about 1860 the Whitworth standard was used in most engineering.

Machine tools made by Maudslay, Whitworth and others were the starting-point for a second stage in the story of British engineering. The machines made by men such as Crompton were clumsy and slow moving. James Watt's steam-engines were powerful but too huge and costly in fuel to drive ships or fast locomotives. To build more efficient engines and to make machinery for complicated tasks needed accurately made metal parts.

The Amalgamated Society of Engineers

Two events in 1851 show how important machine tools were in making Britain the workshop of the world. One was the founding of The Amalgamated Society of Engineers. That was a sign of the spread of a new skilled trade of machine making. Engineering factories were opened throughout the country, specialising in machinery needed by the rest of local industry. In Yorkshire they made machines for textile mills, in Birmingham for factories where metal goods were made, in Glasgow for ship's engines, and so on.

The other event was the display of British industry at the Great Exhibition, which is described in the next unit.

Machine tools and machinery
A *(left)*
Making bricks by hand in 1821.
B *(right)*
The same job done by machinery in about 1850.
C
William Fairburn had been an engineering employer in Manchester for nearly twenty years when he said this in 1861.

3 *What are the main changes that William Fairburn saw over twenty years?*
4 *What do you think workmen would say were (a) the gains and (b) the losses from these changes?*

Sources A–B
1 *Look at the two pictures and list the differences between them. What do they tell you about the effects of new machinery on the workforce?*
2 *Why was a machine likely to be a good investment for brick-work owners at this time?*

"When I first entered this city the whole of the machinery was executed by hand. There was neither planing, slotting nor shaping machines; and, with the exception of very imperfect lathes and a few drills the preparatory operation of construction were effected entirely by the hands of the workmen. Now, everything is done by machine tools with a degree of accuracy which the unaided hand could never accomplish."
Extract from a speech by William Fairburn, 1861

47
The Great Exhibition

The Great Exhibition of 1851 was held in the Crystal Palace, designed by Thomas Paxton. It was opened just when cheap railway excursions were beginning so that six million people had a chance to see the machines which had made Britain into the most industrialised country in the world.

Joseph Paxton (1801–1865)

It was Prince Albert, Queen Victoria's husband, who had the idea for a 'Great Exhibition of the Works of Industry of All Nations'. He chose the site in Hyde Park and the search began for a design for a suitable building. The planning committee turned down 245 schemes before they saw a sketch by Joseph Paxton, who managed the Duke of Devonshire's huge estates in Derbyshire. Paxton was a director of the Midland Railway Company and had made the sketches during a Board meeting. His first doodles were based on a new greenhouse for the Duke's lilies; the final result was a temple of glass set in an iron frame. The magazine *Punch* suggested 'Crystal Palace' as a suitable name – and it stuck.

The Crystal Palace

More than two thousand men were needed to erect the iron framework. Glaziers then worked from wheeled trolleys which ran along the gutters to fit 300,000 panes of glass. The main nave of the building was crossed by a huge domed transept, tall enough to cover three large elms which were left in place. To the west the nave was filled with British exhibits divided into five classes: raw materials, machinery, textiles, metal and ceramic goods, and 'miscellaneous fine arts'. The eastern nave had foreign goods divided in the same way.

Visitors

Between May and October 1851 more than six million people visited the Exhibition. Visiting was arranged according to the social ideas of the time. The Palace was closed on Sundays and the classes were kept apart by making charges vary from £1 to 1s for different days. Newspapers of the time commented on the orderly behaviour of the lower classes who came from all over the country by excursion trains. (Some of these were run for the first Thomas Cook who organised savings clubs and all-in package tours.)

Exhibits

For many of these trippers it was the first ever chance to see parts of their own country, the capital city and the engineering wonders that were beginning to change their world. Ordinary people probably found the fine arts sections rather absurd because most of the items were elaborate and overdecorated. But reporters noted that they spent hours watching steam-engines, textile machines, a mechanical printing press and Nasmyth's huge hammer. Alongside were the precision tools from Maudslay and Whitworth's workshops. It was this combination of great power and precision which showed that British engineering led the world in 1851. But in the foreign section there were signs that a new age was beginning. One could be found in the American gallery. It was Samuel Colt's revolver, made of standardised interchangeable parts.

Two views before the opening
A
A comment in the Illustrated London News, *a weekly magazine which was widely read, especially before the coming of photography.*

"One of the most prominent *social characteristics* of the present time is the growth and progress of pleasure travelling among the people. The working classes of thirty or even fifteen years ago did not know their own country. Very few travelled for pleasure beyond a small circle around the places which they inhabited. But now industrious men of the Midland Counties whose forefathers never saw the sea that encircles these islands are enabled to gain physical as well as mental enjoyment by a view of its mighty waters. Already the working classes in Manchester, Liverpool, Sheffield, Birmingham, The Potteries and the great Iron districts between Glasgow and Airdrie, as well as other places, have commenced laying by their weekly pence to form a fund for visiting London during the Great Exhibition of 1851. Were it not for cheap excursion trains this great source of amusement and instruction would have been unobtainable . . ."
Illustrated London News, 21 September 1850

B
A cartoon in Punch, 13 April 1850.

Sources A–B
1 *Describe the two different views of the effects of industrialisation given in these sources.*

SPECIMENS FROM MR. PUNCH'S INDUSTRIAL EXHIBITION OF 1850.
(TO BE IMPROVED IN 1851).

The Exhibition
C
A painting of one of the halls of moving machinery.
2 *Look back to Source A. How would this hall have been a 'source of amusement and instruction'?*
3 *The profits from the Exhibition were used to start the Science Museum and the Victoria and Albert Museum in London. Suggest why this was done.*

Dickinsons' *Comprehensive Pictures of the Great Exhibition,* 1854

48
The American system

The work of machine-tool makers led to the marvels at the Great Exhibition. It was only a short step to assembly industries where workers put together standardised parts made in other places. This 'American system' began with guns and sewing machines and spread to bicycles.

Large-scale production

Whitworth's standard screw sizes meant that it was worth while making screws on a large scale. In 1840 it took twenty men and boys one day to turn out 20,000 screws on a Whitworth lathe. By 1875 automatic lathes minded by one man could make 120,000 a day. A new industry sprang up, especially in the Birmingham district. The best-known example was the screw-making firm owned by the Lord Mayor, Joseph Chamberlain. Other men started to supply parts for machines, door and window fittings, gas light fixtures and metal parts for guns which were still hand made.

From Colt to Enfield

This is where Samuel Colt fits into the story. He had made a fortune from realising that if you had standard parts you could assemble them into standardised goods. In his American factory he mass-produced revolvers which cowboys could buy at any store. When Britain went into the Crimean War in 1853 the government inspector of weapon production was sent to see Colt's British factory. He bought 150 American machine tools for a factory at Enfield which made a thousand rifles a week. More machine tools were supplied to twenty small firms in Birmingham. They used them to make parts which they supplied to the Birmingham Small Arms Factory which assembled them into guns.

The American system

That was how British engineers discovered the 'American system', which was their name for the idea that some firms could specialise in parts and others in assembling. After small arms came sewing machines. The first to make a standard model, with all the parts the same, was the American, Isaac Singer. His first model in 1850 cost $125. By 1870 he had brought the price down to $64 and opened his British factory in Glasgow.

Bicycle assembly

The American system of the nineteenth century pointed the way to mass-production methods in the twentieth. The link between them was the bicycle assembly industry. It had its small beginnings in 1867 when a salesman from a Coventry sewing-machine firm saw Paris's latest rage, the velocipede. Two years later his firm produced the first British model, the boneshaker with iron wheels and a pedal fixed to the front wheel.

Straight away others saw how suitable it was for an assembly industry. The pioneer was James Starley. In 1870 his Coventry factory assembled the first 'ordinary', nicknamed the penny-farthing. He was quick to see how other firm's products could improve his machines. He designed gears with the help of a new Birmingham invention, ball-bearings, and fitted pneumatic tyres, invented in Belfast by a vet, John Boyd Dunlop, in 1888.

The penny-farthing was difficult to ride, especially in long skirts, and painful to fall off. James Starley's nephew, John, set a new trend with the first Rover safety cycle. He soon had many rivals, including William Hillman, and three Nottingham mechanics who started assembling cycles in a shed in Raleigh Street, Nottingham. By 1896 Raleigh was making 12,000 cycles a year.

Around these assembly firms grew a network of component makers. Apart from Dunlop there was Lucas which made lamps, and the two partners, Sturmey and Archer, who invented and made cycle gears. When motor-car and motor-cycle making began in the late 1890s this combination of assemblers and their suppliers was in an ideal position to move into the new industry.

The Midlands cycle industry
A

An account written by an American in 1912.

1 *What was the difference between the work done in Coventry and Birmingham?*
2 *What reason does the writer give for the growth of specialist parts and accessory firms?*
3 *Why has he put 'Cycle Manufacturers' in quotation marks?*

"The 'Cycle Manufacturers' do not make their own supplies of tyres, wheel rims, chains, accessories – bells, lamps, etc.

(i) The 'parts' and 'accessories' are purchased from firms who specialise in making certain of them, e.g. Dunlop Tyre Company for tyres, wheel rims, pumps, etc.: Lucas Ltd for lamps, bells, etc.; Perry and Company for cycle chains.

It is more profitable to all concerned to purchase supplies of these parts, accessories, etc., from firms specialising in certain kinds of them. These firms are thus finding a larger demand and securing more constant employment for their works. The centre for the manufacture of accessories and parts is Birmingham.

(ii) The 'Cycle Manufacturers' purchase their supplies of steel tubes, bars, wire, accessories, etc., and thence produce the finished cycle. This branch of the industry is centred at Coventry. Here the leading works are situated, and here the industry can be seen at its best. All the leading cycle-makers produce motor cycles as well as cycles and carriers. The present tendency is to include the manufacturer of automobiles also . . ."
C.R. Carter, 'The Cycle Industry', in S. Webb and A. Freeman, *Seasonal Trades*, 1912

American know-how
B

A card showing four Singer factories. The works shown top centre and top left were in Scotland; the other two were in the USA.

4 *Imagine you were 80 years old when the first Singer factory was built in Glasgow and had worked in one of the early textile factories. What might go through your mind when you saw the Singer factory and heard about the even bigger one in America?*

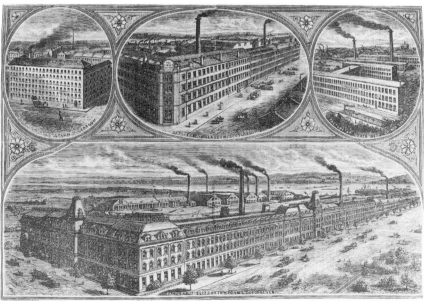

49
Factory Acts

Until about 1850 the word 'factory' or 'manufactory' was used only for textile mills. In the 1830s there were campaigns to shorten the hours of work in these factories. After many enquiries, Parliament passed Factory Acts to protect women and children – but not men. In the second half of the nineteenth century, new Factory Acts were passed to cover working hours and safety in other places.

The pace of mill work

In 1841 it was reckoned that spinners had to make three times as many movements per minute as they did in 1814. Over the same years the number of miles walked by child piecers went up from twelve to thirty a day. Factories were using more machinery, driven by faster steam-engines, in much bigger buildings. Yet the women and children worked longer hours than other workers. The usual average was 12 hours with 1½ hours off for lunch; in the cotton industry it was 12 hours in addition to meal times.

Mill-owners claimed that the work was easier than in other trades and, in any case, the long hours were needed to keep their businesses going. In 1830 their view was attacked by a man who had no connection with textiles. He was Richard Oastler, a Huddersfield land agent. He started a Short Hours Committee in the town. Soon there were others in Yorkshire, Lancashire and Glasgow. Their united aim was for a ten-hour factory day.

Richard Oastler (1789–1861)

The Ten Hours Movement had friends in Parliament, especially John Fielden and Lord Shaftesbury. They persuaded MPs to order two enquiries into children's factory work. Some shocking evidence was turned up about the cruelty used to keep children awake at their machines. In 1833 the enquiry committee's Report said very firmly that the hours were too long for young children. With the Report in front of them, MPs passed the 1833 Factory Act.

Factory Act, 1833

In all textile factories except silk mills:
1 No child under 9 to work.
2 Children 9–12 to work only eight hours.
3 Young people 13–18 to work only twelve hours.
4 Working children to have two hours' education a day.
5 Four government inspectors to check that the law was obeyed.

This was the first time that a law made arrangements for checking that it was obeyed. The four inspectors could be quite thorough because each one had several sub-inspectors. One problem was that mill-owners and parents lied about the ages of children. This was one reason why registration of births and deaths was started in 1837. A birth certificate left no doubt about a child's age.

The inspectors did the mill-owners one favour by agreeing that they could have children working in shifts. This meant that factories could be open for the same hours as before so women had to work as long as ever. The Ten Hours Movement pressed for more changes. Their next success came in the 1844 Factory Act.

Factory Act, 1844

1 The starting age was cut to 8, but from 8–13 children could work only 6½ hours.
2 Women as well as young people to work only 12 hours.
3 Dangerous machinery to be fenced.

Mill-owners could still arrange shifts of child workers, but now women were 'protected persons' it was difficult to keep mills open for longer than twelve hours. The Ten Hours Movement was getting close to its goal. It finally won with the 1847 Factory Act or 'Ten Hours' Act.

Ten Hours Act, 1847

Women and young persons to work only 10 hours.

In many mills that meant a ten-hour day for all. Some owners got round the law by having shifts of evening or night work. That was stopped by Factory Acts in 1850 and 1853 which said that women and children had to put in their time between 6 a.m. and 6 p.m.

Later Factory Acts

The Factory Acts for textile work used three types of control. They made some workers 'protected persons' whose hours were limited. Second, child workers had to receive some education. Third, they made it illegal to have unsafe machinery. In the next fifty years or so these three controls were made to apply to most workers.

The first step was to enquire into children's work in other industries. In potteries, boys were found stacking pots in drying rooms where the temperatures never fell below 120°F. Others were assistants to men who dipped pots in lead glaze; they were often crippled by lead poisoning. 'Phossy jaw' rotted the jawbone of young boys and girls who spent all day dipping matchsticks into phosphorus.

After these findings, the 1864 Factory Act spread the controls to pottery, matchmaking and four other dangerous trades. The 1867 Factory Act made them apply to all places with more than fifty workers. In the same year the Workshops Act began the control of smaller workplaces. From then on the laws about hours, education, and safety got more and more detailed. By 1913 there were 158 factory inspectors, with many assistants, including some women.

For the factory
A

Edward Baines, a Leeds businessman and newspaper owner wrote a book praising the achievements of the cotton industry.

1 *What is Edward Baines's view of factory work compared with domestic trades?*
2 *Do you agree with him that good health is only a matter of not catching disease?*

"Factory labour is . . . less irksome than that of the weaver, less arduous than that of the smith, less prejudicial to the lungs, the spine and the limbs than those of the shoemaker and the tailor. . . .

The only thing which makes factory labour trying even to delicate children is that they are confined for long hours and deprived of fresh air; this makes them pale, and reduces their figure, but it rarely brings on disease."
Edward Baines, *History of the Cotton Manufacture in Great Britain*, 1835

Against the factory
B
A letter from Richard Oastler to Edward Baines's paper, The Leeds Mercury, *1830. (Many cotton manufacturers supported the campaign to end slavery in the West Indies. Anti-slavery pamphlets were dropped on the doorsteps of homes.)*

C
A witness to the Parliamentary Committee on children's work, 1831–2.

Sources B–C
3 *What phrase tells you that Oastler was against slavery in the West Indies?*

4 *What point was Oastler making by describing mill children as 'not half-fed'?*

5 *If you were an MP who could not make up his mind about the 1833 Factory Act, which of Sources B or C would be most likely to make you vote for it? Give your reasons.*

Later in the century
D
A factory inspector's evidence on children's work in a nail factory, 1864.

6 *Do you think the proprietor's explanation of the accidents is reasonable?*

7 *What laws would have been broken if this had been a textile factory?*

E
A book on industry in 1907 explained some of the points of law that a factory manager had to see were obeyed.

8 *What was the purpose of limiting the hours of children aged 12–14?*

9 *Who had the duty to report cases of poisoning to the Home Office? What might be the first action taken by the Home Office?*

"The very streets which receive the droppings of an 'Anti-Slavery Society' are every morning wet by the tears of innocent victims . . . who are *compelled* (not by the cart-whip of the negro slave-driver) but by the dread of the equally appalling thong or strap of the overlooker, to hasten, half-dressed, *but not half-fed*, to those magazines of British Infantile Slavery – *The Worsted Mills in the town and neighbourhood of Bradford!!!*"
The Leeds Mercury, 16 October 1830

"Downe, Jonathan; age twenty-five; examined 6th June 1832 – Have you ever worked in any mills or factories? – Yes. – Where? – I first went to work at Mr Marshall's at Shrewsbury, when I was seven years old. – State the hours of labour in that mill – The regular average was from half-past five to seven, or from six to half-past seven . . . – When you worked in mills, what methods were taken to rouse the children from drowsiness? – . . . provided a child should be drowsy, the overlooker walks round the room with a stick and he touches that child on the shoulder, and says, 'Come here'. In a corner of the room there is an iron cistern; it is filled with water, so that if any fire should occur in the room, they could quench it with that water; then takes this boy, and takes him up by the legs, and flips him over head in the cistern . . ."
Report of the Parliamentary Select Committee on the Bill to regulate the Labour of Children, 1831–2

"Little boys and girls are seen here at work at the tip-punching machines (all acting by steam power) with their fingers in constant danger of being punched off once in every second, while at the same time they had their heads between the whirling wheels a few inches distant from each ear. 'They seldom lose the hand', said one of the proprietors . . ., 'it only takes off a finger at the first or second joint. Sheer carelessness.'"
Children's Employment Commission, 3rd Report, 1864

"Protected Persons
Children. The employment of children under twelve years of age is forbidden. Children between twelve and fourteen years may be employed for half the day . . . or on alternate days.
    Children must not be allowed to clean any machinery in motion . . . . Children must not be employed where dry-grinding of metals or the dipping of lucifer matches is carried on.
Young persons – are those from fourteen . . . to eighteen . . . Young persons and children may not be employed where the silvering of mirrors or the process of making white lead is carried on.
Health and Safety
Dangerous Trades – Notification. Every medical practitioner is bound to notify to the factory department of the Home Office all cases of poisoning by lead, phosphorus, arsenic or mercury . . .
Lavatories and Meals – Where lead, arsenic or 'any other poisonous substance' is used, 'suitable washing conveniences' must be provided . . ."   A. Shadwell, *Industrial Efficiency,* 1907

50 People or machines – textiles

This unit links with Units 12–14 which told the story of textiles up to the 1820s. For another twenty or thirty years hand weaving and knitting went alongside factory spinning. From the middle of the century handwork died, causing unemployment but leading to cheaper goods for the home.

Cotton in the 1820s

The spinning mills of the 1820s towered over the cotton districts like castles of earlier times. The men who owned them ruled the lives of the people in the streets around. It was their clock or bell which called thousands of 'hands', mostly women and children, to start a day's work that began at six in the morning and ended thirteen or fourteen hours later. But the mill-owners' power also stretched to the weavers, the men who sat for even longer hours at hand-looms that clacked away in cellars and attics.

Hand-loom weaving

Once there had been a golden age for hand-loom weavers. Manufacturers had so much yarn that they had to go out and find weavers to turn it into cloth – and pay them good piece-rates. In the best year, 1805, weavers had earned up to 23s a week. By the 1820s such pay was a memory. Now the weavers went to the mills begging for yarn, and they earned only 5s or 6s a week.

One reason was that there were far too many weavers. It took only about three weeks to learn the job, so it was ideal for newcomers to town life. Many had left farm labouring in the hope of higher town wages. In Glasgow they were often the victims of the Highland clearances (see Unit 115). Their landlords had destroyed their homes and crop fields so that they could use the mountainsides for great flocks of sheep.

Power-looms

By the 1820s, too, the power-loom had become a reliable machine. Edmund Cartwright had first invented a power-loom in 1785 but went bankrupt in 1793. Others had tried and failed since then. But now many mill-owners were putting power-looms in weaving sheds built on the sides of their mills. The same steam-engine drove the loom and the spinning mules. After that, they put out yarn to hand weavers only when there was too much work for the power-looms. In this way they could pay even lower piece-rates.

Redundancy

The painful story of redundancy stretched over thirty years. Around 1820 there were 250,000 hand-loom weavers; by 1850 fewer than 50,000. Not many found jobs in the weaving sheds. Employers preferred women because they could pay them less than men. Weavers had to stay near the mills where their wives and children worked. Over the years many found work as general labourers. But new jobs took time and we shall meet unemployed weavers again in the units on workhouses and on Chartism.

Changes in wool

Hand weaving disappeared in other branches of the textile trade only a little later than in cotton. Yorkshire mill-owners put in power-looms for worsted cloth in the 1840s. In the 1860s hand weaving of carpets died out. This had produced strips of carpet which were sewn together to make a complete floor covering for the homes of the middle classes. The carpet-weaving machines could make 'squares' three or four yards wide and created a new fashion which could be followed by the working classes as their housing standards improved. Squares only gave way to fitted carpets again in the 1960s.

The knitters

The weavers' story was repeated among hand knitters in the East Midlands. Knitting was still organised in the eighteenth-century way with putters-out taking yarn from the spinning-mills to homes where there were frames for making stockings and other garments. The knitter rented the frame and had to pay, whether or not there was any work. In the 1830s and 1840s the number of hand knitters grew, especially among men who could not get agricultural work. Putters-out were able to cut piece-rates. Many paid in truck – food or goods from their own cheap store or 'tommy shop'.

Frame-work knitting began to die out when firms such as Mundella and Morley opened power-driven factories in Nottingham in the 1860s. Many of their workers were women. In the countryside some hand-work survived for another fifty years. The last to disappear were a thousand old men who made underpants for the army up to 1908.

Textile specialisation

The end of hand-work in the second half of the nineteenth century meant that textiles was now a steam-driven factory industry using mostly unskilled, female labour. From the employers' point of view the best way to make the system pay was to keep to routine work. So the industry divided into local specialisms. In South Lancashire towns there was spinning and in North Lancashire weaving. In Yorkshire each town had a different specialism in wool.

The hand-loom weavers
In 1834–5 a Parliamentary Committee of MPs listened to evidence after weavers had complained about their conditions.

A
Evidence from an employer.

"With regard to health, having seen the domestic weaver in his miserable apartment and the power loom weaver in the factory, I do not hesitate to say that the advantages are all on the side of the latter. The one . . . confines himself to a single room in which he eats, drinks and sleeps and breathes throughout the day an impure air. The other has not only the exercise of walking to and from the factory but when there lives and breathes in a large roomy apartment in which the air is constantly changed."
Parliamentary Select Committee on the Hand-loom Weavers' Petitions, 1835

B
Evidence from a weaver.

1 *In Source B what does the worker mean by 'discipline'?*
2 *Give reasons why you might sympathise more with the view of the employer (Source A) or the worker (Source B)?*

"no man would like to work in a power-loom, they do not like it, there is such a clattering and noise it would almost make some men mad; and next, he would have to be subject to a discipline that a hand-loom weaver can never admit to".
Parliamentary Select Committee on the Hand-loom Weavers' Petitions, 1835

Power-loom weaving
C

Female weavers and an overlooker in a power-loom shed pictured in Edward Baines's book on the cotton industry, 1835.

3 *Does the picture support the objections of the hand-loom weaver?*
4 *Edward Baines was a supporter of factory industry. In what ways might the picture give an inaccurate picture of scenes in a weaving shed?*

Edward Baines, *History of the Cotton Manufacture of Great Britain*, 1835

Framework knitters
D

William Felkin wrote about his grandfather, a framework knitter, who died in 1838 aged 90.

5 *Why did William Felkin have to work longer hours as he got older?*

Textiles in the early twentieth century
E

An extract from a study made in 1905.

6 *How much training do you think would have been needed for this work?*

F

A mill-girl in Rochdale being taught to weave, about 1900.

Sources E–F
7 *Describe the ways in which the picture acts as supporting evidence for Source E.*
8 *What differences can you identify between this scene and the power-loom shed in source C? Would you trust one source more than the other and why?*

"When he began life, the usual hours of labour were ten, five days a week, and one Saturday was allowed for taking in work and marketing, the alternate one for gardening and domestic matters. In middle life, twelve hours' work was necessary. At its close, fourteen to sixteen hours a day scarcely sufficed for obtaining a bare maintenance by those who depended on this kind of labour."
W. Felkin, *History of the Machine-wrought Hosiery and Lace Industry*, 1867.

"The spinning looms are entirely in the hands of women. Girls of sixteen or eighteen, with a little practice, are quite capable of undertaking such a simple task. From time to time a broken thread needs to be joined or a defective layer of cotton wool must be taken away, but for the rest of the time they have nothing to do but to watch the spindles pursuing their incessant toil."
S.J. Chapman, *The Cotton Industry and Trade*, 1905

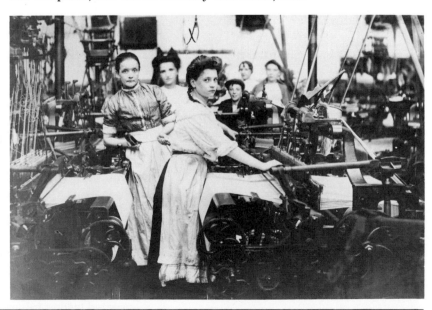

51
Sweated labour

Hand-work survived in many trades after it disappeared in textiles. In tailoring it actually grew, as sweated labour. In other parts of the country sweated workers did the jobs of finishing off work begun in workshops.

Henry Mayhew (1812–1887)

In 1849 a journalist called Henry Mayhew decided to find out how the working people of London lived. His reports appeared over the next two years in the *Morning Chronicle*. Some told what he learned about sweating from the dressmakers and tailors of East London. Many could remember thirty years earlier when garment making had been a job for skilled craftsmen. They were banded together in 'societies' or unions which agreed wages and piece-rates with the masters of the workshops where they worked.

Sweaters

By 1849 and 1850 that was changing. More people wanted cheap ready-made garments known as 'slop' in the trade. So, instead of giving a job to craftsmen, the masters handed it over to a middleman or woman, known as a sweater. He or she would take it round to the home of an unskilled worker, usually a woman, who would do the job for a sweated price. Sometimes sweaters divided a task like trouser-making into several simple processes which could be done by different workers in turn.

In the 1850s sewing machines from America (see Unit 48) increased the power of the sweaters. They could put out jobs to workers who owned or rented a machine and could finish in a faster time. About 1865 a tailor's band-saw could be bought. One man in a workshop could cut through two dozen pieces of cloth at a time so the sweater had even more to take round.

Boots and shoes

This pattern of production with simple machinery turning out materials for sweated workers was found in the Northampton boot and shoe trade. Leather was cut out in workshops by men, known as 'clickers'. The pieces were taken round to women 'closers' who made the uppers in their cottages. These then came back to the workshops to be fitted on to soles by men known as 'makers'.

Straw hats

In the 1850s there were 20,000 women and children straw plaiters in Bedfordshire. They collected bundles of straw from local markets and twisted it into plaits. These were collected by middlemen and taken to Luton and other towns where women sewed the plaits together to make straw hats.

Plaiting went on until the early 1920s when straw hats went out of fashion. Tailoring also had a large sweated section well into the twentieth century. Other sweated trades began slowly to die out after about 1900 as machine methods became more profitable.

Trade Boards

It was only then that the first laws were made to protect sweated workers. In the 1890s women unionists started a campaign which grew into a National Anti-Sweating League in 1906. In 1909 the Liberal government brought in the Trade Boards Act which said there must be trade boards to fix minimum wages in the four main sweated trades: tailoring, box-making, lace-making and chain-making.

Accounts of sweating

A

A report by Henry Mayhew based on accounts from workers.

1 *Describe the differences between 'honourable' and 'dishonourable' tailoring. Why do you think the workers used these terms?*

B

Henry Mayhew gives a sweated woman worker's story.

2 *What did the woman need 'the firing' for? Why did she say she earned only 2s a week?*

C

A report described some of the ways the poor Birmingham families could earn money from sweated work in the 1890s.

3 *What conclusions can you draw from Source C about the effects of sweated labour on (a) health, and (b) family life?*

Sweating in pictures

D *A cartoon from* Punch, *1845.*

E *A drawing from the* Graphic, *1886.*

Sources A–E

4 *Which do you think would have the greatest effect on readers: the articles in the* Morning Chronicle, *the cartoon in* Punch *or the drawing in the* Graphic?

5 *Which of the Sources A–E would be most useful if you had to write an essay on sweating? Give your reasons.*

"The tailoring trade is divided by the workmen into 'honourable' and 'dishonourable'. The honourable trade consists of that class who have their garments made on their own premises, at the supposed rate of 6d per hour – the dishonourable of those who give the work out to 'sweaters', to be done at less than the standard price. . ."
Morning Chronicle, 10 December 1849

". . . I cannot earn more than 4s 6d to 5s per week – let me sit from eight in the morning till ten every night; and out of that I shall have to pay 1s 6d for trimmings, and 6d candles every week; so altogether I earn about 3s in the six days. But I don't earn that, for there's the firing you must have to press the work, and that will be 9d a week, for you'll have to use half a hundred weight of coal. So that my clear earnings are a bit more than 2s . . ."
Morning Chronicle, 6 November 1849

"Three half-pence may be earned at home by varnishing 144 penholders. Each penholder must first be rubbed with sandpaper and then varnished, five coats of the varnish being applied with a sponge. It is dirty and unpleasant work, and you may imagine the comfort of a slum-kitchen full of children in which three-pennyworth of sticky penholders – 288 to wit – are lying . . ."
R. Sheard, *The Child Slaves of Britain*, 1905

Punch, March 1845

Graphic, 20 February 1886

52
The Old Poor Law

Today we use the word 'poor' to mean everything from being hard-up to starving. In British history 'poor' describes those who were also known as paupers. They were people who could not survive without some help because they were widows, orphans, sick or unemployed. This unit describes how paupers were treated under the Old Poor Law.

The Elizabethan Poor Law

Help for the poor has to be paid for by the rest of society. Up to 1834 this was done out of the rates paid by householders in each parish. The government had no part in collecting or spending the money. The system went back to the Poor Law of 1601, at the end of Queen Elizabeth I's reign. It was the job of the parish overseer of the poor to give help or 'relief' to the poor. In most parishes ratepayers took it in turns to be unpaid overseers. Other parishes joined together in a small group, or 'union', which was allowed by Gilbert's Act of 1782. The union then could appoint a paid overseer.

Paupers

People who needed regular relief were known as 'paupers'. At the top of the list were old widows, followed by younger women with children but no man to help support them. In many districts there were large numbers of orphans. Some paupers were too old or 'infirm' to work. The overseer had to see that they got medical relief. Often this was done by paying a yearly fee to a doctor or dispensary to care for all the local infirm poor.

Parishes did not give relief to paupers who had not been born or married there. Under the Settlement Laws of 1662, the overseer could send them back to their own parish and charge its overseer for the cost of removing them.

The able-bodied

The overseer's most difficult problem came from the able-bodied men who were unemployed. The 1601 Poor Law said they should be 'set on work' but it was hard to find jobs for them. The Workhouse Act of 1722 said parishes could set up workhouses with looms and tools where paupers could make goods for sale. But the parishes then had to pay for food and other costs of the workhouse.

Roundsmen

It was usually cheaper to leave the unemployed at home so that they could take odd jobs for a day or two. The parish then only paid relief for the other days in the week. One way of fixing men up with odd jobs was the roundsman system. The overseer gave the pauper a ticket to take round to farmers. If a farmer had a job the labourer would have to do it for the same money as he would get for a day's relief.

Allowances

The much more usual way was the allowance system when the overseer paid money to top up casual earnings. He used a scale which told him how much to pay according to the size of the family and local prices. The best-known scale of allowances was fixed by the magistrates of Berkshire when they held their Easter meeting at the Pelican Inn at Speenhamland in 1795.

Speenhamland

The Speenhamland scale was made to stop local labourers rioting against bread prices which had shot up after war against France began in 1793. But the system spread through the south of England and lasted long after the war ended in 1815. Bread prices did fall but not back to pre-war levels. Many farmers cut down on winter wage bills by buying threshing machines. Some employed fewer regular workers and took casual labour at low rates, knowing that wages would be made up to the Speenhamland scale.

Swing riots

Many ratepayers objected to their money being used to help farmers' wage-bills. They got allowances cut in the 1820s. But this led to greater misery for labourers' families. In 1830 anger exploded in the Swing riots. Across the southern counties bands of labourers raided farms at night. Their first target was the threshing machines. In Wiltshire ninety-seven were smashed and in Hampshire fifty-two. The rioters then set fire to barns and haystacks. Before the raid the farmer usually received a threatening letter signed by 'Captain Swing'. There was no such person and the rioters had no one leader. They were men so desperate that they were ready to face the fierce punishments which were bound to follow. They did no serious harm to any person but 19 labourers were executed, 481 transported to Australia and 644 sent to prison.

The Old Poor Law

A

The account book of an overseer of the poor in Chew Magna, near Bristol, for May 1707. It helps if you read old English aloud.

1 *How many people received relief altogether? How many of them were women?*

2 *Use modern English to write an account of the overseer's work under these headings: relief for paupers, medical relief, removals, pauper funerals.*

Overseer's Accounts, Chew Magna, 1707

"Concerning John Taylor and my espenses in keeping him from being a parrishioner here — 2s 0d

For sending Abigall Cos and her base child to Felton — 1s 6d

Gave Margaret Stone in her sickness — 2s 6d

Paid for a bed 2 blanketts one covered & a thick covering for Moses Dix and for 2 eles of cloath for a bowlster and ye carrige from Bristol — 18s 8d

Pd two men for carrying him to ye church house — 1s 6d

Gave Mary Cox for y Bone setter when her childs arme was broak — 4s 0d

Spent at a parish meeting — 8s 8d

Pd for a coffing bran ale and Grave for Moses Dix — 2s 0d

Gave Sarah Hill towards paying House Rent — 2s 0d

Payde for one apron and two shifts for Huppers Child — 3s 0d

Payd for two shurts and a pear of shoos for John Vigers son — 6s 4d

Gave Tho Kelson to buy spertickels — 6d

Payd to Ospitalls — 14s 0d

Gave to ye Wid Fooll in her sickness at severall Times — 4s 6d

Payd for Caps for Huppers children and neckcloths — 2s 11d

Paid for three sacks of Cole for Moses Dix — 3s 9d"

B

The Speenhamland scale became widely known because of a book, The State of the Poor, *written in 1797. This is part of a page from the book.*

3 *Explain in your own words how the Speenhamland scale worked.*

4 *Before prices started rising a regular day labourer might earn up to 9 shillings a week. What effect would the Speenhamland system have on wages?*

5 *How much, in shillings and pence, did the magistrate allow for each child when the loaf cost (a) 1s 0d and (b) 2s 0d?*

This shews, at one view, what should be the weekly Income of the Industrious Poor, as settled by the Magistrates for the county of Berks, at a meeting held at Speenhamland, May the 6th, 1795.

When the gallon loaf is	Income should be for a Man.	For a single Woman.	For a Man and his Wife.	With one Child.	With two Children.	With three Children.	With four Children.	With five Children.	With six Children.	With seven Children.
s. d.	s. d.	s. d.	s. d.	s. d.	s. d.	s. d.	s. d.	s. d.	s. d.	s. d.
1 0	3 0	2 0	4 6	6 0	7 6	9 0	10 6	12 0	13 6	15 0
1 1	3 3	2 1	4 10	6 5	8 0	9 7	11 2	12 9	14 4	15 11
1 2	3 6	2 2	5 2	6 10	8 6	10 2	11 10	13 6	15 2	16 10
1 3	3 9	2 3	5 6	7 3	9 0	10 9	12 6	14 3	16 0	17 9
1 4	4 0	2 4	5 10	7 8	9 6	11 4	13 2	15 0	16 10	18 8
1 5	4 0	2 5	5 11	7 10	9 9	11 8	13 7	15 6	17 5	19 4
1 6	4 3	2 6	6 3	8 3	10 3	12 3	14 3	16 3	18 3	20 3
1 7	4 3	2 7	6 4	8 5	11 6	12 7	14 8	16 9	18 10	20 11
1 8	4 6	2 8	6 8	8 10	11 0	13 2	15 4	17 6	19 8	21 10
1 9	4 6	2 9	6 9	9 0	11 3	13 6	15 9	18 0	20 3	22 6
1 10	4 9	2 10	7 1	9 5	11 9	14 1	16 5	18 9	21 1	23 5
1 11	4 9	2 11	7 2	9 7	12 0	14 5	16 10	19 3	21 8	24 1
2 0	5 0	3 0	7 6	10 0	12 6	15 0	17 6	20 0	22 6	25 0

F.M. Eden, *The State of the Poor*, 1797

C

Thomas Malthus made this attack on the Old Poor Law in 1798.

6 *What view does he have of the habits of the poor? Does he give any evidence for his opinion?*

7 *Does the Speenhamland scale suggest that the Poor Laws left much money for ale?*

"The labouring poor ... seem always to live from hand to mouth. Their present wants employ their whole attention and they seldom think of the future. Even when they have an opportunity of saving they seldom exercise it, but all that is beyond their present necessities goes, generally speaking to the ale-house. The poor-laws of England may therefore be said to diminish both the power and the will to save among the common people."

Thomas Malthus, *Essay on the Principles of Population*, 1798

The Swing riots

D

In 1830 a pamphlet writer pretended to be 'Swing' to get across his views of the riots.

8 *Does the cover picture suggest the writer was for or against the Swing rioters?*

THE LIFE

AND

HISTORY OF SWING,

THE

KENT RICK-BURNER.

WRITTEN BY HIMSELF.

See page 21.

LONDON:
PRINTED AND PUBLISHED BY R. CARLILE,
62, FLEET-STREET.
1830.

Price Threepence.

The Life and History of Swing, written by Himself, 1830

53
The New Poor Law

In 1832 a Royal Commission looked into the Old Poor Law and said that the allowance system should be abolished. In 1834 the Poor Law Amendment Act set up the 'New Poor Law' which lasted until 1929. This unit shows how it dealt with the unemployed.

The Poor Law Commission, 1832

After the Swing riots the government set up a Royal Commission on the Poor Law. Twenty-six Assistant Commissioners studied 3,000 parishes and the Report was written up by Edwin Chadwick in 1834. It said that Speenhamland allowances made some labourers idle and encouraged large families. It also kept wages down, so hard-working labourers could never earn enough to save.

The workhouse test

It recommended a complete end to 'outdoor relief' for the able-bodied. Any one of them who asked for relief should be 'offered the house'. That meant he must take his family to a workhouse where they would get the smallest amounts of food possible. Men, women and children would live in separate blocks. The idea was to make workhouse conditions 'less eligible', or less acceptable, than those outside, so that labourers would turn down the 'offer' and manage without relief. This was known as the 'workhouse test'.

The Poor Law Amendment Act, 1834

These schemes were made law in the Poor Law Amendment Act. It said the whole country must be divided into poor law unions made up of several parishes. In each union, the ratepayers would elect a Board of Guardians to supervise spending the poor rates. Instead of unpaid overseers there would be full-time relieving officers. They would have to follow regulations made by a three-man Poor Law Commission at Somerset House in London. Edwin Chadwick was their Secretary, heading a team of Assistant Commissioners.

The New Poor Law in the south

In 1835 and 1836 the Assistant Commissioners were busy organising unions in the south of England. New workhouses went up, built to look like prisons. Most were never full. When the workhouse was ready, the relieving officer told out-of-work labourers that he could only offer 'the house'. Very few accepted. Guardians were able to report to Somerset House that the workhouse test had cut the poor rate by a half or more.

Nobody knows the complete story of the tens of thousands who did not get relief after 1834. Some young men joined the army, or became navvies on the railways. Many girls went into domestic service or drifted to London to become sweated workers (see Unit 51). Some were helped to emigrate (see Unit 115). The Commissioners believed their new policy had been a great success, but it must have broken up many families.

So far the New Poor Law had been taken only to farming districts, where many villages had only a few dozen needing relief. They were often men who were out of work for long periods and they got no support against the workhouses from labourers with regular jobs. Most ratepayers were also in favour of workhouses which they reckoned would save them money by driving away the long-term unemployed.

The New Poor Law in the North

It was a different story when Chadwick sent his assistants to the northern factory towns in 1837. There, unemployment was a matter of workers being laid off for a few weeks of poor trade or bad weather. Workhouses might be empty in August and overcrowded in December with workers who were genuinely without a job for the winter. This united working people against the workhouses and they often had the support of ratepayers. The employers did not want their hands driven from the district. The shopkeepers could not afford to lose all the custom from laid-off men sent into the workhouse. So there was a lot of backing for the leaders of the Ten Hour Movement (see Unit 49) when they banded together again, this time against the New Poor Law.

Richard Oastler wrote another pamphlet: 'Damnation eternal Damnation to the fiend-begotten, coarser-food New Poor Law'. Other writers named the workhouses 'Bastilles', after the prison where the kings of France had once put their enemies. The Commissioners were called the 'three tyrants of Somerset House'. There were riots against plans to build workhouses. Some Boards of Guardians simply went on giving outdoor relief. They said it made no sense to build huge workhouses to hold factory workers who would be unemployed for just a few months of poor trade.

The labour test

The Commissioners usually had to climb down and allow unions to pay outdoor relief. In 1842 they gave permission for a 'labour test' instead of the workhouse test. An unemployed man would be given relief after he had spent time in a labour yard attached to the workhouse. In the toughest yards men were made to crush a ton of stone. But some labour yards gave light work to tramps and men not fit for heavy labour. Under the New Poor Law no one got even sixpence for nothing.

The coming of the New Poor Law
A

The workhouse at Andover in Hampshire was built in 1836.

1 *What impression do you think this building was intended to make on labourers in the district?*
2 *Can you suggest a reason for the fencing along part of the main building?*

A drawing from the *Illustrated London News*, November 1846.

B

This report for the last quarter of 1835 comes from the Uckfield Union (in Sussex). The union was formed earlier in 1835.

3 *Who would have been given out-relief in December 1834? What form would it have taken?*
4 *How was relief given at the end of 1835?*
5 *Are there any ways in which the picture of Andover workhouse (Source A) helps to explain the last paragraph?*

"In the month of December, 1834, in the corresponding quarter of the last year, upwards of two hundred and fifty labourers were out of employment, and receiving relief in consequence for their families. . . .

In the quarter just past, at the end of a week's frost and when the snow had stopped most of the operations in agriculture, the greatest number of able-bodied men in the workhouses was twenty-eight. . . .

The well-regulated system of employment, the irksome confinement, the discipline of our workhouses, and I trust a sincere desire to reform, has induced some who were unmarried to enlist as soldiers."

Operations of the Poor Law Amendment Act in the County of Sussex, 1836

C

In the north, things were different.

6 *What clue is there in the passage about the writer's opinion of the men who had attacked John Banks?*
7 *Does the passage suggest reasons why the unemployed were treated more harshly by the Poor Law in country districts in the south of England?*

"On Monday last Mr John Banks, the Relieving Officer of Kirkheaton, presented himself before the Guardians of the Huddersfield Union in a most deplorable plight, his clothes hanging in tatters and his head and face greatly disfigured. It appears that the deluded populace of this district had been on the look-out for him for three days, threatening his life if he durst commence his duties under the new law."

The Times, April 1839

D

A cartoon of the 1830s aimed to make people think about the difference between the New and Old Poor Law.

8 *How does the cartoon explain the idea of 'less eligibility'?*
9 *Was the cartoonist for or against the New Poor Law? Explain your answer.*

McCleans Magazine, 1 December 1836

54
The shadow of the workhouse

In the 1830s the workhouse test for the unemployed was given the most attention. But the New Poor Law was also responsible for the much larger numbers of the old, widows, the sick and orphans. At any one time these made up about one-tenth of all the people in Britain. This section describes how their needs were dealt with before the first steps were taken to build a welfare state.

Relieving officers

Before 1834 needy people went to the parish overseer. He may have known them well and often he dealt with only a few dozen cases. After 1834 they had to go to the relieving officer who could be miles away and handling thousands of cases. So the personal touch was lost, especially because the relieving officer had to follow the regulations of the Poor Law Commission.

He was allowed to give cash as 'outdoor relief' to any paupers who were not able-bodied unemployed. About three-quarters of all relief was outdoor but even here the idea of 'less eligibility' was at work. For instance, right up to the 1880s, relieving officers were forbidden to pay widowed mothers the few extra pence needed to send their children to school. It might give these pauper children a better chance than boys and girls in other families.

The workhouse

Most of the poor dared not complain because the shadow of the workhouse lay behind every outdoor payment. About two out of every ten people on relief were sent there when they could no longer manage on their tiny payments. They were mostly the old, the long-term sick and widowed mothers and children.

Men and women married for fifty years could end their lives in separate dormitories. No visitors were allowed. Even respectable old folk were not allowed a walk outside until the 1880s – and even then they often had to wear uniforms. At first, knives and forks were not allowed and, in the 1860s, one inspector smashed the cups in a workhouse because they were against regulations.

Later improvements

Only in the 1880s and 1890s did some improvements come when officials began to talk of the difference between 'deserving' and 'undeserving' paupers. For the deserving old who had worked all their lives and had not drunk or gambled there were a few 'indulgencies'. They could have separate sleeping cubicles, a locker for their treasures and small rations of tobacco or tea and sugar.

Workhouse children

In the early days children were kept in separate residential workhouse schools or in a part of a mixed workhouse. In the 1880s unions set up the first schemes for fostering and adopting. Some began to copy the scheme of Dr Barnardo who had built a 'village' of cottage homes for orphans in 1870. In 1893 the Sheffield Union went a step further with its 'scattered homes'. These were for up to thirty children and were opened in 'healthy suburbs' where they could mix with others in the local Board school (see Unit 89).

Poor Law medicine

Relieving officers knew that illness caused about half the cases needing relief. Money could be saved by helping people to recover.

It made sense for unions to have medical officers to treat the sick poor. It was a very simple form of family doctor service and the expenses were kept to the lowest. Only in 1864 did the Poor Law Board agree that unions could pay for basic medicines such as cod-liver oil and quinine (which did the job aspirin does today).

Poor Law infirmaries

If the medical officer could not cope, the place for the ill pauper was the sick ward, or 'infirmary', in a workhouse. Most of the patients were too old to care for themselves. About 80,000 a year died in workhouse infirmaries in the 1860s. Their last days were often spent in the same ward as child patients and fever cases.

In 1867 Poor Law unions were allowed to build infirmaries away from the main workhouse and open separate fever hospitals (usually on the edges of towns). By 1900 sick people did not have to go first to the relieving officer before they could be treated free in a public infirmary. Many present-day hospitals began as Poor Law infirmaries built in these years.

Comparisons from the mid-nineteenth century

A

In 1847 the Poor Law Commission was replaced by a Poor Law Board under a government minister. This followed the scandal of Andover Workhouse. It started with reports that paupers fought for rotting meat on bones they were given to crush into fertiliser. This extract is from the statement of 61-year-old Samuel Green.

1 *What evidence does Samuel Green give about the rations at Andover?*

2 *Do you think Samuel Green was likely to have written this statement himself?*

3 *How does the extract explain why the treatment of paupers at Andover became a widely reported scandal?*

"We looked out for fresh bones; we used to tell the fresh bones by the look of them, and then we used to be like a parcel of dogs over them . . . sometimes I have had one that was stale and stunk, and I ate it even then; I ate it when it was stale and stinking because I was hungered I suppose. You see we only had bread and gruel for breakfast, and as there was no bread allowed on meat days for dinner, we saved our bread from breakfast, and because a pint and a half of gruel is not much for a man's breakfast, we ate the stale and stinking meat. . . . I never saw anyone but Reeves and Eaton eat horse flesh. I once saw Eaton take up a horse's leg, and take the hair off it, and eat the flesh. The leg was not cooked."
Report of the Parliamentary Select Committee on the Andover Union, 1846

B

Andover was one of the worst workhouses. In the 1860s a French visitor wrote about one of the better ones in Manchester.

4 *How was the regular diet here different from that at Andover?*

5 *What evidence does Source B give about the treatment of children?*

6 *How would this workhouse be a palace compared with the home of a poor family.*

7 *What does Taine suggest was the main reason for the able-bodied not going into the workhouse?*

"There is no smell anywhere; the beds are almost white, and are furnished with figured coverlets; the most aged and feeble women have white caps and new clothes. . . . In another room the children are taught their lessons, one of the elder children acting as monitor. . . . The daily ration of each inmate consists of two pounds of this oatmeal and a pound and a half of potatoes; four times a week the allowance is increased by four ounces of pie or of meat without the bone. The drink is water, except during illness. We were astounded; this was a palace compared with the kennels in which the poor dwell. . . . Nevertheless there is not an able-bodied inmate of this workhouse at the moment; . . . The workhouse is regarded as a prison: the poor consider it a point of honour not to go there."
H. Taine: *Notes on England*, 1862

Comparisons from around 1900

Even when improvements in the care of aged paupers had begun there were still great differences between workhouses.

C

Dinner-time at St Pancras Workhouse, central London, around 1900.

D

The Women's Day Room in the Cambridge Workhouse. A photograph of about 1890 showing the warden and three of the inmates.

Sources C–D

8 *List all the differences you can see between these two photographs. What does the list tell you about the different living conditions in the two workhouses?*

9 *Look carefully at the second picture. How many signs can you see that the workhouse was still partly run on the idea of less eligibility?*

10 *Can you see any signs that modern ideas about welfare were emerging towards the end of the Poor Law period?*

55
Self-help and helping others

Why are some people poor? How much is it their own fault and how much is it due to things they cannot avoid? Mid-nineteenth-century writers usually put the blame on the habits of the poor. Towards 1900 others showed that poverty was part of the life cycle of many families. This section is about people who had views on this important question.

Samuel Smiles (1812–1904)

A best-selling book in 1859 was *Self-Help* by Samuel Smiles. In the first chapter he wrote: "The spirit of self-help has at all times been a marked feature in the English character, and furnishes the true measure of our power as a nation."

The next three hundred pages were filled with stories of men who had pulled themselves up to fame or riches from a humble start. Samuel Smiles often got his facts wrong but his book shows how many middle-class Victorians explained why people were poor. It was because they did not help themselves to overcome idleness and love of drink, or spending instead of saving.

The Charity Organisation Society

The Charity Organisation Society (COS) believed in self-help. It was started in 1869 to see that charity money went only to the deserving poor who would use it to make a better life. One member explained why it should not be given to the 'undeserving poor': "Alms are given them – a shilling by one, a sixpence by another, a dinner here and some clothing there. . . . The effect of this charity is that . . . people never learn to work or save."

Of course this was true in some cases – and still is. But many Victorians came to see that there were other causes of poverty. One example comes from the story of the Salvation Army.

William (1829–1912) and Catherine (1829–1890) Booth

Many preachers of the time ran missions in the inner cities, hoping to save souls and turn people away from sin. William and Catherine Booth had a mission in East London which went a step further. They went outside the usual meeting-rooms into 'the gutters'. The gutters were public houses, doorways where prostitutes waited and street corners where gamblers met.

The Salvation Army

In 1878 the Booths' Mission had forty-five branches and they named it the Salvation Army. William Booth was its General and full-time helpers were Captains or Majors. Women could hold these ranks, which probably makes the Salvation Army the first equal opportunities organisation. By 1890 the Army had a thousand corps and its officers had learned that many people did not choose sin; they were trapped into it. The Booths first realised this when they found that many young girls became prostitutes simply to avoid starving. They opened thirty-three hostels to shelter them. But this was just one tip of an iceberg of widespread poverty and William Booth wrote: "What is the use of preaching the gospel to men whose whole attention is concentrated on a mad, desperate struggle to keep themselves alive."

'In Darkest England and the Way Out', 1890

Booth asked that question in a pamphlet, *In Darkest England and the Way Out*. He went on to say that everyone should have at least the cab horse standard: "Every cab horse in London has three things: a shelter for the night, food for its stomach and work allotted to it."

It was easy to fill the pamphlet with examples of people who did not have these three things. Shocked readers sent in £100,000. The Army used it to give jobs at its own brickworks, farm and a factory making matches which did not cause 'phossy-jaw'. It started its own labour exchanges to help people find jobs, a well as shelters for the homeless, soup kitchens, and farthing breakfasts.

Socialists

The Charity Organisation Society attacked the Salvation Army for breaking the rules of self-help, but more people were coming to see that public help was needed. Among them were early campaigners for socialism such as William Morris and H.M. Hyndman. In 1892 they wrote: "At this very time official returns prove conclusively that vast masses of our countrymen are living on the very verge of starvation."

Charles Booth (1840–1916)

But was this true? That was the question asked by Charles Booth*, a Liverpool shipowner who had moved his company offices to London. He wrote: "The lives of the poor lay hidden from view behind a curtain on which were painted terrible pictures: starving children, suffering women, overworked men. . . . Did these pictures truly represent what lay behind?"

'The Life and Labour of the People of London', 1891–1903

In 1884 he set out to answer his own question. It took nineteen years to finish the seventeen books in *The Life and Labour of the People of London*. The first volume described a street by street enquiry into all the things which made up living conditions: wages, size of family, the number of rooms a family lived in. From them Booth made two very important findings: the number of loafers and semi-criminals was not quite 1 in a 100, much less than the COS and others said. But against that he showed that 30 per cent of Londoners lived below the 'poverty line': without the money to buy reasonable food, shelter and clothing. This was three times the number who received any kind of Poor Law relief. Booth was quite clear that most of the poverty was due to either low earnings or old age.

Seebohm Rowntree (1871–1954)

But was that true only in London? In 1899 and 1900 Seebohm Rowntree, son of the chocolate factory owner, made his own house-by-house survey of York. He had the results printed in his book, *Poverty*. They showed that 27 per cent of the whole population and 43 per cent of the town's wage-earners were living below the poverty line. Rowntree was a scientist so his poverty line was worked out using the new knowledge about calories to measure diet. He took Booth's idea of the poverty line and added diagrams of the 'cycle of poverty' to show the times in their lives when wage-earners were most in need.

* He was no relation to William Booth.

The work of the Salvation Army
A

1 *Is there anything in the poster which explains why the Salvation Army got large crowds at such gatherings?*
2 *What does the poster tell you about the Army's success in 'taking religion into the gutters'?*

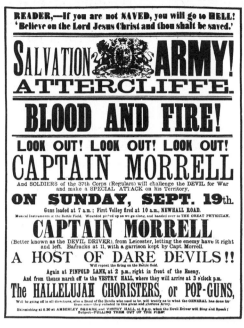

A Salvation Army poster, 1880.

Booth and Rowntree
B

Booth's summary of London's population in 1891. Classes A to D made up 30.7 per cent and were 'in poverty'. Classes E and F made up 51.5 per cent and were 'in comfort'.

3 *Use Booth's description of the classes to explain what he meant by 'in poverty' and 'in comfort'.*

C

Rowntree's diagram of the cycle of poverty.

D *(below right)*

Some causes of poverty based on Rowntree's diagram of 1901.

4 *Use these diagrams to list the main ways in which people fell into poverty.*

Sources B–D

5 *Could it be said that Booth and Rowntree had proved Samuel Smiles's ideas about poverty were wrong?*
6 *In what ways did their findings put a question mark against the work of the Poor Law?*

A. The lowest class – occasional labourers, loafers and semi-criminals.

B. The very poor – casual labour, hand-to-mouth existence, chronic want.

C and D. The poor – including alike those whose earnings are small, because of irregularity of employment, and those whose work, though regular, is ill-paid.

E and F. The regularly employed and fairly-paid working class of all grades.

G and H. Lower and upper middle class and all above this level.

Death of chief wage earner

15.63% of those in 'primary' poverty (1130 persons)

Largeness of family

22.16% of those in 'primary' poverty (1602 persons)

In regular work but at low wages

51.96% of those in 'primary' poverty (3756 persons)

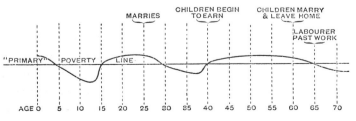

S. Rowntree, *Poverty, a Study of Town Life*, 1901

56
The left-out millions

The Liberal Party was in government from 1906 to 1914. Many laws were passed for state action to help some of the most serious types of poverty. Some people have said these laws made the 'first welfare state', although not everyone had a right to pensions and medical care as they do today.

Poverty in the early 1900s

For millions of people the dawn of the twentieth century brought no hope of better times. Seebohm Rowntree's survey showed just how many were poor from old age, sickness or low wages. In 1902 the army turned down two out of every three young men who had wanted to fight in the Boer War. They simply were not fit enough.

Some people knew that Germany was ahead of Britain. There, the state paid old-age pensions and workers had to be insured against sickness and unemployment. Which party would be first to risk votes by using tax-payers' money in the same way?

The Liberal government, 1906–14

The answer came with the 1906 election when the Liberals had eighty-four more MPs than all other parties. One group of new ministers wanted to use this massive lead to pass laws for state action on welfare. There was a good political reason. The number of Labour MPs had gone up from two in 1900 to twenty-nine in 1906. If the Liberal government did nothing about poverty the Labour Party might go on to win more seats, especially when the poorest working people one day got the vote.

Lloyd George (1863–1945)

David Lloyd George was the leading man among these welfare-minded Liberal ministers. He had been brought up in a Welsh village by his uncle who was a shoemaker and Baptist preacher. He became a solicitor in Wales and an MP for Caernarvon in 1890. Lloyd George came to Parliament with a great hatred of the English upper classes and a lot of sympathy with the struggling poor. His work to help them began when he was made President of the Board of Trade in 1906 but he was in an even stronger position as Chancellor of the Exchequer from 1908 to 1916.

Winston Churchill (1874–1965)

Lloyd George's ally was Winston Churchill, the son of a famous Conservative politician and nephew of a Duke. He had been a soldier, a reporter and then a Conservative MP. In 1906 he crossed over to the Liberals (for a time) saying that 'the cause of Liberalism is the cause of the left-out millions'. In 1908 he followed Lloyd George as President of the Board of Trade. Both men loved power but it was due most of all to them that the Liberal governments of 1906 to 1914 laid the foundations of what was later called the 'Welfare State'.

School meals, 1906

The first step was an Act to allow local education authorities to pay for school meals for the poorest children. Until then penny dinner societies had served about three million meals a year. Under the new law fourteen million meals were provided, and most of them were free. Even more important was the fact that parents did not have to go to the Poor Law guardians for this help. It was the first ever money spent on welfare which a person could take without being treated as a pauper.

School medical service, 1907

In 1907 every education authority was told it must open a school medical service. At first the doctors only inspected children and recommended treatment. Many parents could not pay for the treatment so, in 1912, the government added grants to pay for school clinics. Until 1948 school clinics were the only place where many children could have their eyes, ears and general health cared for.

Children's Act, 1908

The Children's and Young Persons' Act, 1908, made all children into 'protected persons' which meant their parents could be prosecuted for neglecting them. The Act made it illegal to insure a child's life (and it still is). Behind that lay the horrible fact that insurance companies had been paying out to parents whose infants had died in suspicious circumstances or from the carelessness of drunken adults.

Old age pensions, 1908

In 1908 Lloyd George had become Chancellor of the Exchequer. On Budget Day he announced a plan to pay all people aged 70 or over a weekly pension of 5s (so long as they did not have other incomes). The money was to come out of government funds and there was to be no Poor Law test.

In the first year, 650,000 old people collected pensions from their local post office. (The Post Office was given the job because it was the only government organisation with branches in every town and village.) Lloyd George had been told by Poor Law officials that about 500,000 would need pensions. He said that the extra numbers showed how many people had been 'too proud to wear the badge of pauperism'.

School medical service

A

A London County Council doctor examines a boy in 1911 at Holland Street School.

1 *Who are the four adults in the picture?*
2 *Is there any evidence that the County Council kept records of children's health?*
3 *Can you see any clues to tell you whether the boy came from a poor or comfortable family?*
4 *Supposing the doctor found the boy had tonsilitis or poor eyesight, how could he have it dealt with?*
5 *What does the photograph tell you about schools in 1911?*

Three ways of looking at old-age pensions

B

Through journalism.
A reporter interviewed a 90-year-old man in 1912. He and his wife lived with their son and his family.

6 *What does the man mean by 'prayed to be took'?*

7 *What does he mean by going 'on the parish' and why would his children not allow that?*

8 *What did the old couple do with their new pension?*

9 *How does this report illustrate Lloyd George's statement that there were many old people 'too proud to wear the badge of pauperism'?*

"And sometimes a-most 'ave I prayed to be took; for we was only a burden to our children as kep' us; for they be good and wouldna let us go on the parish as long as they could 'elp it. But now we want to go on livin' forever, 'cus we give 'em the ten shilling a week, and it pays 'em to 'ave us along with 'em. I never thought we should be able to pay the boy back for all 'is goodness to me and the missus; but times change sir."
The Nation, 18 May 1912

C

Through statistics.
The number of people over 70 who were given poor relief in 1910 and 1912.

10 *Why did outdoor relief drop so greatly between 1910 and 1912?*

11 *Suggest reasons why indoor relief fell by so much less.*

	Indoor	*Outdoor*
1910	55,261	93,177
1912	49,370	9,530

Figures from The Local Government Board, 1910 and 1912

D

Through a cartoon.
Lord Halsbury was an ex-Lord Chancellor who got a pension of £5,000 a year. He attacked the Old Age Pension as being too small or paltry. The Liberals replied by turning this cartoon from the Westminster Gazette *into a political poster.*

12 *What is the cartoonist saying about the pension?*

13 *From the evidence in Sources B and C suggest one important way in which the pension was a 'wunnerful comfort' to many old people.*

THE BIG DOG AND THE LITTLE ONE.

[From the *Westminster Gazette.*

LORD HALSBURY: I don't think much of that paltry little thing—it's a mockery of a dog.

AGED PENSIONER: Well, my lord, 'tis only a little 'un, but 'tis a wunnerful comfort to me. Us bain't all blessed wi' big 'uns!

Liberal Party Leaflet, published 1 February 1909

57
Liberals, lords and workers

After help to children and old people, the Liberals planned schemes for insuring wage-earners. To do this they needed to collect extra taxes. This started a political row which ended with the House of Lords losing many of its powers. Lloyd George then started national insurance against sickness and unemployment.

The People's Budget

In February 1909 Lloyd George stood up in Parliament to make his budget speech. He told MPs he intended to collect the money needed to fight 'poverty and squalidness'. There would be higher rates of tax on the highest earners and new taxes on cars, petrol, spirits and tobacco. That caused a grumble from opposition Conservative MPs. Then he told them he would tax the profits made by people who owned land which became more valuable if it could be sold for new building. That caused an uproar about interfering with private property. The Conservatives could not defeat the 'People's Budget' in the Commons but they had a huge majority in the House of Lords. At that time all laws had to be passed by both Commons and Lords. The Lords threw the budget out.

Commons v. Lords

The government argued that taxation was a matter not for Lords but for elected MPs to decide. So they called a general election and campaigned for the People's Budget. They won, so the House of Lords gave way and passed the budget. The government said the matter could not end there and drew up a Parliament Bill to cut the Lords' powers for ever. In future they would have no say in laws to do with money and could hold up other laws for only two years.

The question was so important that it was argued in another election in 1910. The Liberals won again, but even so the Lords refused to pass the Bill. The Prime Minister then told the King he would expect him to make 500 new lords, all Liberal supporters, to get the Bill passed. When the King agreed the Lords knew they had lost and passed the Bill in the Parliament Act of 1911.

National Insurance, 1911

Lloyd George used the money from the new taxes to pay for the National Insurance scheme he started in 1911. Insurance itself was not a new idea. Better-off wage-earners often made subscriptions to friendly societies which paid a weekly sum when they were ill (see Unit 64). Big insurance companies, such as the Prudential, had thousands of doorstep agents collecting 1d and 2d weekly for life insurance. This went towards a small death benefit to help a wage-earner's widow and children. But only wage-earners with regular work could afford to insure themselves in these ways. Lloyd George's scheme was compulsory for all workers, men and women, in manual jobs or low-paid white collar work.

He said it gave 9d for 4d. The wage-earner bought 4d worth of stamps to stick on a card. The employer added 3d and the government another 2d. The money went to a friendly society or insurance company chosen by the wage-earner. But the state controlled what they gave in return. Sick pay was ten shillings a week for 26 weeks and the insured person could get free medical treatment. This was given by doctors whose names were on a 'panel' for each district. Doctors earned a fee for each worker who signed on with them. In some districts this was the first time that doctors could be sure of regular payment for treating patients.

It was the first step towards today's national insurance with big differences. Workers' families were not insured and there were no pensions for widows. Lloyd George had wanted these but the insurance companies said they would not help with the rest of the scheme if he threatened their sales of life insurance.

Trade Boards Act, 1909

National insurance was one arm of the Liberals' help for wage-earners. The other came from the work of Winston Churchill when he was President of the Board of Trade. He started with the Trade Boards Act of 1909. It set up Trade Boards to fix minimum wages for women (and some men), who worked in the four most sweated trades.

Employment exchanges, 1910

Winston Churchill then joined with a civil servant, William Beveridge, to plan a chain of employment exchanges across the country. Workers could cut the time they were unemployed by asking about vacancies at a central point instead of trekking from one factory to another. Employment exchanges became the second network of government offices, after the post offices.

Unemployment insurance

In 1912 the employment exchanges took on another duty given in the second part of Lloyd George's Insurance Act of 1911. Unemployment insurance was started for workers in jobs where there was a lot of seasonal redundancy such as building and engineering. The worker's stamp cost 2½d and the employer and the government each paid the same. If they were laid off work the insured workers went to sign on at the employment exchange which paid unemployment benefit.

Working hours

Two other groups of workers were helped by the Liberal governments. In 1908 the Mines Act laid down that underground workers should work no more than eight hours. In 1911 the Shops Act ordered all shops to close for half a day a week to help shop assistants who had become the most overworked employees in Britain.

Lloyd George and welfare
A

In the summer holidays of 1908 Lloyd George went to look at Germany's welfare schemes. This is what he said when he returned.

1 *How important does the visit seem to have been in developing Lloyd George's ideas about welfare?*

"I never realised before on what a gigantic scale the German pension system is conducted. Nor had I any idea how successfully it works. I had read much about it, but no amount of study at home . . . can convey to the mind a clear idea of all that state insurance means to Germany. . . . It touches the great mass of German people in wellnigh every walk of life. Old-age pensions form but a comparatively small part of the system. Does the German worker fall ill? State insurance comes to his aid. Is he permanently invalided from work? Again he gets a regular grant whether he has reached the pension age or not."
Daily News, 27 August 1908

B

This was the Liberal Party poster, based on a Westminster Gazette *cartoon, which defended Lloyd George's plan to tax rises in land value.*

2 *Use the information in the cartoon to explain how Lloyd George's tax would work. How much tax would the landowner have to pay?*

3 *What happened following Conservative opposition to this part of the 1909 budget?*

4 *Are there any clues in the picture about the cartoonist's personal point of view?*

[From the *Westminster Gazette.*]

Mr. Lloyd-George: What are you using this acre field for?

Owner Agricultural purposes. I turn my pony in here!

Mr. Lloyd-George: It can't be worth more than £50 for that purpose—couldn't you do something better with it?

Owner: There's no need for me to do anything—the builders over there are doing it all for me. They'll be wanting to build here soon. Why, I could get £500 to-morrow for this acre!

Mr. Lloyd-George: Then, surely, it won't hurt you to pay a tax of a halfpenny in the £ on an increased value which you have had nothing to do with making!

Liberal Party Leaflet, published 25 June 1909

C

R.W. Harris was a civil servant who produced the first leaflets describing the new National Health Insurance scheme. Here he recalls what happened.

5 *Why did R.W. Harris try out the leaflet on maid servants?*

6 *In what ways was National Insurance an important starting-point in British history?*

7 *What new problems did it create for the civil service?*

8 *Is there any evidence in Source C that some people were hostile to the scheme?*

"In the early days of 1912 it was decreed that there should be delivered by post at every house, cottage, and tenement in the land a paper which should tell every inhabitant of these Islands what his position was under the new scheme. It was the first such wholesale delivery that had ever been undertaken. It fell to my lot to draw up this leaflet. I put it through a series of ten proofs and tried twenty copies of each on all sorts of people, including maid servants. I passed the final proof for press on a Saturday . . . on the Monday morning, I saw too late that the amount of the contribution was set out as sevenpence for men and sixpence for women, without any indication whether the payment was to be made daily, weekly, monthly, or just as the impulse moved the contributors. Most of the printing presses in London had run off between them twenty-five million copies during the week-end. Some retired admirals and generals wrote on their club note-paper, and asked that this slovenly document should be reprinted, and that the cost of reprinting should be deducted from the pay of the responsible official."

R.W. Harris, *National Health Insurance in Great Britain*, 1946

58
The overcrowded city

In 1801 the census showed that three out of ten people lived in towns of over 2,000 inhabitants. In 1851 more than half the population lived in towns of 2,000 or more. This unit describes the problems caused by the population explosion in towns, especially in the 1820s, 1830s and 1840s.

New houses

Imagine moving from a village to a town in the early nineteenth century. The first shock would be the number of people packed into a few square miles. In 1821 Britain had one million houses, by 1851 there were 2¼ million. Cheap new housing was an easy way for small businessmen to make a quick profit. They bought a field or the grounds of an old large home and found an ex-bricklayer turned builder to crowd it with houses. In a matter of months the new landlord would be collecting rents.

To save money most houses were built back to back with tiny windows, and walls only the width of one brick (4½ inches). Floors were made by placing boards or flagstones on top of the damp earth. In hilly districts such as Yorkshire and Lancashire most fields were long and narrow, so houses were thrown up in long terraces facing each other across streets a few yards wide. In Birmingham, Manchester and Liverpool it was more usual to build in a hollow square with all the houses looking into a tiny courtyard. The only way in was through a narrow tunnel. In Glasgow builders preferred tall blocks or tenements. A maze of stairways and corridors led to the one or two rooms which became home for a family.

Housing standards

A family's standard of housing depended on the rent it could afford. A skilled worker might manage a four-roomed house with two up and two down. It was more usual for four or five people to squeeze into a one-up and one-down. To help with the rent very many families even had to take a lodger into these tiny homes.

The poorest never had a house. In Liverpool and Manchester landlords had cellars with separate entrances built below the courtyard houses. They rented these airless rooms to families who often had to prop up their beds on bricks to lift them clear of water. London landlords divided large houses into tiny living-spaces. The lean-to buildings filled up the street spaces until the district became a sort of human rabbit-warren. This was a 'rookery' and the worst were just yards away from the fashionable areas such as Oxford Street. If you couldn't afford a room in a rookery or cellar you might spend the summer nights under a bridge but the winter cold would drive you to a common lodging-house to share a bed with two or three others for a few pence.

Public health

Even with all its evils, town housing was probably better than the crumbling hovels in the countryside. Other sides of town life were probably worse. It was a golden age for the cheating shopkeeper who put alum powder in the flour, dried hawthorn in the tea and water in the milk. Most milk was in any case infected with TB, especially if it came from a street cowhouse. Dairykeepers killed beasts when they became ill and sold the meat cheap to working-class families. Bacon was eaten much more often than beef because there were pigsties in every working-class street.

An even greater health risk was the state of public services. Most towns had separate 'improvement commissions' for pavements, street lighting and drainage. Each commission collected its own rates from better-off householders but their services went to the districts where these ratepayers lived. The new jerry-built* houses usually had no drains or pavements and the road was a stinking mass of mud and rubbish.

Water

Water was supplied by private companies who took it from wells or rivers along wooden mains as far as a single pipe every few streets. The water was turned on sometimes only for an hour every few days, and was sold in bucketfuls. The middle classes had pipes taken into their own homes, although they needed large storage tanks because the water came through at odd half-hours.

Sewerage

Middle-class homes also had water-closets. But the contents often only went as far as a cesspool in the basement. That happened in Windsor Castle too. It was better, if possible, to connect up to a street sewer. This was a square brick tunnel made to collect the sewage, not flush it along. Every so often the sewer was opened, at night because of the smell, and men went in to empty it.

Slum dwellers from several houses had to share a privy which was often just a brick pit. Every few months a night-soil dealer carted the contents away to sell to a farmer. If the night soil was awkward to get at it was left to build into a huge dung-heap. Night soil and cesspools often drained into the rivers and wells where the water companies took their supplies.

It would be interesting to know whether Victorian people noticed the constant smell that came from human sewage and the droppings of thousands of horses. Children could earn a few pence in tips by setting up as crossing-sweepers in fashionable streets to keep a way over the road free from filth. Even without these smells the air was thick with smoke from houses and factories. Chemical and iron works belched out chemicals, gas and ash.

* The term was first used about 1830.

Population
A

Growth of seven towns, 1801–51. In these years the population of Britain grew from 10.5 million to 21.0 million.

1 *Choose three towns and write a few sentences on each saying why you think their population increased.*

Population in thousands

	1801	1851
Birmingham	71	133
Glasgow	77	329
Leeds	53	172
Liverpool	82	376
Manchester	75	303
Portsmouth	33	72
Sheffield	46	135

Home, sweet home, in the 1840s
B

Housing in Preston, drawn and described for a Parliamentary Report of 1844.

2 *Who would live in the Preston houses?*
3 *Suggest why they were built like this.*
4 *Would the builder have any reason to feel proud of his work?*

"Each yard is furnished with a privy by the landlord and, in many cases, with a pigsty and its ... midden by the tenant. The yard – privy, pigsty and midden included – is 13 feet 7 inches long by 11 feet 3 inches wide.... [The] midden-pan is 3 feet 10 inches wide and about 4 feet below the level of the street ... and into it the contents of each privy drain through a hole.... The matter thus collected is removed twice a year from the pan.... When the place was visited, three large heaps of manure were lying within a few yards of the house awaiting purchasers."
Commission on the state of large towns, 1st Report, 1844

C

In 1848 the London Statistical Society did a room-by-room survey of a rookery just behind Oxford Street.

5 *The London Statistical Society obviously used a form to make its survey. See if you can design the form they might have used.*
6 *Draw a rough sketch of the two rooms in Source C and try to work out sleeping arrangements for the occupants.*

"House no 4 – two parlours on Ground Floor. Size of front room, 14 ft long, 13 ft broad, 6 ft high; size of windows, 3 ft 4 in. by 2 ft 2 in. Size of back-room, 11 ft 2 in. long, 9 ft 4 in. broad, less than 6 ft in height; 1 window with 4 whole panes; rent paid, 5s 6d weekly for 2 rooms; ... number of families 5; comprising 4 males above 20, 9 females above 20, three of them single, 2 males under 20, 4 females under 20; total 19. Number of persons ill, 2; deaths in 1847, 1, measles. Country, Irish; trade, dealers and mendicants. State of rooms and furniture bad, dirty; state of windows, 6 whole panes, and 10 broken. Number of beds, 6.... this room opens into the yard, 6 feet square, which is covered over with night soil."
Journal of the Statistical Society of London, 1848

59
The cholera is coming!

Unhealthy town conditions led to a rise in deaths from many everyday diseases and from epidemics of typhus and cholera. This unit tells the story of the four outbreaks of cholera in 1831–2, 1848–9, 1853–4 and 1866.

Rising deaths

Source A shows that the death-rate rose around 1810 after a long fall. One important reason must have been that people in the overcrowded towns were too weak from poor food, damp and lack of fresh air to stand up to disease. Illnesses such as influenza and diarrhoea, which make us 'poorly', were often killers. About one person in three had their lungs eaten up by consumption – or tuberculosis.

These diseases were accepted almost as part of nature. People dreaded far more the epidemics which came and went. Typhus was known as 'gaol fever' from the way it swept through prisons and other crowded places. In most summers in the 1820s and 1830s it struck in one or more industrial towns.

Cholera

Cholera was terrifying because it came from Asia and not even doctors had seen it unless they had worked in India. In 1830 it moved to Europe for the first time. As news came of deaths in Russia, Germany and France the government was scared into action to stop cholera crossing to Britain. It set up an emergency Board of Health which ordered ships to wait in quarantine. At that time any order from the central government was objected to as interference. This one was disobeyed in November 1831 in Sunderland and a docker died from cholera after unloading a boat.

Cholera spread fast along the roads and waterways when the warm weather began in 1832. The Board of Health ordered each district to set up its own local board of doctors, clergymen, magistrates and other local leaders.

Doctors' theories

The doctors could see that cholera struck hardest where people were crowded together, in some villages, at summer fairs, in the poorest parts of towns. But they explained it in two different ways. One group believed it was spread by contagion, through having contact with victims. Others said the cause was poisoned air from the heaps of filth and sewage.

Both theories pointed to the same actions. The local boards opened isolation hospitals in army barracks, old warehouses or tents. They had the dead buried in special pits, and homes fumigated and limewashed. Scavengers were set to work to clear filth.

Doctors were in the dark about the best treatment for patients. The most usual medicine was a mixture of calomel (made from mercury) and opium to speed up the sickness and diarrhoea which was the first stage of the disease. At the end of 1832 cholera disappeared, leaving 31,000 dead. The Boards of Health closed and most people were glad. They had been unpopular for the way they had entered houses and workplaces to clean up.

In the 1840s opinion began to change in favour of cleaner towns. Even so, it took the news that cholera was in Europe again to panic Parliament into setting up a permanent Board of Health in 1848.

Cholera 1848–9

The board's main action to deal with the 1848–9 epidemic in London was to order the sewers to be flushed into the Thames – the main water supply! In this outbreak 62,000 people died, but it led to the first breakthrough in understanding the disease. Two doctors, William Budd and John Snow, observed its spread carefully and decided it was caused by a 'living organism' taken into the stomach.

John Snow

Nearly every other doctor scoffed, but John Snow proved the point in the next outbreak in 1853–4. In Soho fifty people a day were dying in the courts around Broad Street where the only water pump stood. He persuaded the parish vestry to take away the pump handle and there were no new cases of cholera in that district. Snow's 'living organism' was being passed by sufferers into the sewage, which leaked into water which when drunk caused more people to catch cholera.

Cholera came to Britain for the last time in 1866. This time only 14,000 died. That may have been due to the fact that more people were immune to the disease, but Source D suggests another possible reason. John Snow died in 1858 just when his idea of the 'living organism' was being accepted by doctors. Twenty-five years later Robert Koch, a German chemist, was the first to see this living organism under a microscope – the cholera virus.

Births and deaths 1740–1913

A

Birth-rate and death-rate, England and Wales, 1740–1913.

1 *At what point does the first fall in the death-rate begin to level off? At what point does it begin to rise quite sharply? When did the long-term fall begin again?*

2 *Explain as fully as you can how the graph could be used to illustrate the narrative in this unit.*

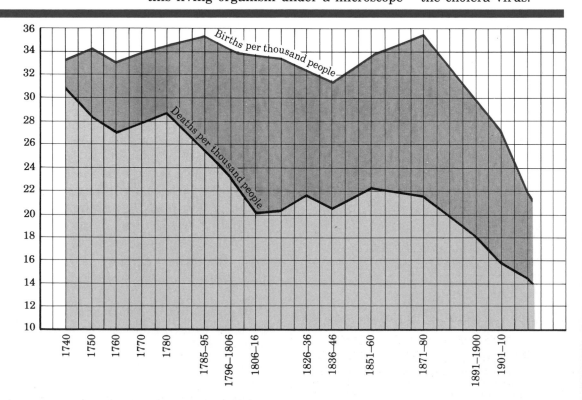

The dread of cholera
B
These two extracts show how cholera caused more fear than other epidemics.

3 *How do these extracts help to explain why people were terrified of cholera?*

4 *How do you think the common people's belief described in the second extract might have arisen?*

Water supply
C
This Punch *cartoon shows how concern about poor public health was growing.*

5 *Is there any evidence that the cartoonist understood the scientific reasons for complaining about the water supply?*

6 *What made the filth in the Thames much worse in 1849?*

D *(below)*
A public health notice in Limehouse (East London), 1866.

7 *What possible reason for the lower death-rate in 1866 is suggested by this notice?*

"To see a number of our fellow creatures in a good state of health, in the full possession of their wonted strength and in the midst of their years, suddenly seized with the most violent spasms, and in a few hours cast into the tomb, is calculated to shake the firmest nerves, and to inspire dread in the stoutest heart."
The Methodist Magazine, 1832

"All the bodies were buried in less than twelve hours . . ., some in two or three hours. The common people firmly believed that the doctors stupify their patients with laudanum and then hurry them off to the grave while yet alive."
Gateshead Board of Health, *Minutes, 1832*

THE WATER THAT JOHN DRINKS.

This is the water that JOHN drinks.

This is the Thames with its cento of stink,
That supplies the water that JOHN drinks.

These are the fish that float in the ink-
-y stream of the Thames with its cento of stink,
That supplies the water that JOHN drinks

This is the sewer, from cesspool and sink,
That feeds the fish that float in the ink-
-y stream of the Thames with its cento of stink,
That supplies the water that JOHN drinks.

These are vested int'rests, that fill to the brink,
The network of sewers from cesspool and sink,
That feed the fish that float in the ink-
-y stream of the Thames, with its cento of stink,
That supplies the water that JOHN drinks.

This is the price that we pay to wink
At the vested int'rests that fill to the brink,
The network of sewers from cesspool and sink,
That feed the fish that float in the ink-
-y stream of the Thames with its cento of stink,
That supplies the water that JOHN drinks.

Punch, 13 October 1849

CHOLERA
AND
WATER.
BOARD OF WORKS
FOR THE LIMEHOUSE DISTRICT,
Comprising Limehouse, Ratcliff, Shadwell, and Wapping.

The INHABITANTS of the District within which CHOLERA IS PREVAILING, are earnestly advised

NOT TO DRINK ANY WATER
WHICH HAS NOT
PREVIOUSLY BEEN BOILED.

Fresh Water ought to be Boiled every Morning for the day's use, and what remains of it ought to be thrown away at night. The Water ought not to stand where any kind of dirt can get into it, and great care ought to be given to see that Water Butts and Cisterns are free from dirt.

BY ORDER,
THOS. W. RATCLIFF,
CLERK OF THE BOARD.

Limehouse District, Board of Works, August 1866

60
Edwin Chadwick and John Simon

Public health is the name given to actions taken by the government and councils to prevent disease. It was a new idea in the 1840s when it was given a boost by a report written by Edwin Chadwick. From 1848 to 1854 he led the work of the first government Board of Health. From 1855 to 1875 the government's chief medical adviser was John Simon.

Chadwick's Report, 1842

In 1838 Edwin Chadwick was in charge of the new Poor Law (see Unit 53). Typhus swept through East London and there was a tragic list of widows and orphans needing Poor Law help. Chadwick said it would be cheaper to spend money on preventing disease. The Home Secretary asked him to investigate.

In 1842 Chadwick finished his report on 'The Sanitary Condition of the Labouring Population'. It shows that he agreed with the doctors who said that the cause of disease was poisoned air from the filth in towns. The theory fitted the facts in his report. People died younger in towns than in the countryside and in working-class districts than in the middle-class suburbs.

The report outlined Chadwick's plan for public health. He wanted the improvement commissions and water companies to be closed down. Instead all towns should have a combined 'arterial system' so that water would flow into every home and sewage would be washed out along earthenware pipes to a safe distance.

'Clean' and 'dirty' parties

Nearly 100,000 copies were sold and the report split politicians and townspeople into two. One Prime Minister called them the 'clean' and 'dirty' parties. The dirty party objected that Chadwick wanted to force them to be clean against their will. Often, these were excuses from improvement commissions or water companies. The clean party campaigned for laws to force towns to make themselves healthier. Parliament delayed until cholera made its way across Europe in 1848 and MPs voted for the Public Health Act.

Public Health Act, 1848

1 There was to be a three man Board of Health in London. (One member was Edwin Chadwick and another was Lord Shaftesbury.)
2 Any town could set up a local Board of health if 10 per cent of the ratepayers asked for it. It had to have one if the death rate reached 23 in the thousand in any year.
3 The local Board's main duty was to arrange for water and sewerage on a plan approved by the Board in London.
4 Local Boards had the power to inspect slaughterhouses and lodging-houses, close graveyards and provide public parks.

The Act at work

The Central Board was given a trial of six years. At the end of that time, 182 small towns had asked for a local board and seventy of these had drawn up plans for a water and sewerage system. Some had begun to clear out cesspools and close pigsties and slaughterhouses. But they were unpopular with shopkeepers who had food destroyed by order, working people who lost their pigsties and ratepayers who had to pay for an arterial system. At the Central Board Chadwick had made enemies. Engineers objected when he meddled in their schemes for water and sewerage and when he handed out part-time work for the Board to his friends.

Public Health after 1854

So the Central Board was closed in 1854 but the work went on, possibly better without Chadwick's interference. He never understood that you could not build an arterial system for Manchester or Glasgow in a few years as you could in a small town. So the cities got Parliament to pass Acts which gave them power to spend ratepayers' money on public health. Liverpool had got its Act in 1847 and was the first town to appoint a medical officer of health.

Most towns started clearing out the privies and giving each home an ash-pail. The first large force of council workers were the men who emptied these each day. By 1870s, sixty-nine towns owned their own water supply, often fed by reservoirs in the country. They made building by-laws (see Unit 61) to say that every new house must have at least one tap and a WC. It was well into the twentieth century before these were found in older houses, so in the meantime councils opened public bath-houses and wash-houses and built public conveniences – for men only!

Sir John Simon (1816–1904)

The government learned a lesson from Chadwick's high-handedness. Instead of an all-powerful Central Board they set up a committee on public health. They chose a doctor, John Simon, as their chief medical adviser. Between 1855 and 1875 he advised on laws which brought about a revolution in public health.

Vaccination

One of his first concerns was smallpox. Ever since Jenner's discovery (see Unit 33) it had been possible to prevent the disease, and the government had issued free vaccine for use by Poor Law vaccinators. This had cut the deaths from smallpox but it could still kill 10,000 in a bad year. In 1853 a law had made infant vaccination compulsory but many parents ignored it. Simon increased the number of vaccine stores and trained vaccinators. In 1871 he advised on a new law which said that parents who refused to have children vaccinated should be fined. There was fierce opposition but the law gave Britain the toughest anti-smallpox legislation in the world.

Food and Drugs Act, 1875

John Simon tackled dangerous food in 1860 through a law which made adulteration illegal. But a ban was not enough to stop such a profitable business, so the 1875 Food and Drugs Act said local health authorities could have public analysts to check food and prosecute law-breakers.

Public Health Act, 1875

Most of all, John Simon was concerned with the patchiness of steps to deal with public health. The Sanitary Act, 1866, said that all local areas should have a board to deal with health matters. Simon was still not satisfied and one of his last tasks was to help write the Public Health Act of 1875. This tidied up and strengthened all the public health laws. Every part of the country had to have a public health authority. Each had to have at least a medical officer and a sanitary (or public health) inspector to see that laws on vaccination, food adulteration, housing and clearing up filth were obeyed.

The campaign for healthier towns

A

In this extract from his Report Chadwick is quoting the research of a Manchester man who had compared living conditions in his town with the tiny farming county of Rutland (now part of Leicestershire).

1 *According to Source A, who lived longest in both Rutland and Manchester? Why do you think this was so?*
2 *Who had the shortest lives of all? Suggest reasons.*
3 *If the death rates in the second table applied today how many of your class would have survived to take GCSE?*
4 *What effect would these tables have on winning middle-class support for expensive water and sewerage schemes?*

B

After Chadwick's Report, a Health of Towns Association was set up with branches all over Britain. This is part of a speech made at the Aberdeen branch.

5 *What evidence does Source B give about support for Chadwick's ideas?*
6 *What theory of the cause of disease does the speaker in Source B support?*
7 *Which organisation paid out most of the £20 million for sickness and death? Where did the money come from?*

Average age of death

	In Manchester	In Rutlandshire
Professional persons and gentry and their families	38	52
Tradesmen and their families	20	41
Mechanics, labourers, and their families	17	38

Of 4,629 deaths of persons of the labouring classes who died in the year 1840 in Manchester:

Under five years of age	2,649 or 1 in 7
Above 5 and under 10	215 or 1 in 22
Above 15 and under 20	135 or 1 in 34
Above 20 and under 25	107 or 1 in 43

E. Chadwick, *Report on the Sanitary condition of the Labouring Population of Great Britain*, 1824

"I state that the air we breathe may be poisoned ... filth ... is accumulated by want of proper drainage and sewerage. The dwelling of every family, therefore, ought to be provided with receptacles for all refuse and a good drain.... But this is impracticable, unless at the same time, water be introduced plentifully into the dwelling of every family.... Sickness is expensive by the cost of medical attendance ... by loss of the labourer's work ... and as causing premature death.... Think of 27,000 cases of widowhood, and 10,000 cases of orphanage arising from removable causes annually. It is calculated that the annual cost of unnecessary sickness and death is ... for the United Kingdom, £20,000,000, all of which might be saved by proper sanitary measures."

I. Gilchrist, *Address to the Health of Towns Association*, Aberdeen, 1848

Half-way there: sanitation in the 1870s

C

In Manchester in the 1870s many working-class homes were supplied with ash-pails by the council.

8 *What evidence does the picture give about improvements in sanitary arrangements compared with those described in Unit 58?*
9 *What would have been your feelings if you had moved in the 1870s to a street where ash pails were provided?*

Supplementary Report to the Local Government Board, 1874

61
The growing city

In the later nineteenth century housing standards began to improve for better-paid working people. Many were able to live in houses built to by-laws. Most of the poor were still crowded into unhealthy slums. Parliament passed two Artisans' Dwelling Acts and two Housing Acts to deal with this problem. Some councils built houses for rent and a few employers put up model villages for their workers, but rehousing from slum homes did not begin on a big scale until the 1920s.

By-law housing

A town council could make by-laws for its own district if it had been given the power by a special Act of Parliament. By-laws were used to lay down building standards for new homes from the 1860s onwards. They were different in each town, but most led to the 'tunnel-back' house. The family had two rooms upstairs and two down. Attached to the back was an extra one-storey building with a scullery, a wash-house and a WC. The houses were built in rows with small yards. Every so often there was a tunnel entry for the scavengers who emptied the dustbins.

Master builders

Most house-building was in the hands of master builders who employed teams of workers to put up several streets at a time. They used standardised windows, doors and fittings and even the patches of fancy brickwork were bought in bulk. The master builder tried to buy a plot of empty land on the edge of the crowded city. His new tenants travelled to work on the new tramways which spread out from the business and factory districts. In the 1860s and 1870s trams were horse-drawn. In the 1890s they began to use overhead electricity. In London, extra underground lines to the new housing estates were opened.

'Model housing'

Only clerks and skilled workers could afford rents for by-law houses and the extra shilling or two for weekly fares. For unskilled workers and sweated labourers housing often became even more overcrowded. One cause was the railways (see Unit 43). One effort to deal with this problem came from the model housing societies such as the Peabody Trust, started with a gift from an American merchant, George Peabody. It built apartments for rent in barrack-like blocks. The bare walls and shared taps and WCs made them unpopular and the rents were anyway too high for the poorest.

Artisans' Dwelling Acts, 1868 and 1875

In 1868 and 1875 Parliament passed two Artisans' Dwelling Acts, both named after government ministers.

Torrens's Act, 1868, gave local councils the power to force a landlord to repair an insanitary house. If he did not, the council could buy the house and pull it down.
Cross's Act, 1875, gave councils the power to clear whole districts, not only single houses.

Birmingham

Both Acts were only permissive; councils were not forced to use the new powers. Most did not do so because of the cost. The biggest scheme to carry out Cross's Act began in Birmingham in 1876. The Lord Mayor, Joseph Chamberlain, persuaded the council to buy 40 acres in the town centre which were crammed with courtyard houses and tumbledown workshops. In their place appeared Corporation Street, running from the railway station to new law courts. The city got a fine new shopping street but at great cost to the people who had been cleared out. Cross's Act said nothing about re-housing and they were left to fend for themselves.

Housing Acts, 1890 and 1909

Re-housing only came into the picture after two Housing Acts, one in 1890 (mostly for London) and one in 1909 (for the rest of the country)

At least half the people evicted in a slum clearance scheme had to be re-housed. To do this, councils could buy land and build on it themselves using money collected from the rates.

Council-house building had already begun in a small way in the 1860s when Liverpool put up some flats for skilled workers. After the Housing Acts Liverpool and other councils, especially in London, built a few homes for people left homeless by slum clearance. Some were blocks of flats and others were estates in the suburbs.

Saltaire

The council estates often copied the model villages built by a few wealthy employers for their workforces. First in the field was a Bradford textile manufacturer, Sir Titus Salt. In 1853 he built a new factory and housing estate a few miles out of town. The eight hundred homes in Saltaire were graded according to the rank and wages of his workers and there were a few rent-free cottages for retired people. All homes had piped gas and water, and a WC.

Port Sunlight and Bournville

Thirty years later the soap manufacturer W.H. Lever made a start on Port Sunlight three miles from the smoke and grime of Birkenhead. Houses were built either semi-detached or in small groups surrounded by open spaces. Each had a bathroom which was still very rare even in grander homes of the 1880s. The same ideas went into the layout of Bournville where George Cadbury had opened a new chocolate factory a few miles from the Birmingham city centre. The difference was that Bournville houses could be rented by people who did not work for Cadbury's. Joseph Rowntree (Seebohm's* father) built his cocoa factory and model village at New Earswick outside York.

Council housing and model villages made only a tiny dent in the number of people forced to live in slum homes. What was needed was a strong government lead and cash help for local councils. These only came after the First World War.

* See Unit 55.

The effects of by-laws

A

Housing in Tooting, South London, built in the 1880s.

B

Charles Masterman became a Liberal MP. Before that he went to live in South London to get to know about the lives of the working classes. This passage gives his opinion of their new estates.

". . . populated streets, roads labelled, curtains in the little bow-windows, a little packed maze of little packed houses . . . tiny back-yards in which a woman can just turn round. At a central site appears a clean attractive gin palace; along one side extends a raw row of red new shops; at a corner sprawls a gigantic elementary school . . . model of the latest educational efficiency; in a less favoured site rises a tiny corrugated edifice with the legend 'Site for the Permanent Church of St. Aloysius. Five thousand pounds required'."
Charles Masterman, *From the Abyss*, 1902

C

By-law housing in York. Seebohm Rowntree called this 'the best type of working class house in 1900'.

Seebohm Rowntree, *Poverty and Progress*, 1941

Sources A–C

1 *Can you identify a district in your own area which in 1902 might have fitted Charles Masterman's description?*
2 *What evidence can you find in Sources A and C for the work of master builders?*
3 *In Source B what is Charles Masterman's attitude to the new district?*
4 *Compare Sources A to C with those in Unit 58. What differences in health and comfort do they suggest? Do they suggest any disadvantages for life in the later nineteenth century?*

Public services in Liverpool

D

In 1907 an historian made this summary of the work of Liverpool council.

5 *List the services which were given in 1907 but not in the earlier years of the nineteenth century.*
6 *What clue is there that Liverpool was a pioneer in council-house building?*

"It offers to see that the child is brought safely into the world. It provides him in infancy with suitable food. It gives him play-grounds to amuse himself in and baths to swim in. It takes him to school . . . it trains him for his future trade. It sees that the citizen's house is properly built and sometimes even builds it for him. It brings into his rooms an unfailing supply of pure water from the remote hills. It guards his food and tries to secure that it is not dangerously adulterated. It sweeps the streets for him and disposes of the refuse of his house. It carries him swiftly to and from his work. It gives him books to read, pictures to look at, music to listen to and lectures to stimulate his thought."
Ramsay Muir, *A History of Liverpool*, 1907

62
Surgeons and science

Before 1847 very few operations were done because there were no anaesthetics. In 1847 James Simpson found that chloroform was safe and operations became painless. But they were followed by deaths from infection until the 1860s when Joseph Lister worked out a method of antiseptic surgery. Later, surgeons changed to aseptic operations.

Hospitals about 1800

A wealthy family in the early nineteenth century never used hospitals because they paid for physicians and surgeons to visit at home. But they subscribed to the costs of a hospital so they could have free admission tickets to give out to servants and the poor. These people would only ask for a ticket if they were desperate. Hospitals were terrifying, especially if surgery was involved.

Operations without anaesthetics were unbelievably painful. Most were amputations because it was impossible to do repair work inside the body if the patient could not be kept still. Even so, many died from infection after an arm or leg was cut off.

Operations

The risks were so great that only a few operations were done each week. They were carried out in the hospital lecture theatre so medical students could watch. Attendants brought in a large box of sawdust and the saws and knives. Next came the surgeon in his oldest coat stiff with blood. Then the patient, hoping the surgeon was skilful enough to cut off the limb quickly. A good surgeon took less than a minute to amputate and another to tie up the arteries with pieces of animal gut he had ready clipped to his coat.

Early anaesthetics

Most surgeons believed that the shock of the knife helped to keep the patient alive. That was one reason why no one took up an idea from Humphry Davy. In 1800 he suggested that nitrous oxide might be given to dull pain. Instead, it was used as 'laughing gas', which was sometimes sniffed for a giggle. The giggle went horribly wrong if the sniffer became addicted. Forty years later an American dentist, Horace Wells, used laughing gas to put a patient to sleep. Another dentist, Thomas Morton, used a different gas, ether, for painless toothpulling. In October 1846 an American surgeon was the first to operate on a patient with the help of ether.

James Simpson (1811–1870)

A letter describing his success reached England in December 1846. Four days later Robert Liston gave ether before amputating a leg – in twenty-eight seconds! Weeks later surgeons were using ether in many European towns. One was Edinburgh, where James Simpson used it in a difficult childbirth. It was successful but he did not like the sore throat it gave the patient. Simpson and a couple of assistants began to experiment on themselves with different gases to find a better anaesthetic. After many failures they discovered chloroform in November 1847. For fifty years it was the most used anaesthetic.

Joseph Lister (1827–1912)

With chloroform the number of operations shot up. Yet more operations meant more deaths from septic infection. No one knew why, although doctors noted that this did not usually happen after operations at home. Septic infection was a hospital disease.

It was studied by Joseph Lister, a surgeon in Glasgow. By 1865 he knew that pus in the patient's veins was formed from dead blood cells. What killed them? He believed it was a poison in the air and began looking for a way to overcome it. His research led him to read about the work of a French chemist, Louis Pasteur.

Louis Pasteur (1822–1895)

Pasteur had been studying why grape juice sometimes went bad and did not make good wine. He found the cause lay in tiny living creatures which he called 'germs' which could float on to the wine from the air. The cure for the winemaker's problem was killing the germs by slow heating – or pasteurisation. Lister saw that it could be germs in wounds which killed blood cells. But he could not attack them with heat.

Antiseptic surgery

Instead he washed the wounds with carbolic acid. But he had learned from Pasteur that the real problem was the germs which floated on to the wound. That needed Lister's great advance, a quite new idea of antiseptic surgery. He shielded all wounds with a dressing of thick plaster soaked in carbolic acid and covered with tin foil. When Lister changed the dressing an assistant sprayed a mist of carbolic acid over the wound and Lister's hands.

The result was an immediate drop in deaths among Lister's patients. Other surgeons did not do as well because they thought carbolic acid was just another chemical to dab on wounds and did not use it as a shield against new germs. Antiseptic surgery only spread widely after Lister moved to work in a London hospital. Then it made many difficult internal operations possible. For instance, an American surgeon first cut out an appendix in 1887 and the operation soon became an everyday affair.

Germ theory of disease

Even so, some patients still died from infection, but scientists were beginning to understand why. Louis Pasteur had been looking into the cause of rabies and had worked out that germs were the cause here too. That led him to develop the germ theory of disease, one of the most important scientific ideas ever. Part of it was the knowledge that a different germ was responsible for each disease. Pasteur used this fact to show how Jenner's vaccination worked and to make vaccines for other illnesses.

Aseptic surgery

A German doctor, Robert Koch, took up the study of germs, or bacteria as they became called. He showed that they did not all live in the air, as Lister had thought, but also in droplets of water from breathing, on the skin and in wooden knife-handles. So instead of surgery being just antiseptic (against infection) it should be aseptic (without a chance of infecting).

To be aseptic surgeons had to use sterilisation. Operations were moved to operating theatres and students watched through a glass wall. Doctors and nurses wore gowns, rubber gloves and masks. Instruments were made of metal only and sterilised in steam. By 1900 many hospitals had sterile operating threatres. For the first time it was safer to have an operation in hospital than at home.

Advances in medical surgery

A

1812   The journals of John Crosse who watched surgeons at work as a medical student.

"The scalpels for the outward incision would not cut and were obliged to be changed a first and a second time. The forceps were pushed about in all directions, inserted and withdrawn and after the three surgeons had been probing with their fingers for forty-six minutes the patient was left in despair, the wound covered with lint and the patient put to bed."
John Crosse's Journal, 1812

B

1846   Letter from Robert Liston to James Miller, a friend of James Simpson.

"Rejoice. . . . An American dentist has used ether to destroy sensation in his operations. Yesterday I amputated a thigh and removed both sides of the great toe nail without the patients being aware of what I was doing."
R. Liston, 22 December 1846, in F.F. Cartwright, *The English Pioneers of Anaesthesia*, 1852

C

1847   An account by James Miller.

"It occurred to Dr Simpson to try a material which he had set aside . . . a small bottle of chloroform. It was searched for and recovered from beneath a heap of waste paper. . . .

Immediately hilarity seized the party – they became bright-eyed, very happy . . . a moment more then all was quiet – and then crash. On awakening, Dr Simpson's first perception was . . . 'This is far stronger and better than ether'."
In E. Simpson, *Sir J.Y. Simpson*, 1896

D

1867   A report by Joseph Lister in the Lancet, *on the first use of antiseptic methods.*

"James Greenlee, aged 11 years, was admitted with a compound fracture of the left leg caused by the wheel of an empty cart passing over the limb a little below its middle. My house surgeon, acting on my instructions, laid a piece of lint, dipped in carbolic acid, upon the wound and applied splints padded with cotton wool. It was left undisturbed for four days when I removed the inner splint and examined the wound. It showed no sign of suppuration."
Lancet, 20 March 1867

E

1868   The doctor at the Dowlais Iron Works wrote to the Lancet.

"The use of carbolic acid in the treatment of wounds and compound fractures has created quite a revolution in the surgical practice at the Dowlais Iron Works: for during the last twelve months I have used it extensively in the treatment of the varied injuries that are of constant occurrence, and I think I may say in every instance with marked success. Formerly, in severe cases of compound fracture, amputation was the rule; latterly it has been the exception."
Lancet, 29 August 1868

F

1870s   Part of a lecture by Louis Pasteur.

"This water, this sponge, this lint with which you wash or cover a wound, deposit germs which have the power of multiplying rapidly. . . . If I had the honour of being a surgeon not only would I use none but perfectly clean instruments, but having cleansed my hands with the greatest care, and subjected them to a rapid flaming . . . I would use only lint, bandages and sponges previously exposed to a temperature of 130° to 150°C."
In R. Dubois, *Pasteur and Modern Science*, 1961

Sources A–F
Imagine you are to give a talk on surgical methods with each of these sources as an overhead projector transparency. Write notes reminding yourself to explain the importance and interest of each one.

63
Nightingale ladies

Until the 1850s a 'nurse' was an unskilled domestic worker in a voluntary hospital or a pauper woman in a Poor Law infirmary. Between 1854 and 1856 Florence Nightingale took charge of a hospital for soldiers wounded in the Crimean War. She spent the rest of her life making nursing into a skilled job.

Hospitals and infirmaries

In the early nineteenth century a hospital was paid for with subscriptions from wealthy people, which is why they were known as 'voluntary' hospitals. The jobs of giving medicines or bandaging were done by the male assistants to the physicians and surgeons. The female 'nurses' appeared in the census forms under 'domestic occupations'. Yet few would have been suitable as a servant in a private home. Hospitals hired them to wash the floors, but not often the sheets or the patients. They gave out food but knew nothing about invalid diets. Many were sacked for drunkenness.

The only public hospitals were the workhouse infirmaries. Pauper women were taken from the female section of the workhouse and set to do the same jobs as the 'nurses' in voluntary hospitals.

Florence Nightingale (1820–1910)

It is not surprising that Florence Nightingale's wealthy parents refused to let her train as a nurse. That did not stop her reading all she could about hospitals and making friends of doctors and public-health experts. In 1853 Sidney Herbert, a politician friend of the family, found her a respectable post as lady superintendent of a nursing-home for retired governesses. Florence Nightingale began her first job at 33.

The Crimean War

In 1854 *The Times* shocked readers with reports about sick soldiers in the Crimean War. They were taken to hospital at Scutari in Turkey and left to die from wounds or typhus. This had always been a soldier's fate, but it was the first time the public had been told the facts. Sidney Herbert was now minister in charge of war supplies and he asked Florence Nightingale to take a team of nurses to Scutari. She could find only thirty-nine suitable women!

At Scutari doctors refused to allow nurses on the wards, even though soldiers were lying on bare boards, being fed chunks of partly cooked meat. Florence Nightingale had money given by *Times* readers and used it to buy sheets, mattresses and night-shirts. She paid for an invalid food kitchen and repairs to the building. Eventually she won some doctors round.

'The Lady with the Lamp'

In a few months the hospital had four miles of beds and Florence Nightingale's nurses were caring for patients, their diet, dressings, savings and letters home. She would not let them on the wards at night but made a round herself carrying a lamp. A *Times* reporter wrote about the 'lady with the lamp' and the story was told over and over again in pictures, poems and pottery statues. A special Nightingale Fund was started and collected £49,000.

In 1856 Florence Nightingale came home worn out. For the next fifty-four years she was never strong enough to work in a hospital but she changed nursing totally. She did it through friends among doctors and politicians, and by dozens of reports and thousands of letters. The first four years she spent on advising on the best way to improve the army medical services. Only in 1860 was there time to think about spending the Nightingale Fund.

St Thomas's

She used it to start a training school at St Thomas's hospital. Here young *women* came for a year's training in caring for the sick. Young *ladies* could pay £30 for two years' training to be sisters and matrons. Florence Nightingale used her network of friends to find them jobs in other hospitals where they could run nursing along her lines. Under a Nightingale nurse, a hospital had separate nurses' homes to encourage parents to allow their daughters to take up nursing. They had to spend time in a training school.

William Rathbone

The Nightingale system spread from the voluntary hospitals to Poor Law infirmaries. In 1865 a Liverpool businessman, William Rathbone, offered to pay for twenty-four nurses to work in the city's Poor Law infirmary. As its matron, Florence Nightingale chose Agnes Jones. She died from typhus after two years but she already had got rid of drunken pauper women and opened a training school for the nurses who replaced them.

New hospitals

Nurses left the Liverpool school to take charge of other infirmaries. They were the start of a great expansion in the number of hospitals and careers for nurses. In 1867 Parliament ordered that the infirmaries in London should be run separately from the rest of the Poor Law Unions' work. Other towns followed suit. Many built new infirmaries, which were grim, barrack-like buildings but far better than the old infirmary wards. They began to admit the general public and not just paupers as patients.

There were other new types of hospital. Most towns built fever hospitals out in the country where infectious diseases could be treated in isolation. As medical skill improved, there were new specialist hospitals for eyes, ear and throat complaints and so on. In country districts groups of family doctors often shared the use of small cottage hospitals. By the early twentieth century hospitals were on their way to being the normal places to go for serious illness whether you were rich or poor. But they were better at dealing with serious illness than with the problems that came from being old, or ill from unhealthy conditions. It was William Rathbone who saw the need to give these people nursing at home.

District nurses

Rathbone divided Liverpool into eighteen districts. Each had a 'district nurse' and a charity committee to raise the money for her pay and the bandages and medicine she used. The idea spread to other towns. In 1887 Queen Victoria gave it a great boost when she handed over the money collected for her golden jubilee to spend on training district nurses.

Nursing and hospitals
A
Florence Nightingale's description of 'nurses', from a letter of 1854.

"The nurses did not as a rule wash patients, they could never wash their feet and it was with great difficulty and only in great haste that they could have a drop of water just to dab their hands and face. The beds on which the patients lay were dirty. It was common practice to put a new patient into the same sheets used by the last."
Florence Nightingale in C. Woodham-Smith, *Florence Nightingale*, 1950

B
Francis Cobbe visited workhouse infirmaries in 1859.

"The sick lay on wretched beds, fit only for able-bodied tramps, and were nursed mainly by old pauper women of the lowest possible class.... I visited an enormous workhouse in a provincial town where there were nearly 500 sick and infirm patients. The Matron told me she had been lately appointed to the post ... 'I never nursed anybody I can assure you except my 'usband before I came here. It was misfortune brought me to this.'"
Francis Cobbe, 1889, in S. Bingham, *Ministering Angels*, 1979

The birth of a legend
C
The man who organised The Times *fund in Scutari wrote this account of Florence Nightingale's work.*

"... as her slender form glides quietly along each corridor, every poor fellow's face softens with gratitude at the sight of her. When all the medical officers have retired for the night and silence and darkness have settled down upon those miles of prostrate sick, she may be observed alone, with a little lamp in her hand, making her solitary rounds."
In E. Cook, *The Life of Florence Nightingale*, 1913

Training under the Nightingale system
D
A lecture on bandaging at a training school for nurses, late nineteenth century.

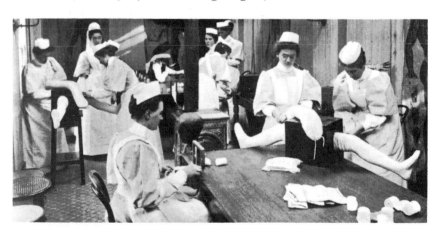

E
Part of a report by Nurse Robinson, the first Liverpool district nurse, who began work in 1860.

"The people whom I have had to do with are most of them so ignorant that they do not know how to take care of themselves, or even prepare the common necessaries of life. I find by suitable advice that there is very great improvement in many houses as to cleanliness, particularly in the bedding, and more air, and in cooking in a common way....

Example No. 1 – Man with wife and six children. Symptoms of consumption; was too weak to work; and the whole family really were starving. I lent them a few shillings (since repaid), procured the woman a little needlework, supplied warm clothing, flannels and nourishment. The man is now apparently quite well ..."
Report of the Liverpool Training School and Home for Nurses, 1860

Sources A-E
1 *After studying these sources, what do you think was Florence Nightingale's most important contribution to nursing?*

64
Doctors

In the early nineteenth century only the rich could afford to pay the fees of physicians and surgeons. Other people went to apothecaries for medicines and medical advice. Gradually apothecaries became known as 'doctors'. From 1858 everyone who worked as a doctor had to be trained in a medical school.

Physicians

In the early 1800s, medical men (and there were no medical women) were divided into three groups. At the top of the tree were the physicians. There were few because the Royal College of Physicians laid down that you had to have been at university before you could train in 'physic' (the art of healing). That kept out people who were not from the upper classes. Physicians' social background meant they could earn good fees from visiting wealthy patients at home and they took all the senior jobs in voluntary hospitals.

Surgeons

Physicians looked down on surgeons, who did not come from the top drawer and often had little general medical knowledge. Most had learned by watching leading surgeons at work and by studying anatomy in a hospital mortuary. (Before 1832 even famous surgeons could only get corpses for study by using hanged criminals or bodies sold by grave robbers.) Some surgeons were too poor to pay for such training and had begun by serving in a regiment where they learned to cut off legs and arms mangled by cannon-balls.

Apothecaries

The humble tradesman of medicine was the apothecary. His specialism was making up medicines. Until the early 1800s he simply sold these over a shop counter. An apothecary was trained rather like a grocer, by serving a five-year apprenticeship.

This three-part division of the medical profession did not trouble the wealthy. If a member of the family was ill they paid for a physician to visit. If he ordered drugs, a servant was sent round to the apothecary. If an operation was needed, a surgeon was called to the house. The ordinary family could not afford fees. They went to the apothecary for advice about treatment as well as to buy medicine. That was one reason for a law in 1815 which said that all apothecaries must pass a medicine examination set by the Society of Apothecaries. Many surgeons took the examination as well so that they could give out medicines as well as do operations.

Doctors

After that, apothecaries and surgeon-apothecaries gradually began to call themselves 'doctors' and to give general medical help from their surgery or by visiting homes. It was often difficult to earn a full living in this way from patients' fees and selling drugs. Many took other work in a public charity dispensary or as medical officer to the Poor Law Union. The doctor needed to be an expert in infectious diseases, minor surgery, midwifery, and drugs. Poor Law doctors were also the public vaccinators.

In fact doctors were beginning to carry out what we now call 'general practice'. But in law they were still apothecaries and surgeon-apothecaries, only a cut above other tradesmen who also served apprenticeships. They pressed for a change in the law and so did others who could see the need for trained doctors. These were the Poor Law Unions, towns which began to appoint medical officers, factory owners who wanted a doctor on their staff and sick clubs whose members paid a few pence per week for treatment.

General Medical Act, 1858

In 1858 Parliament passed the General Medical Act which made general practice the rule. The only people who could treat illness were doctors who had been to medical school and had passed examinations to qualify. Their names went on to the General Medical Register. There was to be a General Medical Council which could strike off the name of anyone they judged was not fit.

After that the medical profession began to divide between consultants and general practitioners. Consultants were the senior doctors who ran the hospitals and controlled all the training of new doctors. As medical knowledge improved, consultants also began to be 'specialists' in a particular part of the body or disease. Some of them opened their own hospitals for specialist complaints.

Pharmacy Act, 1868

Pay was a constant problem for general practitioners. They might have a few patients who could afford to pay a few shillings' fee but not many working people could manage that. Almost all charged lower fees for working-class patients, especially if they came to their surgery. Some still sold medicines but gradually doctors gave this up to make the point that they were skilled professional people, not tradesmen. The Pharmacy Act in 1868 said that drugs could be sold only by trained pharmacists. It slowly became usual for the doctor to write the prescription and the pharmacist or 'chemist' to make up the medicine.

Sickness clubs

A doctor might earn a part-time salary as medical officer of health for a small town or a Poor Law Union. Many mine-owners and factory-owners paid a yearly fee to have their workers treated. Most usual was to try to get work for a friendly society. Many of these, such as the Oddfellows and Ancient Order of Foresters, went back a hundred years or more, but the friendly society movement grew rapidly in the late nineteenth century. Some built their own meeting places but most met in an inn. The societies' job was to collect subscriptions from members (usually skilled working men) and pay out benefits for death, unemployment or sickness. Each year they chose a doctor to see sick members for a yearly fee.

Many doctors quarrelled with factory-owners, who wanted them to declare sick people fit, and with friendly-society patients who wanted more medicine or a sick note for a longer time. To escape these pressures many doctors ran their own sick clubs, using a collector to round up the weekly payments of a few pence.

Women doctors

Women doctors were rare. In 1860 there was only one in Britain and she was an American – Dr Elizabeth Blackwell – , who had qualified abroad anyway. No British medical school would agree to train women, until they were challenged by Elizabeth Garrett.

She faced a long struggle against prejudice. At first she was allowed into lectures but her teachers said it was 'indelicate' for her to go near patients. Once she was driven out of lectures by a male student demonstration. But Elizabeth Garrett refused to give up and in 1866 became the first British woman doctor.

For twelve years there was no other. Then Elizabeth, who was now Mrs Anderson, started her own small hospital for women. Her supporters made a fuss to force London University to change its rules and set up a separate training school for women medical students. Elizabeth Garrett Anderson became its head in 1882. When she retired in 1902 it had nearly two hundred students.

The development of the pharmacy
A
An illustration of about 1800.

1 *What does this picture tell you about the position of apothecaries at this time?*
2 *Suggest why the picture shows a seat.*

B *(below right)*
Jesse Boot, the founder of Boot's the chemist, describes how he started his business in 1877.
3 *Who would be the 'customers' who bought the larger quantities?*

Sources A–B
4 *Use Sources A and B to explain what had happened to (a) apothecaries and (b) pharmacy between the early and late nineteenth century.*

Elizabeth Garrett Anderson
C
A letter from a surgeon to Elizabeth Garrett in 1863.
5 *Pick out two phrases which suggest why the surgeon thought that women should not study anatomy. What do they tell you about his attitude to women?*
6 *What jobs involving 'foul scenes' would other women be doing in the hospital?*

"My idea was simply to buy tons where others bought hundredweights or pounds, thus buying much more cheaply, and making all the articles I sold look as attractive as possible. I made, too, as I could afford to make, a substantial reduction to customers who bought a quantity. Thus I sold bicarbonate of potash at a penny an ounce, but I only charged sevenpence for a pound, and sixpence a pound (less than a halfpenny an ounce) for larger quantities."
J. Boot, in *Great Thoughts*, December 1930

"I must decline to give you instructions in anatomy ... I have so strong a conviction that the entrance of ladies into dissecting-rooms and anatomical theatres is undesirable in every respect, and highly unbecoming that I could not do anything to promote your end. . . . fortunately it is not necessary that fair ladies should be brought into contact with such foul scenes. . . . Ladies would make bad doctors at the best, and they do so many things excellently that I for one should be sorry to see them trying to do this one."
In L. Garrett Anderson, *Elizabeth Garrett Anderson*, 1934

65
Food and taxes in the 1830s and 1840s

In this unit you can read about diet in the 1830s and 1840s and how taxes kept foreign foods out of Britain. Food taxes were at the heart of the debate about whether Britain should protect her trade and industry or change to free trade.

Diet

By the 1830s and 1840s agricultural improvements made it possible to feed many more people than in the 1720s. But the only real change in most daily food was eating potatoes as well as bread. The poorest sometimes had a few slices of bacon. A semi-skilled worker's family might eat a meat soup or stew on Sundays. Families with several wage-earners would eat more meat but most of their extra money was spent on vegetables, butter, cheese and milk.

Food taxes

Apart from luxuries for the rich, the only foods from overseas were tea and sugar. Each person used only tiny amounts. Poor families used tea leaves many times over or bought 'reconditioned' ones. The main reason was the tax on imports. Up to the 1830s the customs duty on tea was 100 per cent of the price; then it actually went up to about 300 per cent. For sugar there were two levels. If it came from a British colony such as Jamaica it was 25s 3d a quarter; from a foreign country it was 35s 9d a quarter.

The Corn Laws

These duties caused great anger but the biggest outcry was against the tax on foreign wheat. This was first put on in 1815, when the war against Napoleon ended. During the war farmers had sold home-produced wheat for very high prices. Afterwards they feared that foreign countries would send a flood of wheat and the price would fall. The largest group of men in Parliament were landowners. They passed the Corn Laws which said that no foreign grain could enter Britain until home-produced wheat had reached the high level of 80s a quarter. In the 1820s the figure of 80s was replaced by a sliding scale which went down as the price of British wheat went up. Yet the scale still kept out most foreign wheat.

For thirty years the Corn Laws were at the heart of a great political debate. On one side were the supporters of 'protection'. On the other were those who wanted 'free trade'.

Protection

Parliament had protected British agriculture, industry and shipping against foreign competition for centuries. It was done by placing a high duty on goods from overseas or passing laws to say they were not allowed in at all. Shipowners and seamen were protected by the Navigation Laws. These stated that goods could not be brought into British ports unless they were carried on ships owned by Britons with mostly British crews.

Free trade

Free traders argued that protection led to other countries protecting their industry. So it made it difficult to find overseas buyers for British products. This point of view had first been put forward in 1776 by Adam Smith in his book *The Wealth of Nations*. By the 1830s factory owners were also complaining that customs duties on raw materials put up the cost of goods manufactured in Britain. They also argued that their wage bills were higher than need be because the Corn Laws kept up the price of workers' food.

Governments came under pressure to change to free trade. The first steps were taken by William Huskisson who was President of the Board of Trade from 1823 to 1827. He began by cutting duties on imported raw materials to almost nothing. Then he lowered duties on imported manufactured goods from about 50 per cent of their cost to 30 per cent.

The Anti-Corn Law League

William Huskisson was MP for Liverpool (until he was the first railway accident victim: see Unit 40). His steps to free trade pleased merchants and manufacturers in the northern towns. But they wanted the government to go further and remove the Corn Laws. In 1839 they started the Anti-Corn Law League which had its headquarters in Manchester. It collected large donations from wealthy supporters. The money was used for pamphlets and *The anti-Bread Tax circular* as well as for paying lecturers to go round the country to speak at public meetings in support of free trade. The League's best-known leader was Richard Cobden, a textile merchant. As MP for Stockport he headed a group of Liberals who demanded the repeal, or cancellation, of the Corn Laws.

Sir Robert Peel (1788–1850)

The Tory government cut most other protection, especially when Sir Robert Peel, a cotton manufacturer (see Unit 13), was Prime Minister from 1841. The 1842 budget ended all duties on raw materials and cut the top rate on manufactured goods to 20 per cent. The government lost money from customs duties and Peel said he would make up the difference by collecting income tax of 7d in the £1 on all income over £150 a year. Income tax had never been collected before except to pay for wars. Peel said his tax would be needed for only a few years – but income tax had come to stay.

In the 1845 budget Peel cut more customs duties but did not touch the Corn Laws. Most of the Tory Party were against repealing them because they would lose the votes of farmers and landowners in the corn-growing districts. Of course, that was why the Anti-Corn Law League wanted them repealed: it would be a clear sign that political power had shifted from landowners to the middle classes. Peel tried to work out a scheme for ending the Corn Laws so gradually that Tory MPs would not object. But before he could do so tragedy struck in Ireland – as you can read in Unit 66.

Two weekly budgets

A

This budget was for a semi-skilled male worker, his wife and three children. It was one of a collection of budgets published in a book in 1841.

	s	d
5 4-lb loaves at 8½d	3	6½
5 lb meat at 5d	2	1
7 pints of porter at 2d	1	2
½ cwt coal		9½
40 lbs potatoes	1	4
3 oz tea, 1 lb sugar	1	6
1 lb butter		9
½ lb soap, ½ lb candles		6½
Rent	2	6
Schooling		4
Sundries		5½
	15s	0d

S.R. Bosanquet, *The Rights of the Poor and Christian Almsgiving Vindicated*, 1841

Sources A–B

1 *What foods are mentioned in the middle-class but not in the working-class budget?*
2 *In what ways would the diet of this household be healthier than the diet of the semi-skilled worker's family?*
3 *What other clues do the two budgets give about different styles of living?*

Dairy produce

C

A painting of a milk shop in London in 1825.

4 *What two ways of selling milk are suggested?*
5 *Why were cows kept in towns at this time.*
6 *What health problems would arise from this sort of dairy?*
7 *What other foods are displayed in the window?*

B

This budget was a model one for 'a Gentleman, his lady, three children and a Maid-Servant' in 1824.

	£	s	d
Bread and flour 1s each		6	0
Butter, 3½ lb at average 1s a lb		3	6
Cheese, ¼ lb each, 1½ lb at 10d		1	3
Milk, 3d each		1	6
Tea, 5 oz at 8s a lb		2	6
Sugar, 4½ lb at 8d a lb		3	0
Grocery, including spices, condiments, etc. 6d each		3	0
Butcher's meat, 18 lb at 7d a lb		10	6
Fish, 6d per day		3	6
Vegetables and fruits, 6d each		3	0
Beer and other liquors 2s a day		7	0
Coals and wood		3	9
Candles, oil, etc. 2 lb a week		1	2
Soap, Starch, etc. 2 lb a week		1	2
Sundries, for cleaning, scouring, etc.			9
	£2	11s	7d

Mrs Rundell, *A system of Practical Domestic Economy*, 1824

George Scharf the Elder, *Golden Lane*, 1825

66
Repeal of the Corn Laws

The Irish potato crop failed and the famine began in 1845. Sir Robert Peel bought American corn to help the starving Irish and then decided to repeal the Corn Laws. He was turned out of power but later governments finished off the work of making Britain a free-trade country.

Ireland

The 1841 census for the United Kingdom showed that just over eight million people lived in Ireland. Roughly three million ate hardly any food apart from potatoes. They were poor tenant farmers, with a half to three acres, and labourers who had no land of their own. In the cold spring of 1845 a virus was working, unseen, throughout Ireland's soil. When the first potatoes were dug in August one in three was rotten. Soon hundreds of thousands of men, women and children were suffering stomach cramp, day and night, from lack of food. They were taking the first steps to death from starvation.

Famine, 1845

The whole of Ireland was then part of the United Kingdom, so dealing with the famine was the British government's responsibility. Sir Robert Peel ordered £100,000 worth of Indian corn (or maize) to be shipped to Ireland from America. It was sold cheaply or given away. The Irish hated the yellow-coloured porridge it made and called it 'Peel's brimstone' but it saved many lives. It also made a nonsense of the Corn Laws. What sense was there in spending taxpayers' money on cheap corn for Ireland when everyone else had their bread prices fixed by the Corn Laws?

Repeal of the Corn Laws, 1846

Peel said he would repeal the Corn Laws even though many Tory MPs would vote against it. It was a brave decision which cost him his job. In June 1846 part of the Tory Party joined with the Liberals to vote for repeal of the Corn Laws. Only hours later the other part of the Tory Party voted with the Liberals against Peel on another matter. He was forced to resign as Prime Minister.

More steps to free trade

In the next fourteen years other governments put an end to all the remaining protection. Just after Peel's fall, the new Prime Minister cut the duty on foreign sugar to the same level as West Indian sugar. The effects on British diet can be seen in the chart in Source B. For West Indian plantation labourers it meant low wages and unemployment. In 1849 the Navigation Laws were repealed. British shipping no longer needed protection. It was already taking the lion's share of the world's business in carrying goods from one country to another.

W.E. Gladstone (1809–1898)

The final stages of free trade were brought about by W.E. Gladstone, when he was Chancellor of the Exchequer from 1852 to 1855 and from 1859 to 1866. In his budgets he removed customs duties from foods and raw materials. Newspaper prices fell after Gladstone allowed in paper and timber free of duty. He sent Richard

Cobden to France to arrange a treaty with the French who agreed to let in British goods at a low rate now that their manufactures came to Britain with no customs duties.

From the time of Gladstone until 1931 Britain was a free-trading nation. The only customs duties left were not for protection but to bring in cash to the government. The most important ones were on alcohol and tobacco.

The results

The first to benefit from free trade were Britain's factory-owners and workers. Raw materials fell in price so they could make cheaper goods to be carried around the world in British ships. Despite all the fuss, the repeal of the Corn Laws made hardly any difference to farmers for thirty years. More foreign corn did come to Britain but the population was still growing and there was a good market for home-grown wheat.

Famine in Ireland, 1846–50

Despite the repeal of the Corn Laws, Ireland's tragedy continued. In the summer of 1846 the potato crop failed altogether. The only way people could tell where potatoes had been planted was by the stench from the fields. The new government did little to help except by opening extra workhouses where thousands died of fever caused by overcrowding. In 1847 it opened soup kitchens to dole out free slops to the starving. Three-quarters of a million Irish were kept alive in this way for three years. Yet it is estimated that four million people died from the famine or diseases it caused.

Emigration

Some landlords did their best to help the poor tenant farmers. Others evicted those who could not pay their rent. For many of these victims of famine the only hope was one of the dreadfully overcrowded ships which took emigrants to Canada and the USA. Between 1849 and 1855 200,000 Irish a year crossed the Atlantic and smaller numbers went on emigrating for the rest of the century.

Free trade

A

In 1841 Richard Cobden spoke in Parliament in a debate on the Corn Laws.

1 *In your own words explain how Cobden could claim that the Corn Laws worked as a tax on bread and earnings.*
2 *In what way did he think the tax was unfair?*
3 *Suggest why he used the example of a nobleman rather than a rich businessman to show that the tax was unfair.*

"The bread tax is primarily levied upon the poorer classes; it is a tax, at the lowest estimate, of 40 per cent above the price we should pay if there were a free trade in corn. The report upon the handloom weavers puts down 10/- as the estimated weekly earnings of a family, and states that in all parts of the United Kingdom that will be found to be not an unfair estimate of the earnings of every labourer's family. It moreover states that out of this 10/- each family spends 5/- on bread. The tax of 40 per cent is, therefore, a tax of 2/- upon every labouring man's family earning 10/- a week, or 20 per cent upon their earnings.

How does it operate as we proceed upwards in society? The nobleman with an income of £500,000 a year, and whose family consumes no more bread than that of the agricultural labourer, pays less than one halfpenny in every £100 . . ."
Parliamentary Debates, 1841

The results of free trade
B

Amounts of tea and sugar consumed on average per person in the United Kingdom.

Year	Sugar (lb)	Tea (lb)
1800–9	19.12	1.42
1810–19	18.06	1.29
1820–9	17.83	1.27
1830–9	17.59	1.37
1840–9	19.45	1.54
1850–9	30.30	2.24
1860–9	38.64	3.13
1870–9	53.90	4.27
1880–9	68.09	4.86
1890–9	78.69	5.58
1900–9	77.99	6.15
1910–19	72.92	6.93
1920–9	78.30	8.94
1930–8	97.57	9.52

In P. Matthias, *The First Industrial Nation*, 1969

4 *Suggest two reasons why the amounts rose between 1800 and 1938.*
5 *Why do you think the table ends in 1938, not 1939?*
6 *Why did sugar consumption rise sharply from 1840–9 to 1850–9?*
7 *Suggest a reason why sugar consumption fell from 1910 to 1919?*
8 *Why might it be more helpful to give figures in averages over ten years?*

C

An extract from a book on Britain's trade which compared the last years of protection in 1840 with thirty years later.

9 *Make simple graphs to show the rise in imports for (a) raw materials and (b) food from 1840 to 1870.*
10 *Write out three phrases or sentences where the writer is making a comment about the advantages of free trade or the disadvantages of protection.*
11 *Suggest why it would have been better for the writer to use ten-year averages?*

"In 1840 there were entered for home consumption in the United Kingdom 4,445,000 cwt cotton, 48,421,000 lbs wool, and 1,896,000 lbs flax and hemp. In 1870 the consumption was 9,836,000 cwt cotton, 171,000 lbs wool and 5,300,000 lbs flax, hemp and jute. The world, we are thankful to say, has ample stores of produce to supply us with food, and, thanks to free trade, our people can get it whenever wanted.... Ever since 1840, the increase in the consumption of foreign articles of food has been very large. The consumption of butter has increased from 1.05 lbs to 4.15 lbs per head; of cheese from 0.92 lbs to 3.67 lbs per head; of corn, from 42.47 lbs to 124.30 lbs per head, of tea, from 1.22 lbs to 3.81 lbs per head; of sugar, from 15.20 lbs to 41.93 lbs per head. What folly, what crime was it by law to hinder the people from getting what will sustain life."
L. Levi, *History of British Commerce and the economic progress of the British 1763–1870*, 1872

Famine in Ireland
D

A drawing of the 1840s. The artist noted that he had left out 'the more revolting features'.

12 *Why do you think the artist omitted the 'more revolting' features?*
13 *What sort of things would he have shown if he had included them?*
14 *What can you learn from the picture about Irish peasant life and about the effects of the potato famine?*
15 *What might be the twentieth-century version of a picture such as this?*

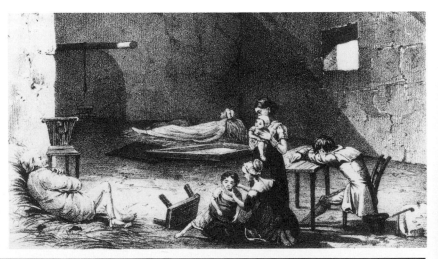

67
A golden age of agriculture

Landowners and farmers had said they would be ruined if the Corn Laws were repealed. But the 1840s turned out to be the first years of a 'golden age' for agriculture which lasted until the 1870s. The best farmers used machinery and scientific methods to produce more food and earn good profits. Agricultural labourers did not share in the good times.

High Farming

In the eighteenth century the best husbandmen had been called 'improvers'. In the nineteenth century the word 'farmer' was used instead of husbandman and improvements were now called 'high farming'. Two things helped the high farmers. One was that most of the land in Britain was enclosed by the end of the 1840s. The other was that new machinery and new science made it easier to carry out changes quickly and on a big scale.

Drainage

A good example was drainage. Up to the 1840s a farmer who had wet soggy land told his labourers to dig ditches and fill them with stones. From the 1840s he could use clay pipes. For a big job he could buy a machine to make the pipes on his own land and even a special earth cutter to dig the trench.

Machinery

For indoor farm work the most important labour-saving machine was the one used to thresh corn in winter. The first models were driven by water or horse power. They were followed by heavy steam-engines which could work a thresher as well as machines which sliced turnips or crushed bones for fertiliser. There were smaller steam-engines which could be used in the fields to drive reapers and mowers. Some farmers tried ploughing by steam. Yet, although they were proud of their steam power, most farmers used horses until the coming of the tractor in the twentieth century.

Science

Scientific knowledge was used to help high farming by chemists such as Humphry Davy. He was one of the first men to show that chemical elements, such as nitrogen or phosporus, were found in all soils. Justus von Liebig, a German chemist, found that different amounts were needed according to the type of plant or animal. A search for new fertilisers and foods followed these discoveries.

The cheapest supplies of nitrogen came in guano, or sea-bird manure, collected on the rocky west coast of South America. In the 1850s 100,000 tons a year were shipped to Britain.

The first processed food for fattening cattle was oilcake. It was made from pressing together the seeds of the flax plant after linseed oil had been squeezed from them.

Rothamsted

In 1843 a young landowner, J.B. Lawes, turned his fields at Rothamsted into an experimental farm. The land was divided up into small plots so that he could try out different seeds with varying kinds of fertilisers. He opened a factory in London to treat crushed bones with sulphuric acid. The result was superphosphates, the first artificial fertiliser made on a large scale.

Prices and profits

Up to the 1870s farmers found it worth while to borrow money from banks to pay for machinery or fertiliser. They knew they would pay it back from the good prices they got. Their profits were helped by the railway which moved large amounts of food quickly.

Country sports

So medium and large farmers led comfortable lives. They improved their farmhouses, bought more furniture and took on extra servants to help their wives run the home and dairy. Landowners shared in the good times because they could charge high rents. These were good years for hunting. Successful farmers and landowners kept horses just for fox-hunting. Gamekeepers cared for pheasants and grouse for slaughter by shooting-parties.

Labourers

For agricultural labourers the times had hardly changed. Ploughmen, shepherds, carters and milkmaids often still found work at hiring fairs. The unmarried ones would take a small wage and a room in the farmhouse or over the stable. Married labourers were given a cottage. The rent was low but the cottage was 'tied' to the job. Injury or old age put them on the path to the workhouse.

Farmers saved on wages by using as much temporary labour as possible. For specialist jobs such as sheep-shearing they hired a travelling gang. For work at harvest or potato-lifting they took on Irish workers who came over for the season, or labourers who spent the winter in town jobs such as coke-shovelling in gas works.

Farm gangs

In eastern England many farmers saved on wages by making a deal with a gang-master. The gang-master employed children and women, who were often working to pay back money he had lent them. The gangs became one of the scandals of the 1860s. Stories were passed round of their heavy work, such as clearing stones from fields, and of children who were underfed and beaten. In 1867 Parliament stepped in with the Gangs Act which said that no child under eight should be in a gang and that if girls were used there must be a gang-mistress for them. These rules dealt a blow to the profits of the worst gang-masters. The rest were driven out of business a few years later when school attendance for children up to ten was made compulsory.

A

This picture shows a thresher with a man feeding the corn into the machine on the right. One man is keeping an eye on the bags of seed at the back of the machine while five others pile up the straw.

1 *What other jobs could a farmer have done with this engine?*
2 *What uses would the farmer have for the straw?*
3 *Which of the men in the picture would be most likely to have a regular job all year round?*

Copeland, *Agriculture Ancient and Modern*, 1866

High Farming

B

Hippolyte Taine, a Frenchman, toured England in 1862. These are parts of the notes he made on one farm.

4 *What is meant by 'byres'; 'arable'; 'oil cake'?*

5 *What evidence is there that the farmer was using 'factory farm' methods?*

C

This writer on agriculture began by describing how animals were driven from Norfolk to London before the railway.

6 *How long did animals take to reach Smithfield (a) before and (b) after the railway?*

7 *Design an advertisement for a railway company to be sent to livestock farmers.*

8 *What evidence is there that Norfolk farmers used the same methods to fatten their beasts as the farmer in Source B?*

D

This diagram appeared in a Scottish handbook on farming first written in the 1840s.

9 *The workers are moving across the field from left to right. What is the job of the right-hand ploughman, the workers next to him and the left-hand ploughman?*

10 *What do you learn about the importance of horses? What animals would have been used a hundred years earlier?*

11 *Which workers would have had regular jobs and which would have been taken on just for the planting?*

H. Stephens, *The Book of the Farm*, 1870 edn

"Bullocks, pigs, sheep, each in a well-aired, well-cleaned stall. We were shown a system of byres in which the floor is a grating; beasts being fattened up there for six weeks without moving.... Steam-engines for all the work of the arable land. A narrow-gauge railway to carry their food to the animals; they eat chopped turnips, crushed beans, and 'oil cakes'. Farming in these terms is a complicated industry ... being perfected, and equipped with cleverly designed tools. .... amused myself by watching the farmer's face: ... the expression was cold and thoughtful. He stood in the middle of a yard in a black hat and black frock-coat, issuing orders in a flat tone of voice and few words, without a single gesture or change of expression. The most remarkable thing is, the place *makes money*."

H. Taine, *Notes on England*, 1862

"cattle and sheep from the Smithfield Monday market had to leave their homes on the previous Wednesday or Thursday week. Such a long drift, particularly in hot weather, caused a great waste of meat. The heavy stall-fed cattle of East Norfolk suffered severely. The average loss on such bullocks was considered to be 4 stones of 14 lb, while the best yearling sheep are proved to have lost 6 lb of mutton and 4 lb of tallow; but beasts from the open yards and old sheep with careful drovers did not waste in like manner. Stock now leaves on the Saturday and are in the salesmen's layers that evening, fresh for the metropolitan market on Monday morning. The cost of the rail is considerably more than the old droving charges, but against that there is the gain of 20s a head on every bullock a Norfolk farmer sends to town."

G.S. Read, *Recent Improvements in Norfolk Farming*, 1858

Potato-planting.

a Ploughman making up single drills in preparation for planting.
b c Single drills on one side of feering.
b c d e Feering for single drills.
d e Single drills on other side of feering.
f Dunghill.
g Cart going with dung.
h Steward hawking out dung for 3 drills.
i Dung-heap in middle drill for 3.
k Worker dividing the dung-heap into the 3 drills.
l m n The 3 drills.
n o p 3 workers, each spreading the dung in 1 drill.
r 3 hindmost planters.
s 3 foremost planters.
t Cart of cut sets of potatoes.
u Ploughman splitting in double drills.

68
The great depression and afterwards

The 'golden age' of farming ended in the 1870s with the beginning of the 'great depression'. This was what some people called the next years of hard times for farmers. It was much worse for grain growers than cattle farmers. By about 1900 new crops had helped farmers to recover and Britain's diet was better than ever before.

American grain

From 1875 there were seven years of cold, wet weather and farmers had smaller crops to send to market. Usually a shortage would put up prices but not this time. The reason was a sharp rise in the amount of foreign wheat that came into the country. Most of it was from the prairies of North America. Here wheat was grown on huge fields, surrounded by barbed wire, a new invention which kept cattle off the crops. The wheat was brought to ports by rail and carried across the Atlantic by steamship. When American wheat merchants found there was a good market in Britain they cut their costs by using more machinery, larger warehouses and bigger ships. The result was that it cost 11/- to bring a quarter of wheat from Chicago to London in the 1870s but only 3/- by 1900.

The 'great depression'

For British corn growers these same years were the 'great depression'. Farmers earned less and began to neglect their ditches, fences and buildings. Some were able to survive by paying lower rents. Others gave up altogether. The amount of land 'under the plough' fell. This brought great hardship to farm workers. Many drifted off to the towns; others emigrated to North America, Australia or New Zealand.

Meat imports

Britain also began to import large amounts of meat. The first canned beef came from Australia and America in the 1860s. In 1880 the SS *Strathleven* arrived from Australia with the first cargo of frozen beef and mutton. But these imports did not have the same effect on farmers. Most of them were sold to working-class people who had never eaten any meat except pork. The better-off still bought home-produced meat.

Dairy farming

Other improvements in working-class diet actually helped many farmers to come through the depression, especially if they could turn to producing milk. Town dairies arranged to collect it each day in churns left by the farm gate. It was usually sold in the street by the canful but the first bottles of pasteurised milk also appeared. Factories were opened to make cheese and butter and bought large amounts of milk from farmers.

Market gardening

Other farmers turned to vegetable growing and market gardening. Many towns opened wholesale markets where food was delivered by cart or railway and sold in the early hours to greengrocers. Fruit was also sent to one of the new factories where jam was made and put into jars for sale. In some parts of East Anglia farmers discovered an altogether new crop to replace grain. They copied the Dutch farmers who grew bulbs for homes and gardens.

Improvement in diet

By 1913 British farmers had come through the depression, mostly by turning from growing grain to fruit, vegetables and dairy farming. Many people were eating a better diet which was a mixture of home-produced and foreign food. Of course that was not true of the poor classes living below the poverty line (see Unit 55).

On the whole food was of better quality. The Co-operative Societies helped by refusing to sell adulterated goods. In 1875 the Sale of Food and Drugs Act gave local councils the power to have samples tested by public analysts (see Unit 60). Shopkeepers who sold impure food were prosecuted. In about twenty years the worst cases, such as mixing chalk with flour, were brought to an end.

The poorest people still bought food in ounces and pinches from corner shops. Many others began to trust the new packages with brand names on them. For cocoa and chocolate there were Cadbury, Fry and Rowntree. Packeted tea was sold by Horniman and Lipton. Thomas Lipton also set up the first large-scale chain of grocery shops in the 1880s, to be followed soon afterwards by Sainsbury.

Tropical food

Important new suppliers of overseas food were the colonies set up by European countries in the hot, tropical areas of the world. Ground-nut oil from Africa and the West Indies was mixed with beef-fat to make 'butterine' or margarine. Fruit merchants learned how to have bananas picked so they were just ripe when they arrived in Britain from Jamaica. Plantations in West Africa and the West Indies supplied cocoa beans. A Dutchman discovered how to take the fat out of these and make it into chocolate or cocoa.

While many of the British people were eating better than ever before, that was not at all true of the people who produced much of their food. Wages in Britain's countryside were still behind those in the towns. But they were far ahead of the earnings of workers on plantations in West Africa and the West Indies. These workers suffered dreadful poverty and ill-health. So did tea-pickers in India and Ceylon, as well as those who worked in the stench and blood of meat-packing factories in Chicago or Buenos Aires.

The 'great depression'

A

1 *What was the main reason for the fall in wheat acreage?*
2 *Suggest reasons why other corns (such as barley) did not fall in the same way.*
3 *What use was made of the extra fallow, grass and pasture?*
4 *What clues does this table give you about improvements in British diet?*
5 *Does it support the view that there was no such thing as a 'great depression' for all farmers but only for some?*

Changes in the acreage used for different farm products (in thousand acres).

	Wheat	Other corns	Fallow, grass and pasture	Market gardens
1867	3,368	5,916	15,062	64
1872	3,599	5,975	17,737	232
1895	1,417	5,983	21,816	352
1913	1,756	5,166	21,933	365

Changes in diet and food selling
B

This table is based on a Board of Trade survey conducted in 1904. It shows the amount and price of food eaten by a family of semi-skilled workers in a week in 1904.

6 *Compare this budget with the one in Source A, Unit 65.*
(a) *What items of food appear here and not in 1841?*
(b) *What evidence is there that meals in 1904 were more enjoyable?*
(c) *Suggest ways in which the 1904 diet would be more healthy.*
(d) *Which foods in the 1904 diet may have been imported?*
(e) *What was spent on tea and sugar in 1841 and in 1904? Give a reason why the spending is so nearly the same for different quantities.*
(f) *Which foods in 1904 were provided by industries which did not exist in 1841?*

		s	d
Average weekly family income		26	11
Average number of children living at home	3.3		

	Quantities	Cost	
		s	d
Bread and flour	29.97 lb.	3	3
Meat (bought by weight)	5.33	3	4
Other meat (inc. fish)		0	8
Bacon	1.11	0	9
Eggs		0	8½
Fresh milk	7.72 pts	0	11
Cheese	0.70 lb	0	5½
Butter	1.5	1	7
Potatoes	15.84	0	9
Vegetables and Fruit		0	7
Currants and raisins	0.5	0	1
Rice, tapioca and oatmeal	2.64	0	5
Tea	0.55	0	11
Coffee and cocoa	0.18	0	3
Sugar	4.62	0	10
Jam, marmalade, treacle syrup		0	5
Pickles and condiments		0	2
Other items		1	3
Total		17	10

Board of Trade, *Second Series of Memoranda, Statistical Tables and Charts*, 1904

C

This photograph appeared on a postcard in the early 1900s. It shows the 'Manor Park Dairy' which stood in a small row of shops in a London suburb.

7 *Which goods are sold by this dairy?*
8 *How was milk sold?*
9 *Where might the shop owner have obtained the butter in the window? What does this tell you about the organisation of food supplies?*
10 *Compare this picture with Source C, Unit 65. How many signs of improvements in health and hygiene can you find?*
11 *Do you know of a shopping parade which might have been built about the time of this photograph? How many changes have taken place there in the past eighty years?*

69
Radicals and reform

In the 1770s MPs were chosen by the wealthiest landowning families. A radical was someone who wanted to change this system radically, at its roots (the opposite of changing it slightly). Remember that Britain was fighting France from 1793 until Napoleon was beaten at Waterloo in 1815.

Major Cartwright

In 1776 British settlers in America said they would no longer be ruled from Britain if they had no say in making the laws. The same year Major John Cartwright wrote a pamphlet saying that Britain would not be a true home of freedom until the system of electing MPs was reformed. There should be an election every year. Everyone (well, at least all males) should have a vote. MPs should be chosen by districts which had the same number of voters.

County elections

Major Cartwright was one of the first radicals and his ideas would have led to quite extraordinary changes for the 1770s. MPs were not at all equally shared out. Each county, no matter whether it was large or small, elected two MPs. Only men who owned land which could be rented for 60/- or more could vote. In small counties a handful of landowners simply met to arrange who would be their MPs and there was no need for an election. In large counties the elections were open to all kinds of pressure. They lasted forty days and each voter had to go on a platform, called the hustings, to put his vote in the box of the man he supported. Candidates' agents bribed voters with money, drink or a meal and then watched how they voted. A mob could be hired to add a little persuasion.

Borough elections

The rest of the MPs came, two each, from places which had been given the title of 'borough' centuries before. By Major Cartwright's time there were twenty-one in Cornwall sending forty-two MPs, while Birmingham and Manchester, with populations of tens of thousands, sent none. In most boroughs only a few had the vote. In some cases they were people who paid an old tax called Scot and Lot. Many would be the tenants of a single landlord and would vote the way he wanted. That was said to put the borough 'in his pocket'. Some pocket boroughs were also 'rotten' because they were in places where a town had crumbled away. The most famous was Old Sarum, once a busy market town but now a deserted hillside where seven voters chose two MPs. In just a few boroughs, such as Westminster, there were many voters.

Radicals

Major Cartwright was a radical leader all his life. He died in 1824. Most of his support came from the country's skilled working men.

Many cobblers, carpenters, tailors or makers of stays (for ladies' corsets) owned their own small businesses. They took the lead in objecting to a system which gave them no share in the government.

Tom Paine (1737–1809)

Radicalism was given a boost when the French revolution broke out in 1789. The revolutionary slogan 'Liberty, Equality, Fraternity' encouraged the radicals and terrified those who had privileges. In 1791 a London staymaker turned customs officer, Tom Paine, wrote *Rights of Man*, saying that the French had every right to change their system of government if it was outdated, and Britons should have the same right. The first edition cost 3s, but a cheap edition was printed in 1792 and sold two hundred thousand copies in two years. It was read by working people such as those who joined the London Corresponding Society. This was started by Thomas Hardy, a shoemaker, and Francis Place, a tailor. It was open to all who wanted to discuss the reform of Parliament.

The French Wars

In 1793 Britain went to war with France. War made life difficult for the radicals because those who sympathised with the French could now be accused of treason. Many were sent to prison and Parliament passed laws to forbid large meetings.

The electoral system before 1832

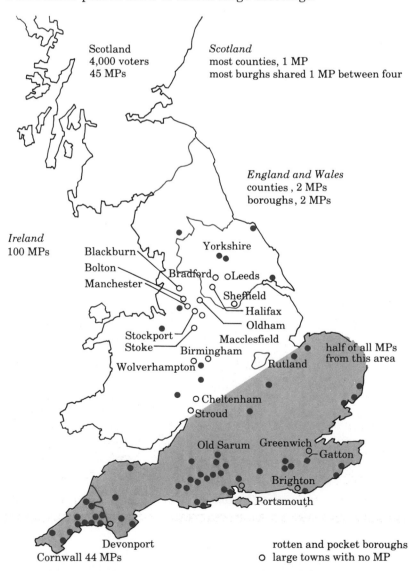

Scotland
4,000 voters
45 MPs

Scotland
most counties, 1 MP
most burghs shared 1 MP between four

England and Wales
counties, 2 MPs
boroughs, 2 MPs

Ireland
100 MPs

Blackburn
Bolton
Manchester
Bradford
Yorkshire
Leeds
Sheffield
Halifax
Oldham
Stockport
Stoke
Macclesfield
Birmingham
Wolverhampton
Rutland
half of all MPs from this area
Cheltenham
Stroud
Old Sarum
Greenwich
Gatton
Brighton
Portsmouth
Devonport
Cornwall 44 MPs

• rotten and pocket boroughs
○ large towns with no MP

The old electoral system: radical views

A

Tom Paine wrote this in 1791.

1 *What are Tom Paine's objections to the systems of county and borough elections?*

"The county of Yorkshire, which contains near a million of souls, sends two county members; and so does the county of Rutland, which contains not a hundredth part of that number. The town of old Sarum, which contains not three houses, sends two members; and the town of Manchester, which contains upwards of sixty thousand souls, is not admitted to send any. Is there any principle in these things?"

Tom Paine, *Rights of Man*, 1791

B

The radical, William Hone, wrote this in a radical paper in 1817.

2 *Describe how Gatton was both a pocket borough and a rotten borough?*

Borough of Gatton

Proprietors	ONE	Sir Mark Wood, Bart., M.P.
Magistrates	ONE	Sir Mark Wood, Bart., M.P.
Churchwardens	ONE	Sir Mark Wood, Bart., M.P.
Overseers of the Poor	ONE	Sir Mark Wood, Bart., M.P.
Vestry men	ONE	Sir Mark Wood, Bart., M.P.
Surveyors of the Highways	ONE	Sir Mark Wood, Bart., M.P.
Collectors of Taxes	ONE	Sir Mark Wood, Bart., M.P.
Candidates at the last Election	TWO	Sir Mark Wood, Bart., M.P. His Son, Mark Wood, Esq., M.P.
Voters at the last Election	ONE	Sir Mark Wood, Bart., M.P.
Representatives returned at the last Election	TWO	Sir Mark Wood, Bart., M.P. His Son, Mark Wood, Esq., M.P.

The Reformists Register and Weekly Commentary, 15 March 1817

C *(below)*

George Cruikshank's view of a hustings.

3 *In the top right a man says 'who would have thought of young Pilfer being so very Liberal!' Can you explain the joke?*

George Cruikshank, *Show of Hands for a Liberal Candidate*, August 1843

70
Radicals and
protest 1815–1822

As the war came to an end in 1815, radicals became more active. The post-war years were times of high prices and unemployment. There were many riots and small rebellions. Severe laws were made against all protest meetings and the government used spies to break them up. In 1819 local part-time soldiers killed and injured many people at a huge radical meeting in Manchester. Afterwards, Parliament passed even harsher laws.

After the war

In the last years of the war the radical movement stepped up its activity. Major Cartwright founded a network of Hampden Clubs for his supporters. William Cobbett, who ran a newspaper, the *Political Register*, cut its price from 1s 0½d to 2d so that his demands for reform could be read by poor people. A Wiltshire farmer, Henry Hunt, spoke to large open-air meetings organised by radicals. His fiery speeches earned him the name 'Orator' Hunt.

Distress

The end of the war brought hard times. Workers who had been making weapons, ships or uniforms lost their jobs or had their wages cut. Parliament passed the Corn Laws in 1815 (see Unit 65). No wheat could be imported until home-produced wheat had reached a high price, 80/- a quarter. High wheat prices meant dear bread. The government was in debt so purchase tax was put on everyday goods. Salt, candles, tea and sugar all became dearer.

Spa Fields

A few radicals believed that the distress would make workers support armed rebellion. They tried to take control of a reform meeting at Spa Fields, near London, where Orator Hunt was to speak. Before he arrived, the plotters led two hundred men to capture the Tower of London. Soldiers easily stopped them but the government used it as an excuse to suspend habeas corpus (Latin for 'have the body produced'). That is the all-important law which says that no one can be held prisoner without being charged. The government was now able to lock up radicals for doing no more than speak or write about changes in the electoral system.

The Pentridge 'rising'

Another government weapon was the people it paid to give information about protest movements. One of these informers, code-named 'Oliver', spread the word among groups of working men that others were about to rebel and needed their help. Jeremiah Brandreth was a victim of this trick. Oliver hinted to him that Nottingham had been captured by the rebels. Brandreth gathered a small band at Pentridge (or Pentrich) in Derbyshire and they marched off to Nottingham. Of course they were met by soldiers. Jeremiah Brandreth and two others were hanged.

The Blanketeers

In 1817 weavers gathered in St Peter's Fields in Manchester, to begin a march to London. They carried a petition for parliamentary reform and the return of habeas corpus. They had no weapons, only blankets to sleep in. Troops broke up their meeting. Some spent five months in prison without ever being accused of a crime.

'Peterloo', 1819

In 1819 Manchester radicals used St Peter's Fields again, for a mass meeting to hear Orator Hunt. They took care to make it orderly. Bands led in men, women and children from different districts. They carried banners calling for 'Liberty and Fraternity' and 'Votes for all'. About 60,000 were listening to Orator Hunt when the magistrates ordered the local yeomanry to arrest him. The yeomanry were volunteer soldiers, mostly businessmen and farmers. The soldiers who arrested Hunt got wedged in the crowd but it was still peaceful. Then other yeomen rode in, slashing with their swords. Panic broke out. In ten minutes eleven people lay dead and 400 were injured, from sword wounds or being trampled.

The Six Acts, 1820

The radicals called it Peterloo, the day when British troops charged at their own people as if they were the enemy at Waterloo. Privately the government blamed the magistrates, but it still used Peterloo as an excuse to attack the whole radical movement. Parliament passed the Six Acts, which forbade public meetings of more than fifty people, put a 6d tax on pamphlets and allowed magistrates to search private homes for political papers.

The Cato Street conspiracy

Just afterwards troops arrested Arthur Thistlewood and six other men in Cato Street, London. The Cato Street conspirators had planned to use grenades to kill cabinet ministers at a dinner party and then take over London. The government made a lot of propaganda out of their success in stopping the plot. What they did not say was that informers had tipped them off a year earlier. The conspirators were hanged and then beheaded.

Peterloo
A, B

The cartoon here and the one on the next page give two artists' different views of Peterloo.

1 *For each cartoon list all the evidence which shows it was either for or against the radicals.*

Death or Liberty!, December 1819

B

Manchester Heroes, September 1819

The Political Register

C

William Cobbett cut the price of his Political Register from 1s 0½d to 2d in November 1816. Here he tells his readers why.

2 *How had workers heard items from the paper before the price cut?*

3 *Why does Cobbett think it good that the new paper could be read at home?*

D

In 1819 one of the Six Acts put a tax on all political papers. Cobbett had to close down and wrote his farewell to readers.

4 *What nickname was given to the cheap Political Register? Do you think Cobbett was proud of it?*

5 *In your own words explain what good Cobbett thought he had done.*

6 *Suggest how a government minister could have defended the newspaper tax.*

"Two or three journeymen or labourers cannot spare a shilling and a halfpenny each week; but they can spare a halfpenny or three-farthings each, which is not much more than the tax which they pay upon a good large quid of tobacco. And besides the expense of the thing itself thus becomes less than the expense of going to a public house to hear it read. . . . The *children* will also have an opportunity of reading. . . . The wife can sometimes read, if her husband cannot. The women will understand the causes of their starvation and raggedness as well as the men . . ."
Political Register, 16 November 1816

"And now, TWOPENNY TRASH, dear little Twopenny Trash, go thy ways. . . . Ten thousand waggon loads of the volumes that fill the libraries and booksellers' shops have never caused a . . . millionth part of the stir that thou hast caused. . . . And thou hast created more pleasure and more hope in the breast of honest men than ever before were created by tongue or pen . . ."
Political Register, 6 January 1820

71
The Reform Act of 1832

In the 1820s men from the middle classes began to play a leading part in the radical campaign for reform. Most of them supported the Whig Party. When the Whigs came to power in 1830 they promised to bring in a law for reform. The House of Lords turned it down and there were riots in several towns. Eventually the Reform Act was passed. It pleased the middle classes but not the working-class radicals.

After Peterloo

Peterloo and the Six Acts made the government very unpopular. Some ministers in the Tory government of 1823–30 began to look for ways of cutting down the number of their enemies. They abolished the laws which said that Roman Catholics or Nonconformists (such as Baptists) could not vote or stand for election. The Home Secretary, Sir Robert Peel, started the London police force. He hoped policemen and not soldiers could be used to deal with riots in future. William Huskisson, minister in charge of trade, altered the Corn Laws so that wheat could be imported when the price began to rise (see Unit 65).

The Tories would not go as far as reform of Parliament itself. Yet this was now being demanded by a new group of radicals from the middle classes. Most of their newspapers called for reform. So did new organisations like the Birmingham Political Union started by a banker, Thomas Attwood. In London Francis Place now owned his own tailor's business. His back room became a meeting-place for leaders of the London Political Union.

The Reform Bill

Attwood and Place had many friends in the Whig Party. In 1830 the Whigs replaced the Tories as the government and in March 1831 Lord John Russell put forward his party's Reform Bill in the House of Commons. He was asking MPs to alter the balance of power away from landowners towards the middle classes in the towns in two ways. First, he proposed that the most rotten boroughs would lose both or one of their MPs. Their seats would be given to towns such as Manchester, Sheffield, Birmingham and Leeds. Second, in all towns the right to vote would go to men living in property which could be rented for £10 a year or more. Source A shows that Lord John Russell knew that this would cut out most workers. The Bill was such a threat to many MPs, however, that they turned it down – by just one vote.

Reform riots

The Whigs called a general election and campaigned on the slogan 'The Bill, the whole Bill and nothing but the Bill'. They won and the new House of Commons passed the Bill. The House of Lords then threw it out. News travelled fast. The same evening there were riots in Derby. The next day crowds in Nottingham attacked the homes of anti-reformers. Nottingham Castle was burned down and the riot went on for two more days. In Bristol crowds attacked the jails, the toll-houses, the Bishop's palace and the town hall. They ended up feasting on looted food in the city's main square.

The 1832 Reform Act

The riots may not have made much difference to what was happening in Parliament. The Lords threw the Bill out once more. But the King promised the Whig Prime Minister that he would make enough new Whig lords to see that the Bill was passed. The threat was enough. The Lords voted for the Bill and it became the Reform Act of 1832.

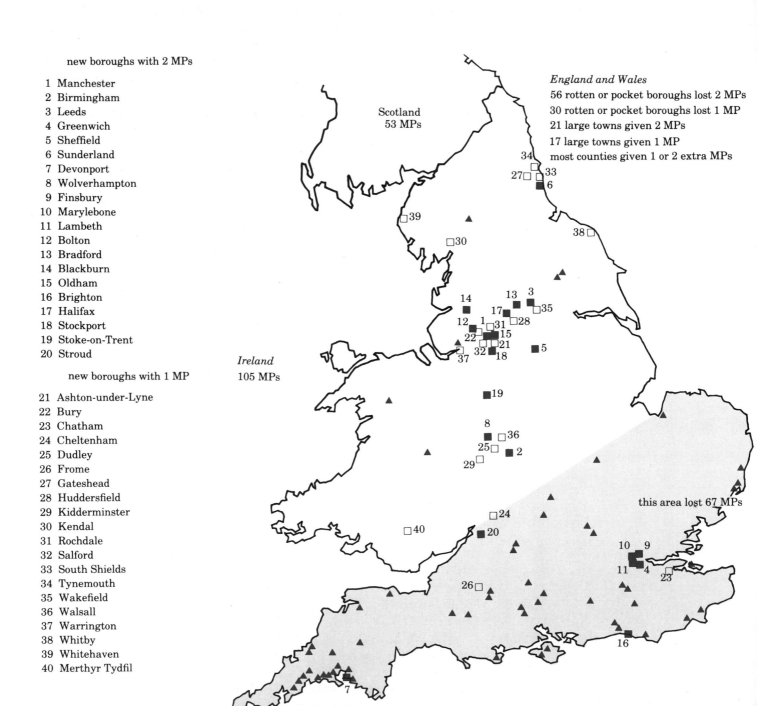

new boroughs with 2 MPs

1 Manchester
2 Birmingham
3 Leeds
4 Greenwich
5 Sheffield
6 Sunderland
7 Devonport
8 Wolverhampton
9 Finsbury
10 Marylebone
11 Lambeth
12 Bolton
13 Bradford
14 Blackburn
15 Oldham
16 Brighton
17 Halifax
18 Stockport
19 Stoke-on-Trent
20 Stroud

new boroughs with 1 MP

21 Ashton-under-Lyne
22 Bury
23 Chatham
24 Cheltenham
25 Dudley
26 Frome
27 Gateshead
28 Huddersfield
29 Kidderminster
30 Kendal
31 Rochdale
32 Salford
33 South Shields
34 Tynemouth
35 Wakefield
36 Walsall
37 Warrington
38 Whitby
39 Whitehaven
40 Merthyr Tydfil

Scotland
53 MPs

England and Wales
56 rotten or pocket boroughs lost 2 MPs
30 rotten or pocket boroughs lost 1 MP
21 large towns given 2 MPs
17 large towns given 1 MP
most counties given 1 or 2 extra MPs

Ireland
105 MPs

this area lost 67 MPs

Cornwall 18 MPs

▲ boroughs which lost MPs

The electoral system after 1832

Results of the Act

The middle classes were pleased with the result. The £10 franchise gave them the vote but kept out the people who worked for them. They were relieved to hear Lord John Russell declare that he would not agree to further changes. Many working-class radicals felt they had been cheated. The Act gave them almost nothing. Their anger grew even sharper when MPs elected under the new arrangements passed their first laws. The Factory Act of 1833 protected children but meant longer hours for adult workers (see Unit 49). The Poor Law Amendment Act of 1834 seemed a direct attack on the unemployed (see Unit 53). In the same year the new government supported persecution of trade unionists (see Unit 75).

Lord John Russell and the £10 franchise

A *Russell asked Edward Baines, editor of the* Leeds Mercury, *to find out what would happen if the vote were given to £10 householders. This is Baines's reply.*

1 *Imagine you are Lord John Russell. Write the letter you think he would have sent to Edward Baines explaining what he wanted him to find out.*

2 *Using Edward Baines's reply, work out a summary of who would get the vote in Leeds after 1832.*

The Bristol riots

B *A drawing of dragoon guards charging the crowd in 1831.*

3 *What were the riots about?*

4 *Were only men involved?*

5 *What aspects of this drawing are likely to be (a) accurate and (b) exaggerated?*

"It appeared that in the parts occupied chiefly by the working classes, not one householder in fifty would have a vote. In the streets principally occupied by shops, almost every householder had a vote. . . . In the township of Holbeck, containing 11,000 inhabitants, chiefly of the working classes, but containing several mills, dye-houses, public houses, and respectable dwellings, there are only 150 voters. . . . Out of 140 householders, heads of families, working in the mill of Messrs Marshall and Co., there are *only two* who will have votes. . . . Out of 160 or 170 householders in the mill of Messrs O. Willans and Sons, Holbeck, there is *not one* vote; Out of about 100 householders in the employment of Messrs Taylor and Wordsworth, machine makers, – the highest class of mechanics, – *only one* had a vote."

Edward Baines, 17 November 1831, in E. Baines, *Life of Edward Baines*, 1859

72
The Chartists

A Chartist supported the People's Charter which had six points for changes in the way MPs should be elected. The Chartist movement had three peak years in 1839, 1842 and 1847 when petitions backing the Charter were sent to Parliament. Each was a year of poor trade and unemployment. Chartists disagreed about whether to use persuasion or the threat of physical force.

Feargus O'Connor (1794–1855)

In 1837 the Poor Law Commission (see Unit 53) began work in the north of England. It was met with a wave of demonstrations. At the centre of many of them was an Irish landowner and ex-MP, Feargus O'Connor. His speeches were full of fire and fury as he blamed the Reform Act for the law on workhouses. He told the crowds that the only way to have fairer laws was to give working-men a vote to elect MPs. Even more people read the same message in his new newspaper, the *Northern Star*, which was printed in Leeds and sold throughout the North and Midlands.

The London Working Men's Association

In London a different sort of working-men's movement was preaching the same message. A cabinet-maker, William Lovett, started the London Working Men's Association (LWMA) in 1836, with the help of Francis Place and six radical MPs. The LWMA's methods were not those of rioting or public demonstrations. They worked through pamphlets and discussion groups. We might call this 'persuasion'; they used the words 'moral force'. Their programme was set out in the People's Charter, written by William Lovett. For its main points turn to Source A.

In 1838 the northern protesters and the London radicals came together to work for the Charter. The Chartist movement was born, and the first scheme was to collect signatures for a petition asking Parliament to make the Charter into law. While that was being done Chartist groups around the country chose men to go to London and sit in their own Chartist 'parliament' or Convention. If MPs did not accept the Charter, the Convention would call all workers out in a month-long general strike or 'sacred month'.

The Convention

Almost as soon as the Convention met in 1839 the question of 'physical force' came up. In some lonely spots men were doing drill with wooden sticks and old guns. Few intended to fight the government but Feargus O'Connor and other 'physical-force' Chartists hoped that the armed bands would panic MPs into accepting the Charter. William Lovett and the 'moral-force' Chartists would have nothing to do with this and walked out of the Convention. The rest of the Convention moved to Birmingham and waited. The government made its preparations and put General Napier in charge of law and order in the north of England with 5,000 soldiers.

The First Petition

On 12 July 1839 MPs turned down the Charter, although forty-six voted for it which shows that not everyone thought it ridiculous. The Convention ordered the sacred month to begin on 12 August.

Then Feargus O'Connor had second thoughts. He did not want to risk clashes with Napier's men. In any case it was foolish to call a strike when thousands of Chartist supporters were already out of work. So the Convention cancelled it. But they were not fully in control of all the Chartists. Around the country there were small bursts of fighting, some started by the police or troops and some by Chartists. The most serious went down in history as the Newport Rising, a grand label for a muddled affair.

The Newport Rising, 1839

Groups of Chartists from several Welsh towns marched into Newport (in Monmouthshire) to free a comrade from jail. Their leader was John Frost, once a Justice of the Peace, who had sided with the Chartists. Some of the marchers wanted a demonstration, the others planned to free the prisoner by force. The army had soldiers waiting in the main hotel. Chartists and soldiers fired at each other. Fifteen Chartists were killed. John Frost and two others were condemned to die for high treason. Later the government changed the sentence to transportation.

The Six Points

A

A chartist hand-bill.

1 *What was the purpose of the hand-bill?*
2 *Make a table in two columns, one explaining what each point meant and another explaining what changes it would mean in the later 1830s.*

The Six Points
OF THE
PEOPLE'S
CHARTER.

1. A VOTE for every man twenty-one years of age, of sound mind, and not undergoing punishment for crime.

2. THE BALLOT.—To protect the elector in the exercise of his vote.

3. No PROPERTY QUALIFICATION for Members of Parliament —thus enabling the constituencies to return the man of their choice, be he rich or poor.

4. PAYMENT OF MEMBERS, thus enabling an honest tradesman, working man, or other person, to serve a constituency, when taken from his business to attend to the interests of the country.

5. EQUAL CONSTITUENCIES, securing the same amount of representation for the same number of electors, instead of allowing small constituencies to swamp the votes of large ones.

6. ANNUAL PARLIAMENTS, thus presenting the most effectual check to bribery and intimidation, since though a constituency might be bought once in seven years (even with the ballot), no purse could buy a constituency (under a system of universal suffrage) in each ensuing twelvemonth; and since members, when elected for a year only, would not be able to defy and betray their constituents as now.

Physical Force

B

William Lovett spoke against physical force at the Convention in 1839.

3 *What two reasons does he give for being against physical force?*
4 *What did Lovett mean by this 'bluster and menace of armed opposition'?*

"The whole physical force agitation is harmful and injurious to the movement. Muskets are not what are wanted, but education and schooling of the working people . . . O'Connor wants to take everything by storm, and to pass the Charter into law within a year. All this hurry and haste, this bluster and menace of armed opposition can only lead to . . . the destruction of Chartism . . ."
W. Lovett, *Life and Struggle of William Lovett*, 1876

C

Benjamin Wilson looked back to the time he became a Chartist in the Halifax district.

5 *What reasons does Benjamin Wilson give for arming himself?*
6 *What was a pike?*
7 *Does the passage give any hard evidence that Wilson or his friend would have used their weapons?*

"A great many people in these districts were arming themselves with guns or pikes, and drilling on the moors. Bill Cockcroft, one of the leaders of the physical force party in Halifax, wished me to join the movement, I consented, and purchased a gun, although I knew it to be a serious thing for a chartist to have a gun or pike in his possession. I had several years practice in shooting, as the farmer for whom I worked supplied me with gun, powder, and shot for the purpose of shooting birds in summer. I saw Cockcroft who gave me instructions how to proceed until wanted, which did not occur as the scheme was abandoned. It might now be said we were fools, but I answer young people now have no idea of what we had to endure. . . . From 1842 to 1848 I should not average 9/- per week wages; outdoor labour was bad to get then and wages were very low."
Benjamin Wilson, *The Struggles of an old Chartist*, 1887

D

General Napier's diaries describe his problem in working out how to deal with the physical-force Chartists.

8 *Why does he call the Chartists 'poor people'?*
9 *What was his estimate of the danger from physical force?*
10 *Why did he advise the magistrates not to interfere with pistol-carrying Chartists?*
11 *In what way does the first entry support the fears of William Lovett?*
12 *What name is given to the sort of books from which Sources B–D are taken?*
13 *What do you think are the advantages and disadvantages of such books as sources of historical evidence?*

"6 August 1839
Poor people! They will suffer. They have set all England against them and their physical force:–fools! We have the physical force, not they. They talk of their hundred thousands of men. Who is to move them when I am dancing round them with cavalry, and pelting them with cannonshot? What would their 100,000 men do with my 100 rockets wriggling their fiery tails among them, roaring, scorching, tearing, smashing all they came near?

12 January 1840
Patrolled all last night. Saw the Chartist sentinels in the streets; we knew they were armed with pistols, but I advised the magistrates not to meddle with them. Seizing these men could do no good; it would not stop chartism if they were all hanged, and they offered no violence; why starve their wretched families and worry them with a long imprisonment?"
Charles Napier, *Life of General Sir Charles Napier*, 1857

73
Chartism: the second and third stages

The story of Chartism continues with the events of 1842 and 1848. The unit goes on to show how many of the Six Points were partly dealt with in the lifetime of many Chartists.

The Second Petition, 1842

In 1840 Feargus O'Connor founded the National Charter Association and the movement began to grow again. By 1842 it had 48,000 members who collected more than three million signatures for a second petition. Fifty men were needed to carry it to the House of Commons in May.

The plug plots, 1842

Parliament turned down the petition. The Chartist protests were swallowed up by the plug plots which started in Midland coalmines and spread into Lancashire cotton factories. In both places owners had cut wages because their sales were falling. The men brought the pits and factories to a standstill by pulling the plugs from engine boilers. Some Chartists believed they could turn the plug plots into a general strike to win the Charter. There were riots and fighting between strikers and troops but the general strike never happened. Poverty forced the men back to work after three months.

The National Land Company, 1845

For five years Feargus O'Connor was busy with a scheme to help Chartists settle on a few acres of land. It was a popular idea, especially with hand-workers who did not want to give up their freedom and work in a factory. About 70,000 Chartists bought shares in O'Connor's National Land Company. The money was used to buy land and the shareholders drew lots to see who would become the first Chartist settlers. About 250 of them got land before the scheme collapsed in a financial muddle.

The Third Petition, 1848

In 1847 Feargus O'Connor was elected MP for Nottingham. The winter that followed was one of the worst ever for unemployment. Anger grew against the new Poor Law and so did support for the Charter. In the spring of 1848 O'Connor claimed that there were six million signatures on a new petition. He called a great London meeting on Kennington Common (near the modern Oval cricket ground). He planned that the crowd would follow him to the House of Commons with the petition.

The government called up 8,000 soldiers, 1,500 Chelsea Pensioners and 150,000 special constables. They had to deal with a crowd which O'Connor said was nearly half a million, *The Times* said was 20,000 and the government said was 15,000. A modern historian has reckoned that the Common could hold 54,000. That suggests that O'Connor was wise to agree when the police told him to call off the march. The petition was sent to Parliament in three cabs. The government had the signatures counted and said there were not quite two million. The names of Queen Victoria, Mr Punch and No Cheese (and others too rude to print in the government report) all appeared several times. The middle-class newspapers make a joke out of it.

Chartism ended in 1848, but not because it was laughed at. A more important reason was an upturn in trade and employment. The railway boom was creating many more jobs on the railways, in ironworks and in engineering. Another reason was that workers joined new movements such as co-operation. (See Unit 76.)

Steps to democracy
A

This table summarises the main changes in Britain's system of democratic government since the Chartists.

1 *Which of the six points has not been brought into force?*
2 *Which of these changes might have surprised many Chartists?*

1867 Second Reform Act. Gave the vote to about one in every three working men; those living in boroughs who occupied a house or paid more than £10 a year for a lodging.
1872 Ballot Act. All voting should be done in secret.
1885 Third Reform Act. Gave the vote to householders and £10 lodgers in counties as well as boroughs.
1885 Redistribution Act. Constituencies sending MPs had to have roughly the same number of voters.
1911 Payment of MPs was decided by the House of Commons.
1911 Representation of the People Act. All men over 21 and women over 30 had the right to vote.
1928 Equal Franchise Act. All women over 21 had the vote.

Women Chartists
B

A report from a Chartist newspaper in 1839.

3 *Give two examples from the 'Objects' which show that this was a Chartist organisation.*
4 *What was the fourth object meant to do?*
5 *Why do you think they used the word 'patriotic' in their title?*

"EAST LONDON FEMALE PATRIOTIC ASSOCIATION
This association held its usual meeting on Monday evening last, at the Trades' Hall, Abbey Street. After the regular business had been disposed of, arrangements were entered into for getting up the tea party. It was also resolved to publish the objects and rules of the association as follows –
1st. To unite with our sisters in the country, and to use our best endeavours to assist our brethren in obtaining Universal Suffrage.
2nd. To aid each other in cases of great necessity or affliction.
3rd. To assist any of our friends who may be imprisoned for political offences.
4th. To deal as much as possible with those shopkeepers who are favourable to the People's Charter."
The Charter, 17 October 1839

Reform after Chartism
C

6 *Suggest which parts of the firm's workforce would be able to vote for the first time in 1868. What law had given them the vote?*
7 *Why was the poster necessary?*
8 *What law made such posters unnecessary?*
9 *Does the poster suggest anything about the attitude of other employers to the political opinions of their workers?*

Election notice, Middleton Ship Yard, 23 June 1868

BOROUGH AND COUNTY
ELECTIONS.
MESSRS. DENTON AND GRAY
Intimate to their Workmen that they are at perfect liberty to Vote for any Candidate they please, and that the side they take in Politics will not in any way affect their employment.
Middleton Ship Yard,
Hartlepool, June 23rd, 1868.

Hartlepool: J. Procter, Printer and Lithographer by Steam Power.   11,745.

12 Labour movements
1820s–1913

74
Trade societies and combinations

This unit tells the story of early trade unions which people of the time called trade 'societies'. When members of a society acted together it was called 'combining'. Parliament passed laws against combinations but they did not stop the societies. In 1811–12 textile workers joined the Luddite movement to destroy machinery which threatened jobs.

Trade societies

In the 1700s, when a craftsman had finished his apprenticeship, he became a journeyman. He would then join his local trade society. He would go to an inn to pay his subscription and to discuss society business. One topic was how to keep down the number of new apprentices so that there was enough work to go round. Most trade societies were also 'friendly societies' and part of the subscription was used to help old or sick members. If a journeyman had no job he could tramp off with a letter from his society. With this 'ticket' he would be helped to find work by a society in another town.

When trade was bad, masters and society men would often send a joint petition to Parliament, asking for help such as a ban on foreign goods. At other times society men would combine against the masters for higher wages or to stop new machinery coming into the workshop. One form of action was to hold a 'turn-out' or a strike. Turn-outs were no use if the masters planned to lay off workers anyway. So another weapon was to riot and attack the workshops or homes of masters. Riots were also a way of warning off 'knobsticks' – men who were brought in to do strikers' work.

Combination laws

When masters found men combining against them they often went to Parliament for help. By 1797 MPs had passed laws which forbade combinations in forty trades. They added three more to stop combination altogether. In 1797 they made it a crime for anyone who joined a society to swear an oath to keep its rules and members' names secret. The penalty was seven years' transportation. In 1799 and 1800 two Combination Acts said that any combination of workmen was illegal. The Combination Acts are often thought to have closed down all trade societies. In fact they just added one more difficulty for workers who were used to having laws passed against them, and over the years the number of societies and society members grew.

The shearmen

One example of men who combined before and after the Combination Acts were the shearmen, or croppers. They did two finishing jobs in the woollen trade. First they brushed the cloth to make the threads stand up, then cropped them with a huge pair of shears to leave a smooth nap. Two years after the Combination Laws, masters brought in machines to brush the cloth. The workmen combined to go on strike as if the laws had not been passed.

Luddism

In 1811 some masters in the Nottingham stocking industry set up new large knitting frames which could be worked by unskilled men. In protest the knitters began to wreck the new frames. They acted in secret, leaving messages that 'General Ludd' or 'Ned Ludd' had been at work. Luddism soon spread to Yorkshire where the shearmen were faced with a threat from a shearing frame to crop the cloth. They too formed Luddite bands which raided workshops and factories. In 1812 there was a pitched battled between the Luddites and soldiers defending a mill. Three Luddites ambushed and killed a mill-owner as he rode by. The murderers were caught and hanged. Not long after, Luddism began to die away.

An illegal combination

A

In 1802 a London magistrate was sent to Wiltshire to investigate reports that shearmen were breaking the Combination Laws. He reported to the Home Secretary on what he had learned from a prisoner.

1 *How does the prisoner's information suggest that the Combination Acts were not working?*
2 *Are there any signs that the shearmen were well organised?*
3 *What was the purpose of the 'ticket'?*

B

This is the ticket the prisoner held.

4 *Look for two symbols of justice and the cap of liberty (which was a symbol used by French revolutionaries).*
5 *What can you learn about the shearmen's work from this ticket?*
6 *If you were a magistrate, would you think that the words around the middle shield broke the Combination Laws?*

"The prisoner . . . says he is a member of the Shearman's Club, and that lately he has been called upon to take an oath 'to be true to the shearmen . . . and not to divulge any of their secrets'. That the committee consists of 13 and meets on Wednesdays – that there is a chairman, a clerk and two stewards, that he has a printed ticket which he states to be the same as is used by the shearmen Clubs in Yorkshire, and if he were to go into Yorkshire it would enable him to get work there. He says the ticket is changed once a year, and that the shearmen will not suffer any man to work who has not got a ticket – that there is a Club in every town in Yorkshire."
Home Office Papers, 1802

75
Societies' attempt to unite

The Combination Laws were repealed (cancelled by Parliament) in 1824. Some of the weaker societies for unskilled workers tried to build their strength by uniting in 'unions' of trade societies. The best-known union was the Grand National Consolidated Trades Union. Its weakness was shown up by the case of the Tolpuddle Martyrs.

Repeal of the Combination Laws, 1824

Not long after Peterloo some politicians began to say that the Combination Laws actually caused striking and violence. There would be much less trouble if workmen could bargain openly with their masters. Francis Place, the radical tailor, pushed this idea hard and got an MP friend, Joseph Hume, to persuade Parliament to hold an inquiry into the Combination Laws. The inquiry recommended that Parliament should allow workers to organise openly. In 1824 all the laws against combinations were repealed, except for the 1797 one which made oath-taking illegal.

Early unions

The repeal helped trade societies of skilled men to grow in strength. But when unskilled workers tried to form societies they suffered from lack of funds and counter-attacks by employers, who sacked society men and easily found other 'hands' to replace them. To fight back, unskilled workers' leaders tried to unite these weak societies into 'unions'. In 1829 John Doherty started the General Union of Operative Spinners. A little later there was an Operative Builders' Union. Neither lasted more than a few months.

The GNCTU, 1834

In 1834 a meeting of working men agreed to start a union which would protect workers in any trade who tried to start a society. They called it the Grand National Consolidated Trades Union (GNCTU). Not long after, two GNCTU organisers were sent to the village of Tolpuddle in Dorset.

The Friendly Society of Agricultural Labourers

They went to advise George Loveless and a handful of other village labourers. Wages in Tolpuddle had just been cut from 9/- a week to 6/-. To fight the cuts, Loveless and his friends had started a Friendly Society of Agricultural Labourers. The GNCTU men helped them draw up rules which said the society would not allow its members to use violence or cause damage (so that no one could accuse Loveless and his men of acting like the Swing rioters of 1830). Soon afterwards the members each took an oath to keep the Society's affairs secret. (That would make sense to anyone who remembered agents like 'Oliver' the spy – see Unit 70).

The local magistrates, all farmers or landowners, wrote for advice to the Home Secretary. He replied saying that it was lawful to form a society now the Combination Laws were repealed. But he reminded the magistrates that the 1797 law against taking oaths was still in force so they had a case for arresting the labourers.

The Tolpuddle Martyrs, 1834

Loveless and five others were put on trial. They did not know about the law against oath-taking but that did not stop them from being found guilty. And the penalty was still seven years' transportation to Australia. There was a great outcry against the harsh treatment of these peaceful labourers. Nearly thirty thousand people joined a protest meeting in London. After two years the Tolpuddle Martyrs were pardoned and brought home. After such unfair treatment it is hardly surprising that five went to live in Canada.

Collapse of the GNCTU

By then the GNCTU had collapsed. It had tried to help too many societies at once and ran out of funds. The case of the Tolpuddle Martyrs had finished it off because the trial encouraged other employers to go on the attack. Some refused to give work to any man who would not sign 'the document', which was a promise not to join a society or union. The 1830s ended without any union in existence, although there were still many trade societies.

A

Part of the front page of the GNCTU newspaper, two months before it had to close. It shows a procession carrying a petition to the Home Secretary to protest at the sentence on the Tolpuddle Martyrs.

1 *What picture was the artist trying to give of the behaviour and organisation of the demonstrators?*
2 *Suggest why the group of men on the left of the picture might have been there.*
3 *What object are the men on the right carrying?*
4 *Comment on the day of the week the meeting was held.*

The Pioneer, 26 April 1834

B

In 1838, back in England from Australia, George Loveless wrote this account of the trial.

5 *In view of George Loveless's comments, what sort of people do you think might have been on the jury?*
6 *Explain the title of Loveless's book.*

"The greater part of the evidence against us, on our trial, was put into the mouths of the witnesses by the judge . . . I shall not soon forget his address to the jury in summing up the evidence: among other things, he told them that if such Societies were allowed to exist, it would ruin masters, cause a stagnation in trade, destroy property. . . . I thought to myself, there is no danger but we shall be found guilty, as we have a special jury for the purpose, selected from among those who were most unfriendly to us."
G. Loveless, *The Victims of Whiggery*, 1838

76
Robert Owen and the idea of co-operation

Robert Owen first became well known for his model village at New Lanark. His ideas on education were a long way ahead of the time. Later he tried to spread the idea of 'co-operation' among working people. It was taken up by the Rochdale Pioneers who started the 'Co-op' movement.

Robert Owen (1771–1858)

Robert Owen was born in 1771 in a Welsh village, the son of a saddler and ironmonger. He left school at 9 and by 18 he had worked in three drapers' shops. With borrowed money he set out to be a manufacturer. Ten years later he was a partner in a spinning-firm which bought the New Lanark mills and its workers' village built by David Dale in Scotland (see Unit 13). Robert Owen married David Dale's daughter and moved to New Lanark to run the mills.

New Lanark, 1800–1815

It took Robert Owen fifteen years to turn New Lanark into a model community. What he did was not always popular. Each worker's house was improved but Owen also sent health visitors round to see that the rooms and the streets outside were kept clean. He closed down all the drink shops in the village. Spinners would not have liked the piece of wood by their machines which showed how their daily work had been marked. Yet all these compulsory improvements made New Lanark a healthier and more orderly place in which to live.

Education

Visitors who flocked to New Lanark were impressed most by the way Robert Owen treated children. No boy or girl was allowed to work before they were 10, after five years in school. Owen would not have only the '3Rs' (Reading, Writing and Arithmetic) crammed into young heads. His school was 'an institution for the formation of character' where young children were taught to live and learn together. He laid down that there should be art, singing and dancing. To help children understand their lessons teachers had to use maps or charts, and coloured blocks for arithmetic (compare this with monitorial schools – see Unit 87).

Villages of co-operation

From 1815 Owen spent his life encouraging working-class families to set up their own model communities. He began with 'villages of co-operation' where people would make their own goods and grow their own food. The idea had little success in Britain so Owen sailed to America to start the village of New Harmony with his own money. Settlers flocked there but they began to work for themselves and the idea of co-operation withered away – and so did most of Robert Owen's money.

Labour Exchanges

He returned to London with a scheme for 'Labour Exchanges', where craftsmen took goods they had made and bought others. Prices were in Labour Notes which stated how much an article was worth according to the hours needed to make it. When the GNCTU was in trouble after the Tolpuddle Martyrs' case he became its president, although he could not stop it collapsing. Afterwards he went on teaching the idea of co-operation.

In Rochdale a group of flannel weavers were impressed by Owen's ideas but the town had few craftsmen who could join together as *producers* as they could in London. Yet they could co-operate as *consumers*.

The Rochdale Pioneers, 1844

In 1844 seven of the Rochdale weavers found twenty-eight people to pay £1 each to start the Rochdale Society of Equitable Pioneers. They used the money to redecorate an old warehouse in Toad Lane and buy goods to open a shop. Customers were given a dividend on each article they bought. The Rochdale Pioneers prided themselves on selling goods which were properly made and food which was not adulterated (which was a common practice – see Unit 58).

The Co-operative movement

The idea spread fast through the north of England. In just seven years there were 130 shops owned by co-operative societies. In 1863 there were enough societies to start their own suppliers, the Co-operative Wholesale Society (CWS).

In 1872 the CWS began to make its own biscuits, boots and soap, and then a wide range of own-brand goods. It was selling standardised and reliable goods long before privately-owned chains like Lipton's. The Co-op improved standards of living for millions of people who went there for their shopping, insurance and the first dignified funerals which working-class people could afford.

The Rochdale Pioneers and the other co-operatives looked on themselves as leaders of a movement to help people to educate themselves and run their own affairs. Most co-ops had reading rooms and meetings where politics and religion were discussed. Women were encouraged to play a full part. Robert Owen died in 1858 but his beliefs were kept alive in the Co-operative movement.

The Co-operative movement
A

George Holyoake was a Chartist who later was active in the co-operative movement. Here he describes the start of the Rochdale Pioneers' Co-operative Society. (A 'doffer' was a young boy who worked in the mills.)

1 *What can you learn about working-class diet from this extract?*
2 *Why did the store open at night?*
3 *From the last paragraph explain how the dividend system worked.*

"On the night when our store was opened, the 'doffers' came out strong in Toad Lane inspecting the scanty arrangements of butter and oatmeal.

Since that time two generations of 'doffers' have bought their butter and oatmeal at the shop, and many a wholesome meal, and many a warm jacket, have they had from that store, which articles would never have reached their stomachs or their shoulders, had it not been for the co-operative weavers.

Mr. Charles Howarth proposed the plan of dividing profits among the members in proportion to their purchases. At the end of the first quarter the Rochdale Society did pay a dividend of 3d in the pound. In 1844 the number of members was 28, amount of capital £28. . . . In 1857 the number of members was 1,850 the amount of capital £15,142."

George Holyoake, *The History of Co-operation in Rochdale*, 1878

B

The CWS fender-making factory in Dudley, shortly after it opened in 1908.

4 *What was the use of the goods being made here?*

5 *How would you use this photograph to illustrate:*
   (a) the development of the co-operative movement after 1844,
   (b) its contribution to working-class living standards?

New Lanark
C

Robert Owen describes how discipline was maintained at New Lanark.

D

Robert Owen describes some of the changes he made at New Lanark.

Sources C–D

6 *What do these sources tell you about the kind of employer Robert Owen was?*

7 *What do you think the workers would have thought of Owen's silent monitors?*

8 *Remember the second passage refers to the years up to about 1815. What was unusual about his treatment of children?*

9 *What results does he claim for his methods?*

10 *Which parts of this description remind you of the way that the Strutts treated their workers? (See Unit 14.)*

"the most efficient check upon inferior conduct was a silent monitor for each one employed in the establishment. This consisted of a four-sided piece of wood, about two inches long and one broad, each side coloured – one side black, another blue, the third yellow, and the fourth white, tapered at the top, and finished with wire eyes, to hang upon a hook with either side to the front. One of these was suspended in a conspicuous place near to each of the persons employed, and the colour at the front told the conduct of the individual during the preceding day to four degrees of comparison. Bad, denoted by black and No. 4; indifferent by blue and No. 3; good by yellow and No. 2; and excellent by white and No. 1."
Robert Owen, *The Life of Robert Owen*, 1857

"The practice of employing children in the mills, of six, seven and eight years of age, was discontinued, and their parents advised to allow them to acquire health and education until they were ten years old. . . . The children were taught, reading, writing and arithmetic during five years, that is, from five to ten, in the village school, without expense to their parents. . . .

Their houses . . . were rendered more comfortable, their streets were improved, the best provisions were purchased, and sold to them at low rates. . . . Fuel and clothes were obtained for them in the same manner. . . . Those employed became industrious, temperate, healthy, faithful to their employers, and kind to each other."
Robert Owen, *A New View of Society*, 1831

77
A new model for trade unions

The first nationwide trade union was the ASE formed in 1851. Its 'new model' was soon followed by other skilled craftsmen. Less skilled workers found it hard to build national unions but they became stronger in local unions and took the lead in starting the TUC.

William Allan

William Allan started work as a piecer in a Scottish cotton factory when he was 12. Other boys went on to become adult factory hands. They might have joined a union for local spinners which would be struggling to keep its members together. At 15 William Allan was apprenticed as a machine-maker. Seven years later he was a journeyman. He moved to Crewe where the Midland Railway Company had just opened its engine works, and joined the Journeyman Steam-engine and Machine-makers Society. In 1848 he became its paid general secretary. Three years later William Allan persuaded other engineering societies to join up in a new larger union, the Amalgamated Society of Engineers (ASE).

The ASE

Afterwards it was said that the ASE was a 'new model' for strong trade unionism. How did it earn that label? First, it was wealthy. Its members were skilled 'artisans' or 'journeymen' who could afford a weekly subscription of a shilling. The ASE offered pensions and benefits for sickness and death. It also built up a large strike fund. Second, it could afford a headquarters in London and full-time officials to put the Union's point of view to MPs, newspaper editors and others who might give their support. Third, the ASE was well organised. Branches dealt with local matters but union members elected a National Executive Committee to handle negotiations and campaigns for changes in the law.

William Allan did his best to see that the ASE earned a name as a union which preferred to negotiate rather than strike. Yet he fought hard for the things that mattered most to his members: keeping down the number of engineering apprentices and shortening the hours of work. He was willing to lead a strike if employers attacked the right of workers to join unions

New Model Unions

That is why the ASE gave £3,000 to building craftsmen striking for shorter hours and the right to have a union. After the strike two more 'new model' unions were started. Robert Applegarth founded the Amalgamated Society of Joiners and Carpenters; Edwin Coulson built up the Society of Bricklayers. Soon there were others, such as the Society of Ladies' Shoemakers.

William Allan, Robert Applegarth and other new model leaders met in a committee known as the London Trades Council. For ten years it acted as a national leadership for the whole union movement. It was much harder for factory workers, miners or railwaymen to afford the new model unions' national organisation. Yet, despite all the difficulties, local trade unions became stronger. Their leaders set up trade councils in many towns.

The TUC

In 1868 the Manchester Trades Council called a meeting or 'Congress' of trade unionists to discuss the problems they shared.

Only thirty-four men came, and there was no one from the London Trades Council. The Congress agreed that meetings should be held every year. Next year the London Trades Council agreed to take part so the Trades Union Congress (TUC) became recognised as the national body for all trade unions. It decided to elect a 'parliamentary committee' to look after union affairs between conferences.

New model unionists

A

A report of benefits paid by the Colchester branch of the Amalgamated Society of Joiners and Carpenters.

1 *Use this account to design a leaflet recruiting members for the union.*

"Each member subscribed 1s per week and for that he received 10s per week when out of employment and 12s per week when sick; and during the time such relief was paid, the weekly subscription was not called for, a feature ... novel in Benefit Societies. Any member meeting with an accident, which permanently incapacitated him from following his trade as a carpenter and joiner, received £100; and for partial disablement, a sum of £50 was paid. The subscription also covered insurance of tools; and on the occasion of the fire at Mr Dobson's premises at Colchester, some men who were members had their tools replaced at a cost of £50. Any person after being a member 19 years was entitled to a superannuation allowance of 7s per week ... On the death of a member his widow or relatives received £12 ..."
The Colchester Mercury, 29 March 1879

B

This illustration of 1870 shows a club for artisans or skilled working men. ('Bagatelle' means a light-hearted game.)

2 *What are the trades of the two artisans shown in working clothes?*
3 *What do the pictures tell you about the the lives of skilled working men?*
4 *Does the picture offer any evidence which might be used to explain the rise of 'new model' unions?*
5 *Suggest what the artist thought about artisans' clubs.*

The Penny Illustrated Paper, 26 February 1870

78
Trade unions and the law

In 1871 and 1875 two sets of laws laid down that trade unions had the same legal rights as other organisations and allowed them to picket at factory gates.

The Sheffield outrages

The years 1866 and 1867 were bad ones for the trade unions. They began with what papers called the 'Sheffield Outrages'. Some workers sabotaged the machinery of men who would not join the union. In the worst case a workman's house was blown up. The Boilermakers' Society sued one of its officials who had pocketed some funds. The judge said that unions could not sue anyone because there was nothing in the law which said that they had the right to exist, or to own property, so nothing could be stolen from them.

The Royal Commission, 1867–9

On top of that, the government set up a Royal Commission to investigate unions. That might have advised Parliament to pass harsh anti-union laws if it had not been for William Allan and Robert Applegarth. They brought witnesses to explain that trade unions wished to protect working people, not to attack employers. Employers such as A.J. Mundella, who owned hosiery factories, gave evidence for the unions. The Commissioners' report came out in 1869 and recommended that the law should give unions legal rights. In 1871 Parliament passed the Trade Unions Act:

Trade Unions Act, 1871

Trade Unions should have the legal right to exist and the law would protect their funds so long as they registered themselves as Friendly Societies.

However, another law in 1871 said it was illegal to picket a factory to persuade workers to support a strike. The parliamentary committee of the TUC worked to get this law changed. In the 1874 general election they sent all candidates a set of questions about it. Many trade unionists had had a vote since the 1867 Reform Act. The TUC advised them to use it for candidates who gave the best answers. Unions were beginning to have political power. In 1875 the new Parliament passed two other Trade Union Acts:

Trade Union Acts, 1875

Peaceful picketing was made legal. Employers could no longer have workmen arrested if they refused to work.

Miners and railwaymen

The changes in the law were one reason why the number of trade unionists grew in the 1870s and 1880s. A single Miners' Federation was built up of local unions. The Amalgamated Society of Railway Servants had started in 1871. But the railway companies discouraged workers from joining and, by 1888, only one in thirteen was a union member.

Farm workers and Joseph Arch

Farm workers faced greater difficulties. The story of their union begins with Joseph Arch, a farm worker and Methodist preacher. In March 1872 labourers in Warwickshire asked him to help form a union, and they tramped miles to attend meetings. Labourers from the south of England asked to join so, in May, the union became the National Agricultural Labourers' Union. By the end of 1873 it had 1,000 branches. It also had enemies among farmers who agreed to give no work to labourers who joined.

Worse problems followed in 1877 when the first shiploads of prairie wheat came to Britain. Many labourers in the corn-growing districts were soon out of work. The union barely held together and Joseph Arch spent his time helping people to emigrate.

Royal Commission on Trade Unions
A

William Allan of the ASE is being asked about strikes or industrial disputes.

1 *What arguments does William Allan give against strikes?*
2 *What impression of the trade union movement is he trying to give?*
3 *What problems are there in using such minutes as evidence?*

The village labourers
B

Families from Meillbourne, Dorset, evicted by farmers in 1874 for belonging to the Agricultural Labourers' Union.

4 *From what had these families been evicted?*
5 *What evidence is there of poverty among agricultural labourers?*
6 *How does this picture explain one of the difficulties for the organisers of unions for agricultural workers?*

C

This extract is taken from Joseph Arch's own life story.

7 *Use Joseph Arch's story to write a conversation between*
(a) *two village women,*
(b) *the rector's wife and a friend to whom she is explaining her work for labourers' families.*

"– I should say that the members generally are decidedly opposed to strikes.... They wish to conserve what they have got ... and we believe that all strikes are a complete waste of money....

Have you found ... that your society has done anything to promote the same feeling ... in other trade societies?
– Many of the societies (the Amalgamated Carpenters and others I could mention) have taken in fact our constitution and our mode of management as their guide."

Minutes of Evidence given to the Royal Commission on Trade Unions, British Parliamentary Papers, 1867

"People used to go to the rectory for soup, but not a drop of it did we touch. I have stood at our door with my mother, and I have seen her face look sad as she watched the little children toddle past, carrying the tin cans, and their toes coming out of their boots. 'Ah, my boy,' she once said, 'you shall never, never do that.' ...

The parson's wife used to sit in state in her pew in the chancel, and the poor women used to walk up the church and make a curtsey to her before taking the seats set apart for them. You may be pretty certain that many of these women did not relish the curtsey-scraping and other humiliations they had to put up with, but they were afraid to speak out. They had their families to think of, children to feed and clothe somehow ..."

Joseph Arch, *The Story of His Life Told by Himself,* 1898

79 Working men in Parliament

Henry Broadhurst was secretary of the TUC parliamentary committee from 1875 to 1890. Some unionists were elected as Liberal MPs. Socialists argued that it was wrong to work with a party which supported the employers. James Keir Hardie stood for Parliament against a Liberal. He lost but in the next unit you will read how he became the first Independent Labour MP.

Henry Broadhurst (1840–1911)

Henry Broadhurst first worked as a stonemason tramping from one town to the next. He ended up in London and became secretary of the Stonemason's Union which he turned into a New Model Union.

In 1875 he was made secretary of the TUC's parliamentary committee just when the government was beginning to accept the union movement as important. Henry Broadhurst led groups of union leaders to put their view to ministers in Whitehall and even at 10 Downing Street.

Lib–Lab MPS

In 1867 the Second Reform Act gave the vote to about one in every three men. It was obvious that working-class voters would be the majority in some districts for the first time. A few local Liberal parties saw they would be more certain of winning elections if they put up working-class candidates. Two miners, Alexander Macdonald and Thomas Burt, were elected in 1874 as the first working-class Liberal (or Liberal–Labour) MPs. In 1880 Henry Broadhurst joined them.

After the third Reform Act of 1884 about two out of every three men could vote. The number of Lib–Lab MPs went up to nine. In 1886 Henry Broadhurst was the first working man to be a government minister, as a loyal supporter of the Liberal Prime Minister, W.E. Gladstone. He also stuck firmly to his view that Lib–Lab MPs should be concerned only with trade union matters. He believed they should not put forward a separate working-class point of view on political questions.

Keir Hardie (1856–1915)

At the TUC conference in 1887 Henry Broadhurst was under attack from James Keir Hardie, an ex-miner who became secretary of a Scottish miners' union. He said that trade unions should back their own working-men's party quite independently of the Liberals. Henry Broadhurst got more support than Keir Hardie but it was a warning to him that ideas were changing.

Back in Scotland, the Liberal Party in mid Lanark wanted a candidate for a by-election in 1888. The local miners wanted Keir Hardie to stand but the Liberals chose a lawyer instead. So Hardie stood against him as an independent candidate. He came bottom of the poll but a few weeks later he took the lead in starting the Scottish Labour Party.

The Social Democratic Federation

But what was the Labour Party for? To Keir Hardie its main task was to press for laws to improve the living and working conditions of all working-class people. He was drawing close to the ideas of the small groups of socialists which sprang up in the 1880s. The best known was the Social Democratic Federation (SDF) which was started by H.M. Hyndman in 1884. Most SDF members took their ideas from the writings of two Germans, Karl Marx and Friedrich Engels.

Marx and Engels

Karl Marx was a German who fled to England in 1849 after taking part in a revolution. He lived in London until his death in 1883 and spent most of his time in the British Museum writing *Das Kapital (Capital)*. In this book he explained his view that wage-earners and employers – capitalists – must always be on different sides in a class struggle. Engels came to Manchester as a businessman and wrote *The Condition of the English Working Classes in 1844*. It described life in London and Manchester in a way which showed his belief that the middle classes would never give up their privileges to make a better life for the working classes.

The Fabian Society

For SDF socialists the remedy was to end private ownership of business and land. All businesses and land should go into public ownership. But not all socialists wanted such far-reaching changes. Most of the members of the Fabian Society, also started in 1884, believed in a more gradual approach to socialism. They wanted to press the government and local councils to improve living conditions step by step. This was sometimes called 'gas and water socialism'.

Elections
A

A polling station, showing working men voting.

1 *Explain how you know this picture was drawn after 1872 (using information in Unit 73).*
2 *What do you think was the purpose of the book on the desk?*
3 *What is the connection between this picture of an election and the history of the trade union movement?*

Illustrated London News, 14 February 1874

B

Part of an election address written by Keir Hardie when he stood as an independent for mid-Lanark in 1888.

4 *Imagine a discussion in a miners' club between men who intended to vote for Hardie and those who would support the Liberal (who was almost bound to win).*

"At present the Members of Parliament returned from Scotland represent the following interests:

Landlords	18
Lawyers	21
Merchants	8
Shipowners	6
Army	5
Manufacturers	3
Schoolmaster	1
Doctors	2
Newspaper proprietor	1
Brewer	1
Various Learned Professors	6
	72

I ask you therefore to return to Parliament a man of yourselves who, being poor, can feel for the poor, and whose whole interest lies in the direction of securing for you a better and happier lot."
Election Address, Mid-Lanark Election, 1888

The Fabians
C

Sidney Webb was one of the first Fabians. He explains his view that Britain's growing public services were really steps towards a socialist society, although men such as his imaginary town councillor would not recognise this.

5 *How many examples of services owned and paid for by the public can you find in this passage?*

6 *Explain how this passage shows why the Fabian Society did not believe there would ever be a socialist revolution in Britain.*

7 *Explain why the Fabians were sometimes called 'gas and water socialists'.*

"The Individualist Town Councillor will walk along the municipal pavement, lit by municipal gas and cleansed by municipal brooms with municipal water, and seeing by the municipal clock in the municipal market that he is too early to meet his children from the municipal school hard by the county lunatic asylum and municipal hospital, will use the national telegraph system to tell them not to walk through the municipal park but to come by the municipal tramway, to meet him in the municipal reading-room by the municipal art gallery, museum and library.... 'Socialism, sir,' he will say, 'don't waste the time of a practical man by your fantastic absurdities. Self-help, sir, individual self-help, that's what's made our city what it is.'"
Sidney Webb, *Socialism in England*, 1889

80
New unions to
new politics

In 1888 and 1889 there were three strikes in London's East End – by match-girls, gas workers and dockers. Out of these strikes came new unions for unskilled workers. Their leaders supported the idea of a separate working-class party and new unionists' votes helped to elect Keir Hardie to Parliament.

The match-girls, 1888

In 1888 the writer Annie Besant talked to girls who worked at Bryant and May's match factory in Bow, East London. She printed their accounts of filthy workshops, long hours, low wages, and 'phossy jaw' in a socialist paper. When the women and girls saw their story in print, 672 of them came out on strike. Annie Besant organised a collection for the strikers and made sure that more people knew about conditions at Bryant and May's. After two weeks the firm agreed to make improvements. The girls went back to work – but they also started a union.

The gas workers, 1889

In March 1889 Will Thorne was a stoker at a gas works in West Ham. He had joined the SDF and was friendly with Karl Marx's daughter, Eleanor, who taught him to write correctly. Stokers worked all winter, choked by fumes, shovelling coke and raking cinders for twelve-hour shifts. In summer many were unemployed.

In March the company said they must work eighteen-hour shifts at weekends. Will Thorne called a mass meeting and got SDF friends to speak to the men: 800 threw money into buckets to start the National Union of Gas Workers and Labourers. In two weeks it had 3,000 members each paying 2d a week. Will Thorne reckoned that low-paid workers could not afford more. At the end of June the company agreed to three shifts of eight hours rather than face a strike. Success brought in more members. By 1890 the Union had 20,000 members and over fifty branches.

The dockers, 1889

Many gas workers in West Ham had dockers for neighbours. Some were specialised ship-loaders (or stevedores) who had a strong union. But most were casual labourers. Each day they waited at

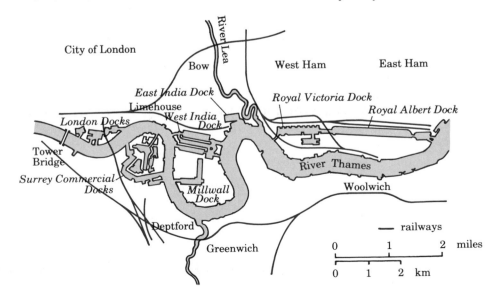

London's East End in 1889

the dock gates for the chance of a few hours' work. It was difficult to get them to join a union as Ben Tillett discovered when he started the tea warehousemen's union in 1887. It made little progress until the dockers were encouraged by the example of the gas workers. They went on strike in the West India dock and then others until the whole of the world's biggest port was idle. The strikers demanded improvements in the casual labour system and a rise in pay from 5d an hour to 6d – the docker's tanner.

To lead such a massive strike Tillett had help from other members of the SDF. John Burns led a daily march of dockers through the business districts of London. Tom Mann took charge of issuing food tickets for the strikers' families. Many people in Britain sent money but the dockers' funds ran out after two weeks. The strike was saved by a first instalment of £30,000, collected by unionists in Australia. This kept the strike going for five weeks, until the dock companies agreed to pay the dockers' tanner. After the victory Ben Tillett started a new union, the Dock, Wharf, Riverside and General Labourers' Union, with 30,000 members.

New unions

The match-girls, the gas workers and the dockers had all formed what people of the time called 'new unions'. They were for general or unskilled labourers, not craftsmen or specialised workers. Their members were mostly living below the poverty line (see Unit 55). Their families lived in the poorest homes, ate the poorest diet and ended their days in the workhouse. This meant they were likely to support socialism and to back the idea of a separate Labour Party. And it was in West Ham, the home of many new unionists, that the Labour Party had its first great success.

New politics

In 1892 there was general election and Keir Hardie stood in West Ham (South) as an independent candidate. He won and was the first working-class MP who refused to join the Liberal Party. In Bradford Ben Tillett also stood for election and lost by just 600 votes.

The effect of the dockers' strike
A

An extract from a socialist newspaper, 1889.

1 *What do the initials* DWR *and* GLU *stand for?*
2 *Suggest reasons why Ben Tillett had been invited to Bristol and Leith.*
3 *Write another slogan which means the same as: 'To combine is to succeed'.*
4 *What does this report tell you about the importance of the London dock strike?*

"we welcome the Deal Porters, to the ranks of the D.W.R. & G.L.U. They meet at Wood's Coffee Tavern, Deptford, and are a credit to any organisation.

BRISTOL ALERT
The wave of enthusiasm in the cause of Unionism which has swept over London, has now inundated Bristol. Ben Tillett has been down there and received a warm welcome . . . all should help to form a good, strong branch of the D.W.R. and G.L.U. To combine is to succeed.

LEITH ALIVE
The men of Leith are moving now. They are going to bear the burden no longer. That's it. They are going to combine, and ask Ben Tillett and Tom Mann to go over and help them."
The Labour Elector, 22 October 1889

81
Birth of the Labour Party

Keir Hardie took the lead in setting up the Independent Labour Party (ILP) in 1893 but the TUC still backed Lib–Lab MPs until 1900 when it set up the Labour Representation Committee (LRC). After the Taff Vale Judgement in 1901 many more unions supported the LRC. In 1906 there were twenty-six Labour Party MPs.

The ILP, 1893

In the House of Commons the new MP, Keir Hardie, attacked the Conservatives and Liberals for their lack of feeling for working people. Outside Parliament he organised a conference in Bradford. There, in January 1893, twenty-four unionists and socialists agreed to start the Independent Labour Party (ILP) to put up candidates for Parliament and local councils. The new party also declared that it believed in public ownership. It called for a welfare programme to give state care for widows, the sick and the old.

In the general election of 1895 the ILP put up twenty-eight candidates. All lost, including Keir Hardie. But support for a separate Labour Party was growing. ILP members were elected to many local councils. In 1898 they won control of West Ham council. In other London districts, ILP councillors were active in schemes to build the first council houses. In Bradford, Margaret Macmillan was elected for the ILP on to the School Board. She persuaded it to open the country's first nurseries. In London's Poplar, ILP members Will Crooks and George Lansbury were elected as Poor Law Guardians. Socialist ideas were spread by newspapers such as the *Clarion* and by young people in Clarion Cycling Clubs who toured the country holding meetings and sticking up posters.

Each year at TUC conferences in the 1890s Keir Hardie and the new unionists called for the TUC to back a separate party. Each time they were voted down by the older unions. Then the Amalgamated Society of Railway Servants (ASRS) changed its mind. It could not get the railway companies to recognise it and blamed this on the number of MPs who had shares in railways. The ASRS now could see the advantage of Labour MPs. In 1899 it put a proposal to the TUC for a Labour Representation Committee (LRC) to find the cost of fighting elections.

The LRC, 1900

The LRC met for the first time in 1900 but only a few unions with 350,000 members backed it. Six months later there was a general election. The LRC quickly found fifteen candidates but only two won. Keir Hardie was elected for Merthyr Tydfil and Richard Bell, secretary of the ASRS, won in Derby.

The Taff Vale Judgement

The LRC might have fizzled out if workers on the Taff Vale Railway had not gone on strike to support signalmen who had been sacked after asking for more pay. The ASRS made the strike official and Richard Bell went down to Wales to organise pickets. The strike lasted eleven days and the Taff Vale Railway sued the Union for £23,000 it had lost. The Company took the case to the House of Lords who declared in July 1901 that the Union had acted against the law and must pay.

The Labour Party

All unions knew that their funds might be in danger unless they could get a new law to protect them. That meant having Labour MPs elected to the House of Commons. By 1903 unions which together had more than eight million members had joined the LRC and set up a special campaign fund. The next election came in 1906 and the LRC won twenty-nine seats. These MPs changed the name of the party from the LRC to the Labour Party and elected Keir Hardie as their leader. Because it had done so well the new party was strong enough to persuade the Liberal government to support a Trades Disputes Act. This changed the law so that unions could not be held responsible for any loss which might follow from a strike, such as the one at Taff Vale.

The Osborne Judgement, 1909

After this success the Labour Party seemed set to grow in strength until it was struck a blow in another court judgement in 1909. W.V. Osborne, a railwayman who was also a Liberal, claimed that it was wrong for the ASRS to give part of his subscription to the Labour Party. As with Taff Vale, his case ended in the House of Lords, who gave the judgement that such a 'political levy' was illegal.

Trade Union Act, 1913

Without union money the Labour Party would soon have been in difficulty. It was saved by two changes in the law. From 1911 MPs were paid by the state, which meant that unions no longer had to pay wages to working-class MPs. Many unions continued to 'sponsor' MPs, however, and to pay part of their election expenses. This was just one of the ways in which unions kept a central place in the Labour Party.

In 1913 Parliament passed the Trade Union Act. This said that it was legal for unions to make a 'political levy' if their members voted for it. Anyone who objected had the right to opt out of paying the political part of their union subscriptions.

The ILP's early days

A

Philip Snowden joined the ILP in the 1890s. Later he became the first Labour Chancellor of the Exchequer. In his autobiography he remembered the early years.

1 *What did Philip Snowden mean by the 'ethical appeal of Socialism'?*

2 *In what ways was the ILP 'something new in politics'?*

3 *Why should Nonconformist local preachers and working men give their time to speak for the ILP?*

4 *Imagine you were living in the 1890s. Would you have been in sympathy with the ILP? Give your reasons.*

"The Party quickly developed a large number of local speakers. Many young men who were Nonconformist local preachers were attracted to the movement by the ethical appeal of Socialism.... Working men who had toiled all day at arduous work went out at nights into the streets to preach in their simple way the new gospel.... The movement was something new in politics. It was politics inspired by idealism and religious fervour. Vocal Unions were formed which accompanied cycling corps into the country at weekends, and audiences were gathered on village greens by the singing of the choirs; then short and simple addresses on Socialism were given. On their country jaunts the cyclists distributed leaflets and pasted slips on gates, and sometimes stuck them on cows, bearing such slogans as 'Socialism the Hope of the World', 'Workers of the World Unite'."
Philip Snowden, *An Autobiography*, 1934

The Taff Vale Strike
B

5 *What is the purpose of this poster?*
6 *What information and assistance might a workman get if he called at the strike headquarters?*
7 *Why was this strike so important to the history of the Labour Party?*

STRIKE !
ON THE
Taff Vale Railway.

Men's Headquarters,
Cobourn Street.
Cathays.

There has been a strike on the Taff Vale Railway since Monday last. The Management are using every means to decoy men here who they employ for the purpose of black-legging the men on strike.

Drivers, Firemen, Guards, Brakesmen, and
SIGNALMEN, are all out.

Are you willing to be known as a

Blackleg ?

If you accept employment on the Taff Vale, that is what you will be known by. On arriving at Cardiff, call at the above address, where you can get information and assistance.

RICHARD BELL,
General Secretary.

The Trade Disputes Act, 1906
C

'The prospect of a Trade Disputes Bill to protect the unions intimidates the Prime Minister.'

This cartoon was drawn while Parliament was discussing the law on trade disputes. The man is the Prime Minister, Herbert Asquith.

8 *What does the cartoonist suggest about the Liberal Party's attitude to the Bill?*
9 *Does the cartoon suggest why the Liberal Party agreed to support it?*
10 *What did the Trade Disputes Act say?*

82 Punishment

Eighteenth-century convicts spent only a short time in foul conditions in prison before they were hanged, whipped, dumped in the hulk of an old ship or transported overseas. John Howard and Elizabeth Fry pressed for clean, well-run prisons where prisoners would be reformed.

Eighteenth-century criminals

Judges sent very few people to prison in the early 1770s. Far more were fined or whipped 'tied to a cart's tail'. Two-thirds of all convicts were sentenced to transportation to the American colonies for seven or fourteen years, or life. Even more were actually sent overseas because death sentences were often changed to transportation. Nearly 200 crimes could be punished by death but usually only murderers, forgers and riot leaders were hanged. Condemned Londoners were kept in Newgate prison, near the Old Bailey, until they were taken in carts to the public gallows at Tyburn. Hangings were grisly festivals with spectators buying copies of the prisoner's life story – and often having their pockets picked.

The hulks

In 1775 the British settlers in America went to war with Britain. Transportation came to a stop. The government quickly beached old warships around the coast. Each hulk held several hundred convicts. In 1787 transportation started up again, this time to Australia. But the hulks stayed in use and many criminals sentenced to only seven years' transportation were never sent overseas.

The hulks were the first prisons run by the government. But they could not hold all the prisoners. Judges began to sentence the others to gaols run by counties and towns. But they were unsuitable, according to John Howard, who visited them all and wrote up his findings in *The State of the Prisons* in 1777.

The state of the prisons

Howard found that more than half the prisoners were debtors, kept there until they could pay. Buildings were often ramshackle so the criminals had to be chained to stop escapes. The gaol keeper and his assistants, the turnkeys, lived by charging a fee before a prisoner was released. Better-off prisoners could pay for comfortable rooms on the 'master's side'. On the 'common side' chained criminals, debtors and their families were crammed into small filthy rooms. In hot weather many died from typhus or 'gaol fever'.

John Howard wanted to punish criminals and persuade them to reform. He said they should be kept in separate cells and work in the daytime. Men and women, hardened criminals and first-timers should never be mixed. Prisoners should wear uniforms and have regular but simple meals. Keepers and turnkeys should be paid.

Elizabeth Fry (1780–1845)

Yet prisons had hardly altered when Elizabeth Fry visited the women's section of Newgate in 1813. She was a wealthy Quaker and had already done a lot of charity work among the poor. But that did not prepare her for the scenes reported in Source B. The horrible picture stayed in her mind while she had her ninth and tenth children. In 1817 Mrs Fry returned and persuaded the keeper to agree to changes. There was to be a female 'matron' or warder; children were to have lessons and the women to do useful sewing. The women were put into plain uniforms.

Sir Robert Peel (1788–1850)

Like John Howard, Elizabeth Fry believed that strict discipline should take the place of cruel punishments. Whipping for women was stopped in 1820. Between 1822 and 1830 Sir Robert Peel was Home Secretary. He persuaded Parliament to abolish hanging for a hundred crimes. (By 1837 the death penalty was kept for only murder and treason but it was not until 1868 that public hanging was stopped.) In 1823 Peel's Prison Act said that prisons should become an 'object of terror' to law-breakers. Keepers were forbidden to take fees. Women prisoners were to have women warders.

In 1835 the first prison inspectors was appointed to organise a new system. More than fifty gaols were built in the next fifteen years. Most were grim buildings, with high walls. Inside there were more than 12,000 single cells. The keepers and turnkeys were replaced by governors and warders. All prisoners had to work. The lightest tasks were sewing and picking oakum* but many convicts spent their time on the crank (Source C). There were harsh punishments such as flogging and bread and water diets.

In 1878 all prisons were put under government control. The first person in charge of HM Prisons said that gaol should offer 'hard labour, hard bed and hard fare'. Australia refused to take any more transportees in 1853 so seven years' transportation was changed to four years' penal servitude. That meant 'hard labour' in places like the stone quarries outside Dartmoor.

Juveniles

Little was done to try to reform prisoners as John Howard and Elizabeth Fry had hoped, except for children. From 1854 they were sent to reformatory schools instead of prison. Later the prison at Borstal, in Kent, began to give work training to prisoners aged between 16 and 21. In 1902 the Borstal system was made nationwide.

* Tarred ropes used for sealing the gaps between the planks of wooden ships.

Thomas Rowlandson, *The journey to Tyburn*, 1700

Punishment – old style

A *(above)*

A painting of the journey to Tyburn.

B *(right)*

Elizabeth Fry's first visit to Newgate is described by a supporter, Thomas Buxton.

Sources A–B

1 *What would you say were Rowlandson's views on public hanging?*

2 *Look at the title of Thomas Buxton's pamphlet. Do you think he believed places such as Newgate produced or prevented crime?*

Punishment – new style

C

A prisoner turning a crank handle which might have been connected to a grinding stone outside his cell.

3 *What does Source C tell you about improvements in prison sanitation?*

4 *List any other evidence that this was one of the new prisons built after 1835.*

5 *Suggest, with reasons, what John Howard might have thought of this prison.*

"Nearly three hundred women, sent there for every gradation of crime, some untried, and some under sentence of death, were crowded together in the two wards and two cells. . . .

They slept on the floor, at times one hundred and twenty in one ward, without so much as a mat for bedding; and many of them were very nearly naked. She saw them openly drinking spirits. . . . Everything was filthy to excess, and the smell was quite disgusting."

Thomas Buxton, *An Inquiry whether Crime and Misery are Produced or Prevented by the Prison System*, 1818

H. Mayhew, *The Criminal Prisons of London*, 1861

83 Police

In the eighteenth century it was the job of parish constables and street watchmen to cope with crime and disorder. Then the small teams of Bow Street Runners became London's first detectives and armed police. In 1829 Sir Robert Peel started the unarmed police force in London. In 1830 and 1856 police forces were set up in the rest of the country.

Parish constables

Britain's police system in the eighteenth century dated from the Middle Ages. Every parish had to choose a constable for a year. The job was part-time and unpaid. A village constable might have to leave his farm or workshop only a few times: to break up a fight, send a few beggars on their way or arrest someone on a magistrate's orders. But the job could be a great burden if the village had grown. More industry and more public houses meant more disturbances and a turnpike road was a temptation to highway robbers.

Watchmen

Big towns, such as London, were made up of many parishes but there was no possibility of their constables coping with the amount of crime and disorder. In the smart districts the parishes paid watchmen to stand in watch-boxes at night and keep an eye on houses. Every hour they called the time: 'Two o'clock and all's well'. This told the householders that the watchmen were awake – and was probably quite helpful to burglars too!

Bow Street Runners

Watchmen were not intended to track down criminals or find stolen goods. The magistrates were responsible for seeing this was done. In the 1750s two brother magistrates, Henry and John Fielding, set up a team of 'runners' to work from their court in Bow Street. The idea caught on and by 1820 London had teams working from eight magistrates' courts. The Bow Street Runners had a special place in the system. They were really Britain's first detectives because they had the right to follow clues and criminals all over London and outside. The Bow Street court also organised the first uniformed police, easily recognised by their red waistcoats. For the highways there was a horse patrol and for the streets in daytime a foot patrol. Both were armed with swords and pistols.

Sir Robert Peel

When Sir Robert Peel became Home Secretary in 1822 there were 4,500 watchmen but only 450 runners and patrolmen. He could see three problems. First, there were not enough trained police to deal with crime among London's one million people. Second, some districts had neither watchmen nor runners. Third, troops had to be called in to deal with demonstrations which often made matters worse. Sir Robert's solution was a single large police force for the whole city. It was not a popular idea as many people believed the police would interfere with their freedom. So it took seven years of persuasion before Parliament passed the Metropolitan Police Act.

The Metropolitan Police Act, 1829

On 29 September 1829 three thousand 'peelers' or 'bobbies' appeared on London's streets. Every effort had been made to show they were civilians. Their uniform was blue, not scarlet, and they wore long tail coats and tall hats – which were strengthened so that they could stand on them to look over walls. Swords were locked away in police stations and men on the beat carried truncheons.

London was divided into divisions, each run by a superintendent. Inspectors took charge of daily work and sergeants checked on constables as they walked around at $2\frac{1}{2}$ miles an hour. The new police were popular when they were seen to be preventing crime and 'moving on' undesirables. But they had their critics, especially for the way they handled political demonstrations and for their raids into slum 'rookeries' and public houses for suspects.

A nationwide police force, 1830 and 1856

Larger cities set up copies of the London police. In 1830 a Police Act gave counties the power to start forces, headed by Chief Constables. The Chief Constable of Essex was the first to give policemen a cottage which was also the village police station. Yet, by the 1850s, only half the counties had police forces. So a third Police Act in 1856 made county forces compulsory and three inspectors were given the job of seeing that the new forces were efficient.

Peel's Police
A

Sir Robert Peel wrote this letter to the Prime Minister, the Duke of Wellington, in 1829 giving information he would need to speak in Parliament about the scheme for a new police force.

1 *What two main reasons does Peel give for a new police force?*
2 *How did the Metropolitan Police Act deal with the problem described in the last two sentences?*

B

Here are some of the orders sent to all police divisions by the Commissioners in charge of London police in 1829 and 1830.

3 *Is there any evidence that some policemen were not observing the rules of 19 September 1829?*
4 *From the orders of 17 October 1829, and 19 October 1830, suggest which class of people the Commissioners wanted to keep sympathetic to the police.*
5 *Explain the order of 3 June 1830, in your own words.*

"My dear Duke, – I sent you . . . a statement of the number of criminal offenders committed to prison in the last seven years . . . in London and Middlesex. In 1822 there were 2,539 committals; in 1825, 2,901; and in 1828, 3,516. There is strong proof of the rapid increase of crime, and the necessity of some determined measure for its repression. In 1822 there were 20 committals for breaking into a dwelling house; in 1825, twenty-three; and in 1828, 102. . . . Just conceive the state of one parish in which there are eighteen different local boards for the management of the watch. . . . Think of the state of Brentford and Deptford, with no sort of police by night!"

Robert Peel, 1829 (*Peel Papers*, British Museum)

"September 19, 1829. Police Constables are particularly cautioned not to pay attention to any ignorant or silly expressions of ridicule that may be made use of towards them personally. . . .

October 17, 1829. Some instances of rudeness on the part of individuals of the Police towards persons asking them civil questions have been reported to the Commissioners of Police. The Commissioners therefore call upon the Superintendents to instruct their officers and men.

June 3, 1830 . . . the Police Constable is not authorised to take anyone into custody without being able to prove some specific act by which the law has been broken. No Constable is justified in depriving anyone of his liberty for words only, and language, however violent, towards the Police Constable himself is not to be noticed . . .

October 19, 1830. It is particularly desirable that individual Police Constables, when walking the streets, should not shoulder past respectable people, but give way in a mild manner . . ."

Instructions to the Metropolitan Police, Part III, 1836 edn

84
Victorian women

In 1837 eighteen-year-old Princess Victoria became Queen. She ruled until 1901. In this unit you can read about Victorian women at work and at home.

Factory women

Early Victorian Britain was the 'workshop of the world'. The only women whose work was made easier by machinery were spinners and weavers in textile factories. Even here they only worked as 'hands' and did not become engineers or overseers. Yet the work was less tiring than spinning at home. It also gave them a chance to earn wages and spend time away from their tiny houses.

Women in other trades

In most other trades women were pushed into the jobs where machinery was not used. In tailoring and shoemaking they did the sweated work of stitching while men did the cutting out with machines. In the iron trade men went into the factories while women took over the hand-trades of nail-making and chain-making. In farming men operated the threshers and harvesters while women were the weeders, hoers and stone-pickers.

Domestic service

The largest group of women workers was the domestic servants: a million in 1851, 1½ million in 1881 and 2 million in 1911. For middle-class Victorians a sign of getting on was that their wives and daughters need do no work. A wealthy family would have a dozen or more servants. The head servant would be male but most others would be female – cooks, housemaids, parlourmaids and launderesses. Even the wife of a clerk would have a maid-of-all-work living in the attic. The maid would wash and mend clothes and sheets while the mistress would do the embroidery.

Education

Middle-class men looked with horror on the idea that their daughters should be educated to earn a living. Most girls were taught at home by governesses, or in small private schools. Their lessons were to do with the 'accomplishments' needed to catch a husband. This was not always easy because there was a shortage of suitable men as so many had jobs overseas as army officers, officials and traders. So girls learned singing, drawing, dancing and French. Subjects to do with understanding the wider world, such as science, mathematics and geography, were seen as being for boys only.

Working-class women

When it came to working-class women, politicians and writers thundered against female labour in mines, factories and farm gangs. They said it made young women coarse and immoral. These arguments were used to support laws which controlled hours and conditions for women workers. Some employers who used cheap female labour said it did no such harm and that it was essential to industry. Few men looked at the question from the point of view of the women themselves who often did believe they had the right to earn badly needed money and have the freedom to be outside the home.

Working wives

The Victorian middle classes were quite sure that a married woman's place was in the home. Working wives were said to make bad homes which meant their husbands spent their free time in the ale-house. Working mothers were reported to neglect their children's diet and health. This might have been true where children were sent to dames who kept them in overcrowded rooms, fed them badly and kept them quiet with a pennyworth of Godfrey's Cordial. You could buy this from any corner shop and it contained opium.

Many employers would not keep women on after marriage, which often made home conditions worse if their husbands were low earners. In any case, the Victorians were slow to do anything about the women who suffered most by working at home in the sweated trades (see Unit 51). Through all Victoria's reign there were no laws to help domestic servants.

The debate about women's factory work

A

The view of leaders of the campaign to shorten factory hours, 1842.

"They grow up in total ignorance of all the true duties of woman. Home, its cares and its employments, is woman's true sphere; but these poor things are totally unfitted.... They neither learn, in the great majority of cases, to make a shirt, darn a stocking, cook a dinner or clean a house.... They are married early. Many are mothers before twenty.... Through these means is engendered a vast amount of immorality and misery."
The Ten Hours Question, A Report addressed to the Short Time Committee of the West Riding, 1842

B

A factory inspector's opinion, 1840.

Sources A–B

1 *What are the main disagreements between the two sources about factory work for women?*
2 *Using both sources, say how old you think a factory girl might have been when she married.*
3 *Which of these two passages do you think was nearest to the way that factory girls would think themselves? Give reasons for your judgements.*

"The great drawback to female happiness, among the middle and working classes, is their complete dependence and almost helplessness in securing the means of subsistence.... In Lancashire profitable employment for females is abundant. Domestic servants are in consequence so scarce, that they can only be obtained from the neighbouring counties. A young woman, prudent and careful, and living with her parents, from the age of sixteen to twenty-five, may, in that time, by factory employment, save £100 as a wedding portion. I believe it to be to the interest of the community that every young woman should have this in her power."
Report of the Commission on the State of Handloom Weavers, 1840

Marriage
C

The Registrar-General gave these figures for the average age at which men in certain trades married in 1884–5, together with the age of their wives.

Occupational group	Bachelors, years	Spinsters, years
Miners	24.06	22.46
Textile hands	24.38	23.43
Shoemakers and tailors	24.92	24.31
Artisans	25.35	23.70
Labourers	25.56	23.66
Commercial clerks	26.25	24.43
Shopkeepers and shopmen	26.67	24.22
Farmers and farmers' sons	29.23	26.91
Professional and independent class	31.22	26.40

The Registrar-General's Annual Report, 1886

4 *What does this tell you about the average age of marriage of girls who married textile hands compared with the other groups? What light does this throw on Sources A and B?*

5 *Suggest a reason why girls in mining areas married earlier than others.*

6 *Why would the last two classes marry later?*

Lancashire pit-brow girls
D

The drawing shows pit-brow girls, who sorted coal above ground, at a Lancashire colliery. The photograph of workers in Wigan in 1865 gives a different view of the same subject.

7 *List the differences in the way these two pictures portray pit-brow girls. Suggest reasons for the differences.*

8 *What do the differences tell you about the value of photography as a historical source?*

9 *Which law said that women should not work underground? Do the scenes suggest that women in mining districts had an easier life after it was passed?*

The *Pictorial World*, 18 April 1874

85
The Ladies of Langham Place

After 1850 some women began to campaign for the right to be educated and to work. More jobs opened up for them, but only when they were no threat to men's work.

An office in Langham Place

Barbara Leigh-Smith, Bessie Parkes and Emily Davies were all aged around 30 and from middle-class homes. In 1858 they took an office in Langham Place in London and started the *Englishwoman's Journal*, the first paper owned by women. In the first numbers they wrote that it was untrue that women did not need education for work. One proof was the low pay of women who became governesses because they were not trained for anything else.

Married Women's Property Acts

Barbara Leigh-Smith led the ladies' campaign to change the legal position of women. In a pamphlet she wrote that it was unjust for a man to have the right to use all his wife's money as he pleased. A man could divorce his wife for adultery but she could only divorce him for cruelty or desertion and, even then, he had custody of the children. In 1870 and 1882 Parliament passed two Married Women's Property Acts to allow women to keep their property and earnings separate from their husbands'. But male MPs were less willing to change the divorce laws and it was not until 1923 that a woman could divorce a man for adultery.

Education

Emily Davies's aim was to put girls' education on an equal footing with boys'. She began by backing two pioneers, Miss Buss and Miss Beale. Emily Buss started the North London Collegiate School for Girls. Her pupils studied the same subjects as boys and she would not allow 'accomplishments'. Dorothea Beale took over a small school and turned it into Cheltenham Ladies' College, the first girls' public school. There was soon a small network of schools run on the same lines as Miss Buss's and Miss Beale's.

Emily Davies's first personal success was to get Oxford and Cambridge Universities to agree that girls could sit for their 'local examinations', a sort of early GCSE and A level. In 1873 she founded Girton College which took Cambridge's first female students. A year later there was a women's college in Oxford. By the end of the 1870s a trickle of women were leaving after a full university education. They were not the sort to sit at home. Many went as teachers into the new girls' grammar schools (see Unit 90).

New jobs

Girls who had been to one of these schools had little trouble in finding work. Social change was on their side. The 1870 Education Act doubled the number of pupils in elementary schools and most of their teachers were women. In 1868 Florence Nightingale had started the first training school for nurses. In the 1860s and 1870s Britain was crisscrossed by telephone wires and female fingers were thought very suitable for the switchboards. There was a boom in counter work: in stores selling the new packaged foods, drugs and other goods, or in the post offices found in every village and shopping street. There was an even greater need for clerks after post offices started paying old age pensions in 1908.

The greatest number of girls went into clerical jobs. Government departments were swelling to deal with regulations on factories, education and public health. Private companies needed clerks to deal with paperwork connected with sending goods by rail and sea.

Shorthand and typing

The 1870s and 1890s were good years for private schools which taught shorthand and typing. Sir Isaac Pitman had worked out his scheme in 1837 and Gregg's was published in 1888. In 1882 Remingtons opened a new works to mass-produce type-writing machines. In the same year an American showed how touch typing could be faster than the hunt-and-peck method.

Separate work and pay

By the First World War working women had got nowhere near equality with men. They were always paid less for the same jobs but usually were slotted into work for women only. The Post Office had a special grade for 'girl clerks' – no matter how old they were! There were fixed ideas about what was suitable for each sex. Men were assistants in hardware stores and in groceries; women worked in dress, millinery and cake shops. Banks believed their customers would not trust women with money.

Very few women rose to senior positions. Some became matrons, head teachers or supervisors of girl typewriters (as typists were called). Few were made assistant inspectors of factories or schools. Women could not break into law and engineering. One small success was in medicine. The story of Elizabeth Garrett Anderson who was encouraged to be a doctor by Emily Davies is told in Unit 64.

Working women

A

A cartoonist's view of women at work.

1 *What does the cartoonist expect readers to laugh at?*
2 *What does the cartoon tell you about attitudes towards women at work?*
3 *Why would the Post Office need more clerks in 1914 than five years before.*

INVENTION FOR ATTRACTING THE NOTICE OF POST-OFFICE LADIES.
(Patent applied for.)

Punch, 12 November 1914

B

Census figures show changes in the number of people at work.

4 *Why did the number of teachers jump between 1861 and 1881.*
5 *Suggest as many reasons as you can for the rise in the number of clerks.*

	Teachers		Nurses	Clerks	
	Women	Men	Women	Women	Men
1861	79,980	30,280	24,821	279	91,012
1881	122,846	46,076	35,175	6,420	236,125
1901	171,670	58,675	64,214	57,736	518,900
1911	187,298	68,670	77,060	124,843	658,998

86
Votes for women

The word 'suffrage' means a vote. The Reform Acts of 1832, 1867 and 1884 gave the suffrage to more men, but not to women. From the 1860s women campaigned for the vote. The *suffragists* used peaceful methods. Then in 1903 the Pankhursts started the *suffragette* movement.

The first suffragists

One friend of the ladies of Langham Place was Harriet Taylor whose step-father, John Stuart Mill, became an MP in 1866. Harriet Taylor and some of the ladies collected 1,500 signatures on a petition for the same voting rights as men. John Stuart Mill spoke up for the petition but Parliament turned it down. That was the start of the suffragist movement. Women's suffrage societies sprang up all over the country with their own newspapers, pamphlets and lecturers. Over the next thirty years there were to be many more petitions to Parliament.

Anti-suffragists

Most men and many women believed that politics was man's work. Political leaders were nearly all against female suffrage. Conservatives believed it would upset their supporters. Liberal leaders feared that women would give their votes to the Conservatives. The Independent Labour Party believed that women should not have the same voting rights until every man had the suffrage.

The WSPU

Four Manchester members of the ILP disagreed with their party. They were Mrs Emmeline Pankhurst and her daughters, Christabel, Sylvia and Adela. In 1903 they founded the Women's Social and Political Union (WSPU). They argued that it was important to get votes for some working-class women to put pressure on MPs for laws to ease their hard lives. Their plan was to win publicity by militant action. Christabel started at a public meeting where the Foreign Secretary was speaking. With her went Annie Kenney, a cotton mill-hand. They shouted suffrage slogans. Police tried to remove them and got spat at. Both women were sent to prison for a few days. Sylvia Pankhurst and other WSPU women then took turns at disrupting meetings and going to prison. As they had planned, the WSPU became headline news. The *Daily Mail* called them 'Suffragettes' and the name stuck.

The suffragettes in London

In 1906 the Pankhursts and Annie Kenney moved to London. There they were helped by Mrs Pethick-Lawrence and her husband who looked after the funds while the Pankhursts organised public meetings and marches and found volunteers to chain themselves outside 10 Downing Street. At each demonstration suffragettes got themselves arrested and often roughly handled by the police. Public sympathy grew for the women who were willing to suffer.

Hunger-striking

In 1909 the suffragettes stepped up their activity by damaging government office windows. Those in gaol went on hunger-strike. Thirty-seven became so weak that they were freed. The government ordered that future hunger-strikers should be fed by force. But stories of brutal forced feeding only won more support for the women.

In 1910 and 1911 the suffragettes called a truce while there were two general elections and the government gave a vague promise to consider a suffrage law. It was not kept and, in the next two and a half years, suffragettes broke hundreds of shop windows, slashed paintings in art galleries, set fire to schools and railway stations. They also poured ink and acid into letter boxes around Britain.

Emily Davidson

Emily Davidson led a party to burn a house being built for Lloyd George. She was arrested, but not long after she was let out of prison she dashed on to the course at the 1913 Derby with a WSPU banner. The King's horse ran her down. She was killed and the WSPU turned her funeral into a suffragette demonstration.

Cat and Mouse Act

Hunger-striking went on in prison and the government replied with a new law, known to everyone as the 'Cat and Mouse Act'. Hunger-strikers were let out when they were dangerously ill and re-arrested as soon as they were strong. Many suffragette 'mice' escaped the police 'cats' by hiding in WSPU 'safe houses'.

By summer 1914 the WSPU was almost an underground organisation of middle-class women fighting a private war against the government. Its 'generals' were Mrs Pankhurst hiding in England and Christabel sending orders from France. Some thought they had become more like dictators. They had expelled the Pethick-Lawrences because the latter did not agree with their campaign of violence, and Sylvia Pankhurst who complained they had lost interest in the problems of working-class women.

Votes for working-class women
A

A cartoon of 1900.

1 *When would the man probably have first had the vote?*
2 *Suggest ways in which the franchise had made an umbrella for working-class men.*
3 *What argument is the man using against votes for women?*
4 *How could you use this cartoon to explain the beginnings of the WSPU?*

IS THIS RIGHT?

THE OPEN MARKET

Woman. Why can't I have an umbrella too?
Voter. You can't. You ought to stop at home.
Woman. Stop at home indeed! I have my Living to earn.

The First World War

On 3 August 1914, Britain joined in the First World War. The government released all suffragettes in prison and Mrs Pankhurst called off the violence. Soon she and Christabel were in the limelight again. This time it was at meetings calling on men to join the army and women to take their places in factories. They used up most of the WSPU funds but women's war work was an important reason for politicians giving the suffrage to women in two stages, in 1918 and 1928.

Mrs Pankhurst and the police
B

In 1931 Sylvia Pankhurst wrote a history of the suffragette movement. Here she describes how a group of women tried to see the Prime Minister at the House of Commons in 1909.

5 *Is there any evidence that Mrs Pankhurst tried to get herself and others arrested?*
6 *Suggest reasons why the crowd grew sympathetic to the women.*
7 *If Inspector Jarvis had written his own account in 1931 how do you think he would have described the same event?*
8 *How reliable do you think Sylvia Pankhurst's account of the Suffragette Movement is likely to be?*

"Mrs. Pankhurst led a small deputation, including the aged Mrs. Saul Solomon, who was making her third attempt to secure arrest, and Miss Neligan, an old school mistress of seventy-six . . . to the very door of the House. Here stood the stout, red-faced Inspector Scantlebury, the head of the police force attached to the House, with a company of his men. He handed Mrs. Pankhurst a letter from the Prime Minister – a curt refusal to accord an interview. 'I am firmly resolved to stand here till I am received!' she cried, with blazing eyes, and threw the missive to the ground. Inspector Jarvis then began to push her away, and his subordinates laid hands on the other women. To end the struggle and protect her elder companions from the violence usually preceding arrest, she struck the Inspector lightly on the cheek with her open hand. 'I know why you did that,' he said, but the hustling continued. 'Must I do it again?' she asked quietly. He answered: 'Yes.' She struck him on the other cheek, and he called to his subordinates: 'Take them in.'"
Sylvia Pankhurst, *The Suffragette Movement*, 1931

THE MODERN INQUISITION TREATMENT of POLITICAL PRISONERS under a LIBERAL GOVERNMENT

ELECTORS! *Put a stop to this Torture by voting against* THE PRIME MINISTER

Force-feeding
C

A suffragette poster, probably for the 1910 election.

9 *Was the poster aimed mostly at men or women? Give reasons for your answer.*
10 *Suggest why the government was not prepared just to let hunger-strikers die.*

87
Schools in the early 1830s

This unit is the first of four which tell the story of education in the nineteenth century. It begins with a tour of the different kinds of school in the 1830s. Then it shows how the churches were trying to provide cheap education for the poorest classes in monitorial schools.

The wealthiest homes

Infants of very wealthy parents were looked after by a governess. Later, for the boys, she was replaced by a tutor who taught mostly Greek and Latin. If parents wanted children to learn mathematics and French they would hire a visiting master. Other masters would come to teach girls the 'accomplishments': music, drawing and dancing. Some boys were sent to boarding-school, although wise parents would know that the 'public school' of the time taught little but 'manly' habits such as fighting and gambling.

The middle classes

Most middle-class boys went to small private schools. A clergyman might open a 'classical academy' in his home and teach Greek and Latin to half a dozen boys. The owner of a 'writing school' might have thirty or forty sons of local businessmen learning arithmetic, book-keeping and English. There were some academies for young ladies, but most learned writing, embroidery and household management at home.

The working classes

Some working mothers paid 3d or 6d a week to send their toddlers and young infants to a Dame School. It was often no more than a child-minding service run by a woman who crowded the children into her single living-room. The same mother might send older children to a common day-school. The 'teacher' was usually a man, sometimes a struggling cobbler or blacksmith who looked after the children in his workshop. Parents who could afford 9d a week might find a common day-school which would teach their son the 3 Rs well enough to become an apprentice craftsman or shop assistant.

The Ragged School Union, 1844

Some orphans and children of the really poor were cared for by ragged schools. The first was started by John Pounds, a sailor who took up shoemaking after an accident. His workshop in Portsmouth became a friendly place for hungry, ragged children who roamed the streets. He found time to teach reading and writing as well as cookery and shoemaking which gave them a chance to find work as domestic servants or cobblers' assistants. Ragged schools were started in other towns by charities. In 1844 Lord Shaftesbury started the Ragged School Union to help spread the idea.

Dame, common day and ragged schools were always tiny and most labourers' children had no education. Few people had bothered about that when boys and girls helped their parents in the fields or workshop. But when labouring families were crowding into the factory districts the middle and upper classes were disturbed by the sight of groups of wild boys and girls. The worries made them dip into their pockets to pay for schools for the poor.

Sunday schools

This kind of charity education began in the 1780s with the Sunday School movement. One of its pioneers was Robert Raikes who owned a Gloucester newspaper. Sunday Schools spread quickly. Some factory owners forced young workers to attend on their only free day. The people who paid usually laid down that the children were to be taught to read Bible stories. Some forbade writing in case children learned enough to find jobs outside their factory.

Joseph Lancaster

Monitorial schools

British and Foreign School Society

Because they were paid for by charity, Sunday Schools had to be cheap. In 1798 Joseph Lancaster found a way of running a weekday school which cost hardly any more. He put more than two hundred children into one room with only one paid master. He divided them up into small groups taught by an older child or 'monitor'. The monitor might be just one step ahead of the group but every child was busy and under control. This was the start of the monitorial system. King George III said he approved. Royal support helped Lancaster collect enough money to start the British and Foreign School Society to set up more monitorial schools.

The National Society

Most backers of the British and Foreign School Society were non-conformists: they belonged to churches which did not conform to the beliefs of the Church of England. The Church of England was not going to let education slip into rival hands. In 1811 it set up the 'National Society for educating the poor in the principles of the established Church'. It found its own expert in the monitorial system, the Revd Andrew Bell. By 1830 the National Society had about 400 monitorial schools to the 100 run by the British and Foreign School Society, all paid for by local donations. Together, in thirty years, these two societies had given Britain the starting-point for a nation-wide system of elementary education.

Sunday schools

A

Robert Raikes wrote this letter in reply to an enquiry about his schools. The man who received it sent it to the Gentleman's Magazine, *which was widely read by the wealthy classes.*

"SIR   Gloucester, Nov 25 [1783]

Some business leading me one morning into the suburbs of the city, where the lowest of the people (who are principally employed in the pin-manufactory) chiefly reside, I was struck with concern at seeing a group of children, wretchedly ragged, at play in the street ... Ah! Sir, said the woman to whom I was speaking, could you take a view of this part of the town on a Sunday, you would be shocked indeed; for then the street is filled with multitudes of these wretches, who, released on that day from employment, spend their time in noise and riot, playing at chuck, and cursing and swearing.... I then enquired of the woman, if there was any

1 *What does this passage tell you about Robert Raikes's reasons for starting Sunday schools in Gloucester?*

2 *What clues are there about the reasons for the spread of Sunday schools?*

3 *Is there any evidence that Sunday schools were entirely Robert Raikes's idea?*

decent, well-disposed women in the neighbourhood, who kept schools for teaching to read. I presently was directed to four: to these I applied, and made an agreement with them to receive as many children as I should send upon the Sunday, whom they were to instruct in reading, and in the church catechism. – For this I engaged to pay each a shilling for their day's employment."
Gentleman's Magazine, 1783

J. Lancaster, *The British System of Education*, 1810

Lancaster's system
B *(above)*

Joseph Lancaster wrote a handbook on his monitorial system. This illustration showed how one book could be used to teach many children to read.

Sources B–C

4 *How was the single book used in this school?*

5 *Suggest whose picture is on the wall and what 'patron of education' means.*

6 *How does this Source C help to explain why Lancaster used the word 'monitor' for the children in charge?*

7 *What did Joseph Lancaster mean by 'British' in the title of his book?*

8 *What does Source C tell you about Lancaster's view of education for girls?*

9 *What do the sources suggest about the advantages and disadvantages of monitorial schools?*

C *(below)*

Lancaster also explained how arithmetic should be taught.

"The monitor takes the book of sums – suppose the first sum is as follows:

(No. 1)	lbs.
	27935
	3963
	8679
	14327
	54904

He repeats audibly the figures 27,935, and each boy in the class writes them; they are then inspected, and if done correct, he dictates the figures, 3,963, which are written and inspected in like manner: and thus he proceeds till every boy in the class has the sum finished on his slate. He then takes the key, and reads as follows:

FIRST COLUMN. 7 and 9 are 16, and 3 are 19, and 5 are 24: set down 4 under the 7, and carry 2 to the next."
J. Lancaster, *The British System of Education*, 1810

88
Elementary schools 1833–1870

In 1833 the government began to pay part of the cost of schools run by the societies; because the government paid, it could make the schools replace monitors with pupil-teachers and see that children reached higher standards.

The grant to education, 1833

In 1833, for the first time ever, the government began to spend money on education. This was because of the Factory Act of 1833, which said that workers aged between 9 and 12 must have two hours' education each day. The government gave a grant of just £20,000, divided between the National Society and the British and Foreign Society. They were to use it to pay half the cost of new school buildings.

After six years ministers began to worry about whether the money was well spent. So they started a small department known as the Committee on Education. The man in charge was its secretary, James Kay-Shuttleworth. He set up a team of HMI (Her Majesty's Inspectors). The societies got grants only after HMI had checked the buildings, the number of pupils and the teaching.

Pupil-Teachers

James Kay-Shuttleworth knew that monitors were there to control children more than teach them, so he had them replaced by pupil-teachers. These were boys and girls who were apprenticed to the school's teacher for five years from the age of 13. In school hours they helped with the teaching; before and afterwards they studied with the teacher. Each year they were examined by an HMI and got a small wage if they passed. After five years they were given a certificate which meant they could take charge of their own school. A few pupil-teachers won a Queen's Scholarship to go to a training college. The extra training meant they could take charge of a larger school and have pupil-teachers of their own.

The Newcastle Commission

By the late 1850s the government was spending £400,000 in grants. MPs asked whether it was well spent and set up a Royal Commission, headed by the Duke of Newcastle, to find out. The Newcastle Commission reported that there was much to be worried about. School managers bumped up the number of pupils on the day the inspector called. In most schools only a third of the pupils attended for more than 100 days a year. About three-quarters left without being able to spell simple words or make out a shop bill.

Revised Code, 1862

In 1862 Robert Lowe, the minister in charge of education, announced a Revised Code of rules for paying grants. Instead of making a general check on schools, HMI would examine each pupil. Children were divided into six standards with different tests for each. Part of the grant was given for attendance, but most of it was worked out from the number of passes at each standard. The Revised Code put teachers on to a system of 'payment by results'. Was this a good thing? Certainly more children reached a higher standard. In 1864 only 58,000 passed standards IV to VI; in 1870 the number was 96,000. On the other hand, many children spent the whole year being drilled in the 3 Rs for the inspection.

The Revised Code

A

Joseph Ashby was at school in the 1860s at the time of payment by results. He gave this account to his daughter, M.K. Ashby. (Notice that he uses 'teacher' for pupil-teacher and 'master' for the teacher in charge of the school.)

1 *How did the schoolmaster feel about the HMI's visit? What evidence in the source supports your answer?*

2 *How many rooms were there in this school?*

3 *What evidence does this passage give about the effects of the Revised Code?*

4 *Choose a word or phrase which most summarises Joseph Ashby's feelings about his time in school.*

5 *Would you regard M.K. Ashby's book as a primary or secondary source of evidence?*

B

Matthew Arnold was an HMI. This is what he wrote about the Revised Code.

6 *What is meant by: 'ciphering', 'teaching by rote'?*

7 *What is Arnold's main criticism of the Revised Code?*

8 *List the aspects of the system about which Arnold and Joseph Ashby were in agreement.*

"You did almost nothing except reading, writing and arithmetic. What a noise there used to be! Several children would be reading aloud, teachers scolding, infants reciting, all waxing louder and louder until the master rang the bell on his desk and the noise slid down to lower note and less volume.

. . . you might wait the whole half-hour of a reading lesson while boys and girls who could not read stuck at every word. If you took your finger from the word that was being read you were punished by staying in when the others went home.

Two inspectors came once a year and carried out a dramatic examination. The schoolmaster came into the school in his best suit; all the pupils and teachers would be listening till at ten o'clock a dog-cart would be heard on the road even though it was eighty yards away. In would come two gentlemen with a deportment of high authority, with rich voices. Each would sit at a desk and children would be called in turn to one or another. The master hovered round, calling out children as they were needed. The children would see him start with vexation as a good pupil stuck at a word in the reading-book he had been using all the year, or sat motionless with his sum in front of him. The master's anxiety was deep, for his earnings depended on the children's work."

M.K. Ashby, *Joseph Ashby of Tysoe*, 1961

"The great fault of the Revised Code, and of the famous plan of *payment by results*, is that it fosters teaching by rote. . . . It is found possible, by ingenious preparation, to get children through the Revised Code examination in reading, writing and ciphering, without their really knowing how to read, write and cipher.

. . . a book is selected at the beginning of the year for the children of a certain standard; all the year the children read this book over and over again, and no other. When the inspector comes they are presented to read in this book; they can read their sentence or two fluently enough, but they cannot read any other book fluently. Yet the letter of the law is satisfied."

M. Arnold, *General Report for the year 1869*

C

The annual inspection of Higher Bebington School, Cheshire, 31 January 1868.

9 *Use the source to explain the importance of the examination in paying the running costs of the school.*

10 *What does the source tell you about the differences between the Master's and Mistress's classes?*

11 *What was meant by Half-Timers?*

Schedule of Grants.

	(7)	(8)	(9)	(10)	(11)	(12)
GRANT CLAIMABLE.		Boys (or Mixed) under Master	Girls (or Mixed) under Mistress	Infants	TOTAL Day School	Evening School
On average Attendance		12 8 -	16 16 -	6 -	29 4 -	
On Examination		20 13 4	17 17 4		38 10 8	
On Infants presented		13 -	10 1 6	9 8 6	10 14 6	
On Half-Timers, Art 47 (b)						
On Examination, Min. 20/2/67						
—Twelfths since, At 1/4			6 13 4		6 13 4	
1st April, 1867) At 8/- (Ex. VI.)			1 4 -		1 4 -	
Gross Total of Claim		33 14 4	52 12 2	4 16	86 6 6	

89
Inside the Board schools, 1870–1902

Education for all started with the Education Act of 1870 which set up School Boards. In the next thirty-two years there were many developments: compulsory and free schooling, later leaving ages and improvements in teaching.

Schools in 1870

In 1870 HMI counted pupils in schools in Leeds, Liverpool, Manchester and Birmingham. The total was just a third of all children in these towns. They found others in common day and ragged schools but that still left about half in no school of any kind.

That was one reason why governments began to consider a system to cover all children. Robert Lowe gave another when he reminded MPs that uneducated children might one day be adults with the vote. Already the 1867 Reform Act had given it to many working men. He told Parliament: 'It will be absolutely necessary to prevail upon your future masters to learn their letters.'

Forster's Education Act, 1870

The job of seeing this was done was given to another Cabinet minister, W.E. Forster. He was under pressure from two groups. One wanted the churches to run all the extra schools that were needed. The other wanted the churches to have no say in education. Forster's Education Act of 1870 found a middle way.

The aim, he said, 'was to cover the country with good schools'. The first step was to be a survey in each district to see how many extra schools were needed. The Church societies (now called the 'voluntary' societies) would have six months to 'fill the gaps'. If they failed, local ratepayers would elect a School Board. It would provide all the schools still needed and pay for them out of local rates. Board schools were to give simple Bible lessons but not teach the creed of any one church.

School Boards

School Boards turned out to be needed in nearly every district even though the Act did not make attendance compulsory. London's Board decided straight away to make it compulsory by a local by-law and had to provide schools for half a million extra pupils. Other Boards waited until 1880 when a national law said that all children must attend school up to age 10. In 1891 this was raised to 11 and in 1899 to 12. The only pupils who could leave earlier were 'half-timers', who spent their last one or two years half in school and half in the factory. School Boards had officers to round up children roaming the streets and those doing illegal work. Some parents could not afford the fee which was often only 1d a week in the poor areas. This was solved in 1891 when Board School education was made free.

Free schooling did not stop large numbers of children coming to school weak from hunger. Cheap Dinner Societies provided meals for 1d; in Birmingham a nasty greasy soup was sold for ½d. Poverty also meant that many children came with body-lice and ring-worm or just plain filthy. Some School Boards had part-time medical officers who inspected children for disease.

Thirty years' progress

By 1900 life in most Board Schools was very different from what it had been in the 1870s. Most children were no longer divided into 'standards' all working in the same room. They were in classes in rooms leading off the school's central hall. Lessons had changed too. New subjects had been added such as needlework, drawing, history and geography. In 1897 the Revised Code examinations were dropped. Many boys did woodwork and girls did domestic science at special centres. For some there were science lessons by demonstrators who pushed equipment in a handcart round the schools.

Board Schools gave some physical education. Sometimes this was only drill with marching and arm swinging exercises. But teachers also played an important part in the spread of organised games. They set up school football and cricket leagues just when these were becoming popular games for spectators. (The Football League with two divisions, a North and a South, was founded in 1888.)

The London School Board at work
A

These two photographs of boys from Lant School, London, were used to illustrate changes in children's physical health between 1874 and 1902.

1 *How do you think the Committee used these photographs for evidence of social progress?*
2 *What family connections might there be between some of the boys in the first and second photograph?*

LANT ST. BOARD SCHOOL (SOUTHWARK), 1875.

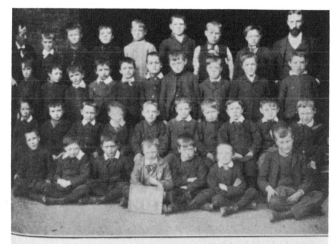
LANT ST. BOARD SCHOOL (SOUTHWARK), 1902.

Parliamentary Committee Report on Physical Deterioration, 1904

B
A report by the Board's inspectors, 1903.

3 *From Source B what would you decide was the most important result of the 1870 Education Act?*
4 *How does Source A provide evidence to support the claims made by the Board's inspectors?*

"London is now dotted all over with magnificent school buildings that are well staffed, well equipped, and in which, as a whole, splendid educational work has been done. . . . The results achieved by the board have not been confined to the children. The influence of the schools has had a very wholesome and civilizing effect upon parents in the poorer quarters of London. We, who have had to visit the schools in the slums of London, have been greatly struck with the change that comes over a district when a Board School had been fairly established."

Report of the School Management Committee, London School Board, 1902–3

90
Secondary education

This unit deals with changes in secondary education. In the nineteenth century it was thought of as being a separate system of fee-paying schools for families who did not use the elementary schools. The 1902 Education Act took the first steps to link the two systems.

Endowed grammar schools

Middle-class parents who wanted to send their eleven-year-old child to school had a poor choice in the 1850s. Most of the ten thousand private schools had a single owner-teacher who offered only one or two subjects. There were a thousand endowed grammar schools but they were no better. The endowment was money that men and women had given to start the school centuries before. The schools still had to be run as their founder had instructed. Often they could teach only Latin and Greek to twenty or so boys.

Endowed Schools Commission, 1869

One solution was for local businessmen or a religious group to subscribe together to open a proprietary school. Another came in 1869 when the government set up the Endowed Schools Commission and gave it legal power to alter the founder's wishes so that money could be used to make the school suitable for the modern nineteenth-century child. By the 1880s, six hundred grammar schools had been reorganised, including ninety-one for girls.

Science classes

The question which worried many people was how Britain could catch up with Germany (see Unit 38) in science education. A Department of Science and Art (we would say 'craft') was set up to give grants to secondary schools and night schools which organised science classes. In 1889 a tax was put on spirits and the money was handed to local councils. Many used this 'whisky money' to start the first technical colleges, mostly for evening classes.

Higher-grade schools

Meanwhile, in most industrial towns, the Boards had one or more 'higher-grade schools'. The brightest pupils in ordinary Board schools transferred there when they had reached grade six and stayed for two more grades. They concentrated on technical and commercial subjects needed in local business. Many went on to study at night and take one of the examinations started in the 1880s by the City and Guilds of London Institute or the Royal Society of Arts. By 1900 most pupil-teachers went to a higher-grade school and then started a three-year apprenticeship. Half

Pupil-teacher centres

their time was spent working in school and the other half at the Board's pupil-teacher centre. At 18 most went on to training college.

The Cockerton Judgement

Education in a higher-grade school or pupil-teacher centre was often as good as in a grammar school. But there were furious arguments about whether it should be paid for from public funds. The 1870 Education Act said Boards could use ratepayers' money only for elementary education. In 1900 an auditor, Thomas Cockerton, who was checking the London School Board's accounts, said it had broken the law in spending on higher-grade schools. A court case followed and the judges agreed with him. Cockerton had been encouraged to make his judgement by Robert Morant, a government education official. It was a move in Morant's plan for a new law to bring all schools, elementary and secondary, Board or Voluntary, into one system.

The 1902 Education Act

In 1902 Parliament passed the new Education Act Morant had asked for. It made town and county councils into Local Education Authorities (LEAs) and abolished School Boards. At elementary level, the LEAs took over the Board schools and the running costs of Voluntary schools. At secondary level the LEAs now controlled the higher-grade schools and pupil-teacher centres.

In the next few years LEAs turned the higher-grade schools and pupil-teacher centres into city or county grammar schools. They also built some new ones. Elementary school pupils took a transfer examination at 11. In 1907 a new law said that LEAs were to make a quarter of their grammar-school places free to boys and girls who won a scholarship in the transfer examination.

Four out of five pupils stayed on in elementary school until 13. Their time was spent on the 3 Rs, a little history and geography, with woodwork or domestic science. School led straight on to domestic service, unskilled work or, at best, a craft apprenticeship.

The grammar schools

For the grammar-school pupil there was Latin, modern languages, maths and lots of English, the subjects needed for white-collar jobs. For the rest of their time schools usually divided pupils between 'arts' (such as history and geography) and science courses. For most girls that meant no science. Even boys who studied physics and chemistry learned little about the technical side. Grammar schools saw themselves, first and foremost, as the place for preparing students for university and teacher-training colleges. From 1917 their pupils began to sit for School and Higher School Certificates which were run by examining boards set up by the universities.

Bradford Grammar School, 1868–95

A

1 *What tells you that this was an endowed grammar school in 1868?*
2 *How relevant would this kind of education be to life and work in Bradford at the time?*

"Bradford Grammar School has an endowment estimated by the trustees at £900 per annum. I found in this school 42 pupils of whom two are reading a Greek play, and otherwise studying with a view to admission into one of the universities. Eight only were able to translate a simple passage from a Latin author.... The staff consists of two clergymen and one assistant master ..."
Report of the Schools Enquiry Commission, 1868

B

3 *How does the 1895 source illustrate the work of the Endowed Schools Commission?*
4 *What evidence is there that the school received grants from the Science and Art Department?*
5 *Suggest reasons why Bradford parents would be prepared to send their sons to this school.*

"The school is situated in good buildings with large airy class-rooms, a fairly good playground and a good gymnasium.... There is a well-appointed chemical laboratory, a small physical laboratory and a good chemical lecture-room.... The school has a remarkably good staff of assistant masters.... The number of boys in the school is 420, and their ages vary from 8 to 19, while the fees vary from £10 up to £16 a year ... the upper school is divided into two departments, classical and modern. The modern side is an organised science school ..."
Royal Commission on Secondary Education, 1895

16 Communications

91 Sending messages

Fast and cheap communications were vital to industry and trade in the nineteenth century. Four improvements followed each other: the new postal service, telegraphs, telephones and wireless.

The old post

In 1839 the Post Office carried an average of three letters per person. Most people sent none because they could not write and because of the charges, which rose with distance. Payments were collected by the 'letter-carrier' on his round, which made it very slow. Many people refused to pay but this was often because they only needed to know where the letter came from to understand a prearranged message. Well-connected people had their own free system. MPs could send mail free if it was written on franked paper they signed. (No envelopes were used: letters were folded and sealed with wax.) Most MPs signed franked paper and sold it.

Rowland Hill (1795–1879)

In 1837 Rowland Hill wrote a pamphlet: 'Post Office Reform; its importance and practicability'. Its 'importance', he said, was that the country needed a cheaper mail service. Its 'practicability' came in Hill's idea of speeding up the mail by charging the same for any distance and making the sender pay. In 1840 the prepaid postal service started at a cost of one penny for each half ounce. Hill first charged senders for stamped paper. A few months later he changed to selling gummed stamps.

In 1913 the Post Office carried an average of sixty-six letters per person a year. Industry and business gained because documents, orders and cheques could be sent quickly and cheaply. Ordinary people found new ways of keeping in touch by letters (usually sent in envelopes after the 1850s), Christmas cards (which began in 1845) and postcards (from 1870).

Telegraphs

By the 1860s there was a network of 1,900 post offices. This put the Post Office in a strong position to take over a new system, the telegraph. Two inventors, Cooke and Wheatstone, had made the first electric telegraph in 1835. Electric signals were sent along wires to make needles point to letters on a dial at the receiver's end.

Wires were strung beside railway tracks to telegraph offices at stations and along poles in the streets to post offices. In 1851 the British wires were linked to France by underwater cable. In 1866 Brunel's last ship, the *Great Eastern*, laid a telegraph cable to America.

Telephones

In 1876 Alexander Bell sent the first voice message along a telegraph line in America. For a time Britain had some private telephone companies but most had to use the Post Office trunk wires between towns. It also made sense to have one organisation in charge of the telephone exchanges. So, in 1911, Parliament gave the Post Office full control of all telephones (except in Hull).

Marconi (1874–1937)

By then many inventors had been busy trying to send signals without wires. The most practically minded was Guglielmo Marconi who had an Italian father and Irish mother. He showed how electromagnetic signals could be collected on a wire he called an aerial. In 1896 Marconi came to Britain where the Post Office paid him to carry on with his experiments.

In 1897 Marconi formed his own company to make equipment and run wireless stations. He paid special attention to ships which could not be connected by wires. The new service made its mark in saving lives, but more people became aware of it in 1910 when a ship's captain radioed that he had the murderer, Dr Crippen, on board. Two years later radio messages brought ships to save many passengers when the *Titanic* sank on her first journey.

The new post

A *(left)*
The new post began 10 January 1840.

B *(right)*
By April there had been an important change in the method of payment.

1 *Imagine you were in charge of a town post office. Explain how you would have to reorganise the jobs of your staff in January and again in April.*
2 *Suggest what the public might think of these changes.*

POST OFFICE REGULATIONS.

ON AND AFTER THE **10th January**, a Letter not exceeding HALF AN OUNCE IN WEIGHT, may be sent from any part of the United Kingdom, to any other part, for ONE PENNY, if paid when posted, or for TWO PENCE if paid when delivered.

THE SCALE OF RATES,

If paid when posted, is as follows, for all Letters, whether sent by the General or by any Local Post,

Not exceeding ½ Ounce .... **One Penny.**
Exceeding ½ Ounce, but not exceeding 1 Ounce **Twopence.**
Ditto   1 Ounce .... 2 Ounces **Fourpence.**
Ditto   2 Ounces .... 3 Ounces **Sixpence.**

and so on; an additional Two-pence for every additional Ounce. With but few exceptions, the WEIGHT is limited to Sixteen Ounces.
If not paid when posted, double the above Rates are charged on Inland Letters.

COLONIAL LETTERS.

If sent by Packet Twelve Times, if by Private Ship Eight Times, the above Rates.

FOREIGN LETTERS.

The Packet Rates which vary, will be seen at the Post Office. The Ship Rates are the same as the Ship Rates for Colonial Letters.

As regards Foreign and Colonial Letters, there is no limitation as to weight. All sent outwards, with a few exceptions, which may be learnt at the Post Office, must be paid when posted as heretofore.

Letters intended to go by Private Ship must be marked " *Ship Letter.*"

Some arrangements of minor importance, which are omitted in this Notice, may be seen in that placarded at the Post Office.

No Articles should be transmitted by Post which are liable to *injury by being stamped,* or by being crushed in the Bags.

It is particularly requested that all Letters may be *fully* and *legibly addressed,* and *posted as early as convenient.*

January 7th, 1840.

By Authority :—J. Hartnell, London.

TO ALL POSTMASTERS AND SUB-POSTMASTERS.

GENERAL POST OFFICE,
25th April, 1840.

IT has been decided that Postage Stamps are to be brought into use forthwith, and as it will be necessary that every such Stamp should be cancelled at the Post Office or Sub-Post Office where the Letter bearing the same may be posted, I herewith forward, for your use, an *Obliterating Stamp,* with which you will efface the Postage Stamp upon every Letter despatched from your Office. *Red Composition* must be used for this purpose, and I annex directions for making it, with an Impression of the Stamp.

As the Stamps will come into operation by the 6th of *May,* I must desire you will not fail to provide yourself with the necessary supply of Red Composition by that time.

Directions for Preparing the Red Stamping Composition.
1 lb. **Printer's Red Ink.**
1 Pint Linseed Oil.
Half-pint of the Droppings of Sweet Oil.
To be well mixed.

. By Command,

W. L. MABERLY,
SECRETARY.

Post Office Regulations, 7 January 1840   Notice to postmasters, 25 April 1840

92
Sound and vision

This unit describes broadcasting since 1922 when the first public station was set up in Britain to the 1980s. It also looks at the effects of broadcasting on the cinema.

Wireless

In the First World War the Marconi Company made thousands of wireless sets for the forces. To stay in business after the war it needed to sell wirelesses to home listeners. In 1922 it got a licence from the Post Office (which controlled all ways of sending messages) to start the first regular broadcasting service. Station 2LO soon had 30,000 listeners and rival wireless makers naturally wanted broadcasting licences to build up their sales. But many people feared that Britain would become like America where 219 stations cluttered up the airways and some listeners complained that advertising spoilt the programmes. So Marconi and five other firms were told to join into one British Broadcasting Company. The money for programmes would not come from advertising but from a 10/- receiving licence paid by listeners through the Post Office.

Station 2LO and the first BBC

John Reith (1889–1971)

The Company's general manager was a young engineer, John Reith. He decided that it should provide a public service, free of anything to do with money-making and not linked with the government. Parliament agreed, and the Company became the British Broadcasting Corporation in 1927. The new BBC had no connection with wireless-making firms but it was still paid for by licence fees.

When Reith left the BBC in 1938, three-quarters of homes had wireless sets. The single BBC wireless channel started to make people think of themselves as belonging to one country and not just one town, village or district. That was not very much to do with news because the BBC was not allowed to broadcast it until after 6 p.m., so as not to take business from newspapers. It was more to do with bringing national events, from Cup Finals to the King's funeral, into every home. Reith believed that it was the BBC's job to improve the taste of listeners by broadcasting classical music, talks and discussions as well as stories and plays by leading writers. Every evening there were some of these programmes as well as the dance music, comedy shows and sports broadcasts which were more popular. Sundays were kept mostly for religious and serious programmes. Many listeners felt that the BBC knew little about everyday life. By the mid 1930s six million of them listened each day to Radio Luxembourg and Radio Normandy.

Cinema in the 1920s

Movie-makers believed that people who worked five and a half days a week wanted romance and thrills during their time off. By the 1920s the cinema chains had built picture palaces in every part of Britain. Until 1927 all films were silent, although the smartest cinemas had electric organs for background music. Then came the first talking picture, or 'talkie', with Al Jolson in *The Jazz Singer*.

By 1938 40 per cent of people went to the cinema once a week and a quarter went twice. The cinema killed off the music-halls which had been the main public entertainment until the early 1920s.

Most of the films were made in Hollywood, even though Parliament tried to stop this Americanisation in 1927 with a law that said that a quota of films had to be British made.

Television

John Logie Baird (1888–1946)

In 1924 John Logie Baird sent the first television picture, a simple test card. The idea was straightforward; it was a matter of turning the light and dark in pictures into electromagnetic waves. They could be picked up by an aerial and turned back into a picture which was built up line by line. The problem was to get enough lines on the screen to make a sharp picture.

The first TV

The BBC used Baird's system in experiments. But the EMI company found ways of making clearer pictures. It was their equipment which the BBC used to open the world's first television service, for London only, in 1936. By 1939 there were nearly 80,000 TV sets picking up the daily programmes. They stopped the day that the Second World War began. The BBC had more important jobs: broadcasting news around the clock, sending radio programmes to countries occupied by Germany, and starting a second radio channel, the Forces Programme.

Media after 1945

The Forces Programme specialised in request programmes and comedy. It was the first sign of the idea that separate channels might be used for audiences with different tastes. In 1946 the BBC turned it into the *Light Programme* to go alongside its *Home Service* and a new *Third Programme*, for listeners who wanted classical music and serious talks. In 1946, too, the BBC started up television again.

ITV

The BBC kept its monopoly of broadcasting until Parliament passed the Television Act in 1954. The Independent Television Authority was given the job of choosing a commercial TV company to broadcast in each region and seeing that it kept to rules about political bias and the amount of advertising.

More channels

By the 1980s people had even more viewing choice with four TV channels. Television had forced thousands of picture palaces to close but the film industry actually got a boost from the coming of the video-recorder in the 1970s. A new development of the 1980s was 'teletext'. Both the BBC and ITV began to send 'pages' of news and information in the lines between those used for pictures.

Radio in the 1980s

Choice in listening began to widen in the 1960s when pirate stations such as Radio Caroline broadcast pop music and advertisements from ships moored just over three miles from the shore, outside British-controlled seas. The government found a way to close them down but their programmes had become so popular that the BBC opened Radio 1 as a pop channel. It also started local radio. A few years later these were joined by independent local radio stations. Broadcasting had become very different from the single channel of John Reith's days at the BBC.

Public Service v. Commercial

A

The government committee which looked into broadcasting after 2LO was started gave its views on advertising.

1 *How did the committee think newspaper and radio advertising would differ?*

2 *List the reasons it gives for not having advertisements.*

B

Captain Plugge ran IBC which made commercials for radio in the 1930s. This is part of a brochure selling advertising time in the new early-morning slot.

3 *To whom do you think Captain Plugge would have sent this brochure?*

4 *What arguments is he using to sell the new advertising time?*

5 *What evidence has he that it would be a good time to advertise?*

"The broadcasting of advertisements on a large scale would tend to make the service unpopular, and thus to defeat its own ends. In newspaper advertising the small advertiser as well as the big gets his chance, but this would not be the case in broadcasting. The time which could be devoted to advertising would in any case be very limited, and, therefore, exceedingly valuable; and the operating authorities, who would want revenue, would naturally prefer the big advertiser who was ready to pay highly, with the result that only he would get a chance of advertising."
Report of the Broadcasting Committee, 1923

"we asked the electricity engineer of a thriving London suburb and he, very kindly, had a look at his supply load-chart which, to our surprise, indicated that 74% of the population in his district got up between 7 and 8 while 24% got up before 7. This certainly seemed interesting, so we went to his competitor – (Mr Therm's engineers), and he told us that 75% of the gas consumers were up before 8 o'clock.

Finally, we asked the listeners themselves over the air, and an overwhelming majority said they'd like to hear Radio Normandy start at seven. . . .

All those business people whom you could only reach on Sundays can now hear your advertising message before they leave for work."
IBC Pamphlet, 1930s

Cinema and television

C

Two tables from the government's annual study of social change.

6 *How far would you agree that there is a connection between the two charts?*

7 *Write two statements which could be made after studying the first chart. Write a possible explanation for each.*

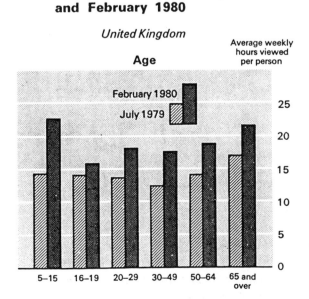

Television viewing: July 1979 and February 1980

United Kingdom

Social Trends, 1982

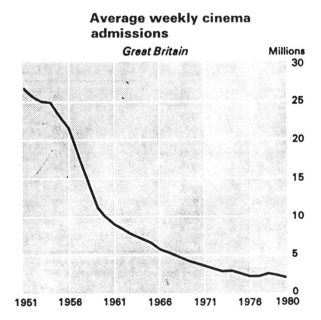

Average weekly cinema admissions

Great Britain

Social Trends, 1982

93
The first motor cars

The internal combustion engine was a French invention and the first cars were German. Ten years later car making began in Britain, first catering for wealthy customers and then using assembly methods to make cheaper models.

Internal combustion

In the 1860s British engineers were still improving steam-engines and miners were bringing up more coal every year. France and Germany were short of steam coal and their engineers were looking for another form of power. A Frenchman, Etienne Lenoir, made the first gas engine. He squirted mains gas into the engine's cylinder and exploded it with a flash made by a sparking plug. The gas expanded to push the piston. Lenoir's engine was an *internal* combustion engine because the gas burned inside. (Steam-engines had *external* combustion because the boiler was outside.)

Benz and Daimler

After the first oil wells were sunk in the USA it was possible to use petrol vapour instead of mains gas, which meant engines could be portable. About 1885 two German engineers, Karl Benz and Gottlieb Daimler, each fitted one to a horseless carriage. It was the start of the motor car industry. In the next ten years other French and German engineers solved the problems of making gears, cooling engines, stopping and starting.

Locomotive Acts

Before 1895 no cars were made in Britain. Yet there were plenty of enthusiasts driving French or German models. Every journey broke the Locomotive Acts which had been passed to make it hard for steam-powered road carriages to take business from horse-drawn wagons. The first Act (1865) said that a 'self-propelled' vehicle must have a man in front carrying a red flag. The second Act (1875) said the red flag was not needed but the man was and it fixed a 4 mph speed limit. Car owners joined the Self-Propelled Vehicle Association (SPVA) to get the law changed. In 1896 Parliament raised the speed limit to 14 mph and the SPVA celebrated with an 'emancipation run' from London to Brighton.

Early car makers

The freedom encouraged 270 firms to try making cars in the next ten years. Many had only a large garage where a few workers put the engine and chassis together before handing them over to a carriage maker. He built the body to the owner's design just as if it was a horse-drawn carriage. Such cars were usually sold to people who could afford a chauffeur to drive them.

Rolls-Royce

Gradually a few regular models replaced these custom-built cars. Lanchesters and Daimlers got a name for being stylish and reliable. Very wealthy families could go a step further and turn their stables into a garage for a Rolls-Royce. The firm began when the Hon. H.F. Rolls, a rich motoring and flying enthusiast, linked up with Charles Royce's engineering company in 1905. In 1906 they moved to Derby where the first Silver Ghost was made in 1907.

New British firms

Many other makers of hand-built cars went bankrupt, while French firms such as Renault were turning out hundreds of cars each year and selling many in Britain. Their secret was to build standardised models at prices which doctors and salesmen could afford. After about 1905 or 1906 some British firms began to do the same. Humber, Singer, Hillman, Rover and Wolsey all grew out of the bicycle industry in Birmingham and Coventry. Herbert Austin was manager of the Wolsey Works before he set up his own factory. Cars were made in the same way as bicycles with about half the components coming from other factories.

Component makers such as Lucas and Dunlop had begun as suppliers to the bicycle industry. Other companies started in the Midlands to make engines, radiators and gearboxes. The vehicle works themselves were huge sheds where teams of assemblers each had a space to build up a car from the parts stacked near by.

Henry Ford (1863–1947)

In the nineteenth century such assembly methods were known as the American system. Now, in Detroit, Henry Ford was making them out of date. In 1909 his factory turned out the first 'Model T'. It cost $850. By 1915 it cost $440 and production was up to 100,000 each year. Ford's workers were spread out in 'assembly lines' and each did a different job on an engine or car brought by conveyor. Henry Ford had begun mass production, twentieth-century style.

William Morris (1877–1963)

In 1911 Ford opened a factory in Manchester. In one year he became the country's biggest car maker producing 1,485 cars, all cheaper than British models. The competition forced other firms to begin making lighter cars at lower prices. The man who came nearest to Henry Ford's methods was a newcomer, William Morris, who owned a small cycle-making business in Oxford. He saw that he could make a reliable model entirely from parts supplied by other firms. He rented a disused army barracks in Oxford and took on unskilled workers who each did a small part of the assembly. Many were farm labourers from the surrounding countryside. They could be paid less than trained engineers. In 1913 they made a thousand Morris Oxford cars even without a moving assembly line.

Wartime, 1914–18

The war ended private car making and the factories went over to making guns, shells and aircraft as well as vehicles for the army. Factory owners ended up with new large factories paid for by the Ministry of Munitions and they learned a lot about mass production. In many factories half the workers were women who had come straight from domestic service and similar jobs.

Car assembly

A

A factory making Iris cars in London, 1907.

B

The chassis assembly shop at Austin's works in Longbridge, 1913. There is no moving assembly line but parts could be carried to the benches by overhead rail.

Sources A–B

1 *What are the differences and similarities between the two systems of car assembly?*
2 *What would be the differences from the point of view of the people who worked there?*
3 *Why would a factory such as Austin's be suitable for war production?*

Motoring hazards

C

The speed limit went up to 20 mph in 1903. Sydney Davis, an early car engineer and pioneer driver, remembered motoring in those years.

4 *What does Sydney Davis say lay behind the outcry against tarring the roads?*
5 *What reason does Sydney Davis suggest for the growth of the motor industry in France? Can you suggest another?*
6 *Would you regard Sydney Davis's book as a reliable source of evidence?*

"Two worries existed, the dust and the Police. . . . Get caught exceeding the 20 mph limit and it might cost four or five pounds. . . . But the dust was something all of us will remember, for it billowed out in dense clouds astern, covering everything. Some farmers put up notices 'Please drive slowly and raise less dust', to be justified by the state of such fruit trees as could be seen from the road. You could almost hear the windows being closed when a car was approaching a village. . . . No wonder women wore extraordinary veils that looked like cones point downwards, or that leather clothes were a prized possession. . . . So long as the dust lasted there was no chance of the Motor Industry really developing in this densely inhabited country, whatever it might do in France.

But what an outcry there was when the authorities commenced tarring the roads. You can see the point of view, 'Why all the expense to let rich men play with their toys?'"
Sydney Davis, *Memories of Men and Motor Cars*, 1967

94
Britain on pneumatic wheels 1919–39

This was the age of private cars for the middle classes, and bus and coach travel for everyone else. Cars affected where people lived and spent their free time. Lorries took business away from railways.

After the war, car making began again. By 1924 there were four times as many cars as in 1913. The number had doubled again in 1934. Prices fell so that a car cost about six months' wages for a senior bank clerk, a head teacher, or a shopfloor manager.

William Morris

The rise in numbers and fall in prices came because the leading car firms used moving assembly lines. By 1930 a car was leaving William Morris's factory every two minutes. To make sure of a steady flow of parts he had bought up most of the factories which supplied him. In 1926 he helped start the Pressed Steel Company where car bodies were stamped out in single pieces. This cut down the need for skilled workers such as welders.

Morris became a very rich man by making it easy for middle-class families to buy and run motor cars. He set up a chain of garages which had to carry stocks of standard spares. His cars could be bought on hire purchase. There was a magazine to get people interested in the improvements which were added each year: dipping headlights, chrome bumpers, safety-glass windscreens.

Herbert Austin 1866–1941

The mass-production methods pioneered by William Morris meant that only his company and five others succeeded as popular car makers. Other firms were driven out of business unless, like Rolls-Royce, they made much higher-priced cars. Morris's leading rival was Herbert Austin. In the 1930s his Longbridge factory in Birmingham needed six train-loads a day to supply 6,000 machines and 6 miles of conveyor belts minded by 20,000 workers. There were two other British-owned firms, Standard and Triumph, and two American-owned, Vauxhall and Ford.

Effects of the motor car

By 1939 there was one car to every twenty-four people, and it changed the pace of life and work for its owner. Before supermarkets, salesmen drove round taking orders from small shops. Doctors used cars for their rounds while other white-collar workers just drove them to work. It was no longer necessary to live near a tram or railway so new estates of detached and semi-detached houses spread around cities. In some cases they were strung out in a 'ribbon development' on each side of the road out of town.

Town planning

Leisure habits were changed. Journeys to the country or seaside did not need the same careful planning as by rail. Trips and picnics became popular. Many small country alehouses turned into motorists' inns. For a time, motoring seemed a good thing for the environment. Fumes were less bothersome than the stink and droppings of millions of horses. Rubber tyres made better road surfaces necessary. The first tarmac was laid in 1910 but it was not until the 1920s that it was used widely.

Accidents

Between the two wars, 120,000 people were killed on the roads. The yearly death-rate rose most sharply when the old 20 mph speed limit was dropped in 1930. This called for new regulations from the Minister of Transport, Leslie Hore-Belisha. The 1934 Road Traffic Act laid down a speed limit of 30 mph in built-up areas, made the driving test compulsory for new drivers, and led to the first pedestrian crossings marked by 'Belisha beacons'.

Motor buses

Only the middle classes could afford private cars but everyone else benefited from the bus and the coach. The bus and the council estate went together. In the days of the tram, working-class estates were built with straight streets leading off main roads where the trams ran. Buses made it possible to build in the spaces between these early estates. They also made it more sensible to build curved roads so that the buses could move easily.

The coach and long-distance bus brought new freedom of movement. Their fares were cheaper than those of the railways and you could board them at more convenient places. It became an everyday matter to visit relatives or go shopping in a town several miles away. When the coach was called a 'chara' or 'charabanc' it was being used for day trips or tours, a new way of holiday-making.

Goods vehicles

In 1939 nearly half a million goods vehicles had begun to replace the railways for carrying goods over middle-length journeys. Many manufacturers had their own fleets, others used carrier businesses, such as Pickfords, who had turned from horse to lorry. Goods vehicles could not carry freight over long distances as cheaply as trains. They were also more expensive to use in towns. So most delivery men used an electric or horse-drawn float, and pubs were supplied by horse-drawn 'drays'. The age of the horse was not completely over until the 1940s.

Mass production

A

The finishing shop at Morris's works, in the mid 1930s.

1 *Compare the photograph with Source B in Unit 95. How had production changed since 1913?*

B

William Morris said this about his car prices in 1924.

2 *Try making a diagram to show what Morris meant by the 'pyramid of consumption power'. (Remember that weekly wages were around £2–£3 for unskilled workers, £4–£5 for skilled, £6–£10 for better-paid white-collar workers.)*

"We have never waited for the public to ask for a reduction. We get in with the reduction first. It is not quite sufficiently realized in this country that every time you make a reduction, you drop down on what I may call the pyramid of consumption power to a wider base. Even a ten-pound price reduction drops you into an entirely new market. If the man cannot pay the last £10 in price, he cannot buy the car. When the £10 is knocked off, he very often can and will. The only object in life of many makers seems to be to make the thing the public *cannot* buy. The only object of my life has been to make the things they *can* buy."
W. Morris, *Policies that built the Motor Car Business*, 1924

C

Changes in the average index price of cars, counting the price in 1924 as 100.

3 *How much would you have paid in 1930 and in 1936 for a car which cost £200 in 1924?*
4 *Use Sources A and B to give two explanations for the change. Can you think of any other explanations?*

End of Year	Index price
1927	91.6
1928	80.6
1929	75.0
1930	68.1
1931	60.8
1932	59.6
1933	61.4
1934	51.8
1935	49.8
1936	49.0

Society of Motor Manufacturers and Traders, *The Motor Industry of Great Britain*, 1939

D

Road accidents, 1928–38

5 *What law was passed in 1934? What did it say?*
6 *What is the trend of the accident figures (a) before 1934 and (b) after 1934?*
7 *What changes in the number of vehicles had taken place in these years?*
8 *What do your answers to 6 and 7 suggest about the 1934 law?*

	Killed	Injured	Total
1928	6,138	164,838	170,976
1930	7,305	177,895	185,200
1932	6,667	106,450	213,117
1934	7,343	231,603	238,946
1936	6,461	227,813	234,374
1938	6,648	227,711	233,359

Figures from Ministry of Transport Statistics

95
The car in our life

After 1950 car owning spread to all classes. It gave new freedoms but created risks to health and to town life. The industry suffered badly from foreign competition in the 1970s.

After the war

Car making stopped in the Second World War and there was no petrol for private motoring. After the war, Britain was desperately short of steel. She needed to re-start overseas trade. The government told car makers they could have steel provided they made cars for export. It was a great boost for the industry which made more than half the cars in war-shattered Europe in 1950.

New models

In 1953 petrol rationing ended. Renault and Volkswagen were back in business so British firms turned back to the home market, which wanted even larger numbers of cheap small cars such as the Austin A40, the Morris Minor and then the Mini. Especially when men and women worked, often with overtime, families had more money to spend than ever before. Manufacturers brought prices down by using more automatic machines and longer assembly lines. But their profit was only a few pounds on each car, so even the largest firms could not survive on their own. Austin and Morris joined together in 1952 and Standard, Triumph and Leyland combined into another large firm. In 1968 it united with Austin-Morris to become British Leyland, which produced 95 per cent of the cars and 90 per cent of the goods vehicles made by British-owned firms. Their rivals were the American-owned Ford and Vauxhall.

New car owners

By the early 1960s millions of families were using cars for holidays (which was good for caravan and camp-site owners), day trips (which helped many stately-home owners with their repair bills) and shopping (which led to the start of the supermarkets). A car made it possible to buy a house in a new estate. But for every extra one per cent of workers who changed to private driving there was a 12 per cent increase in vehicles at rush hours.

The Buchanan Report, 1963

In 1963 a civil engineer, Colin Buchanan, wrote *Traffic in Towns*, a report for the Ministry of Transport. It warned of coming problems. Since 1953 the number of cars had risen from one for every 24 people to one for every 7 and there would be three times as many cars by 1980. (The actual figure was twice as many.) Many towns were cut in two by roads which no one could cross safely. There were rising health dangers from noise, fumes and accidents. The report went on to show how traffic inside and outside towns would have to be planned to stop them being strangled.

Motorways

One solution had begun when the first 75 miles of the M1 motorway opened in 1959. It had set new records in building: a bridge every three days and a mile of road every eight. By the 1970s there were 750 miles of motorway. They helped traffic to move faster and drew cars and lorries away from town bottlenecks.

But they disturbed many lives. Houses were cleared, especially for the London 'Motorway Box', and people were forced to live near ugly sound-baffle walls and to use double glazing to cut out the noise. Motorways were also wasteful of land.

Controlling traffic

In town centres, planners used ring roads, bypasses and underpasses to separate people and cars. They put double yellow lines and parking meters in busy streets. Multi-storey car parks went up like concrete mushrooms. Another way of easing congestion was to spread the area over which people moved. New housing estates, hypermarkets and garden centres appeared outside towns.

Britain spent thousands of millions of pounds to make it easier to travel by car. Not nearly as much was spent on improving public transport. The number of passengers fell and fares went up. So there were even fewer passengers and many services were cut – which meant that even more people turned to the private car.

Foreign competition

In the 1970s many cars on British roads were made in France, Germany or Japan, while few British cars were seen abroad. Even British Leyland was a tiny company compared with the leading foreign car-makers. Figures showed that more automated machinery was used to make foreign cars. By the mid 1970s British Leyland had huge debts. The Labour government handed it over to the National Enterprise Board which spent hundreds of millions of pounds to give it a chance to start earning profits again.

The Buchanan Report

A

Part of the preface to the Buchanan report, written by Geoffrey Crowther.

1 *Suggest what Geoffrey Crowther meant by saying that the car would 'spoil our civilisation'.*

"Car-affording has worked itself down the pyramid of incomes until there is now an enormous group of them just coming into range. . . . We are nourishing a monster of great potential destructiveness. And yet we love him dearly. Regarded as 'the traffic problem', the motor car is clearly a menace that can spoil our civilisation. But translated into terms of the particular vehicle that stands outside the door, we regard it as one of our most treasured possessions or dearest ambitions, an immense convenience, . . . a symbol of the modern age."

G. Crowther, Preface to C. Buchanan, *Traffic in Towns*, 1964

B

2 *What do the figures tell you about the motor car since 1951?*
3 *What problems have the changes caused for other forms of transport?*
4 *Write a note to each year explaining the background to the figures given.*

Motor vehicles in use, 1913–83

	All vehicles	Private cars
1913	305,662	105,734
1919	330,518	109,715
1923	1,105,388	383,525
1928	2,038,000	884,645
1939	3,084,896	1,944,394
1946	3,106,810	1,769,952
1959	8,661,980	4,965,774
1969	14,751,900	11,227,900
1983	20,698,000	15,925,000
1984	20,773,000	16,055,000

Ministry of Transport

96
Railways in our century

Railways were first built to link nineteenth-century towns and villages and to carry goods for the main industries. Since the First World War there have been great changes in industry and competition from motor transport.

The First World War

The First World War was a war which depended on supply. The government needed to move raw materials to munitions factories and to shift shells, guns, and troops to the ports. This huge stream would not flow smoothly if it had to pass along the lines of 140 separate companies. So the government set up the Railway Executive Committee (REC) with powers to control the whole network. The REC had to give 700 locomotives and 30,000 wagons to the army in France. Even so, it managed to move one and a half times the freight the railways had carried in peacetime.

Amalgamations, 1921

After the war many MPs wanted to keep national railway planning so they passed the Railway Act of 1921. This forced the companies to amalgamate into just four, but they faced difficulties in the 1920s and 1930s. Heavy industry and coalmining were depressed and produced fewer goods for the railways to carry. New factories were often built away from railway lines. Road transport was usually cheaper and more convenient for moving people and goods over shorter distances. Less business meant less income to spend on modernisation. Some lines in the south were electrified but most railways were running in 1939 just as they were in 1919.

Nationalisation

When war broke out in 1939 the railways were again handed over to the Railway Executive. Careful planning meant that they carried more goods and passengers than in peacetime. But the lack of spending before 1939 left its mark; by 1945 lines and locomotives were in a bad state and one in five wagons needed repair.

In 1945 Labour leaders gave three reasons for wanting to nationalise transport. First, two wars had shown that planning made it more efficient. Second, the railways badly needed modernisation and the companies lacked funds to do the work. Third, the railways would only have a future if they were planned together with road services. So, in 1947, the Transport Act set up the British Transport Commission to run the nationalised railways and a state road haulage business known as British Road Services.

BRS only controlled part of road haulage because most large firms had their own long-distance lorries. So the joint planning of road and rail never had a proper chance to work. The idea was given up in 1953 when the Conservatives denationalised BRS and left the railways in competition with private road transport.

Modernisation

In 1955 British Railways began a modernisation programme. At that time diesel engines were a rare sight but, from 1968, steam-engines have been seen only in museums or on private lines. Jointed lengths of track were replaced by lines welded into a continuous strip. Semaphore signals worked by levers gave way to coloured lights controlled by computers.

Dr Beeching

Modernisation had to be paid for. The job was given to Dr Richard Beeching who was in charge of British Railways from 1962 to 1965. In 1964 his report, 'The Reshaping of British Railways', gave some blunt facts. There were 17,000 miles of rail but half of this was used by only one-twentieth of the traffic. That half cost more in staff, repairs and signals than the money it earned. Some 2,000 stations handled freight but more than half of it went through just 118. Only a third of all passenger coaches were in regular use; the rest were needed only for holidays and rush hours.

Following the Beeching report came the Beeching cuts: a third of the lines and locomotives, more than half the stations and nearly half the staff. The railways were left with three main jobs: carrying people to and from work in London, intercity express trains and a new freightliner service where goods are moved in containers delivered by lorries to thirty or so terminals.

Streamlining
A

These figures illustrate the effects of the Beeching cuts.

1 *Which of the cuts do you think would save the most money? Give your reasons.*
2 *What was the effect of the cuts on road traffic?*
3 *Suggest why there was a bigger cut in coaches which were loco hauled than diesel or electrical units.*

	Dec. 1962	Dec. 1970
Locomotives	12,628	4,449
Passenger coaches:	33,821	18,678
loco hauled	22,715	7,699
diesel and electrical units	11,106	10,979
Freight vehicles	862,640	370,917
Stations	6,802	2,868
Marshalling yards	602	146
Route mileage for traffic	17,481	11,749
Employees (rail only)	475,222	251,797

British Railways Board, *Annual Reports and Accounts*, 1962, 1970

Paying for the railways
B

This advertisement compares the cost of British Rail with the railways of other countries.

4 *What does the advertisement tell you about the difference between railways in Britain and other countries? Do you think the figures are likely to be truthful?*
5 *Why do you think British Rail published this advertisement? How useful is it as a source of evidence? In which newspapers do you think it most likely that it appeared?*

Compared with other railways, ours don't need much support.

BELGIAN TAXPAYER   GERMAN TAXPAYER   FRENCH TAXPAYER   BRITISH TAXPAYER

Every railway in Europe needs some support from the taxpayer.

But ours needs less than most.*

Each year the Government requires British Rail to run passenger services which, although unprofitable, are socially vital.

Like the commuter services in the South East.

For three hours every working day they bring 400,000 people in and out of Central London, but inevitably for the rest of the time the trains are under utilised.

Our contract with government is to run these services at a price which we agree each year in advance.

In fact, we've met our contract for the second year running, and beaten it in 1977 by £27,000,000.

Which is no mean achievement in these inflationary times.

Pound for pound British Rail are giving the nation good value for money.

Especially when you take into account the social and environmental advantages that can't be measured in money alone.

British Rail
The backbone of the nation.

97
From Kitty Hawk to Costa Brava

In the early 1900s it was not clear whether air travel would be by airship or heavier-than-air machines. The latter won, especially because of their importance in two wars, yet air travel only became common from the 1950s.

Lighter than air

In 1900 many engineers believed the twentieth century would be the age of the airship. Lighter-than-air machines had come a long way since hot-air balloons with a basket underneath. 'Rigid' airships had hydrogen-filled balloons in a frame which also held a passenger and crew deck. In 1912 the German Ferdinand von Zeppelin made a petrol-driven dirigible (steerable) airship.

Heavier than air

Heavier-than-air machines went back to people who tried to glide like birds. Wilbur and Orville Wright, brothers who owned a cycle repair business in America, spent years trying to discover how to control a gliding machine. They worked out the system of flaps on the wings which is still used. In December 1903 they fitted the first tiny petrol engine to an aircraft and Wilbur flew for 12 seconds along a field at Kitty Hawk, North Carolina. By 1908 their best time and distance was 75 minutes and 77 miles. By then the Wrights were selling aircraft to wealthy experimenters. One was Louis Blériot, who first flew the English Channel in 1909. Another was C.F. Rolls. He was killed in an air accident in 1910, but Rolls-Royce went on to be leading aero-engine makers.

War in the air

The Wrights' most important customers were the armies of Britain, France and the USA. When war came in 1914, aeroplanes were used for spotting and then for bombing and air fighting. Aircraft design leapt ahead and so did the number of young men who knew how to fly. After the war they wanted to carry on. Bombers were fitted with four passenger seats and used to give joy rides over Blackpool and take the Prime Minister to talks in Paris.

Alcock and Brown, 1919

One was used by Captain Alcock and Lieutenant Brown to make the first non-stop flight across the Atlantic from Canada. Brown had to leave the cockpit during the flight to chip ice away, but 16 hours later they crash-landed safely in an Irish bog. Brown said that airships would always be more suitable than aeroplanes for long-distance travel. Zeppelins, 200 metres long, had crossed the North Sea to bomb Britain in the war. After 1918 these giants were fitted out like luxury liners and gave a smooth ride. But pilots had trouble flying in bad weather. Designers tried to improve them too fast and many crashed on their trials. Britain gave up airships when the R101 crashed and killed forty people in 1930.

Civil aviation between the wars

By then the government had decided to back civil aviation by aeroplane. It wanted Britain to have a share of the world's air traffic and a network to carry mail, businessmen and officials to the countries of the British Empire. From 1924 it paid an annual subsidy each year to a new company, Imperial Airways. In 1938, it forced private companies to join into the state-owned British Airways to run services to Europe.

There was steady progress up to 1939. Four-seater planes grew into twenty-eight-seater airliners. A London airport was opened at Croydon. Radio beacons were set up to help navigation. In 1939 Imperial Airways and British Airways were joined to become the British Overseas Aircraft Corporation (BOAC).

Yet the number of passengers going through Croydon in an average week could be fitted on to a few of today's Jumbo jets. Flying was for a very few who could afford it. For most others it was like the cinema, a bit of glamour they could watch but not take part in. There were plenty of publicity stunt stories like Amy Johnson's solo flight to Australia in 1930, which took 191 days. Aeroplanes were also at the heart of the great fear of the late 1930s, when war looked likely, that 'the bomber will always get through'.

The Second World War

Every year in the 1939–45 war, bombers were made larger and more powerful so that 60,000 people were killed in Britain and many more in Germany. One defence against them was radar which was later used to make post-war flying much safer. Another was fighter planes. Out of the search to increase the speed of aircraft came Frank Whittle's invention of the jet engine in 1941.

Jet engines

Jets were not used in the war but they replaced propellers from 1952 when BOAC was the first airline to fit them on its new fleet of Comets. With pressurised cabins they flew higher and faster. With new airports such as Heathrow, and improved radar, the Comets could fly in almost all weathers. Regular services to America and the Far East took business away from the shipping companies who turned their liners over to luxury cruising.

'Tourism'

Larger planes can only make a profit if most of their seats are filled. In the 1960s airlines joined up with tour operators to provide package holidays. This pushed up the number of Britons who spent their holidays abroad from 2 million in 1951 to 8 million in 1973, and 15 million in 1983.

Cheap fares

Airlines provided cheap fares for holiday-makers but they were less good at catering for the person who wanted to fly to a job in Germany or see a cousin in America. One reason was that their international organisation insisted that each airline charged the same high fares to cut down competition. In the 1970s this began to change. Some private airlines ran services with no luxuries, no advance bookings and cut-price fares. Freddie Laker found this was the way to fill his 'Skytrains' to North America. He later went bankrupt but other operators carried on with similar services. The government allowed private airlines to compete with British Airways (the new name for BOAC) on the intercity routes. In the 1980s fares began to fall and travellers could board a 'shuttle' service without booking for flights inside Britain.

Concorde, 1976

Air travel was putting aside its image of glamour, except for Concorde. Built with money from British and French taxpayers, Concorde was the first supersonic airliner. It carried fewer passengers than ordinary airliners and fares were three or four times higher. Only a few were built as many airports would not let it approach because of the shock waves from its 'sonic boom'. In the 1980s it was not clear whether other supersonic planes would follow or whether Concorde would be, like Brunel's wide-gauge railway, a brilliant idea which did not fit into the general trend.

A prophecy
A

Major Baden-Powell wrote about a visit to the USA to see the Wright brothers.

1 *What kind of shocks do you think the Major had it mind?*

"If only some of our people in England could see or imagine what Mr. Wright is now doing I am certain it would give them a terrible shock. A conquest of the air by any nation means more than the average man is willing to admit or even think about. That Wilbur Wright is the possessor of a power which controls the fate of nations is beyond dispute."
New York Herald, 6 October 1908

The effects of war
B

The Bristol Aircraft Company's works in 1918. It had 3,000 workers. In 1914 there had been 300.

2 *What does this photograph suggest about the importance of the war in the aircraft industry?*

3 *In what ways does this factory appear different from those for older British industries?*

Between the wars
C

An Imperial Airways manager recalls passengers travelling in Africa in the 1930s.

4 *What does this tell you about the numbers and types of people using long-distance air travel?*

5 *What are the advantages and disadvantages of using recorded interviews as evidence?*

"They were what would today be called the jet-set, the very rich who are constantly perambulating about the world. Africa was, of course, a mecca for the Safari business. There was big business in transporting very rich people down to Africa, Kenya and Uganda particularly. That was perhaps two per cent of the passengers. The balance was made up almost exclusively of colonial civil servants going to and from leave and members of His Majesty's Services going to and from postings . . ."
BBC TV interview, 1978

Post-war flight
D

Percentage of passengers using air and sea, 1948–1970.

6 *Explain why sea travelling fell so sharply between 1953 and 1963.*

7 *What did shipping companies do with ships?*

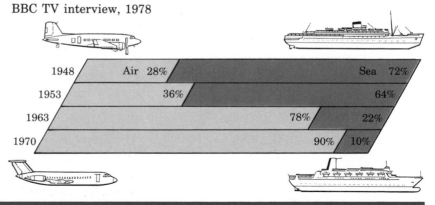

	Air	Sea
1948	28%	72%
1953	36%	64%
1963	78%	22%
1970	90%	10%

98 Edwardian summer — or autumn?

The next ten units are about the British economy in the twentieth century. This one deals with Edwardian times when Britain still had the benefits of her earnings as the world leader in trade and industry through the nineteenth century. But there were signs that she was losing her lead.

Edwardian Britain

Edward VII was king from 1901 to 1910. Life in Edwardian times was hard for many people, especially if they were farm labourers, sweated city workers, widows in the workhouse or 13-year-old girls in service. But on a world scale Britain was the richest country of all, the only one where most people had shoes on their feet, a bed to sleep in and glass in their windows. Hardly anyone starved and food came to nearly every table from all corners of the earth.

Britain's balance of payments

Britain was reaping the harvest from leading the world's industry and trade since the 1760s and the balance of payments looked better than ever (Source B). At the top of the earnings league were the dividends which came back on money invested overseas by British people, to pay for railways in China and Argentina, new docks in the Red Sea, tea farms in Ceylon, and rubber plantations in Malaya. The next biggest earners were 'services', starting with the steamers which 'tramped' from one country to another carrying goods. Then there were all the profits made by merchant and insurance companies with branches round the world.

The gold standard

These dividends and profits were *invisible* earnings, made on selling services, not goods which you could see. One reason why 'invisibles' were in such a good position was the gold standard. This meant that £1 sterling could be exchanged for a fixed amount of gold (a few grams) and that there was enough gold in Britain to pay anyone who asked for it instead of notes. Most other currencies were priced in gold, too. The same few grams would be exchanged for 4.86 US dollars and there were rates for Italian lira, Japanese yen and so on. So Americans, Italians, Japanese and Britons knew they could be paid in gold if they had dealings with each other.

Balance of trade

The figures for invisibles show how rosy life was for bankers, merchants and maiden aunts who got a steady dividend on money which they had invested in a mine in Australia for example. When it came to the *balance of trade* on *visible* goods Britain's balance sheet showed a loss; the money earned from selling exports was less than she paid for imports. The loss on visibles was not important so long as it was small. But many Edwardians feared that it would grow. The exporting industries were the same as they had been for fifty years: textiles, coal, steel, machinery, ships and locomotives. In all these, Britain's slice of world trade was shrinking, against competition from the USA and Germany.

Nearly one-fifth of American coal was cut by machine but only one-fiftieth of Britain's. Germans supplied all the artificial dyes used in Britain, down to the khaki for army uniforms. Behind the two rivals of British industry was another league of countries such as Belgium, Hungary, Russia and Canada, who were all starting their own industries and buying less from Britain. She was forced to sell more to Africa and Asia. Even here there were worries: Japan and India had growing industries in factory-made textiles.

The new industries

Some people worried that Britain was not doing well in developing new industries of her own. She made cars in tiny numbers while Henry Ford in the USA had them rolling off the first assembly lines. The German, Rudolf Diesel, made the first powerful oil engine which could replace steam in factories, and German firms made four times as much electrical equipment as British.

Opinions

There were many views about the reasons for this slow growth. Some said that British firms did not sell their goods hard enough. Others blamed investors who put their money into foreign railways rather than new machinery or electricity for a British factory. There were complaints that too many firms were run by men who had inherited them and were content to let them tick over instead of pushing on with new methods. Managers were less likely to have scientific knowledge because Britain's universities gave only a handful of science degrees against Germany's 3,000 a year.

Some manufacturers blamed free trade. Since the 1860s there had been no customs duties or tariffs on imports. Other countries had also been free traders, but in the 1880s and 1890s America, Russia, Germany and France began to put tariffs on imported goods. In 1903 Joseph Chamberlain started a campaign to make Britain protectionist as well. His 'Tariff Reform League' wanted customs duties on good from abroad, except for countries in the British Empire. Supporters of the Liberal and Labour Parties were firm free traders, and Chamberlain's plan split his Conservative Party. Britain remained a free trading nation until the 1930s.

Opinions
A

In 1907 an economist, Alfred Marshall, looked back at British industry in the 1850s.

1 *Summarise in your own words the point of view in Source A.*

"She had the full benefit of railways, and no other country at that time had. Her coal and iron, better placed relatively to one another than elsewhere, had not begun to run short . . . and in distant lands there was a rapidly increasing demand for manufacturers, which she alone was able to supply in large quantities. The combination of advantages was sufficient to encourage the belief that an Englishman could expect to obtain a much larger real income to live much more luxuriously than anybody else . . . and that if he chose to shorten his hours of work and take things easily, he could afford to do it. . . ."
Memorandum on the Fiscal Policy of International Trade, 1903

The nation's earnings 1911–13
B

A simplified table of the balance of payments just before the First World War.

2 *What is the difference between (a) visible and invisible trade, and (b) balance of trade and balance of earnings?*

3 *Why was (a) the balance of trade 'in the red', and (b) the balance of payments 'in the black'?*

4 *If economists had looked at these figures in 1913, which would they say were, (a) satisfactory, and (b) unsatisfactory?*

Invisibles	£ million
Dividends on investments overseas	187.9
Services: Shipping	
Merchant companies working overseas	
Insurance	152.6
Total earnings on invisibles	**340.5**
Visibles	
Imports	623.2
Exports	488.9
Balance of trade	**– 134.3**
Balance of Payments	
Profit on invisibles	340.5
Loss on trade	– 134.3
Overall balance	**206.2**

Figures from Board of Trade Statistics, 1913

Invisibles, 1913
C

The countries in which Britain invested ($ million).

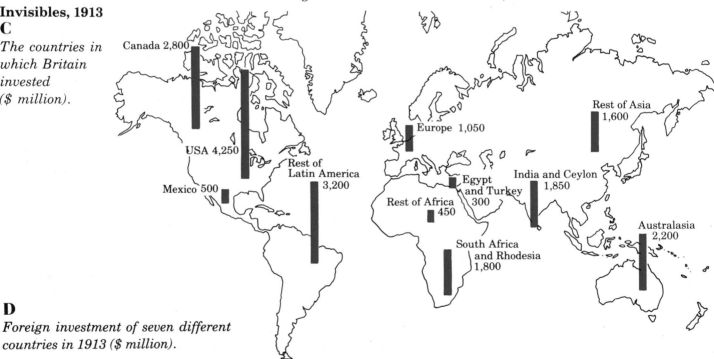

D

Foreign investment of seven different countries in 1913 ($ million).

Sources C–D

5 *What do Sources C and D tell you about Britain's investment in 1913?*

6 *Give as many reasons as you can to explain why her overseas investment was so large and so world-wide.*

7 *What were the main advantages and disadvantages of having so much money tied up in foreign investment?*

99
The home front
1914–1918

The First World War forced British governments to be involved in planning and running industry for the first time. Women workers were brought in to factories, transport work and offices from less well-paid jobs or from no paid work at all. The war-time need for extra money made Britain leave the gold standard and get into heavy debt.

Wartime powers

One in three men joined the forces between 1914 and 1918. Three-quarters of a million died and twice as many were gassed or wounded. Such death and destruction meant a massive effort to produce everything from sandbags to boots, rifles to heavy guns, wireless sets and barbed wire. This led to a new thing, government control of industry, mining and transport – as well as their workers. Most of it was done through powers given in the law which everyone called DORA – the Defence of the Realm Act. By 1918 the government controlled 20,000 workplaces. (It had also done other things such as rationing foods and cutting pub opening times.)

Industrial changes

The railways were run as a single system. Engineering factories were told to turn over to munitions and many new ones were built with government loans. The government took over parts of the chemical industry to step up explosive-making and started a dye-making business. Science-based industries were helped by a new Department of Scientific and Industrial Research. The war boosted new industries, especially aircraft, wireless and vehicles. Because the government was the biggest buyer, it was able to insist on modernisation. Factories which made machine tools for making arms often only got orders if they used more automated methods.

The government department for electricity supply sorted out the pre-war problem of too many small power stations. It marked a few as main suppliers to a large area and lent them money to build up their equipment. Much of the new power went into the countryside where, because of the danger, munitions factories were built.

Women workers

With so many men at the front the government needed workers for munitions factories, trams, buses and office jobs. The only choice was to employ women. Most of the women who worked in war factories came from domestic service and other poorly-paid work. The government made special arrangements with trade unions for 'dilution', which meant that the women could replace skilled men for wartime only. On the whole the women worked in bad conditions but they were better paid than before. The war also gave a great boost to their chance to work alongside men, or even replace them, in clerical jobs and the civil service.

Going off gold

The war needed huge sums of money. The government borrowed some from the public as war bonds, which became the first national savings certificates. Some came from 'going off gold'. Banks no longer printed their own notes which they guaranteed to change 'on demand' for gold (in sovereign pieces). Instead the government printed notes (£1 and 10s) in greater quantity than the value of gold in the country. It was making money by printing it. This led to inflation but there was full employment and higher wages so most people's standard of living did not change.

More serious was the fate of British money overseas. Britain lent huge sums to Belgium and France, but she had to borrow even more from the USA. The Americans also had four years, 1914–18, when Britain and Germany were cut off from world trade. US industry and overseas sales boomed and Britain never caught up again. One of the most important results of the war was that the world had a new top industrial and trading power – the USA.

Women's war work
A
A Birmingham manufacturer's comments in 1917.

1 *What two main reasons does the writer give for women not wanting to return to housework after the war?*

Two views of shell workers
B
A drawing of 1916.

"Typical cases which have come to my personal observation show that women prefer factory life. They like the freedom, the spirit of independence fostered by their new-found earning power, the social life. The children, they say, are better off than before, better fed, housed and clothed. These women will not want to return to their domestic duties after the war."
A. Kirkcaldy, *Industry and Finance*, 1917

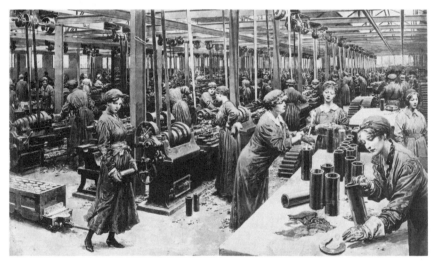

Illustrated London News, 1916

C
A photograph of 1917.

Sources B–C
2 *What different impressions do you get from these two pictures?*
3 *List the differences in the evidence each gives about the work and the workers. Which do you consider more reliable?*
4 *Can you suggest reasons for the differences?*
5 *If you could use only one to illustrate an essay on women's work which would you choose and why?*

100
Between the wars

The oldest trades were shrinking or growing very little. Their problems are described in Unit 101. This unit looks at the new industries which took off in the 1920s and 1930s.

Electricity

Wartime experience showed how electricity could be supplied from a few large power stations. In 1926 the Central Electricity Board (CEB) was set up to build a national grid with a standardised voltage. A few huge power stations were linked in a network of cables which carried electricity everywhere except the most remote farms. The power stations were owned by private companies or town councils but the CEB controlled the supply. CEB load dispatchers asked for more power when the skies darkened or Gracie Fields was due to sing on the BBC and less when there was a burst of sunshine.

National grid

Factories could now have many small electric motors instead of one fixed steam-engine which drove all the machinery. It would have been impossible to carry out the hundreds of separate operations in making cars or wireless sets without them. The grid also made it possible to build factories away from coalfields. By 1938 nearly two-thirds of homes were wired up for electricity (usually with only one or two power points). That was healthy for the electrical goods industry. In 1923 only 5,000 homes had electric cookers; by 1939 there were $1\frac{1}{2}$ million, as well as 7 million electric irons, and vacuum cleaner sales of 400,000 a year.

Chemicals

In the war the government had led the move to make up for lost time in the chemical industry, especially in dye-making. After the war British scientists were sent to defeated Germany to find how their chemists made nitrogen from the air. The result was a new factory making nitrogen fertilisers at Billingham-on-Tees. It worked at temperatures of 5,000°C and was just one of the ways in which the chemical industry was changing. Photography and medical drugs used chemicals and so did the glass and paint trades which were growing because of a boom in house-building.

The chemical industry supplied the first plastics made by turning wood-pulp or coal-tar into celluloid and 'bakelite', which was a brittle material used in electric light fittings and radios. Wood-pulp was also used for the first artificial fibre, rayon. It was often known as artificial silk and was used for stockings and underwear.

Amalgamations

All these products came after millions of pounds spent on research. Most needed completely new factories. This is why chemicals became an industry of giant firms. Largest of all was ICI, formed when Brunner-Mond (who had built the nitrogen works) joined with three rivals in 1926. Four years later Lever Brothers, who owned many soap and food companies in Britain, combined with a Dutch group of companies to become Unilever. Courtaulds, who made nearly all the rayon in dozens of mills, had been a struggling silk-ribbon firm in Coventry in 1904.

House-building

Four million homes were built between the wars which led to a need for schools, churches and shops. Nearly 4,000 cinemas were built as well as hundreds of new chain-store branches. So building did well, especially in the new industrial areas in London and the Midlands. Builders mostly used traditional methods and needed large numbers of apprenticed tradesmen. Backing the building-site workers were factories turning out bricks, wooden frames, metal pipes as well as toilets, baths and electrical fittings.

Food

People on average ate less bread and potatoes and more packaged food of all kinds: breakfast cereals, canned and bottled fruit and vegetables and factory-made sausages. Most shops changed from making up their own packets of tea, flour and sugar to selling branded ones. Food preparation was a fast-growing industry giving new jobs, especially to women. It was a business with a few large companies who pushed sales in massive advertising campaigns.

Retailing also was led by large firms (even though there were still 40,000 private butchers in 1939). Most high streets and town shopping centres had branches of chain stores. The co-operatives made up an even larger organisation, rising from 4 million members in 1918 to 8.5 million in 1939. They had a big share of another booming trade, delivering milk and bread.

New centres

Vehicle-making had the biggest growth of all (see Units 93 to 95). Road transport influenced the position of the new electricity-based factories which were usually built near roads, not canals or railways. Most were in the South and Midlands of England.

Industrial change between the wars
A

A new Marks and Spencer store in Brixton, 1931.

1 *List the ways in which this picture provides clues about the rise of new industries and new jobs between the wars.*

B

The average yearly rate of growth or decrease of output and jobs in twelve industries between 1920 and 1938.

2 *What can you see in common between the last four industries on this list?*

3 *Can you suggest any connections between the rise in vehicles and the rise in electricity and building?*

4 *On the basis of this table, where would you expect unemployment to be a serious problem?*

	output	jobs
Vehicles	6.6	3.0
Building	5.4	1.8
Electricity, gas, water	5.0	2.5
Electrical engineering	4.7	3.6
Building materials	3.7	2.1
Food processing	3.5	1.5
Tobacco	2.2	0.5
Chemicals	1.9	0.4
Iron and steel	1.1	−2.4
Textiles	0.2	−1.4
Mining and quarrying	0.2	−2.3
Ship building	−2.7	−4.6

D.H. Aldcroft, *The British Economy Between the Wars*, 1983

C

The distribution of unemployment, 1937.

5 *What connections can you see between Sources B and C?*

101
Old industries on hard times

The old heavy industries were in decline after 1920. Most of them had schemes for joint action to deal with the difficulties and governments played a small part in plans for recovery in the 1930s. That was a step towards the present-day government involvement in industry.

After the war Britain's old industries had a good year or two making goods which had been in short supply. After that they shrank or made only very slow progress.

Coal

There was still plenty of coal in the ground but the markets were shrinking. Coal was burned in power stations to make electricity but far less was used to run steam-engines or make gas. Lorries and cars rivalled steam railways. The world's shipping went over to oil, which destroyed the Welsh miners' market for steam coal. Heavy users of coal, such as textiles and steel, were shrinking industries. Small markets meant small profits and small profits meant little money for improvements in the mines. Some progress was made between 1913 and 1939. The amount of coal hewed mechanically went up from about 10 per cent to about 60 per cent but, by 1939, German mines used machinery for 97 per cent of their output. Britain still had 70,000 pit ponies at work.

It was also an old-fashioned industry from a worker's point of view. Accidents happened every day. Miners still provided their own clothes and tools and went home to tin baths. Union leaders and managers haggled to decide how many pennies should be paid for hewing coal or putting up props.

Steel

The steel industry did badly in the 1920s. Foreign countries were making their own steel; Britain had too many small factories which were long distances apart. In the 1930s the industry began to pick up. Smaller firms combined so that ten made two-thirds of all steel. Some opened new continuous plants like the one on top of a new ironfield at Corby in Northamptonshire. The iron was smelted and stayed liquid until it came through the rolling mills in a continuous stream.

In 1932 the steel firms joined in the British Iron and Steel Federation. It arranged for some old mills to be scrapped and new ones built. The threat from Hitler after 1935 brought orders from the arms-makers as Britain began to prepare for war.

Shipbuilding

Shipbuilding had a short boom just after the war and then the deepest slump of all industries. Other countries began to build their own ships and took the lead in launching new vessels such as oil tankers. The industry was saved from total collapse only by reorganising itself. Every firm paid one per cent of the price of each ship to a fund to buy up the oldest yards so they could be closed down. In 1935 the government's 'scrap and build' scheme gave loans to ship-owners to scrap an old vessel and order another. Government loans also helped the Cunard-White Star Line to order two new liners, the *Queen Elizabeth* and the *Queen Mary*, from John Brown's shipyard on the Clyde.

Cotton

Cotton had a bad war; Lancashire's exports slumped while Japan's rose. After the war Japanese firms bought looms and spindles from Lancashire by the shipload. In Japan they were mostly run on electricity while Lancashire mills mostly stuck to steam. Japanese wages were low, as they had been in the early days of cotton in Britain. India, too, began to turn out factory-made cotton and buy less from Britain. There was some justice in that because Lancashire goods had destroyed Indian cottage spinning and weaving in the nineteenth century. In India, Mahatma Gandhi organised a boycott of foreign-made cloth.

As with steel and shipbuilding, the industry took steps to help itself. Nearly a hundred firms joined in the Lancashire Cotton Corporation which closed down about half the machinery in Lancashire to keep the other looms and spindles busy. The government started the Spindles Board to buy up part of the machinery in each mill.

Cotton and Blackburn

A

Mahatma Gandhi visits Blackburn, 1931.

B

A mill-owner recalled the visit in an interview in 1983.

"He was shown how serious the situation was. In Blackburn alone there were seventy-four mills closed within about four years. Well,' he said, 'you come to the villages in India, we're a lot poorer than what you are', and there wasn't really much to say about that."
BBC TV interview *All our Working Lives*, 1983

C

The writer, J.B. Priestley visited Blackburn in 1933. (The present-day spelling of 'dhootie' is 'dhoti'.)

"The tragic word round there, I soon discovered, is dhootie.... A dhootie is the loin-cloth of India, which even Gandhi does not disdain to wear, and it is also the name of the cheap cotton fabric from which these loin cloths are made. Blackburn expected every man to do his dhootie. This fabric was manufactured in the town and surrounding district on a scale equal to the needs of the gigantic Indian population. So colossal was the output that Blackburn was the greatest weaving town in the world. . . . Millions and millions of yards of dhootie cloth went streaming out of this valley. That trade is almost finished."
J.B. Priestley, *English Journey*, 1933

Sources A–C

1 *What part had Gandhi's political ideas played in Blackburn's troubles?*
2 *Does the mill-owner's account help to explain why Gandhi and the mill-workers seem to be getting on well?*
3 *Where were 'dhooties' made before Blackburn became a weaving town?*

102 Governments and the depression

Between 1920 and 1939 unemployment never fell below 9 per cent of workers, and was 23 per cent in the slump of 1931. This unit looks at how governments dealt with benefits for the jobless and how the problem broke up the Labour government in 1931.

Unemployment

By early 1921 a third of all workers in shipyards and steel mills were unemployed and so were a quarter of all engineers. With hard times in other industries the total of jobless workers was 1½ million and it never fell below 1 million until 1940.

Benefits and the dole

It was a human tragedy and a problem for governments. Lloyd George had started national insurance for a few workers in 1911. The scheme had been extended in 1920 so that most workers and their employers paid into the fund which gave fifteen weeks' benefit when someone was unemployed. Before the war the fund was big enough to cover this unemployment benefit. Now it was not, especially when workers were jobless for many months. The government had to allow 32 weeks of extra payment, from money collected in taxes. This hand-out was quickly named 'the dole'.

The American boom

While Britain's industry was sagging, the USA's was booming with ever larger numbers of cars, fridges and vacuum cleaners, cinemas, fast foods and new homes. Many Americans did not stop at spending. They were bewitched by the chance of making money on the Wall Street stock exchange. The price of shares was always going up, so you borrowed money to buy some. A bit later you sold them at a profit and then you bought some more . . .

The American crash

. . . until 1929 when there were signs that the American boom was over. Overseas trade was falling. Shareholders decided to sell before the prices went down. On Black Tuesday in October 1929 so many tried to sell shares that panic set in and prices crashed. Huge losses were made. Banks could not get back all they had lent to buy shares so they had to stop lending to industry which put it into a depression. That meant that American firms did not need foreign materials, which led to a slump around the world.

Cabinet crisis

The Great Slump began a few months after the Labour Party won the 1929 general election. It had promised to deal with unemployment but by 1931 British exports had fallen by a half and nearly three million were out of work. In the summer, the Prime Minister, Ramsay MacDonald, and his Cabinet faced a crisis.

There was a gap between the money coming in from taxes and the money the government needed to spend. The biggest single reason for this gap (or budget deficit) was the soaring cost of the dole. At the same time bankers in the City of London reported that foreign lenders were taking their money back because it was needed in their own countries. The Bank of England was handing out £2m of gold a day. It told the government that it needed to borrow from French and American government banks to cover this loss. But they would only lend if they could see that Britain was going to cut her debts by closing the gap in her budget.

The National Government

The Cabinet met to discuss saving in government spending. Could they cut the dole? Most ministers refused to cut as much as Ramsay MacDonald and the Chancellor of the Exchequer wanted. The Prime Minister went off on his own to lead a new National Government, a coalition of mostly Conservatives with a few Liberals and just four Labour ministers who stood by him.

Dole cuts

The National Government now went ahead with pay cuts for government-paid workers such as judges (10 per cent) and teachers (15 per cent). They saved a bigger sum on the unemployed. Insurance benefits were cut by 10 per cent and paid for a shorter time. That meant more people went on to the dole, which was also cut by 10 per cent. Before they could get the new smaller dole unemployed people had to pass a means test.

The means test

The testing was done by officials from the Public Assistance Committees which had taken over when the Poor Law was ended in 1930. The unemployed had to disclose the earnings and savings of everyone in their household, even lodgers. Many failed the means test because another member of the family was working or even because they owned goods which could be turned into cash.

Unemployment 1919–39
A *(right)*

1 *Copy this graph and add these explanatory notes in the right place:*
Post-war production boom
Britain back on gold
Wall Street crash
Cabinet crisis in Britain.

Living on the dole
B *(below)*

An advertisement page from the News Chronicle, *December 1933.*

2 *What do the* News Chronicle *advertisements suggest about the spread of unemployment in the early 1930s?*

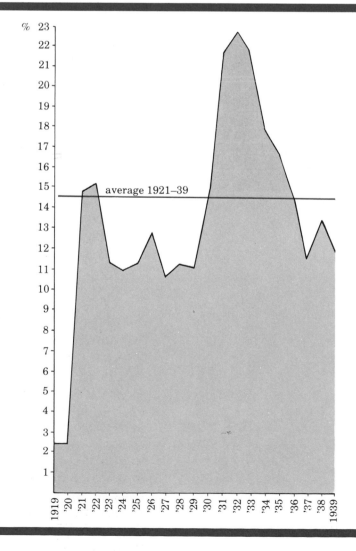

average 1921–39

DOOR-KEEPER for "Social Club," hours 3-5 p.m. and 7-11.45 p.m., Sundays, 7-11 p.m.; wages £2 per week. Apply by letter only, giving full particulars, Secretary, Bridgeway Club, Bridge-rd., W.6.

The Secretary,
Bridgeway Club,
Bridge Road, W.6,

requests us to announce that he had

1,425 APPLICATIONS

in response to a position advertised in the "News-Chronicle" on Tuesday last.

The vacancy has now been filled, and the Committee of the Club in thanking all disappointed applicants trusts they will soon obtain employment.

103
J.M. Keynes

Up to 1931 Conservative and Labour governments believed in keeping public spending down and fixing the pound at a high value compared with the money of other countries. This unit describes why J.M. Keynes disagreed with them.

Back on gold

Many jobs depended on exports. Politicians believed that the first step to help them was to put Britain back on the pre-war gold standard, when the pound equalled $4.86 and there were fixed rates for other currencies. This was done in 1925 by the Chancellor of the Exchequer, Winston Churchill. Officials told him that once dollars, yens, francs and pounds were at fixed levels, world bankers would have more confidence in their worth and step up lending and borrowing, so world traders would then buy and sell more. This would bring extra orders to British industry in the long run.

J.M. Keynes (1883–1946)

But the economist John Maynard Keynes, said, 'In the long run we are dead!' In the short run he was sure the gold standard would add to unemployment. To begin with, the rate of £1 = $4.86 was too high. It should have been nearer $4.40 to make every £1-worth of British goods sell cheaper in countries which used dollars.

Keynes's second reason was that the merchant banks in the City of London (the ones which specialised in overseas business) would not do much lending until they had built up stocks of gold and other foreign money. To encourage foreigners to lend to them they would give high interest rates. But industries in Britain would have to pay the same high rates to borrow money for new equipment and factories.

The General Theory

In 1936 Keynes's book, *The General Theory of Employment, Interest and Money*, drew his ideas together. He wrote that the economy is made up of a chain of activities, and each link acts as a *multiplier* on the next. When someone borrows money to build a new factory it will give work to people who will have wages to spend on goods (furniture) and services (a haircut). That will mean that cabinet makers and hairdressers have money to spend on other goods and services.

That was how a healthy economy worked. When it was healthy the government could leave it alone. But when it was sick the government must act. Sickness began at the beginning of the chain when no one was borrowing to spend on new building. To bring about a cure the government must itself borrow and spend. It did not matter what it spent on – but roads, hospitals and houses would be best. The government should also make it easy for private employers to borrow by seeing that interest rates were low.

Britain off gold, 1931

Most of Keynes's ideas were taken up after 1945 but a few were tried in the 1930s. In 1931 the Government gave up the gold standard. High interest rates were no longer needed to attract foreigners to use British banks so companies here could borrow more cheaply.

Special Areas Act, 1934

The government gave some help to industries in trouble, like the scrap and build scheme for ships (see Unit 101). Closest of all to Keynes's ideas was the Special Areas Act. This gave small sums to four distressed areas: South Wales, Tyneside, West Cumberland and Scotland. An example of spending by the scheme was the new steel works at Ebbw Vale in South Wales. Sadly this meant that there was no new steel works for Jarrow on Tyneside.

Spending on rearmament

The biggest public spending was not part of Keynes's schemes but it worked in the same way. It was the orders for new weapons, in case Hitler turned out to be untrustworthy. From 1935 to 1939 spending on arms went up nearly three times. Two results were a spurt in steel-making and many extra jobs in engineering.

The story of Jarrow

Two hundred men set out from Jarrow to take a petition to Parliament to let industry come to their town.

A

A Special Branch report.

"The march throughout the Metropolitan Police District was well organised, and the men well disciplined. The general public were sympathetic and generous, and the demonstration was kept free from political propaganda. During the marchers' stay in London their conduct was exemplary and no incident occurred necessitating police action."
Special Branch, Report on the Jarrow March, November 1937

B

The government would not allow the marchers to present their petition to Parliament. Instead it was presented by their MP, Ellen Wilkinson. This is part of it.

"During the last fifteen years Jarrow has passed through a period of industrial depression without parallel in the town's history. Its shipyard is closed. Its steelworks have been denied the right to reopen. Where formerly 8,000 people, many of them skilled workers, were employed, only 100 men are now employed on a temporary scheme."
Parliamentary Debates, November 1937

C

The marchers arrive in London.

Sources A–C

1 *What chance of help for Jarrow had gone to another place before the march?*
2 *Why do you think the Special Branch would have been keeping an eye on the march?*
3 *What were the two main causes of unemployment in Jarrow according to Source B?*
4 *Imagine you were a government minister. How would you have explained that the government was not prepared to spend a great deal of money in helping Jarrow?*

104
The people's war

The Second World War lasted from September 1939 until Germany was beaten in May 1945, and Japan in August 1945. From 1940 the country was run by a coalition government with Winston Churchill (Conservative) as Prime Minister and Clement Attlee (Labour) as his deputy.

A nation at war

Enemy bombers and rockets brought the Second World War to the people of Britain. Nearly as many civilians were killed as troops. Men and women joined the ARP (Air Raid Precautions) and the Home Guard. The Women's Volunteer Service stood by with tea wagons and helped to evacuate 1½ million city children to new 'billets' in the country. The BBC helped with its news broadcasts, tips on how to cope with rationing, and 'music while you work', as well as speeches from Winston Churchill and other national leaders.

Government direction

As in the First World War, it was a struggle between the production machines of the fighting countries. The Emergency Powers Act, 1939, did the same job as DORA (Unit 102). Ernest Bevin was asked to leave his job of Secretary of the Transport and General Workers' Union to be Minister of Labour. There he organised five million people to serve in the forces, the Land Army, factories making munitions, aircraft and parachutes. 'Bevin Boys' – 22,000 of them – were sent to help miners dig up more coal.

Women workers

By 1945 there were an extra quarter of a million women in both munitions and the civil service, an extra three-quarters of a million in engineering and 111,000 more in farming. Very many also did voluntary work or part-time jobs in places such as the new works' and schools' canteens.

Rises in production

Aircraft production rose from 2,800 planes in 1939 to 26,000 in 1944. By then they were the large heavy bombers which developed into the post-war airliners. The war gave a modernising shot in the arm to other important industries. Electric furnaces were built to smelt the highest quality steels, more loading equipment was put in mines and tens of thousands of high-quality machine tools were made to turn out weapons.

Science-based industry

Scientists played a leading part. In 1941 Frank Whittle invented the jet engine. The new fibre, nylon, saved hundreds of lives when it was used for parachutes. The atomic bomb grew out of discoveries of British physicists (and many went to join the teams which made it in the USA). Radar guided planes and ships, and tracked down the enemy. A house in Buckinghamshire held Colossus, the world's first electronic computer. It had no storage memory but it made thousands of rapid calculations to crack enemy codes.

Wartime welfare

The war brought great hardships but many benefits. Very few people were unemployed. Women going out to work meant that family earnings could usually keep ahead of rising prices. Rationing meant that some families got more milk, eggs and meat than they had eaten before the war. People doing heavy jobs got larger rations and there were issues of orange juice, cod-liver oil and milk for infants. Planning in industry led to the 'utility' scheme for low-cost furniture and clothes made by standardised methods. Factory inspectors ordered employers to open canteens and a national system of school meals was started.

Post-war planning

Some wartime civil servants believed that these improvements showed that planning for the nation as a whole should be continued after the war. They prepared schemes for education (Unit 123), town planning (Unit 114), as well as William Beveridge's plan for a new welfare state (Unit 112). Beveridge also wrote a report on *Full Employment in a Free Society* which took ideas from J.M. Keynes, who worked as a civil servant during the war.

The 1945 general election

Winston Churchill and some Conservative ministers were not so keen on keeping government planning. Labour leaders, however, believed that most people wanted change. After Hitler was defeated in May 1945 they insisted on holding a general election without waiting for victory over Japan. In the campaign the Labour Party promised full employment and welfare schemes. They said they would bring these about by keeping the most important wartime controls and nationalising some key industries. The election was on 5 July with a three-week wait while soldiers' votes came in by post. At the count on 26 July the Labour Party had 180 more MPs than the Conservatives. Clement Attlee became Prime Minister of a Labour government.

Planning, persuasion, propaganda

A

*Rationing.
The front page and page 7 of a 1942 government pamphlet explaining clothes rationing.*

7. Number of coupons needed for the principal articles of adults' and children's clothing

The following table sets out the number of coupons needed for various articles of clothing, other than the following :—Infants' clothing (para. 8) ; industrial overalls (para. 9) ; industrial footwear (para. 10) ; officers' special uniform garments (para. 11) ; nurses' special garments (para. 12). The figures in the last column apply only to young children's wear which is exempt from Purchase Tax because of its size and character (not merely because it is Utility) ; the number of coupons needed depends on the garment—*not* on the age of the child.

	Man	Woman	★Child
Group I covers the following types of goods :—Woollen (i.e. containing more than 15 per cent. by weight of wool), fur, imitation fur, leather, imitation leather, corduroy (except Utility fustian cloths nos. 309, 310, 3090-1, 3100-3107), velvet, velveteen, and all pile fabrics except towelling. All other goods are in Group II. Saddle-lined garments are rated as unlined. Fur includes imitation fur.			
Overcoat, Raincoat, etc.			
¶ Mackintosh, raincoat, overcoat, cape (except cycling cape), cloak—			
(a) if unlined, single texture, and Group II	9	9	7
(b) if fully lined and Group I	18	18	11
(c) other than those in (a) and (b)	16	15	10
Detached lining for overcoat, raincoat or mackintosh	7	7	4
Jacket, Cardigan, Waistcoat or Pullover			
§ Jacket, blouse-type jacket, sleeved waistcoat, coat, blazer, cycling cape, woman's half-length cape, woman's bolero—			
(a) if lined and Group I	13	12	8
(b) if unlined, single texture, and Group II	6	6	4
(c) if unlined, blouse-type and knitted	8	8	5
(d) other than those in (a), (b) or (c)	10	10	6
† Bolero, short jacket, short cape—			
(a) if Group I and with sleeves of not less than elbow length		5	
(b) if Group II and with no sleeves or with sleeves of less than elbow length		2	
(c) other than those in (a) or (b)		3	
Sweater, jersey, jumper, pullover, cardigan, woman's bedjacket— if Group I and weighing at least 10 ozs. (7 ozs. for children)	8	8	5
Cotton football jersey	4		2
Waistcoat, pullover, jumper, cardigan, woman's bedjacket, jersey, sweater—other than those described above	5	5	3
Trousers, Shorts or Skirt			
**Trousers, slacks, over-trousers, **breeches, jodhpurs—			
(a) if lined and Group I	11		8
(b) if unlined and Group II	5	5	4
(c) other than those in (a) or (b)	8	8	6
Shorts—			
(a) if fully-lined and Group I	6	6	4
(b) if not fully-lined and Group II	3	3	2
(c) other than those in (a) or (b)	5	5	3
Skirt, divided skirt—of Group I		6	4
Skirt, divided skirt—of Group II		4	3
Kilt (with or without bodice)	16	14	8

★ Young children's wear of a size, style and character, which is exempt from Purchase Tax, even if not Utility.
¶ Women's coats and capes fall into one of these categories if over 28 in. long.
§ Women's coats, capes and jackets fall into one of these categories if over 16 in. but not over 28 in. long.
† Not over 16 in. long, and not fur.
** Until December 31st, 1942, men's and youths' corduroy trousers and breeches may be sold at the Group II Coupon rating, even though not made from Utility fustian cloth, provided the price does not exceed 30s. retail (22s. 6d. wholesale) including Purchase Tax.

Foreword
from the President of the Board of Trade

The people of this country can congratulate themselves on the results of clothes rationing. In the first twelve months more than a quarter of a million tons of shipping space were saved in textiles alone. Nearly four hundred thousand men and women have been released from making cloth and clothing for civilians, and have gone into the Services or on to war production, while the workers that are left can be confident that they are making only the necessaries of war-time life.

The increasing strain of war on our supplies has made inevitable a cut in the clothing ration. But the cut is least for those whose needs are greatest, the children and the industrial workers.

Any sacrifice of comfort or appearance, which clothes rationing may bring to any of us, will, I am sure, be cheerfully borne, in order that victory may come sooner. Many patriotic people have returned unused coupons to the Board of Trade thus helping our war effort by saving precious shipping space, material and labour. I hope that many more will do the same.

Hugh Dalton.

B *(left)*

Evacuation. Bombing did not start until nearly a year after the war had broken out. By then many women had sent for their evacuated children to return home. The government issued this poster in 1940.

C *(right)*

Economising. The Railway Executive ran the railways for the government.

D

Planning. Hugh Dalton, the President of the Board of Trade, looks back. An extract from his autobiography.

"I regarded some national control of industrial location as vital; by giving information to employers ... and by the use of building licences which, for new industrial buildings, the Board of Trade controlled.

In August 1943 Sam Courtauld came to see me. He wished to act in conformity with the Government's plans for post-war employment; I suggested that he should put some of the new factories which his firm were going to build in Distressed Areas. I sent him particulars of a number of suitable sites and he adopted some of my suggestions."
H. Dalton, *The Fateful Years*, 1952

E

Censorship. This photograph was taken after heavy bombing on Derby. The government censor would not allow it to be published at the time.

Sources A–E

1 *What do all these sources tell you about the role of government in wartime?*
2 *In what ways do Sources A and C deal with the same problem?*
3 *What different approaches to public opinion can be seen in Sources B and E?*
4 *Imagine a mother and father looking at the poster in Source B. Write the conversation which might take place.*
5 *What argument would there be for and against publishing Source E?*
6 *Which distressed areas would most interest Sam Courtauld as sites for his new factories? Give your reasons.*

105
The austerity years

The Labour Party was in power from 1945 to 1951. In these years of shortages and 'austerity', industry recovered and there was full employment. A public sector in the economy was built up by nationalising large industries.

The effects of war

In 1945 the country was in a bad way, with factories, homes and docks smashed by bombs. Railways and roads, carriages and lorries, were worn out. Britain had lost £1,000 million of overseas investments, and earnings from trade had shrunk to tiny figures. She had £3,300 million of debts to other countries. J.M. Keynes was sent to the USA to ask for a loan. Canada chipped in with another. But now Britain owed more. To get out of the red in five years she would have to increase her exports by 75 per cent.

Post-war controls

So the Labour government had two aims: full employment and an export drive. For both they used controls left over from wartime. Motor firms were told they could have steel only if they made cars for export. Building licences were needed for new factories and offices. The government gave them to firms who would open factories in areas of pre-war unemployment. Hoover went to Merthyr Tydfil. Ford was sent to Liverpool and Chrysler to Scotland.

Progress 1945–50

By 1950 the country was well on target. Exports were 77 per cent up on 1946 and they were mostly in the heavy industries: machinery, chemicals, steel, vehicles and ships. At the same time home production was keeping out imported factory-made goods. British-made television sets were flowing into the shops.

It was expensive to buy petrol from the USA. Instead refineries were built around the coast to make it out of cheaper crude oil bought from Arab countries (who were paid in pounds, not dollars). Oil refining gave the raw material for man-made fibres such as nylon, rayon and terylene. Jobs in this industry helped to make up for losses in cotton which stayed on hard times.

Austerity

To meet the export drive meant doing without luxuries – or 'austerity' as Stafford Cripps liked to call it. He was Chancellor of the Exchequer from 1947 to 1950. Some rationing was tighter than in wartime. Fuel was hard to get and people shivered in homes, schools and factories through the coldest winter of the century in 1947. Tens of thousands were on waiting-lists for new houses.

The first sterling crisis

In 1948 and 1949 the government tried to make life a bit easier with a 'bonfire of controls'. Some goods were no longer rationed and some licences were scrapped. More imported goods came into the country. But not for long. In 1949 Stafford Cripps announced that the imports were causing too much money to be sent out of Britain to the USA and other dollar-using countries. He devalued the pound from $4.00 to $2.80. This helped exports by making British goods cheaper in dollar countries. But it put up prices of imports and forced people to do without many of them.

The trade unions

The years of austerity had another side. There was full employment. In many families, earnings stayed ahead of price rises because there was more work outside the home for women (see also Unit 121). The trade unions agreed to share in austerity by not making high wage demands. The only long strike was in the docks where men were still treated as 'casual' workers.

Election campaigns

Yet, by 1950, austerity was making the Labour Government unpopular with some voters. In the June general election it held on to power by a majority of just eight. There was another election in 1951 which the Conservatives won. One great argument in these elections was over the programme for nationalisation.

Nationalisation

The Conservatives had nationalised some industries before the war: the electricity grid, and two airlines as well as London Transport which ran the underground and buses. After the war Labour added to these with British European Airways (BEA) and the Bank of England. But these were tiny steps compared with making a large public sector out of coal, gas, electricity, transport and steel. These industries gave jobs to a fifth of all Britain's workers.

The public-sector industries

The industries were taken over from local councils or private owners (who were paid compensation). They did not go into government ownership but public ownership, run by their own boards. The boards were chosen by the government but they had to make their own decisions about how to run the business.

The government did not expect the boards to make big profits for many years. Its main reason for nationalising industries was to modernise them so that they could offer a better service. For instance, there were still 500 separately owned power-stations feeding into the national grid. Nationalising coal gave a chance to end the bitter disputes between miners and owners. It was possible to mechanise small pits and make overdue improvements, such as providing pit-head baths.

There was a single Transport Commission to make overall plans for roads, rail, canals and ports. British Road Services built up a goods-carrying service which used thousands of lorries. It began to make a profit while the railways made a loss because the government would not let them borrow all the money they needed.

The Conservatives did not object to nationalising coal, gas, electricity and transport. But they fought strongly against public ownership of steel. They said it was an efficient industry which did not need reorganising. The Labour Party said it was too important to the rest of industry to leave alone, and nationalised steel in early 1951. The Conservatives promised they would de-nationalise it – which they did in 1953, along with the road services.

A new spirit
A

J.B. Priestley wrote a novel about three men 'demobbed' from the army. One of them says:

1 *How does the extract from J.B. Priestley's book help to explain (a) why Labour had so much support in the 1940s, and (b) the post-war economic recovery of Britain?*

B

Miners congratulating themselves on beating their target, 1946.

2 *Why were many factories and pits given weekly targets?*
3 *Why was coal output particularly important?*
4 *Can you explain the most obvious difference between production on different days?*
5 *Can you see any connection between this scene and the views of the man in Source A?*

"We don't talk about liberty when what we really mean is a chance to fleece the public. We don't go back on all we said when the country was in danger. We stop trying for some easy money. We do an honest job of work for the community for what the community thinks we're worth. We stop being lazy, stupid and callous. . . . Instead of guessing and grabbing, we plan. Instead of competing, we co-operate."

J.B. Priestley, *Three Men in New Suits*, 1945

Nationalisation
C

This cartoon was called 'Let Battle Commence'. The Daily Herald *was owned by the trade union movement.*

6 *Imagine that you were the person who drew this. Explain what message you were hoping to get across and whom you would most expect to believe it.*
7 *Design a poster which puts the anti-nationalisation point of view.*

Daily Herald,
17 October 1948

106
From affluence to decline

Between 1950 and the mid 1970s the economy grew faster than at any time in the twentieth century. This led to better living conditions but industry was becoming less efficient and losing its share of world trade.

The economy of the 1960s

In 1957 when Harold Macmillan, the Conservative Prime Minister, said 'You've never had it so good', many believed him, even while they knew it was a boast to gain votes. Unemployment stayed low and even in bad years it only reached about 400,000. More women were going out to work, so family earnings were often high enough to pay for motor cars, kitchen equipment and electrical goods. Many people began to buy their own homes. Pay for wage-earners rose more than professional people's salaries. This seemed to bear out Keynes's view that if ordinary people had money to spend it would keep industry busy and employment high. Of course, some people did not share in the new 'affluence' as it was sometimes called. Many were immigrants who had been encouraged to come to Britain because there was a shortage of workers (see Unit 117).

Britain had an important business in building new aircraft, helicopters and hovercraft. Her chemicals industry led the world in inventing new fibres and polythene products. There were booms in fertilisers, medicines and paints. In the new field of electronics Britain specialised in communications equipment – which helped the change-over from telephone operators to automatic exchanges.

Power supplies

Fuel and power were modernised. Coal output fell from 227 million tonnes in 1954 to 124 million tonnes in 1981 but the workforce dropped from 700,000 to 230,000. Fewer miners could produce more coal per worker. Most of them worked in newer pits so nine-tenths of the coal was cut and loaded by machine.

By 1970 two-thirds of every tonne of coal went to power stations. The air above Britain's towns became free of the smoke and grit which had covered them for 150 years. The clean air programme was helped by the closing of gasworks as the Gas Board tapped natural gas from under the North Sea. By the 1970s there were thirteen nuclear power-stations where uranium atoms were split to make heat which produced steam to turn electricity generators. Then development slowed down, because of high costs and because of evidence that nuclear power-stations were not absolutely safe.

North Sea oil

In the 1960s oil and petrol were becoming the cheapest fuel for railway locomotives, heating and other uses in industry. Then in 1973 the cost shot up when Arab countries raised prices in protest at Western nations' support for Israel in the Arab-Israeli wars. But two years earlier a test drill in the Forties Field in the North Sea had found oil which was worth the heavy cost of drilling and piping ashore. The government divided the North Sea into blocks where oil companies paid for the right to drill from their rigs.

In 1975 the first regular supplies of North Sea oil were brought to Aberdeen and by 1981 Britain was getting more oil than she needed for home use. Oil created many new jobs, especially in Scotland. The companies paid taxes to the government and royalties (payment per barrel) to the British National Oil Corporation. The money helped to close the gap in Britain's balance of payments. That pushed up the value of the pound against the dollar.

Yet the overall gain to Britain was small. A 'strong' pound meant that countries who paid in dollars had to pay more for British exports so they bought fewer. Industry did not get cheap fuel because oil prices were fixed at the high world level.

Service industries

Each year more people turned to jobs in servicing and maintenance, helping the change-over to North Sea gas, installing new telephones, laying TV cables. Others went into selling, in shops and mail-order firms, or into advertising. Industry needed fewer workers because of mechanisation, especially when computers were used to control machines or look after warehouse stocks.

This switch-over to service industries was happening in other countries too. But while Britain's economy had been growing at about 2½ per cent some of her rivals had advanced two or three times as fast. She actually had a lower standard of living than many other European countries. The key problem was productivity. British workers in industry were increasing the amount they produced at a slower rate than people in other countries. Britain's share in world trade fell from a sixth in the early 1960s to under a tenth in the mid 1970s. Poor productivity also meant a huge rise in imports of cheaper manufactured goods.

In 1965, 95 per cent of all cars on British roads were made in British factories; in 1980 it was 43 per cent. In the same years Britain's share of world car sales fell from 11 per cent to 4 per cent. The ship-building industry had been the world's largest in 1950. By 1980 it was in eighth place, mostly because other countries used more automated methods and built more specialised ships such as oil tankers. In 1950 the British steel industry provided 10 million tonnes. It built new mills turning out continuous 'strips' of steel. By 1970 output had reached 27.9 million tonnes. By 1980 this had fallen back to 11.4 million.

Productivity
A

Changes in output in industry per hour worked, 1960–74.

1 *Use this chart to explain what productivity means.*
2 *What effect does productivity have on (a) imports, (b) exports, (c) the balance of trade?*
3 *What explanations would you give for Britain's low increase in productivity?*

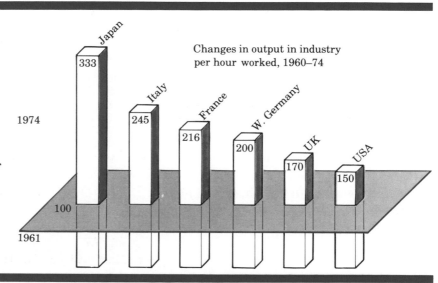

Changes in output in industry per hour worked, 1960–74

Sixty years of the same job
B *(above)*
A sixteen-man crew which laid the Birmingham–St Albans telephone cable in 1914.

C *(right)*
The same job being done in Oxford in 1957.

D
Laying a fibre optic cable for telephones in 1976.

Sources B–D
4 What do these three photographs tell you about
   (a) changes in the nature of work,
   (b) changes in employment,
   (c) changes in social class?
5 What evidence is there in Source D for changes that have taken place in other industries?

107 Governments and the economic decline

Up to the mid 1970s Conservative and Labour governments tried to manage the economy with stop–go and incomes policies. In 1974 there was a serious slump. The unit ends with a look at Labour and Conservative policies since then.

Stop–go

Both Conservative and Labour leaders agreed by the mid 1960s that one important cause of the decline was their own policy of 'stop–go'. It arose from J.M. Keynes's teaching that it was the government's job to keep the economy growing. When industry seemed to need this kind of push, the Chancellor of the Exchequer signalled 'go'. He lowered tax and bank rates and allowed easier terms for hire purchase. His hope would be that, as people bought more goods, companies would borrow more to invest in up-to-date equipment.

'Go'

A 'go' lasted only a year or two before there was a jump in imports. That was bound to happen if firms were going to use more raw materials, but money went out to pay for them, so there was a larger gap in visible trade. That led to a sterling crisis. Since 1918 Britain had been more important in the world as a banker than as a manufacturer. As a banker with not too many goods to sell, she was watched carefully by foreigners who had money earning interest in the British 'reserves'. If they thought her trade gap would widen they decided to put their money in another country.

'Stop'

But the government could not allow these reserve to shrink. So the Chancellor signalled a 'stop'. He put up taxes and bank rates and limited hire purchase. The high bank rates brought money back into the country but they made it expensive for industry to modernise. So when the time came for another 'go', workers were using equipment which was a couple more years out of date.

Income policies

Because they knew that stop–go was harmful, governments tried to get together with the unions and employers to agree on other schemes. The Macmillan Conservative government set up 'Neddy', the National Economic Development Council (NEDC) in 1961. The Wilson Labour government followed in 1966 with a National Prices and Incomes Board (NPIB).

The NEDC and NPIB were linked with the governments' belief that they needed 'incomes policies' to stop wage rises pushing up prices. One way was to weaken the power of unions to carry out damaging strikes (see Unit 110). Another was wage freezes, or pauses. The first freeze came in 1961 when the Chancellor, Selwyn Lloyd, tried to persuade everyone to agree to no more than a 2 per cent rise. In 1967 the Labour government tried to get the Prices and Incomes Board to disapprove of all wage rises over a 'norm' of 3 per cent. When this failed the government put on a total freeze for six months. Edward Heath's government began with a freeze in 1972 followed by pay limits. He could not make the limits work and lost an election which he called in 1974 to judge whether or not the miners were right to strike for a 17 per cent pay rise.

The world slump

That was the end of twenty-five years in which unemployment had never been more than 3 per cent and inflation was usually below 5 or 6 per cent. But then the world was in a slump, triggered by the sharp leap in oil prices in 1973. In Britain that pushed inflation up to nearly 30 per cent by the end of 1974.

Labour policies, 1974–79

The crisis brought an end to any agreement between the parties. From 1974 to 1979 Labour was in power. To tackle inflation they relied on the unions to carry through drastic incomes policies. To deal with unemployment the new National Enterprise Board pumped millions of pounds into British Leyland and other firms. The government refused to let the British Steel Corporation close down steelworks even though sales were slumping.

For four years, from 1974 to 1978, these policies kept the support of the unions (and many other people), even though government spending on other public services was cut. Inflation was brought down to 8 per cent and unemployment had gone up to only 5½ per cent. But there were two big questions. First, had the policies of hanging on to sick industries really helped for the future? Second, how much longer would the unions go along with wage policies? In the 'winter of discontent' in 1978–9, unions struck for wage increases which were soon running at about 15 per cent.

Conservative policies, 1979–86

In May 1979 the Conservatives, led by Margaret Thatcher, won the election. Her government believed it should make beating inflation its main priority. To do this they tried monetarism, the idea that inflation comes about because there is too much money circulating. So the government cut the amount of money spent on local government, roads, education and nationalised industries. It refused to help industries pay more wages and keep more workers than they could afford. A new chairman of British Steel, Ian MacGregor (an American), was brought in to close steelworks which he did after a long strike. After that the government transferred him to the National Coal Board which it believed had too many pits which were not making profits. The Coal Board had built up enough stocks to keep the power-stations going and to defeat a year-long strike against closures by more than two-thirds of the miners' union. At British Leyland (BL), Michael Edwardes was able to make workers redundant. After much resistance, the unions accepted that there would be no extra government help and agreed to his pay offer.

Another Conservative aim was to encourage more private investment in industry. It hoped to do this by cutting taxes so that people would have more savings to invest. But it could afford only small cuts, partly because of the costs of unemployment benefit. It had more success with 'privatisation', or selling parts of nationalised industries to private shareholders. This could be done only with profit-making industries such as Jaguar (which was split off from BL), British Telecom and parts of the aircraft and oil industries.

The Conservative policies caused a chain of unemployment and bankruptcies. By 1986, unemployment was over 3 million (or more than 13 per cent). Inflation was down to around 5 per cent. That was important for people who had to live on small incomes. But the same question-mark hung over the Conservative government as over Labour. Had it really made industry ready for a revival?

Stop–go
A
The Labour Prime Minister, Harold Wilson, spoke to Parliament in 1966.

1 *Was Wilson announcing a 'stop' or a 'go'?*
2 *What would be the effect of the changes for people who made household goods?*

"The down payment on cars, motor cycles and caravans is raised to 40 per cent and the repayment shortened by 24 months. The down payment on furniture is raised to 20 per cent and repayment period shortened to 24 months. The down payment on domestic appliances is raised by $33\frac{1}{3}$ per cent . . . it is estimated that this will cut hire-purchase borrowing by £160 million."
Parliamentary Debates, 20 July 1966

Inflation
B
The retail price index, 1961–83.

3 *What caused the first peak in the graph?*
4 *What led to the fall in inflation after 1981?*

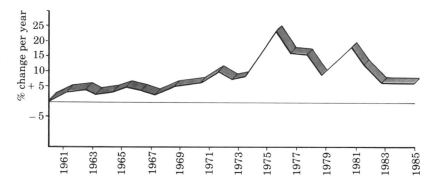

C
Stan Taylor, a lecturer at Warwick University, described the effect of Labour and Conservative policies on Conventry.

5 *How does his account illustrate the difference between the policies of the Labour government from 1974 to 1979 and the policies of the Conservatives after 1979?*

"In 1975 Coventry's Chrysler plants were only saved from closure by a government loan of £162 million, British Leyland with five major plants in the city was nationalised, and the Coventry tool making firm, Alfred Herbert, was taken under the wing of the National Enterprise Board. This effectively meant that in the late 1970s, one in four Coventry workers was directly or indirectly dependent upon the state for his job. . . .

In 1980, the city's industrial base began to collapse. BL's rationalisation programme led to the closure of its plant at Canley (5,500 jobs), and the loss of 1,600 jobs at the Jaguar factory as well as a further 250 at the Climax works. This job-cutting was, of course, a condition of continued government aid to the company. On the government's insistence, the National Enterprise Board sold the Alfred Herbert firm to a private company, which made redundancies (which eventually totalled 900) a condition of purchase. . . . The problems of these major firms meant the contraction or closure of many minor firms. . . These losses, added to the lack of jobs for school-leavers, raised the rate of unemployment from 6 per cent in January 1980 to 10.9 per cent in September."
B. Crick (ed.), *Unemployment*, 1981

108
Conciliation or strife

In the 1890s governments took the first steps to help unions and employers sort out disagreements. The unit also describes how the railwaymen, dockers and miners (who made up a Triple Alliance in 1914) fought employers and the government just before and after the First World War.

Conciliation Boards

In 1893 the government set up a Labour Department. Its civil servants were given the job of trying to get peaceful settlements between unions and employers. They usually set up a Conciliation Board where the two sides could meet with a neutral chairman. Employers in large industries often ignored the Labour Department. They formed their own national organisations to fight unionism.

Industrial unions

The union reply was to build large 'industrial' unions, one for each industry. In 1910 Ben Tillett and the seamen's leader joined their unions into a National Transport Workers' Federation (NTWF). The NTWF then began to draw in other transport workers. In Bristol a young man who delivered soft drinks, Ernest Bevin, started a branch for local carters. In 1912 four railway unions came together in the National Union of Railwaymen (NUR).

The Miners, the NTWF and the NUR made up the three biggest unions. Between 1910 and 1912 each led a strike which closed the ports, railways or mines. They were the first nationwide strikes and far too big for the Labour Department to handle. The Chancellor of the Exchequer, Lloyd George, took over the job of peace-making. Each time, he got the two sides together to draw up an agreement. In all three cases the employers later broke part of their promises. So the three unions agreed in June 1914 to work together. This was the Triple Alliance and it was important in the 1920s. But first there was a war to fight.

1914—18

In 1915 unions agreed to allow 'dilution' or letting unskilled workers do craft jobs. Union leaders were given places on committees planning the war effort and three became government ministers. In 1917 the Ministry of Labour started Joint Industrial Councils (or Whitley Councils) of unionists and employers to advise the government on everything to do with their industry. By 1920 there were sixty-eight.

All these changes helped trade unions to double their numbers during the war. Yet some unionists thought their leaders were selling out to the government. The strongest complaints came from shop stewards on the Clyde. They formed their own Clyde Workers' Committee which ignored union leaders in London and led strikes against dilution and for wage rises. The government's reply was tough. Seven shop stewards were arrested and sent to prison.

Triple Alliance

In the war the mines and railways had been under government control. This was not given up until 1921. So when the Triple Alliance showed its strength in 1919 it was acting against the government. By standing together, the three unions forced it to give up plans for a wage cut on the railways and won a temporary rise for miners. The NTWF had its own success. Dock employers refused to pay a wage claim in 1920 and the union took them to an industrial court. The NTWF's national organiser was now Ernest Bevin. For twenty days he cross-examined witnesses for the employers. One said that a docker's wage would pay for a healthy diet. Bevin proved him wrong by cooking food to show just what scrappy meals it would buy. The court gave the dockers their rise.

In March 1921 the government handed the mines back to the owners and their first act was to cut pay. The Miners' Federation called on the Triple Alliance to back a strike. The railwaymen and transport workers agreed. Then on 'Black Friday', 15 April, they backed down because they believed the miners should have at least tried to negotiate with the owners. The Triple Alliance was dead.

Rise and fall of the Triple Alliance

A

The President of the Miners' Federation wrote this in 1916.

1 *What does the writer suggest was the background to the Triple Alliance?*

2 *Which was the largest group of workers in the NTWF?*

3 *What would be the programme of events before the Triple Alliance acted?*

"One definite concrete result of the industrial unrest of recent years is the formation of the Triple Industrial Alliance proposed at a conference of the Miners' Federation of Great Britain, the National Union of Railwaymen, and the National Transport Workers' Federation, held on April 23rd, 1914. . . .

The predominant idea of the alliance is that each of these great fighting organisations, before embarking upon any movement . . . should formulate its programme, submit it to the others, and that upon joint proposals joint action should then be taken."
R. Smillie, *Labour Year Book*, 1916

B

From the Daily Herald, *a paper paid for by trade unions.*

4 *What event is the* Daily Herald *writing about?*

5 *Which of the unions mentioned was not a member of the Triple Alliance? Suggest why it had been drawn into the strike plans.*

6 *What justification was there for the phrase 'a smashing frontal attack upon the workers' standard of life'?*

"Yesterday was the heaviest defeat that has befallen the Labour Movement within the memory of man.

It is no use trying to minimise it. It is no use trying to pretend it is other than it is. We on this paper have said throughout that if the organised workers would stand together they would win. They have not stood together, and they have been beaten. . . .

The National Union of Railwaymen, the Transport Workers' Federation, the Associated Society of Locomotive Engineers and Firemen have called off their strike, the Miners are fighting on. . . .

The owners and the Government have delivered a smashing frontal attack upon the workers' standard of life. . . .

The Triple Alliance, the Trades Union Congress, the General Staff, have all failed to function. We must start afresh and get a machine that *will* function."
Daily Herald, 16 April 1921

109
1926: 'National' or 'General' strike

In the early 1920s several new large unions were set up and the TUC was given a General Council to help in disputes. In 1926 it called a nine-day strike in support of the miners.

Larger unions

After Black Friday the miners had to take a wage cut, but so did dockers, railwaymen, building workers and others. Union membership fell from 8 to 5½ million. Ernest Bevin led the fight back. The first need was for even larger unions. Bevin's NTWF joined with other unions into the Transport and General Workers' Union with half a million members. Gasworkers and manual workers followed with the General and Municipal Workers' Union and the engineering unions combined in the Amalgamated Engineering Union. In 1921 Bevin got the TUC to set up a General Council with power to call union leaders to discuss plans if a major strike seemed likely.

Pit wage cuts

In 1925, after Britain went back to the gold standard (see Unit 103), the miners were again told to take a wage cut by the owners. The General Council got union leaders to stop all movements of coal. This would have brought industry to a standstill. The government bought time by agreeing to pay a subsidy to the mine-owners so that miners could keep their wages for nine months. In that time a Commission, led by Lord Samuel, would look into the industry.

The unions called that day 'Red Friday'. But the Prime Minister, Stanley Baldwin, was under pressure from mine-owners and Tory MPs, as well as people who asked whether Britain was to be ruled by Parliament or a handful of union leaders. His government prepared. It divided the country into districts which would be run in an emergency by Commissioners who could swear in special constables. The OMS, or Organisation for the Movement of Supplies, drew up lists of volunteers.

Samuel Report, 1926

In March 1926 the Samuel Commission recommended cuts in wages but not longer hours. The miners would not accept the first and the owners would not agree to the second. To force the miners to take cuts and longer hours they locked them out of the pits. The General Council called a meeting where union leaders agreed a 'national strike' of key workers on 3 May. They hoped the threat would force the government to a settlement. On Sunday 2 May they thought they had an agreement with the Cabinet. Then Stanley Baldwin called off the talks because he was angry that printers refused to print an anti-union article in the *Daily Mail*.

The nine-day strike

The strike was on and lasted for nine days. Workers in transport, iron and steel, electricity, gas, building and newspaper printing all stopped work. The government called it a 'general' strike and said it was a move by the unions to take over the running of the country. It printed its views in an official paper, *The British Gazette*, run by Winston Churchill. Thousands of special constables were sworn in, although there was little trouble between strikers and police. OMS volunteers drove a few trains and lorries. They were usually protected by large numbers of police or troops and did very little to dent the standstill in transport. The TUC said it was a 'national' strike in sympathy with the miners and it was not about winning political power. These views were printed in their news-sheet, *The British Worker*. In every town there was a local strike committee which tried to keep essential supplies moving by giving tickets to lorries carrying essential food and medicine.

The strike ends

After nine days the TUC called off the strike. It wanted the miners and owners to negotiate but the miners' leader, A.J. Cook, stuck to his slogan of 'not a penny off the pay, not a second on the day'. The owners were just as obstinate. The miners stayed locked out for seven months before they went back on the owners' terms.

The strike weakened the unions. In 1927 MPs passed the Trade Disputes Act which made sympathetic strikes (in support of another union) illegal. It also changed the rules about paying the political levy to the Labour Party. Unions could now only pass on part of the subscriptions of members who had signed a form 'contracting in'. That was a blow to the funds of the Labour Party.

By 1939 the union movement and the Labour Party were recovering. There were 154 Labour MPs and union numbers were rising. Unions had two respected leaders: Walter Citrine, the TUC general secretary, and Ernest Bevin. In 1940 the Labour Party joined the war coalition and Bevin became Minister of Labour. After the war he was Foreign Secretary in the Labour Government which had the 1927 Trade Disputes Act repealed in 1946.

Moving supplies
A *(right)*
A food convoy passing through East London, May 1926.

B
A cartoon in the bulletin of the St Pancras strike committee.

POLICEMAN: "We don't seem to get many passengers."
VOLUNTEER: "But we are making a good IMPRESSION!"

Sources A–B
1 *What kind of vehicle is leading the convoy in Source A?*
2 *Is there any evidence that it was needed at the time the photograph was taken?*
3 *What comment is the bulletin (Source B) making about scenes such as that in Source A?*

General strike
C

An attack on the unions in the British Gazette.

4 *Summarise Lord Grey's view of the strike in your own words.*
5 *Does he give any evidence to support his view?*

"Neither in fact, nor, I believe in law, is the course adopted by the Trade Unions a strike in the proper sense of the term. It is an attempted revolution.

Were it to succeed the community would thenceforth be ruled by a relatively small body of extremists who regard trades unions not as the machinery for collective bargaining but as a political instrument . . . "
Lord Grey, *British Gazette*, May 1926

National Strike
D

An extract from the British Worker.

"We are entering upon the second week of the general stoppage in support of the mine workers against the attack upon their standard of life by the coalowners.

Nothing could be more wonderful than the magnificent response of millions.

From every town and city in the country reports are pouring into the General Council headquarters that all ranks are solid, that the working men and women are resolute in their determination to resist the unjust attack upon the mining community."
British Worker, May 1926

E
A table of wages from the British Worker.

Sources D–E

6 *What is meant by 'the lock-out' in Source E?*
7 *What did the owners expect miners to do before they were allowed back to work?*
8 *Suggest reasons why there were such differences between miners' earnings.*
9 *What do these two sources tell you about the General Council's reasons for calling the strike?*

OWNERS' DRASTIC PROPOSALS

The Miners' Federation prepared a table showing a comparison of wages payable to certain representative classes of day-wage workers before the lock-out and the wages that would be paid under the terms of the owners' demands posted at the pit-heads.

The following figures were taken from the statement. Similar reductions were demanded in other districts.

On the basis of a 5½ day week the reductions range from 3s. 9d. to 17s. 2d. a week.

	Present wages s. d.	Owners' terms s. d.	Reduction per day. s. d.
Scotland			
Coal hewers	9 4	7 6	1 10
Labourers	6 8¼	6 0	8¼
Northumberland—			
Hewers	10 4	7 7	2 9
Labourers	7 7½	4 9	3 1½
Durham—			
Hewers	9 8	6 10	2 10
Labourers	7 6½	4 11¾	2 6¾
South Wales and Monmouthshire—			
Hewers	9 9¼	7 2½	2 6¾
Labourers (day)	8 0¾	*6 8	*1 4¾
South Yorks			
Hewers	10 7½	9 6¾	1 0¾
Labourers	8 8½	7 6½	1 2
Lancashire			
Hewers	9 6½	8 1½	1 5
Labourers	8 8½	6 2	2 5½
North Wales			
Hewers	9 4½	7 8	1 8½
Labourers	6 5	5 0	1 5
Derbyshire			
Hewers	11 8¾	10 6¾	1 2
Labourers (surface)	8 8½	7 6½	1 2
Notts—			
Hewers	12 1¼	10 10½	1 2¾
Labourers (surface)	8 5½	7 3¾	1 1¾

*If married. For single men the rate would be 5s. 9d. a day, a reduction of 2s. 3¾d. a day.

British Worker, May 1926

110
Unions and government

In the years after 1945 union membership grew particularly among women and white-collar workers. Parliament passed many laws dealing with the rights of union members. Others dealt with industrial relations. There were also many attempts to find a way to keep wage claims down, and the story of these pauses and freezes is told in Unit 107.

Growth of unions

From 1945 to 1979 the number of people in unions went up from $7\frac{3}{4}$ million to over 11 million. The number of women union members nearly doubled. Unionism spread among people who did white-collar jobs as well as footballers and musicians. The biggest unions were still the TGWU and the GMWU, but the miners and railway workers were well down the list behind public employees, civil servants, shopworkers, teachers, and many others. Most workplaces had a shop steward or union representative.

The old unions paid most of the Labour Party's expenses and their leaders had a strong voice in its policy. But some newer unions did not join the Labour Party. If they did, large numbers of their members 'contracted out' of paying the political levy.

Anti-union opinion

Many public opinion polls showed that, while more people were joining unions, the trade union movement was thought to have too much power which it used badly. One reason may have been that members in one union thought that workers in another were getting too big a share of the cake. Another may have been that the popular daily newspapers were usually anti-union. A third was that some unions crossed over the line from industrial action against an employer to political action against the government.

'In Place of Strife'

Both political parties considered laws on industrial relations – bargaining between employers and unions. The first attempt was set out in a 1968 White Paper (a discussion paper) called 'In Place of Strife'. It was written by Barbara Castle, the Minister of Labour in Harold Wilson's Labour Government. She suggested that there should always be a ballot of members before a union went on strike and that the government should have the power to order a 28-day 'cooling off' time before it took place. The TUC led a strong union opposition and some Cabinet ministers feared that the Labour Party would lose union support. Harold Wilson ordered 'In Place of Strife' to be dropped.

Industrial Relations Act, 1971

Edward Heath's government was more prepared to tackle the unions. In 1971 their Industrial Relations Act said the 'closed shop' would not be legal, and that unions and employers should sign binding agreements on wage increases. It set up a National Industrial Relations Court to judge cases where employers said that unions had broken an agreement. The Court was used mostly in cases where unionists took 'unofficial' strike action. The TUC told unions to ignore the Act and organised strikes and a 'day of action'. The Engineering Union was fined heavily for refusing to obey the law. Many employers also thought it was a bad law which interfered with their relations with unions.

The 1974 election

Union power finally brought down Edward Heath's government in 1974. The miners put in a claim for wages well over the limit the government had set to try to control inflation. The government refused to let the National Coal Board pay the increase. The miners banned overtime and were joined by the railwaymen and power workers. The government declared a state of emergency which gave it powers to put all industry on to a three-day week to save energy. Edward Heath then called an election in February 1974 saying the electorate should decide on the right of the government to try to limit union power. His party lost and Harold Wilson came back as Prime Minister of a Labour government.

Three Labour laws 1975

The new government quickly gave the miners nearly all they had asked for and repealed the Industrial Relations Act. Labour then went on to pass three important laws in 1975. The Employment Protection Act brought workers' rights up to the level of that in other countries: it gave maternity leave with pay and guaranteed pay for workers put on short time. It also made much simpler arrangements for tribunals to judge cases where workers claimed they had been unfairly dismissed. The Health and Safety Act said that unions must be involved in the safety arrangements at work. The Sex Discrimination Act made it illegal to offer women lower pay and poorer chances of promotion.

ACAS

The most important move of this Labour government was new machinery for conciliation, which had been the job of government ministry staff since 1893. In their place came ACAS, the Advisory and Conciliation Service. The hope was that ACAS would be respected if it was not connected with a government department. In 1975 it helped with 2,500 industrial disputes.

'The winter of discontent'

These laws were one sign of a close partnership between the Labour government and the unions. The other side of the bargain was that union leaders backed wage limits of a few per cent or a small money increase up to mid-1978. In 'the winter of discontent' in 1978–9 the partnership broke down and there was a series of long strikes. They caused much anti-union feeling, especially when health workers' strikes led to longer waiting lists and difficulties for some patients. Critics of the health workers seemed to ignore just how low their pay was, and a fairer complaint was against secondary picketing when strikers in one industry tried to persuade workers in another to stop work.

Employment Acts, 1980 and 1982

The winter of discontent weakened the Labour Government just as the three-day week had weakened the Conservatives. In June 1979 Margaret Thatcher won a general election after promises to control union activities. Two Employment Acts followed in 1980 and 1982. The first made secondary picketing illegal. It also allowed closed shops only where 80 per cent of the employees in a workplace voted for it. The second said that employers who lost trade because of secondary picketing could sue the union for damages in court.

The Unions since 1945

A

Size and numbers of unions 1900–1980.

1 *Write a note to the table in Source A to explain: (a) the drop in numbers of unions, (b) the fall in numbers and members in 1930, (c) the fall in numbers in 1980, (d) the general increase in women unionists.*

	No. of Unions	No. of members (in 000s)		
		Men	Women	Total
1900	1,323	1,808	154	2,022
1910	1,269	2,287	278	2,565
1920	1,384	7,006	1,343	8,348
1930	1,121	4,049	793	4,842
1945	781	6,237	1,638	7,875
1950	732	7,605	1,684	9,289
1960	664	7,884	1,951	9,835
1970	540	8,440	2,740	11,179
1980	438	9,162	3,790	12,852

B

A cartoon of 1950. The three men are Stafford Cripps, Clement Attlee and Herbert Morrison, the Foreign Secretary.

2 *What comment is the cartoonist making about trade unions in 1950?*
3 *From your reading of this unit and Unit 105 on the Austerity Years, how fair a comment do you think Low was making?*

"I'LL ATTEND TO THE FOUNDATIONS LATER"

C

A cartoon on union power, April 1979.

4 *Whose heads had the unions collected in 1974 and 1979 and how?*
5 *How would you fill the third space?*

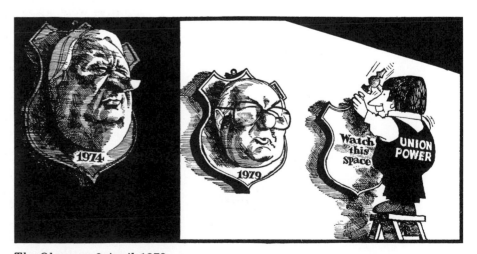

The Observer, 6 April 1979

111
Health between the wars

This is the first of four units on health, welfare and social conditions from 1913 to the present. It looks at general health between the wars and shows how average standards improved. However, causes of ill-health due to poverty and poor diet were still easily found.

Average living conditions

Between the wars the *average* person in Britain was better housed, better fed, less overcrowded and a good deal cleaner than before 1913. One reason for this was that wages for the *average* family rose higher than prices. Another was that the number of children in an *average* family fell from about three to two. Fewer children meant healthier mothers, more money to spend on food, heating and holidays and less overcrowding. The overcrowding problem was also helped by the great amount of house-building (described in Unit 114). Along with this went the work of carrying on the improvements in water supply and sewerage started in the nineteenth century. By the late 1930s most town houses had both, although only half had hot water taps and fixed baths. Even so they often had sculleries where clothes could be washed with water boiled on the fire or gas stove.

Diet and recreation

The *average* family in the 1930s was spending twice as much on fruit as on bread. This was just one of the signs of healthier eating compared with the nineteenth century. People from these earlier times would have been astonished to find one in every three families went away for a week's holiday every year. They might have been even more amazed to see men and women sea-bathing together, changing on the beach, lying in the sun. Farm workers would find it difficult to understand that young people actually enjoyed walking and cycling through the country to spend nights at youth hostels, started in 1930.

Better sanitation, housing and diet, as well as more leisure, all helped to improve the general health of the *average* person. They also cut down the numbers who caught the common diseases: tuberculosis, typhoid, diphtheria and scarlet fever.

Preventing disease

By 1922 enough was known about the bacillus which caused tuberculosis for the Ministry of Heath to order all milk to be pasteurised or sterilised so that the infection could not be passed on from cattle. From the 1930s vaccines to *prevent* diphtheria were given to most children. Success in *curing* disease was slower to come, although medical scientists knew what they were looking for: the 'magic bullet'.

New drugs

The idea came from the early twentieth century when a German scientist discovered that certain dyes could be used as medical drugs. The disease virus mistook the dyes for a vitamin it needed for food and poisoned itself on them. By the 1930s scientists in several countries found several of these magic bullets, which were known as sulphonamides or sulpha drugs. The British firm May and Baker's M&B drug was used to fight severe influenza and pneumonia, two common English diseases which often had been killers. But each sulphonamide usually worked for only one type of disease and the key to making a drug to cure most illnesses lay hidden in Alexander Fleming's notebooks from 1928 to 1938.

Alexander Fleming (1881–1955)

Alexander Fleming was a doctor in the research laboratories at St Mary's Hospital in London. To investigate ways of destroying harmful bacteria he grew germs on culture plates. In 1928 he noted that a mould was spreading from airborne spores which settled on the plate and killed the bacteria he was trying to grow. He had seen penicillin (which is the scientist's name for the mould that grows on jam or cheese) and guessed that it would make a good antibiotic (which is the scientists's name for microbes which destroy others).

Chain (1906–78) and Florey (1898–1968)

Alexander Fleming did not make enough mould to test out his guess and soon went back to other important work. Full study of penicillin only began again in 1938 when Dr Ernst Chain, a Jewish refugee from Nazi Germany, started work at an Oxford laboratory. In 1940, while British troops were fleeing Dunkirk, he showed that it could cure seriously ill mice. But humans are 3,000 times bigger than mice. Through the Battle of Britain and the 'Blitz', Dr Chain and his laboratory head, Dr Florey, worked day and night with six girl assistants to make enough penicillin for a human trial. In spring 1941 they could just manage six trials on dangerously ill humans. All were nearly totally successful.

Penicillin's inportance to the war effort was clear and tremendous efforts went on to mass produce it. Boots tried to grow it in a million milk bottles but the real breakthrough came after Florey and Chain visited the USA. Just before the Japanese attack on Pearl Harbor the Americans found a way to make penicillin in large tanks. By 1942 it was in the hands of doctors at the battle fronts and saving the first of thousands of lives. Only after the war was there enough for use on civilian patients.

Below the average

All these improvements in diet, social conditions and medicine helped to better the health of the *average* person. Yet no one is average and, in the 1930s, many people made studies which showed up wide differences.

In his book, *Food, Health and Income*, John Boyd Orr claimed that a tenth of the population was severely undernourished. A survey in Newcastle on Tyne in 1933 showed that poorer children suffered eight times as much pneumonia and five times as much rickets as children from middle-class families. In 1935 Seebohm Rowntree made a second survey of York.* When he used the same poverty line as in 1899 he found that 'primary poverty' had certainly fallen by nearly a third (Source D). But then he tried a poverty line based on higher spending on food to take note of what was thought a satisfactory diet in the 1930s. Nearly one in six of all people fell below it and nearly one in three of working-class people.

*The first was in 1899, see Unit 55.

Social conditions

A

Effects of the Water Board's work in filtering London water through sand to get rid of bacteria.

1 *What connection does the chart make between water supply and typhoid fever?*
2 *Suggest reasons why the fall levelled off in the last few years.*

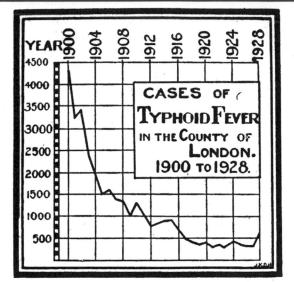

THE DECLINE OF TYPHOID FEVER in the County of London from 1900 to 1928 is shown in the graph above. It should be noted that the Metropolitan Water Board was set up by the Metropolis Water Act, 1902.

Morning Post, December 1935

B

H.A. Mess studied health in the industrial districts of Tyneside in the late 1920s.

3 *List four ways of preventing tuberculosis given by the author.*

"The prevention of tuberculosis is far more important than its treatment. Bad housing conditions are only one set of factors, and it is impossible to measure exactly their effect upon health, but there can be no doubt that the improvement of Tyneside housing would do an immense deal to lower its death-rate from this disease. It is all to the good that most of the new housing is on high ground, away from the damp and the fog of the river. If tuberculosis is to be tackled effectively, there must be no relaxation of effort when the immediate shortage of housing is overtaken; and the reconditioning of old houses is important as well as the building of new houses.

Anything that will help to abate the smoke nuisance, and so allow more generous access of sunlight, will help to diminish tuberculosis. Anything tending to improve the purity of the supply of milk will preserve health, especially in children."

H.A. Mess, *Industrial Tyneside*, 1928

Health from surveys of the 1930s
C

This comparison of the infantile mortality rates (the number of infants under one year dying out of every thousand born) for three poor and three wealthier towns was made in 1935.

	1928	*1929*	*1930*	*1931*	*1932*	*1933*
Wigan	93	129	107	103	91	110
Liverpool	94	97	82	94	91	98
St Helens	98	114	80	88	89	116
Bath	47	48	48	39	40	52
Brighton	50	54	51	54	41	47
Oxford	38	64	41	44	61	32

4 *Imagine you were a Ministry of Health official. What would be your four most important recommendations to cut infant deaths in Wigan?*

"We fail to see why the Ministry of Health is satisfied with infantile mortality rates of over 100 in towns like St Helens and Wigan. Cannot the influences which send up the figures be discovered and overcome? Or do we and the Ministry condemn 100 or more infants out of every thousand born to die annually in, let us say, Wigan, while only 50 die annually in Brighton?"
G. McNally, *Public Ill-Health*, 1935

D

In this extract from his 1936 survey of York, Seebohm Rowntree compares causes of primary poverty between 1899 and 1936.

	1899 per cent	*1936 per cent*
Death of chief wage-earner	1.42	0.61
Illness or old age of chief wage-earner	0.79	1.60
Unemployment	0.36	3.04
Irregularity of work	0.44	0.40
Largeness of family, i.e. more than four children	3.43	0.54
In regular work, but low wages	8.03	0.63

5 *What cause of poverty had grown most and which had fallen most between 1899 and 1936?*

6 *Suggest reasons why the proportion in regular work but with low wages changed so much.*

7 *What two kinds of unemployment benefit has Seebohm Rowntree joined together to get his figure of 41 per cent in paragraph 3?*

The following facts in the table merit attention:
(1) Nearly half the persons in primary poverty (1,755 out of 3,767) are children under 14 years old.
(2) 67.9 per cent of the income of the families in primary poverty is derived from social services. This compares with 6 per cent in 1899.
(3) Of the total amount received from social services of one kind and another, 41 per cent was unemployment benefit, 2 per cent health insurance, 33 per cent State pensions, and 23 per cent public assistance, which is equivalent to the old 'poor relief'."
B.S. Rowntree, *Poverty and Progress*, 1941

A medical breakthrough
E

A doctor, interviewed in the 1980s, recalled the 1930s.

8 *Explain why the doctor saw M and B as such a dramatic cure.*

". . . no general practitioner of my generation will ever forget the first time they used what was called M and B in those days, in the case of a roaring pneumonia. It was *dramatic*. We used to call two or three times a day or more, and there was a chap sitting up in bed, panting for breath, looking blue, temperature of 105, you gave him these things and I'd say, 'Give him four of these now and then two every four hours', and you'd call next morning carrying your death certificates with you and you'd have a chap sitting up in bed . . . and he was a good colour, cough was loose, he wasn't panting for breath. *Dramatic*."
J. Gathorne Hardy, *The Doctors*, 1984

112
Beveridge and the second welfare state

This unit looks at the gaps in benefits and welfare in the 1920s and 1930s. Then it shows how William Beveridge's scheme aimed at giving equal treatment and equal benefits for all and how it was carried out between 1944 and 1948.

National Insurance, 1912–38

The best seller in December 1942 was a *Report on Social Insurance* by Sir William Beveridge. He had been a civil servant from 1908 to 1920, first in charge of the new Labour Exchanges and then helping to set up Lloyd George's 1911 and 1912 insurance schemes. Between the wars he had been head of two university colleges.

Social insurance had changed a lot since 1912. Then, about twelve million workers had paid into two funds, one for health treatment and one for unemployment. By 1942 new laws had spread health insurance to 20 million and unemployment insurance to 14 million. In 1925 an important improvement had said that health insurance must include benefits for a widow and orphans. The fund also had to pay workers a pension from 65 until 70, when they were old enough for the state pension.

Even so, there were huge gaps in the schemes. Only workers, not their families, were insured for treatment from a panel doctor. Many workers covered their families by paying into a sick club or private insurance fund. Most insurance did not pay for visits to dentists or opticians. If you needed glasses you tried to find a suitable pair at a Woolworth's counter. You visited a dentist to have teeth pulled to cure an ache, not to have them filled to stop decay. When unemployed workers had used up their benefits they had to go on to the dole (see Unit 102).

When all else failed the sick or unemployed went to the Public Assistance Committees which took over from the Poor Law Unions in 1929. They were no longer sent into workhouses (which were often turned into geriatric hospitals) but paid 'assistance', the new word for outdoor relief. The rule of 'less eligibility' lingered on and assistance was less than the lowest wages.

The Beveridge Report

William Beveridge's report said that there should be an end to all the differences between people who were insured and those who were not, or between those on benefits and those on public assistance. He recommended a single *national* system run by a Ministry for National Insurance and not by private companies. Everyone should pay the same flat-rate contributions and have the same *flat-rate benefits* which should be high enough to stop the need to turn to assistance. He made it clear his scheme would not solve the problem of 'want' (or poverty) unless there were child allowances, a full national health service and full employment.

Wartime welfare

Some government leaders were worried about the costs but the wartime mood was strongly for welfare improvements. Parliament recognised this in 1944 when it set up a Ministry of National Insurance (with headquarters in Newcastle). In 1945 it passed an Act to pay family allowances in the future. After the war Clement

Attlee's new Labour government said it would pay family allowances as soon as possible. In Newcastle, 2,000 civil servants worked to see that each mother had an order book by August 1946. She could use it to collect 5/-a week for every child after the first.

National Insurance Act, 1946

In 1946 the National Insurance Act said that the rest of Beveridge's schemes would be ready by July 1948. The work needed 40,000 more staff at Newcastle. They had to close down the old insurance scheme where benefits were paid by 'approved societies'. Future payments were to be made by the Ministry of National Insurance, through the post offices for old age pensions, and through employment exchanges for sickness and unemployment benefits. Every worker got a national insurance scheme and a card for contribution stamps. That still left out people who could not pay contributions, and therefore, could not have benefits. For them, the National Assistance Board took over the work of the old Public Assistance Committees, but its means test checked only on the person and not on the rest of the family.

Aneurin Bevan (1897–1960)

The Minister for Health was an ex-miner, Aneurin Bevan. In 1946 he announced his plans for a national health service. First the plan nationalised all the hospitals and shared them out between twenty regional groups. Future treatment was to be free and hospital doctors would be paid a salary. Next, there was the 'primary' care given by GPs, dentists and opticians. They would get a fee for each patient on their panel, whether or not they came for treatment. Third, there were local authority medical services: vaccination, maternity and child care, health visitors and district nurses, ambulances. All these would now be free.

National Health Service Act, 1946

The doctors began by voting not to join the National Health Service (NHS). They feared they would be told where to work and would end up with poorer incomes. Bevan got them to join by agreeing to allow doctors to work only part-time for the NHS and to have pay-beds in hospitals for their private patients.

The 'appointed day' for the start of National Insurance, National Assistance and the NHS was 5 July 1948. It was the start of a new kind of welfare state, based on the idea that everyone should receive the same services and benefits. In the first year National Insurance actually cost less than expected because unemployment was low. On the other hand the NHS was busier because the planners had not realised the amount of neglected health. They had budgeted for £1 million in opticians' work; in fact it cost £32 million and 5¼ million pairs of spectacles were provided. By 1951 doctors were giving 19 million prescriptions a month; compared with the 7 million given to panel patients in 1947.

All this meant rising NHS costs and, in 1951, the Labour government decided to make patients pay part of the costs of dentists' and opticians' work. Aneurin Bevan resigned in protest. A few months later the Conservatives were back in power. They added a small charge for doctors' prescriptions. But they had no plans to dismantle the three-year-old welfare state.

The Beveridge Plan

A

An extract from the Beveridge Report.

1 What did Beveridge mean by (a) the first sentence? (b) 'the road of reconstruction'?

"Social insurance fully developed may provide income security; it is an attack upon Want. But Want is one only of five giants on the road of reconstruction and in some ways the easiest to attack. The others are Disease, Ignorance, Squalor and Idleness."
W. Beveridge, *Social Insurance and Allied Services*, 1942

B

The wartime Ministry of Information drew up this report on the attitude of Clydeside workers.

"Interest in the Beveridge Plan on its publication was really tremendous. For a week or two the war news tended to take a back seat and one report says: 'There has been possibly more widespread discussion on this than on any single event since the outbreak of the war.' The publicity given to the scheme by the radio and Press together with the explanatory pamphlets on the subject, which appeared almost overnight, aroused a quite remarkable enthusiasm."

C

The Prime Minister, Winston Churchill, wrote to the Cabinet in January 1943.

Sources B–C

2 Invent five characters who could be used in the script for a play which you are writing to show how the Beveridge Report appealed to the public.
3 Is there any evidence that Churchill was against the Beveridge Plan?

12 Jan 1943

"Ministers should, in my view, be careful not to raise false hopes, as was done last time by speeches about 'homes fit for heroes', etc. The broad masses of the people face the hardships of life undaunted, but they are liable to get very angry if they feel they have been gulled or cheated."
W.L.S. Churchill, *The Second World War*, 1951

Paying for health

D

A memory of the 1930s, written in 1964.

4 What does Lena Jeger's account tell you about the main weakness in national health insurance before 1948?
5 Imagine you were the doctor: what thoughts would be going through your mind as you slipped the money into your pocket?

"My mother used to sit in a misery of embarrassment on the edge of a chair in the consulting room on the rare and desperate days when one of us had to be taken to the doctor – opening and shutting her purse, waiting for the right moment to extract the careful, unspareable half-crown. She never knew whether to just slide it across the desk, which she said might make the doctor feel like a waiter, or to actually put it in his hand and make him feel as if he worked in a shop. Sometimes we dropped the money and that was the least dignified of all, especially if the fat doctor let my mother pick it up. And sometimes he would shout at my mother for not having come before, like the time we had to wait for my sister's sore throat to turn unmistakably into diphtheria before she was pushed off in a pram to his surgery. 'Good God woman, why didn't you bring this child days ago?'"
Lena Jeger, *The Guardian*, 1964

E

A Ministry of Health announcement, 1947.

6 Imagine you were a mother like Lena Jeger's. How would you have reacted to the Ministry announcement?
7 Use Sources D and E to explain why the NHS cost more than expected in its first few years.

"Your doctor will give you a prescription for any medicines and drugs you may need. You can get these free from any chemist who takes part in the Scheme. In some country areas the doctor himself may dispense medicines. The same is true of all necessary appliances. Some of them will be obtainable through hospitals; some your doctor can prescribe for you. There will be no charge, unless careless breakage causes earlier replacement than usual."
Ministry of Health, 1947

113
Health and social security

This unit looks at health and social security in the UK in four sections on National Insurance, Social Services, the National Health Service and changes in health since 1948.

National insurance

By 1960 about half the workers in the country had some pension from their employers; they could look forward to more than the old-age pension when they retired. The government started its scheme of graduated insurance in 1961. Instead of flat-rate *contributions*, workers paid a varied amount according to their earnings. Instead of a flat-rate retirement *pension* they would be getting one which varied according to their contributions.

Supplementary benefits

The other side of the story was that flat-rate pensions were not big enough to keep people from falling into poverty because of old age, long-term sickness or unemployment. No one knew this better than National Assistance Board (NAB) staff. As early as 1953 one in four of all widows or old-age pensioners went to them for help. In 1968 the NAB was joined with the Ministries of Health and National Insurance into the Department of Health and Social Security (DHSS). The DHSS replaced national assistance with supplementary benefits. By the 1980s more than five million people needed them to supplement other benefits or pensions. Supplementary benefit was paid according to fixed scales which were a sort of poverty line. No one needed to fall below it. Yet the welfare state has a large proportion of people only just above it.

Social services

William Beveridge thought out his ideas in terms of the cash needed to give social *security*. After 1948 the idea grew that the state ought also to give social *services* to those who could not manage altogether on their own. They included children in care, infirm old people and the handicapped. The job was done by separate council departments. Their staff were often dissatisfied with a policy which allowed them to give help only after an old person had become ill from neglect or a child had got into serious trouble with the law. They often could do nothing for the thousands of old or mentally handicapped people who had to stay in hospital.

New services

One answer was to improve the number of personal services to people living at home: home helps, meals on wheels, wardens for old people's housing. Another was to provide more hostels where disabled and handicapped people could live. In 1968 the Seebohm Committee reported on its enquiry into personal social services. It said that each local authority should have a single Social Services Department. Its social workers should be trained to bring together all the different kinds of help that a 'client' needed and be responsible for day nurseries, hostels and training centres. In 1971 Social Services Departments were set up in all local authorities.

The National Health Service

In 1973 the NHS was twenty-five years old. Since 1948 the number of hospital doctors had more than doubled and each region of the country had nearly an equal share of specialists. Their work had been helped by important advances. Anaesthetics had improved so it was possible to do operations lasting several hours. New machinery helped doctors to 'scan' a brain for injury, monitor a heartbeat or burn out a tumour with laser beams. New drugs could deal with rare diseases or stop the body rejecting a transplanted liver or heart. Transplant operations got the headlines but new skills put thousands back into active life. There were artificial hips, delicate operations to stop blindness and surgery for the injured in accidents.

Reorganisation of the NHS, 1974

The 380,000 hospital beds could be divided into two groups. Three-eighths of them were for acutely (or severely) ill people who were treated and sent home in days or a few weeks. Five-eighths were for long-stay patients who were mostly the old, and the mentally handicapped. Many of these beds were in run-down hospitals.

These facts were one of the reasons why the NHS was reorganised in 1974. Instead of it being divided into three sections (hospitals, community health and primary care), each district had a single health authority for all services so they could balance community care with hospital care. Some old people could live at home and be visited each day by a district nurse. Health visitors could help new mothers at home after a day or two in hospital for the birth.

Rising costs of the NHS

Everyone expected health care standards to go on rising. Each year new hospitals were built and old ones were modernised. Dentists began to get the better of rotten teeth and it became accepted that regular check-up visits were needed. But improved health care meant increased costs, and this was made worse by the growing proportion of old people. In 1978 the average cost per year of health care for the under 65s was £85; for the over 65s it was £210.

Ministers of Health tried to get doctors to prescribe less expensive drugs. Health education campaigns tried to cut illness caused by smoking, heavy drinking and bad diet. Margaret Thatcher's government made some hospitals privatise their cleaning or laundry services. The Conservatives also encouraged the growth of private health schemes. By the mid 1980s about 4½ million people were covered by schemes – which were mostly paid for by employers. But most used it to cover the costs of long-stay care in nursing homes. When it came to the family doctor or treatment for a serious illness nearly everyone relied on the NHS.

Health since 1948

Since 1948 the most obvious improvement has been the final victory against fevers which killed thousands, especially children, as recently as fifty years ago. Immunisation has wiped out diphtheria, scarlet fever and typhoid. For a time there were growing numbers of victims of poliomyelitis until that was beaten by new vaccines discovered by Dr Jonas Salk in the USA in 1954. Rising living-standards and free medical treatment have brought about a big improvement in general health. People with various kinds of physical and mental handicap have benefited from new ideas about community care. Yet in the 1980s there was evidence that Britain was not doing as much as other countries to treat and prevent disease.

Health Service
A *(below)*
A mobile van giving anti-polio vaccinations, 1958.

Sources A–B

1 *Explain how each of these sources could be used to support the view that prevention is more important in medicine than cure.*
2 *Who discovered the vaccine being used in Source A?*

C

In the 1970s a team of social scientists set out to investigate poverty in Britain. This is one table they used to work out who was deprived.

3 *What questions would you ask to build up a deprivation index for today?*

B

An extract from a book published in 1979.

"In Britain we spend £500 million a year on patching ourselves up after road accidents, and over £100 million to treat smoking related complaints. Even if we escape a road accident or cancer we are still prey to another modern epidemic, worry. In 1973 alone there were 46 million prescriptions issued for tranquillisers. . . .

. . . stress was the predominant problem in everyone's lives whether it took the form of worry about school, friction with parents, despair at the political situation, depression over unemployment and redundancy or money. In order to combat the national gloom the Health Education Council launched a big campaign aimed at getting people to take more exercise, reasoning that . . . people might sleep better and worry less."

L. Garner, *The N.H.S. Your Money and Your Life*, 1979

Characteristic	% of population
1. Has not had a week's holiday away from home in last 12 months	53.6
2. *Adults only.* Has not had a relative or friend to the home for a meal or snack in the last 4 weeks	33.4
3. *Adults only.* Has not been out in the last 4 weeks to a relative or friend for a meal or snack	45.1
4. *Children only* (under 15). Has not had a friend to play or to tea in the last 4 weeks	36.3
5. *Children only.* Did not have party on last birthday	56.6
6. Has not had an afternoon or evening out for entertainment in the last two weeks	47.0
7. Does not have fresh meat (including meals out) as many as four days a week	19.3
8. Has gone through one or more days in the last fortnight without a cooked meal	7.0
9. Has not had a cooked breakfast most days of the week	67.3
10. Household does not have a refrigerator	45.1
11. Household does not usually have a Sunday joint (3 in 4 times)	25.9
12. Household does not have sole use of four amenities indoors (flush WC; sink or washbasin and cold-water tap; fixed bath or shower; and gas or electric cooker)	21.4

P. Townsend, *Poverty in the UK*, Allen Lane 1979

114
Housing in the twentieth century

After both wars there was a spurt in council house-building followed by a slum clearance programme. Since 1919 private home ownership has been rising. Ideas about town planning go back to 1902 but were mostly acted on after 1945.

Garden cities

In 1902 Ebenezer Howard wrote *Garden Cities of Tomorrow*, his vision of new towns which would bring together the facilities of the city with the pleasant features of the countryside. He, and others, put the ideas into practice by starting the first garden city at Letchworth in 1903, followed by Welwyn Garden City in 1920.

Inter-war housing

Ebenezer Howard's ideas for design were copied by civil servants in the new Ministry of Health (which included local government housing). They had to advise councils on carrying out the Housing Act taken to Parliament by their Minister, Dr Addison. It said councils must build houses and would get a government grant if the ministry approved the design. In 1924 a new Minister, John Wheatley, drew up a new Housing Act. This said councils could have £9 a year for forty years for each house they put up.

Private building went on even faster. Builders put up semi-detached homes which were bought with mortgages. Building societies go back to the 1830s when they had mostly been formed to raise money for a single housing scheme. After 1918 they became large-scale organisations with High Street offices.

Housing costs

Altogether about three million private and one million council houses were built. They were a sign of a rising standard of living but it was not shared by all. Mortgages for small houses were around 14/- a week while council house rents were between about 8/- and 15/-. This was at a time when three-quarters of all workers earned no more than 30/-. All too often the poorest lived in the worst kind of nineteenth-century slum without toilet or bathroom. They were the families who were most likely to share with lodgers. In the mid 1930s the health dangers from overcrowded housing led to a change in government policy. New Housing Acts said that grants would go only to slum clearance.

Town planning

In the 1939–45 war, schemes for post-war housing dealt first with town planning. In 1944 a plan for Greater London showed a green belt where no building would be allowed and places where new towns could take London's 'overspill'. In 1947 the New Towns Act said that new towns should have a Development Corporation to plan separate zones for industry, shopping and open spaces. Fourteen new towns were started in the 1940s and another fourteen in the 1960s. New towns were only part of a package of laws on planning. The Town and Country Planning Act said that all councils must keep 'town maps' to show zones for different kinds of building as well as open spaces. All new buildings would need planning permission to certify that they fitted the overall scheme.

Post-war housing

In 1945 there was a desperate housing shortage after wartime bomb damage. The quick answer was to turn out metal frames and panels of wood and asbestos to build 'prefab' (or prefabricated) houses on waste ground. They were intended to last ten years but many were lived in for forty. Prefabs were followed by a new programme of council house building with the help of government grants. While Labour was in power up to 1951 hardly any licences were given for private housing. The Conservatives then came to power with a promise to build even more houses, both council and private. The result of Labour and Conservative concern was $2\frac{1}{2}$ million new homes in just over ten years.

Then, just as in the inter-war years, the government began to spend most of its share of money for council building on slum clearance. By 1967 900,000 houses had been pulled down and $2\frac{1}{2}$ million people rehoused. Because slums were mostly in inner cities, councils decided to re-house people near their old homes. To fit them in they built high-rise tower blocks, even though they were more expensive than houses or low-rise flats. The result was a miserable life for tens of thousands of people. Tower-block building slowed down after the disaster at Ronan Point in south London in 1968 when the side of a block fell out after a gas explosion.

Private ownership

The poor quality of much council housing was one reason for a boom in private ownership. Another was that higher family earnings meant that more people could take out mortgages, helped by the fact that many married women went out to work. Building firms began designing smaller houses which were sold complete with 'luxury' fittings. Conservative government laws forced councils to sell houses to tenants who wished to buy them. By 1984 over half the houses in Britain were privately owned.

Planning
A

This diagram appeared in Ebenezer Howard's book Garden Cities of Tomorrow *in 1902.*

1 *Use this diagram to explain why Ebenezer Howard believed that the best place for new building was a combination of town and country?*
2 *Using his words, list what you think would have been the three worst and three best aspects of life in 1902 in (a) the town, (b) the country.*
3 *Under town-country, what did he mean by 'no sweating'?*

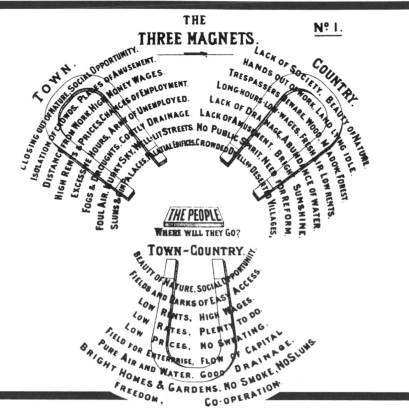

THE THREE MAGNETS.   Nº 1.

Housing between the wars

B

Plans for a council house, 1920.

4 *What does the council house plan tell you about how the occupiers were expected to use the rooms and facilities?*

5 *How was the council house to be heated?*

C

An advertisement for private housing, 1937.

6 *Compare the plans for the two houses. List the differences under accommodation, size of rooms, etc.*

7 *Why might the private house be suitable for a London office worker?*

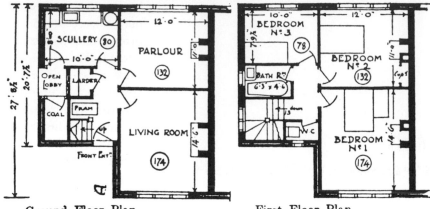

Ground Floor Plan.   First Floor Plan.

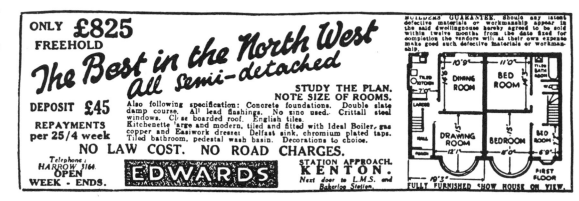

ONLY **£825** FREEHOLD

The Best in the North West All Semi-detached

DEPOSIT **£45**
REPAYMENTS per 25/4 week

STUDY THE PLAN.
NOTE SIZE OF ROOMS.

Also following specification: Concrete foundations. Double slate damp course. All lead flashings. No zinc used. Crittall steel windows. Close boarded roof. English tiles. Kitchenette large and modern, tiled and fitted with Ideal Boiler, gas copper and Easiwork dresser. Delfast sink, chromium plated taps. Tiled bathroom, pedestal wash basin. Decorations to choice.

NO LAW COST.   NO ROAD CHARGES.

Telephone :
HARROW 3164.
OPEN WEEK - ENDS.

EDWARDS

STATION APPROACH.
KENTON.
Next door to L.M.S. and Bakerloo Station.

FULLY FURNISHED SHOW HOUSE ON VIEW.

Post-war housing

D

In 1981 and 1982 the journalist Paul Harrison visited council estates in Hackney.

8 *What was the purpose of building external balconies in the 1940s and 1950s?*

9 *What evidence does Paul Harrison give in favour of tower blocks?*

10 *What does he say about their disadvantages?*

"On the estates of the 1940s and 1950s . . . access to individual flats is by external balconies, so that each flat has a door giving on to the world outside. Yet there is something indefinably ugly about these narrow alleyways in the sky . . . most pre-war problems remain: high child density, inefficient heating and insulation, lack of car space and play space. . . .

As the 1960s rolled on . . . this was the era of tower blocks. The idea: stand the streets on end so as to liberate the open space and greenery that the city needs. The reality: malfunctioning lifts; vertigo, mothers terrified for children."
Paul Harrison, *Inside the Inner City*, 1984

Housing facts and figures

E

Number of houses built since 1919.

11 *Make a copy of this chart and label it with the following in the correct places: Addison Act, Wheatley Act, inter-war slum clearance begins, Second World War, restrictions on private building, post-war slum clearance begins.*

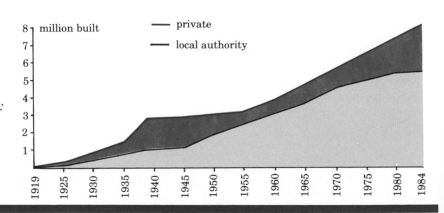

21 Migration

115
People on the move

This is the first of three units on migration. It starts with 'pull' migration which attracted people from the countryside to towns. Then it looks at the causes of 'push' migration where people moved longer distances. Many emigrated overseas. Up to the 1850s most emigrants were Scots and Irish going mostly to North America. Then English and Welsh were attracted by emigration. In this movement overseas the favourite places were the countries of the British Empire.

Internal migration

In 1851 more than three-quarters of people over 20, in Manchester, Bradford and Glasgow, had been born somewhere else, mostly in the country. A survey in 1900 showed that two-thirds of London police and transport workers had been born there too. These were just two examples of *internal migration* from rural areas to towns – a movement which went on up to 1913.

One cause of migration was the 'pull' of better earnings. Most migrants made their homes in the nearest town and usually only the educated or specially skilled moved longer distances. 'Push' migration took place when people were forced to move by very poor living conditions. Things were no better a few miles away so they had to go much further and often went overseas.

Highland clearances

Around 1800 a sharp population rise in the Scottish Highlands cut the amount of land that each family could farm. Around the same time landowners began to evict families from their tiny potato patches to clear large stretches of land for sheep grazing. They paid for some tenants to sail to America but most victims of the Highland clearances walked south. Some stopped in Glasgow; the rest moved on to towns or gangs of travelling workers in England.

The Irish

In 1835 two million Irish had no work for thirty weeks of the year. Many peasant families lived off just half an acre. Cottage spinning and weaving died out because the country was flooded with English factory-made cloth. Often the best hope was to cross to England on one of the new steamers which charged a few pence for deck passengers.

Single Irish men often joined the navvies and harvest gangs but many families moved to industrial towns. In the 1841 census there were 400,000 Irish-born people living in England, Scotland and Wales. By 1851, after the potato famine, there were twice as many. One in ten in Manchester and one in six in Liverpool were Irish. The penniless newcomers settled in the districts with the cheapest housing and worst overcrowding. For several years the extra numbers made health conditions much worse. Then, from the 1870s, the stream of Irish migration to Britain slowed down. With the worst of the famine behind them, it became more common for Irish families to save up to make their way to America.

Pauper emigrants

Before the 1850s the number of English who emigrated was small – and many were paupers. The Poor Law Commission paid for about 25,000 to go to Australia to get them off the relief books. Charities paid passages for young women and orphaned children to become domestic and farm servants overseas.

Emigration to the Empire

In the 1840s the idea of emigration began to be more attractive. Trade unions and the Salvation Army had schemes to help the unemployed start again overseas. Shipping-lines advertised faster services and gave free advice on emigration. New mail services meant that emigrants kept in touch and invited relatives and neighbours to join them. The governments of Canada, Australia, New Zealand and South Africa opened recruiting offices in Britain. More and more emigrants preferred the open spaces in these countries of the British Empire to the cities of the USA which were already crowded with new arrivals from Europe. Australia became more popular when transportation of criminals was ended, first to New South Wales in 1840 and finally to Western Australia in 1868.

Since 1913

Right up to 1913 there was *net emigration* with more people going out to settle overseas than coming to live in Britain. After the First World War this continued except for two periods of *net immigration* when more people entered Britain than left. In the 1930s the flow of immigrants was made up of people returning as they lost overseas jobs because of the world-wide slump. After the Second World War there was also a few years of net immigration because of the numbers who came to Britain for work (see Unit 117).

After 1919 the movement in Britain was no longer from the rural areas to the towns but from old to new industrial areas. The biggest internal migration was from the north of England and South Wales into the Midlands motor-making districts.

A

This was written in M.K. Ashby's account of her father's life in Tysoe, a Warwickshire village.

1 *Would you describe the migrations as due to 'pull' or 'push'?*
2 *What evidence is there that towns would grow faster than the rate of immigration into them?*

"In 1892 the causes of removal were unemployment, low wages and bad cottages. The attraction of the towns was a myth; men were not so much drawn away as propelled out. There was an increased tendency for girls to leave the countryside for 'service'. . . . Indeed what else could a labourer's daughter do? There was no attractive life or work at all for a bright grown girl. Once gone she seldom came back. What then of the next generation of village mothers?

. . . From one small area the migrants flowed to Birmingham and its neighbourhood, from another chiefly to Coventry and again to the railway works at Crewe and the breweries of Burton-on-Trent. A certain number of young men, encouraged by the clergy, were joining the Metropolitan Police Force."

M.K. Ashby, *Joseph Ashby of Tysoe*, 1961

Internal migration
B

The map shows the internal migration in England and Wales between the 1851 and 1861 censuses. The thickness of the arrow shows the net numbers of people migrating between counties.

3 *Find the six leading centres of internal migration, and give a brief reason why each was attracting newcomers.*
4 *Suggest why so many from the South West and East Anglia went to London.*
5 *What other migration was especially strong within Great Britain at this time?*
6 *Describe how the map supports M.K. Ashby's account in Source A.*

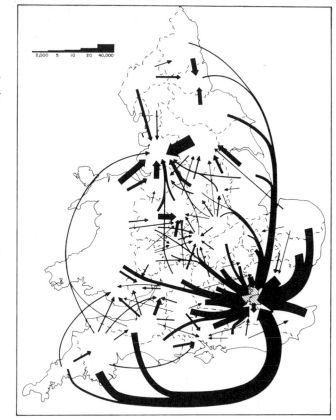

Emigration
C

Extracts from the Government of South Australia's regulations for giving assisted passages to emigrants, 1851.

7 *Imagine you are the South Australian civil servant who drew up these regulations. Write out two lists of notes to remind you of (a) who the Australian Government wanted to keep out and (b) who it wanted to encourage to come to Australia.*

"1. The Emigrants must be of those callings which, from time to time, are most in demand in the colony. They must be sober, industrious, and of general good moral character; of all of which decisive certificates will be required. They must also be in good health, free from all bodily or mental defects; and the adults must, in all respects, be capable of labour, and going out to work for wages. The candidates most acceptable are young married couples without children.

2. The separation of husbands and wives, and of parents from children under 18, will in no case be allowed.

3. Single women cannot be taken without their parents, unless they go under the immediate care of some near relatives. Single women with illegitimate children can in no case be taken.

4. Single men cannot be taken except in a number not exceeding that of the single women by the same ship."

British Parliamentary Papers, 1852

Emigration
D

Emigration from Britain.

8 *What might you have thought about the emigration figures for 1905–13 if you had been (a) the minister in charge of the army or (b) an official responsible for the Poor Law?*

1815	2,000	1850	281,000	1885	208,000
1820	26,000	1855	177,000	1890	218,000
1825	15,000	1860	128,000	1895	185,000
1830	57,000	1865	210,000	1900	169,000
1835	44,000	1870	203,000	1905	262,000
1840	91,000	1875	141,000	1910	398,000
1845	94,000	1880	228,000	1913	470,000

Figures from W. Page (ed.), *Commerce and Industry*, 1919

116
Refugees

Until the 1940s many immigrants to Britain were refugees. In the late nineteenth century they were often Russian or Polish Jews fleeing from persecution. These newcomers led to the first immigration laws in 1905 which were strengthened in 1919. In the 1930s there was another wave of refugees as Jews fled from Nazi rule in Europe.

Emigration from Europe

In the nineteenth century forty million people left Europe for the USA. One group came from the western part of the Russian Empire and Poland, which was then ruled by Russia. Many of these refugees were Jews. From the 1880s the Russian government limited the places where Jews could live and work. In the 1890s it encouraged pogroms, or murderous attacks, on their homes.

Between 1880 and 1905 about 200,000 Russian and Polish Jews came to Britain instead of the USA. There were no laws against free entry. Most Jews came without money, working tools or household goods. They were bound to live where housing was cheap and they could find low-paid work. A few thousand went to Manchester and Leeds but nearly all settled in the East End of London. Desperate for a home, the new settlers were willing to pay more rent and soon other Eastenders were having to do the same.

East-End Jews

Jewish families worked hard in the sweated trades (and some became sweaters or landlords themselves). They were blamed for taking work from English and Irish Londoners just as they were for filling the Board Schools with Jewish children. They were often disliked (or feared?) for their customs: Jews kept the Sabbath on Saturday, they ate fish and poultry, not pork, put sand instead of oilcloth on their floors and slept outside on warm nights.

The complaints did not add up to a fair picture. Many East Londoners were gladly leaving for new homes along the tramway routes and soon there was no serious overcrowding. Jews helped the clothing trade to undercut foreign competition and saved the jobs of other workers. Public health officials noted that the newcomers improved the cleanliness of the streets. Immigrants were ten times less likely to end in the workhouse at public expense.

The anti-immigration campaign

The story of the Jewish settlement might have been like that of the Irish in the 1840s – a few years of strain followed by acceptance. Instead it was the cause of a political campaign to limit the right to enter Britain freely. In the East End the British Brothers' League organised groups to whip up anti-immigrant and anti-Jewish feeling. It held political meetings which opened with 'patriotic' songs and continued with stewards throwing out anyone who did not agree with its speakers. The British Brothers' League got little support for its methods. But the idea of restricting immigration was taken up by protectionist politicians who believed that keeping out cheap foreign labour was the same as keeping out cheap foreign goods. Against that, many liberals and socialists pointed out that the immigrants were blamed for social problems that had existed long before.

Aliens Act, 1905

There were larger numbers of politicians in favour of keeping out Jewish immigrants – or aliens – and Parliament passed the Aliens Act in 1905. It gave a new official, the immigration officer, the power to refuse entry to those who had no money or no job to go to, as well as criminals and victims of serious diseases. It was an unfair Act because the officials dealt only with certain types of ship, the ones most used by Polish and Russian Jews. Other immigrants still came in freely.

The 1919 Aliens Restrictions Act was tougher but also fairer. It laid down that there was no longer a free right of immigration for anyone not holding a British passport. (It was this Act which made carrying passports for foreign travel compulsory.) Every port had to have an immigration officer to refuse entry to those who could not support themselves in Britain and put limits on the stay of holiday-makers and business travellers.

Refugees from Hitler

In 1933 immigration officers first met Jewish refugees fleeing from Nazi persecution. They arrived without money because their savings had been seized by the Nazis. Up to 1938 the Jews already in Britain gave an undertaking to care for refugees until they could support themselves. After 1938, when Hitler added Austria to his racist Empire, the refugee numbers rose to a hundred a day. The Jewish Aid Committee could no longer care for them all but private organisations, including non-Jewish groups, joined in the work. This often meant bringing children to British foster homes and leaving their parents to the concentration camps.

The work of those who helped Jews was to Britain's credit. To her discredit were a number of anti-semites, people who discriminated against Jews. Even more shameful was the British Union of Fascists (BUF). This was started in the depression by Oswald Mosley, once a rising Labour leader. Many early members joined the BUF because it promised solutions to the slump. By about 1934 they had left Mosley and he turned to cruder ways to win support. Each week he led marches of black-shirted followers through the East End of London. Their slogans and speeches began to concentrate on attacking the Jewish settlers. There were also fights with objectors. In 1936, Parliament put an end to the worst threats and violence with the Public Order Act, which made it illegal to wear military-style uniforms.

The Second World War

In 1940 all adult German and Austrian Jewish refugees were interned, mostly in camps on the Isle of Man. When the fear that they might be spies had died down, they were released. Many did war work or fought in the Jewish Battalion. By then other aliens were coming to Britain, such as many of the 190,000 Poles who fought alongside the Allies in the Second World War.

After the war Britain was severely short of industrial workers. The government began a recruiting drive amongst 'displaced persons'. Some were Italians but most were from eastern European countries which had fallen under Communist control in 1944–5. About a third of a million (half of them Poles) settled here. About the same number of citizens of the Irish Republic came to Britain.

The Royal Commission, 1903

A

In 1903 a Royal Commission collected evidence on immigration. It found many different opinions. This extract from its Report summarises many of the complaints it heard.

B

The Commission, however, heard evidence from specialists who often gave a different view. One was the London County Council Medical Officer who looked at death-rates in Jewish districts in 1900.

C

Another witness was a member of the London School Board.

1 *In which ways does the evidence in Sources B and C contradict that in A?*

Jewish Londoners

D

A drawing by T. Heath Robinson of immigrants arriving in London, June 1905.

2 *Imagine you were one of the children in the picture, and are now around 30. Write a piece of autobiography looking back on your first years in London.*

Refugees from Hitler

E

One of two Jewish sisters, who were brought to Britain during the Second World War, gave this account nearly thirty years later. . . .

3 *What did the girls need to bring the parents to safety?*

4 *What fate did their parents suffer?*

"In respect of the Alien Immigrants it is alleged:

1 That on their arrival they are (a) in an impoverished and destitute condition (b) deficient in cleanliness and practise insanitary habits . . .

2 That amongst them are criminals, anarchists, prostitutes and persons of bad character

3 That many of these being and becoming paupers and receiving poor law relief, a burden is thereby thrown upon the local rates."

Royal Commission on Alien Immigration, 1903

"When I came to examine the death rates, which I had expected to find very high in view of the conditions of the houses and the prevailing conditions of the district, I found them very low. . . . the only conclusion I could come to was that the difference in the death rate was due to the better care the inhabitants took of themselves and their mode of life."

Royal Commission on Alien Immigration, 1903

"The Jewish children have proved excellent scholars, far the most regular in London, usually well-fed even in poor families, and bright in school. This is due largely to the excellent domestic character of their parents, never drinking and devoted to their children."

Royal Commission on Alien Immigration, 1903

"IMMIGRANT JEWS."

"My sister managed to get a domestic permit for our mother and also managed, heaven knows how, to find a guarantor for our father, who was already over sixty. I still have in my possession the cable we received from our parents 'Arriving Croydon Airport Wednesday 6th September'. On Monday war broke out – we had lost the race by three days . . . We received the usual Red Cross messages after that for a couple of years, then they stopped. After the war we learned that they had shared the fate of six million others."

K. Gershon (ed.), *We came as children*, 1966

117
Post-war settlers

This unit describes the background to the immigration of settlers from the old colonies of Britain. It briefly tells the story of black people in Britain before the 1940s and then explains the Acts which limited Commonwealth immigration and made laws for racial equality.

West Indians

The East European and Irish immigrants of the later 1940s did not solve the shortage of labour in Britain. So London Transport, the NHS and other employers advertised for workers in the British West Indian islands, which were colonies of the Commonwealth up to the 1960s. All these West Indians could have passports saying they were 'Citizens of Great Britain and her colonies' so they had full rights to enter and leave Britain. In the 1940s and 1950s several thousands came each year, although large numbers also returned to the Caribbean after working in Britain for a time. In the 1950s the West Indians were joined by people from different parts of India and Pakistan (and later Bangladesh). Other arrivals came from Malaysia, Hong Kong, Cyprus and parts of Africa.

Early black settlements

They were not the first black people to live and work in Britain. In the eighteenth century black people had sometimes been brought here by slave-owners. In the nineteenth century Africans and Indians (called 'lascars') were employed on ships. By 1900 there were settlements of black people, as well as Chinese, in ports such as London, Liverpool, Cardiff and Bristol.

Towards colonial freedom

During the Second World War, the Allied Forces included soldiers from every part of the British Empire and Commonwealth. After the war, leaders in the colonies began to force Britain to agree to giving them their independence. India and Pakistan became independent in 1947, and by the end of the 1960s most colonies had gained their independence. Most chose to remain as equal members of the Commonwealth. But the British Empire was dead.

The immigrants in Britain

So Britain was recruiting labour just when she was giving up rule over the homelands of the immigrant workers. But was the change in attitude to the Empire matched by a change in attitudes towards black people? The new arrivals were soon facing the problems met by the Irish in the 1840s and the Jews in the 1880s. They were offered the lowest-paid jobs and many spent years on permanent night shifts. Educated immigrants often had to take manual work because their qualifications were not recognised.

Most immigrants had been recruited for jobs in the industrial cities. That meant living in old inner city houses which landlords (some of them immigrants themselves) often turned into flats or rooms. It was really the old story of the new settlers getting the worst houses, the poorest jobs and the oldest schools.

In 1958 there were anti-immigrant riots in Notting Hill in London and Nottingham. In 1959 the National Front was formed out of groups which had links with the pre-war Fascist movement.

Its policies were racist and threatening to the newcomers. Few people voted for the National Front in elections. But opinion polls showed that many believed that Britain was accepting too many immigrants. Both Labour and Conservative governments took steps to cut immigration to a trickle.

Commonwealth Immigration Acts, 1962 and 1971

The first step was the Commonwealth Immigration Act of 1962 which took away the automatic right of entry for anyone who had a British passport. If they came from colonies or ex-colonies, their numbers would be limited by a quota of employment vouchers. This did not apply to passport holders from the white Dominions, such as Canada. The 1962 law limited the number of black immigrants just as the 1905 law restricted East European Jews and not anyone else.

The 1971 Commonwealth Immigration Act ended the quota of employment vouchers and said that only relatives and dependants of settlers already here could come to Britain. That rule led to much hardship as elderly people, children, wives and fiancées waited to enter Britain. At the ports there were some disgraceful cases of insulting treatment to Commonwealth people. These rules do not apply to many white people from the Commonwealth countries. Provided they have British-born parents or grandparents they can move freely in and out of Britain.

Race Relations Act, 1965

Clearly the immigration laws were discriminating against black people. For those who were already in Britain, Parliament took some measures against blatant discrimination. In 1965 the Race Relations Act made it illegal to discriminate against people of any race in a public place. That put a stop to petty-minded actions such as refusing to serve black people in pubs, but there was strong evidence that they were heavily discriminated against when looking for a home, or trying to get a job on equal terms with white people. In 1968 such discrimination in housing and employment was made illegal. Unfortunately that did not close the doors on all the ways that employers, landlords and housing managers could ignore black people.

Racial Equality Act, 1976

In 1976 the Racial Equality Act tried to end such indirect discrimination. It also outlawed racially offensive comments in writing or speeches. People who felt there had been discrimination could take their case to a race relations tribunal. The Act set up the Commission for Racial Equality to investigate discrimination. Many thought its powers were not great enough and in the 1980s there was still a lot of evidence that racial minorities were at a disadvantage in housing, education and employment. After riots in Brixton (London) and St Paul's (Bristol) in 1980, an enquiry was led by Lord Scarman which suggested that the poor conditions in Brixton were further worsened by the prejudice on the part of some police. Police made efforts to improve officers' understanding of ethnic minorities, and government money was given to develop jobs in the inner cities. Further riots in Toxteth (Liverpool) in 1981, and in Handsworth (Birmingham) and Tottenham (London) in 1985 indicated that much was still to be done.

Prejudice and tolerance

A

Many people in the UK first saw a black person in 1942: probably a soldier in the US army. The Sunday Pictorial *reported a talk given by a vicar's wife to village women and then gave its own views.*

"1 If a local woman keeps a shop and a coloured soldier enters she must serve him, but she must do it as quickly as possible and indicate that she does not desire him to come there again.

2 If she is in a cinema and notices a coloured soldier next to her, she moves to another seat immediately.

3 If she is walking on the pavement and a coloured soldier is coming towards her, she crosses to the other pavement.

The vast majority of people here have nothing but repugnance for the narrow-minded, uninformed prejudices expressed by the vicar's wife. There is – and will be – no persecution of coloured people in Britain." *Sunday Pictorial*, 6 September 1942

B

Walter Kobak was a Pole who served with the Polish Parachute Regiment, married a Scots girl and became a miner in 1948. He remembered his early days in Britain in a TV interview.

1 *How would you explain the examples of prejudice in these two passages?*

2 *Do they suggest any ways in which it can be overcome?*

". . . of course there was resentment of me coming in and probably taking away [someone's] job. Not at the time, because there was plenty of work, but his son probably was in danger of not being accepted in that pit because I would work until I was sixty-five years of age. Through time, of course, it became better, because we were hard workers – well, I can only speak for myself. I was a hard worker and I was gradually being accepted as a good worker, not as a Pole. Then of course, with me being able to express myself a little better, I tried to point out to them that down below, when there is a fall, it doesn't say, 'I'm not going to fall because I've got a Britisher underneath me, I'll fall now because there's a Pole', and of course the boys understood that."

P. Addison, *Now the War is Over*, 1985

Population tables

C

The effects of the Immigration Act which came into force on 1 July 1962.

3 *From Source C suggest reasons for the rise in immigration in 1960 and 1961.*

4 *How does the table explain the effects of the Commonwealth Immigration Act?*

Immigrants from three Commonwealth countries

Year	West Indies	India	Pakistan	Total
1955	27,550	5,800	1,850	35,200
1956	29,800	5,600	2,050	37,450
1957	23,000	6,600	5,200	34,800
1958	15,000	5,200	4,700	25,900
1959	16,400	2,950	850	20,200
1960	49,650	5,900	2,500	58,050
1961	66,300	23,750	25,100	115,150
Jan–Jul. 1962	31,800	19,050	25,080	75,930
July–Dec. 1962	3,241	3,050	−137	6,154

S. Patterson, *Immigration and Race Relations in Britain*, 1969

D

The estimated population of New Commonwealth and Pakistani origin in Great Britain. By 1978 more than 40 per cent had been born in Britain.
(These statistics involve some estimations, as most censuses of UK population statistics are not collected on the basis of ethnic origin or colour.)

5 *Suggest why the Commonwealth and Pakistani population continued to grow after the Immigration Acts.*

Mid year		% of GB population
1966	860,000,000	1.7
1968	1,087,000,000	2.0
1970	1,281,000,000	2.4
1972	1,453,000,000	2.7
1974	1,615,000,000	3.0
1976	1,771,000,000	3.3
1978	1,920,000,000	3.5

From Office of Population Censuses and Surveys, *Population Trends*

118
Agriculture in war and peace

Before 1914 agriculture went through the depression described in Unit 68. In the First World War the government helped with payments for growing extra grain. After the war cheap foreign corn put farming back into depression until the government again helped with cash. Government help boosted agriculture even more in the Second World War.

In 1914

Before the First World War the world's largest merchant fleet went out with coal, textiles and other manufactures and came back with wheat from the American prairies and Russia, fruit from the Canaries, meat from Argentina and Australia, cocoa from West Africa. Cheap imported food meant that farmers often gave up. By 1914 only one-fifth of wheat was home grown. Farmers who produced milk, fruit and vegetables did less badly but even they had less than a half share of food eaten in Britain.

In wartime

This nearly led to disaster in war. In the winter of 1916–17 there was less than six weeks' food in the country. The German fleet blocked the way to Russian and American wheat. The lines of people outside food shops grew longer and angrier. The government's answer was to appoint a Food Controller. Lord Rhondda set about rationing sugar, meat, tea and butter. In 1917 the government tackled the main problem: shortage of grain. Through the Corn Protection Act it promised farmers that when the war ended and cheap foreign grain came back the government would pay them at least what it cost them to grow home produced corn. There was also a new deal for farm labourers who were given a Wages Board to fix minimum rates of pay. With this guarantee, farmers ploughed up disused land. By 1919, they were growing three-fifths instead of one-fifth of Britain's wheat.

Depression again

In 1921 the government broke its promise. Foreign corn was flooding in at half the price of home wheat. The government would not pay the huge bill to make up the difference. Farming quickly dropped into an even deeper depression than before the war. By 1931 only a seventh of wheat and less than four-tenths of all foods were home grown. Many farmers went bankrupt. Others neglected parts of their farm and turned the rest into small-holdings. The main dairy and fruit growers did not suffer so much but that was because they often used mostly family labour.

Farm labourers

The only help the government gave to farmers was to close down the labourers' Minimum Wages Board. That meant farm workers' pay could be cut step by step. In 1918 it was 42s for a 48-hour week; in 1920 36s for 50 hours. Women earned even less. In 1923 Norfolk farmers tried to cut it to about 14s. Six thousand labourers went on strike and got 26s after the Labour government gave back their Wages Board in 1924 but they still left farming in large numbers. There were a million in 1919 and about half that number in 1930.

Those who stayed worked hard for their low pay. Ploughing was done by men and horses, cows were milked by hand. For threshing there was machinery but it was steam driven while the rest of Britain was turning to petrol engines. Many labourers still lived in cottages tied to the job; they were almost always without electricity or water.

Marketing boards

Farming was saved from total collapse by the industrial slump of 1929–31. In 1932 the government decided that the only way to start recovery was to end free trade and go over to protection, putting customs tariffs on foreign goods. That left it with the problem of keeping food cheap without free trade. The government went back to paying guaranteed prices for wheat. Second, they set up marketing boards. The Milk Marketing Board bought up all farmers' milk at a fixed price and then sold it to dairies. Soon there were boards for eggs, potatoes, bacon and hops.

Improvements in the 1930s

Farmers could now began to open up land again. In 1936 a quarter of Britain's wheat was home grown. Farmers had money to modernise. Almost every farm in the 1930s still had horses but most had a tractor or two as well. Electricity from the national grid supplied milking machines. Some council houses were built for labourers who got small wage rises and seven days' annual holiday. Country buses kept people in touch with nearby towns. By 1939 farming was healthier than at any time since the 1870s.

The Second World War

In 1939 the government set up a War Agriculture Committee in each county. These laid down targets for each farmer. Those who objected might find their petrol ration cut or have their land confiscated. The Women's Land Army was built up to a much bigger size than in the First World War. When that was not enough, prisoners-of-war were set to work on farms.

The number of tractors and combine harvesters (mostly given by America as part of lend-lease) went up four times. Government-controlled chemical factories turned out fertilisers and weedkillers. Government scientists helped farmers with advice. By 1945 Britain produced 80 per cent of its own food – and it had not done that since the eighteenth century.

Wartime
A

The Women's Land Army was started in 1917 and added 33,000 women to the 80,000 already working as agricultural labourers. Here a member is ploughing.

1 *Why would this have been an unusual sight before the First World War?*

Between the wars
B

The journalist Philip Gibbs describes a visit to East Anglia in the late 1920s.

2 *What does Philip Gibbs say was at the root of the farmers' difficulties?*
3 *What steps were taken to improve the situation in the 1930s?*

"It was a tragic situation. Here are some of the finest and largest farms in England, into which these men have put all their fortune and labour of mind and body. Those far-stretching harvests of wheat and oats should have been a source of wealth to themselves and the nation. But on every acre of wheat they would lose five pounds at least. They were losing on almost every other crop. . . . There had been a frightful slump in the price of potatoes. It did not pay to rail their cabbages. They dropped four to five shillings a head on every sheep. They could get no paying price for eggs. For five years their capital had been withering away by these continual losses, while their land fell in value to a quarter of what they paid for it."
P. Gibbs, *England Speaks*, 1935

Wartime
C

Clearing land in the fenland between 1939 and 1941.

4 *What two important wartime steps to improve food production are illustrated in Source C?*
5 *Compare Sources A and C. What do they suggest about agricultural progress over thirty years?*

119
A new agricultural revolution?

After the Second World War farmers got guaranteed incomes, first from the 1947 Agriculture Act and then from the EEC's Common Agricultural Policy. This encouraged mechanisation and specialisation, with fewer farm workers. By the 1980s Britain was producing much of her own food and eating a great deal of it from convenience packages.

Diet in wartime

By 1945 full employment and higher wages meant most families could buy up all their rations and eat food they could not have afforded before the war. Far more people had meals in canteens at factories or in cheap-priced 'British Restaurants'. These helped to spread the idea that a full meal should always have vegetables and a pudding which added fruit and milk to the diet.

Agriculture Act, 1947

After the war it was unthinkable to return to the standards of the 1930s, so the government could not repeat the policy of 1921 when they had stopped wartime help to agriculture. There was a new deal in the 1947 Agriculture Act. Prices paid to farmers would be agreed the autumn before, in an Annual Price Review based on the price of foreign food. If this was cheaper than home-produced food, farmers would get a deficiency payment to make up what they would lose by selling at low prices. In 1973 there was a bigger change when Britain joined the European Economic Community.

Common Agricultural Policy

The EEC already had its own system of paying farmers under the Common Agricultural Policy (CAP). There were target prices for food sold to wholesalers or marketing boards. Foods outside the Common Market had levies added to their price to bring them up to EEC targets which were fixed to give farmers a good income. Sometimes farmers produced too much which could have brought the price in the shops down. To check this the EEC had an organisation which would buy food from the farmer at just below target price. This was called 'intervention buying'. The EEC then stored the food until it could be sold at the target price or exported.

The CAP meant that food became more expensive in Britain because there were no more cheap foreign products, especially from the Commonwealth. But what mattered to farmers was knowing what they could earn the following year. They could work this out just as well from the CAP target prices as the Annual Price Review's deficiency payment. Some politicians objected that both methods 'feather-bedded' farmers by making them the only producers with a guaranteed income. On the other hand, both systems encouraged farmers to be more efficient because the more food they produced on each acre the more they earned. The result was that food output grew by more than 6 per cent a year up to the 1980s, while industry managed only 2 per cent a year.

Mechanisation

In the 1940s the horse was a common sight alongside the country's 200,000 tractors. By the 1960s there were half a million tractors and hardly any horses. The tractors were dwarfed by the monster machines which harvested grain, baled tons of hay, or ripped beet out of the soil. Farm buildings hid other examples of mechanisation. Broiler hens lived in cages where they were automatically fattened before being slaughtered, prepared and frozen.

In the 1960s came automatic milking parlours, where cows could be washed, milked and fed special foods while standing on a slowly moving turntable. Winter food for most animals came from airtight silos which kept grass and barley fresh. Haystacks, which took days of heavy work to build, became things of the past.

Science

Science played a big part in the changes. Experts in genetics bred animals which would fatten quickly, with the aid of 'balanced' diets. In the 1940s there were about 200,000 bulls on farms. In the 1980s nearly all calves came from fifty very expensive bulls kept at AI (artificial insemination) stations. Scientists improved the 'strains' of seeds so that farmers could get a bigger yield per acre.

Specialisation

In the 1940s most farms were mixed Specialisation developed in the 1960s and 1970s. In parts of East Anglia and southern England sheep disappeared and farmers specialised in grain. Some was used for bread and cereals but most of the barley went to specialist animal farmers as feed. Specialisation often meant the end of old rotations. With the help of fertilisers the same field was used for many years to grow grain. This could also mean that farmers ripped out eighteenth-century enclosure hedges.

One reason for specialisation was the growing connection between farmers and food processors. It began with canners who built factories near fruit and vegetable farms and bought up the whole local crop. In the 1960s there were freezing plants to supply the one in two households which had bought a freezer by 1970.

Farm workers

Mechanisation and specialisation led to a fall in the number of farm labourers from 600,000 in 1945 to 150,000 in 1985. Those who stayed had very different lives. Back-breaking jobs disappeared and they had to become experts on machinery or the controls in animal houses. Farmworker's pay however stayed lower than in many other jobs which needed less skill.

Farmers

The number of farms fell and the average size of each one grew. This was a result of the coming of extremely expensive machinery which would not repay its cost on a small farm. So many farmers sold land to neighbours who enlarged their holdings. The second change was the disappearance of landowners whose families had rented land to farmers for centuries. In the 1980s only a third of farms were rented. In some ways this stood for all the changes that had taken place since Defoe's day. Wealth and power had passed to industry and commercial business and away from land ownership.

Criticisms

The agricultural changes had many critics who argued that the countryside was under threat from weedkillers and the disappearance of hedges and patches of waste land. Some believed that factory farming methods which kept animals and poultry in closed spaces were cruel and also produced less healthy meat. At times of famine in other parts of the world, there were plenty of people who asked why surplus food bought under EC intervention rules were kept in stores and not sent to help the starving.

Consequences of agricultural change

A

A development of the 1970s was the round baler which could deal with 8 cwt of hay at a time.

B

Changes in the proportion of Britain's food which was home produced.

Sources A–C

1 *Using Sources A–C list the evidence for the idea that there has been an agricultural revolution since 1945.*
2 *Compare the information in Source C with that in the sources in Units 65 and 68. What conclusions can you draw about gains (or losses) in healthy diet?*

self-sufficiency

75%

50%

25%

1980–1
1953–4
1936–9

wheat · barley · sugar · beef · mutton · pork · bacon · butter · cheese · eggs

C

Amounts eaten per head in 1982, according to family income.

Families earning:	over £240 pw	£127–£240	£77–127	less than £77	OAPs
Milk (pints)	4.09	3.83	3.90	3.82	4.42
Cheese (ounces)	4.20	3.98	3.71	3.25	3.73
Beef & veal (ounces)	8.72	7.20	6.86	5.59	7.80
Bacon & ham (ounces)	3.96	3.59	4.01	3.95	3.96
Fresh fish (ounces)	1.18	1.06	1.02	1.21	2.61
Frozen fish (ounces)	1.46	1.67	1.64	1.34	1.71
Eggs	3.43	3.22	3.49	3.72	3.51
Sugar (ounces)	8.01	8.71	10.33	12.49	10.31
Potatoes (ounces)	29.65	36.92	43.89	49.11	41.11
Fresh vegetables (ounces)	29.03	26.16	25.61	23.04	33.52
Frozen & processed vegetables (ounces)	14.89	19.09	18.87	18.95	11.65
Fresh fruit (ounces)	26.13	19.73	16.29	14.02	20.86
White bread (ounces)	14.85	19.16	25.26	27.30	20.99
Other bread (ounces)	10.53	10.38	8.10	7.69	12.90

National Food Survey Committee, *Household Food Consumption and Expenditure*, 1982

120
Feminine or equal?

Parliament gave the vote to women in 1918 and 1928. New laws created a fairer system of divorce. More jobs were open to women in new industries. But it was still unusual for married women to work outside the home in many parts of the country — even though most families had fewer children.

The vote

The part played by women in the First World War meant that male political leaders felt bound to give them a part share in political rights. In 1918 all men could vote and so could six million women, but they had to be over 30. Women could also become MPs. The first was an Irish Sinn Feiner who refused to come to Parliament. So the first woman MP in the House of Commons itself was Nancy Astor*, the American-born wife of the English businessman, Lord Astor. In 1928 women over 21 got the same voting rights as men. Until 1945 there were never more than fifteen women MPs. Perhaps it is not surprising therefore that there were only a few laws in the 1920s and 1930s which directly helped women.

Divorce

One was the Matrimonial Causes Act of 1923, which put men and women on the same footing over divorce. A woman could now divorce her husband for adultery and no longer had to prove that he had been cruel as well. The law did nothing to help women whose husbands had deserted their families. They had to wait until 1937 when another Matrimonial Causes Act allowed men and women to divorce if they had been deserted for three years.

Women at work

In 1919 many women had to give up their wartime jobs to men coming out of the army. In the 1920s there was a smaller number of manual jobs for women. It was much less common for middle-class families to have servants. There was some new work in light industry, such as assembling electrical equipment, but often these replaced jobs lost in older industries such as textiles. The biggest growth was in white-collar work as clerks, teachers and nurses. In the 1920s and 1930s it became more usual for women to stay at work for a year or two after marriage but some organisations, such as the Civil Service, did not allow this. In 1911 only about a third of all women and only a tenth of those who were married had jobs outside the home. In 1931 there were about three-quarters of a million more women workers but they were still only a third of all women and still only a tenth of the married.

* She stood for her husband's seat after he became a lord.

Smaller families

After the First World War women were more likely to get married because fewer men took jobs overseas. A woman who married in the 1880s had an average of 4.6 children. Her daughter who married in the 1900s had 3.37 and her grand-daughter would have 2.19 children in the 1920s. Obviously many couples decided to limit the size of their families. Enquiries at the time suggested that half of them did so by 'being careful' in various ways. Since these are the most risky methods of avoiding pregnancy, families would have been even smaller if contraceptives had been used. The sheath was available from around 1914 and diaphragm caps came in around 1919. It was another thing to feel it was right to use them. This is where a doctor of biology, Marie Stopes, enters the story.

Marie Stopes (1880–1958)

In 1918 Marie Stopes wrote *Married Love* and *Wise Parenthood*, two books which suggested that birth-control was the key to a happy marriage. Some people disapproved but letters poured in from women of all classes asking for advice. In 1921 she opened the first birth-control clinic (in North London) and in 1930 she joined with others to start the National Birth-Control Council. In 1939 it had more than sixty clinics and changed its name to the Family Planning Association.

Family life

Parents came to expect most of their babies to survive. The new school-leaving age of 14 meant that children could not become early wage-earners and would cost more to keep. If families were kept smaller, parents and children could share in greater spending on food, clothes, hot water and separate bedrooms. Some parents wanted to be able to keep their children at grammar school until they were 16. Many women simply realised that it was quite unnecessary to spend so much of their lives in the hard work of bringing up children. The mother of the 1880s had her last child on average aged 33; the mother of the 1920s had hers at 28 – and she would live longer. Smaller families meant that parents had more leisure time for visits to the cinema, a dance hall or to one of the new pubs with lounge bars.

Housework

Almost all women found housework easier after the spread of electricity and piped water and the coming of more packaged food. But class differences showed up sharply. Women in the old industrial districts still worked long hours over the wash-tub and cooking stove. The family earnings were simply not enough to pay for an easier life. It was the woman in the more prosperous districts who had hours to spare from basic housework. Even her shopping was made easier when delivery vans brought milk and bread daily.

More freedom

These same women were likely to be emancipated from other things as well as housework. As teenagers they could go to dances at the local Palais, or to the cinema or tennis club. For the most daring there could be holidays at Youth Hostels (started in 1930) or a Butlins Holiday Camp (started in 1937). But these new freedoms were not leading to equality with men so much as making a new type of feminine person. Clothing fashions began to change every year. One-piece backless swimming suits appeared in 1930 and tennis shorts for women soon afterwards. The cosmetics industry boomed in the 1930s when few women felt dressed without lipstick and usually face powder. The cinema was a powerful way of drawing attention to new fashions. Magazines for women carried advertisements and articles on new recipes and dressmaking as well as giving advice on bringing up children. Their stories were almost all romances which ended with a shy young secretary or nurse marrying her boss or the doctor.

Housework

A

In 1939, Margery Spring-Rice wrote a report on the evidence collected by a Woman's Health Enquiry Committee on the lives of wives of manual workers.

1 *How many examples are there to show that conditions had not improved much for these women compared with women in the nineteenth century?*

2 *In what ways would a Woman's Health Enquiry Committee today find that the lives of these women had improved?*

"If their husbands and/or sons are miners or bakers, or on any nightshift, they may have to get up at 4 (possibly earlier), make breakfast . . . go back to bed for another hour's rest. The same woman who does this has probably got a young child or even a baby who wakes up early. . . . Her bed is shared not only by her husband but, in all probability, by one *at least* of her young family.

. . . if she has only the average family of this whole group, four or five children, she is probably very poor and therefore lives in a very bad house. . . . She may have to go down (or up) two or three flights of stairs to get hot water . . . she may have to heat it on an open fire. . . . The school-children will be back for their dinner soon after 12 so she must begin her cooking in good time. . . . She has not got more than one or two saucepans and a frying pan, and so even if she is fortunate in having some proper sort of cooking stove, it is impossible to cook a dinner as it should be cooked.

Then comes tea, first the children's and then her husband's. . . . If she is a good manager she will get all into bed by 8, perhaps even earlier and then . . she sits down again, after having been twelve or fourteen hours at work and perhaps she then has a 'quiet talk with hubby', or listens to the wireless, 'our one luxury' . . . she doesn't go out because she can't leave the children unless her husband undertakes to keep house for one evening a week while she goes to the pictures . . ."
M. Spring-Rice, *Working Class Wives*, 1939

Family planning

B

A letter written to Marie Stopes in 1926.

3 *Use the letter to suggest three reasons for setting up family planning clinics.*

"I am a young Mother of two beautiful children a Girl, born January first 1925 and a Boy born December 21st 1925 both born in the same year. I had terrible times for both, having to have instruments and chloroform and the dear littles mites cut about. The Dr told me when my baby boy was born I wasnt to have any more children as I should never deliver them myself, I am now dreading the thoughts of having any more children. My husband is only a working man and we feel we can't afford more children on our money it would mean misery. Can you please give me some advice how to prevent any more little ones coming. I am yours truly"
Marie Stopes, *Mother England*, 1929

121
A lot more equal?

During the war and afterwards, the government took important steps to improve family welfare and health. In the 1950s and 1960s it became common for married women to work, but no laws dealt with equal pay and sex discrimination until the 1970s. There was a great rise in the number of divorces after they became cheaper in 1949 and easier to get in 1973.

Wartime

In the Second World War women were directed to essential war work in the same way as men although the government took steps to care for their families. Looking ahead to peacetime, William Beveridge wrote that caring for homes and families was 'vital unpaid service'. His report recommended that women and children, not just men, should be insured (see Unit 112). In 1945 Parliament agreed that family allowances should be paid directly to mothers.

After the war, many people were catching up on the five years when men in their twenties and thirties had been away from home in the forces. So 1946 and 1947 were boom years for weddings or starting married life. Quite naturally this led to a 'bulge' in the birth-rate and many younger women were fully occupied in looking after their husbands and families at home.

Work

Older women often wanted something different. Many objected when they had to give back their wartime jobs. They found other jobs as soon as possible so, in 1947, 18 per cent of married women had work compared with 10 per cent before the war. The percentage rose to 29 per cent in 1957, 38 per cent in 1966 and 60 per cent in 1979.

Most women did one of three sorts of job. They could go into one of the light industries making household appliances. Pay was low but they could often work part-time or in shifts, which suited their family life. The new welfare services were growing to cope with the children of the bulge and other needy groups. So women went into classrooms, nurseries, old people's homes and hospitals where they became radiographers and physiotherapists as well as nurses. Third, women took the place of men who moved from shops and service work to higher-paid jobs in other industries.

Equal pay

In almost every job women were paid at a lower rate than men. Until the 1950s this was not thought unfair. Ideas began to change first in the Civil Service and teaching. Between 1955 and 1961 women teachers' pay increased in stages to match mens'. In industry, employers said that paying more to women would drive them out of business (which is what mill-owners said about shorter hours in the 1830s). Unions argued that equal pay would lower men's wages. In 1970 a new law said that equal pay for the same jobs had to come in steps by 1975. Many employers gave new descriptions to jobs done mostly by women so that they could not be said to need the same kind of skill as work done mostly by men.

For some people this showed that the real problem was 'sex discrimination'. There were old-fashioned attitudes which said that only men could cope with certain skills. Women were penalised for needing time off to have children. They were kept out of clubs or rooms in pubs. The education system was said to discriminate by discouraging girls from getting higher qualifications.

Equal Opportunities Act, 1975

These concerns led to the Equal Opportunities Act of 1975. It now became illegal to label jobs for either men or women only, or to discriminate against women in any other way. The Equal Opportunities Commission (EOC) was set up to investigate sex discrimination and advise on ways of stopping it. It has helped individual women to take employers to court and has used its powers to get some organisations to end discrimination.

Divorce

Along with the move to greater equality went other changes in the relationship between men and women. In 1949 men and women could get legal aid for divorce cases. It was no longer only the well-to-do who could afford to end a marriage. In 1954 there were six times as many divorces as in 1949. But you still had to give a 'cause', such as adultery, cruelty or desertion. A Royal Commission found that many people believed that men and women should be allowed to make their own choice about divorce and not have to prove there was a cause. But Parliament took no action.

The number of divorces went on rising. In the 1930s one in ten women married before 20; in the 1960s it was one in four. It was these early marriages which were most likely to end in divorce. But these young divorces were usually followed by a second marriage. So it was said that marriage and family life were still respected. This shift in ideas led to a new law in 1969 which ended the need to give a cause. After 1973 couples could divorce after declaring that they had not lived together for twelve months.

One-parent families

In the 1970s the number of divorces had gone up six times since the 1950s. Enough time had passed to see that second marriages were more likely to break up than first marriages. There was also evidence of hardship following divorce. Some men were paying maintenance to their ex-wives' children and trying to finance a new family as well. Others dodged paying and left their first family in poverty. A Royal Commission in 1974 found an increase in one-parent families; by 1981 they numbered 5 per cent of households. Some were women who did not want to marry but most were cases where mothers (and some fathers) had been divorced and not re-married. In almost every case single-parent families were badly off because the mother (or father) could not cope with a full-time job and caring for children.

Attitudes

A

William Beveridge in 1943.

1 *Do you think that the year had any bearing on the last sentence?*

"the attitude of the housewife to gainful employment outside the home is not and should not be the same as that of a single woman. She has other duties ... in the next thirty years housewives and mothers have vital work to do in ensuring the adequate continuance of the British race and of British ideals in the world."
W. Beveridge, 1943

B

Maureen Colquhoun, MP, speaking in the House of Commons in 1965.

"The Sugar Board has five men and no women. The Agricultural Training Board has 27 men, no women. Is it to be said that the only role of the woman in agriculture is that of the farmer's wife?

The Committee of Investigation for Great Britain has seven men, no women. I do not know how Great Britain can be investigated without the help of women.

The National Bus Company has seven men, no women. Of course women do not travel on buses. Neither, apparently, do they travel on trains, because the British Railways Board has twelve men, no women."

Parliamentary Debates, May 1965

C

A cartoon in The Guardian, *1981.*

Sources A–C

2 *Explain for each of these sources how it illustrates different attitudes of the 1940s, 1960s and 1980s.*

Working women

D

In his third survey of York, Seebohm Rowntree found many more working-class women going out to work. He asked 1,278 of them for their reasons.

3 *Put into your own words the most common reason for women working given in Source D.*

"171 did so to enable them to buy furniture etc for the home, twenty-seven to pay for children's education, eighteen, most of whom were qualified nurses, did so from a sense of duty, 441 'to make ends meet', 351 to buy luxuries, and 270 for the pleasure of meeting other people instead of being cooped up in their home . . ."

S. Rowntree and G. Lavers, *Poverty and the Welfare State,* 1950

E

The Royal Commission on One-Parent Families, headed by M. Finer.

4 *What major changes in the character and age structure of the female labour force are described in Source E?*

"Today, mothers have more than half their active adult lives to lead after their youngest child has reached school leaving age. One result has been a transformation in the character and age structure of the female labour force upon which the economy has been dependent for cheap labour ever since industrialisation. On the eve of the second world war, the representative woman worker was young and single, doing a job between leaving school and getting married. Now, she is married, over 35 and with a grown up family."

The Royal Commission on One-Parent Families, 1974

122
At school 1918–1939

The Fisher Act of 1918 said that steps should be taken to improve elementary education after age 11. The Hadow Report in 1926 said there should be three different types of secondary school. The main result was modern schools which were a new kind of elementary school for 11–14-year-olds.

Post-war planning

In 1917 a new Minister of Education was given the job of planning for better post-war schools. He was H.A.L. Fisher, a well-known historian and vice-chancellor of Sheffield University. He met strong demands for improvements in education after the age of 11. Of all children in elementary schools only one in eleven got a free place to a secondary school. Ten out of eleven pupils stayed at elementary school until 13 when they could leave if they had a job; otherwise they left at 14. A few still became half-timers at age 12. Even among those who did get a free place to secondary school, many left at 14 rather than 16, because their parents could not afford to keep them there for longer.

The Fisher Act, 1918

In 1918 Fisher's Education Act pointed the way to improvements.

1 All children were to attend school from 5 to at least 14. Early leaving and part-timing were abolished.
2 It was the duty of local authorities to improve the education of older elementary pupils. This should include opening some schools where they could stay after 14.

The Hadow Report, 1926

The Act did not say how these foundations should be built on. That job was given to a committee headed by W.H. Hadow (who followed H.A.L. Fisher as head of Sheffield University). In 1926 the Hadow Committee published its report on 'The Education of the Adolescent'. It said there should be a break in education at 11. Schools for children under that age should be called 'primary' and there should be three kinds of 'secondary' education. As before, some pupils who passed a test at 11 would have free-place scholarships to secondary schools, re-named 'grammar' schools. The rest would go to a separate 'modern' school and the leaving age should be raised to 15. At 13 they should have the chance to pass a test to transfer to a technical, or central, school.

Governments said it would cost too much to raise the leaving age to 15. At last this was planned for 1 September 1939. Two days later war broke out and the change was postponed. Only a few technical and central schools were built. There was a small rise in the numbers winning scholarships to grammar schools. Most progress was made with what was called 'Hadow reorganisation'. By 1938 nearly half of elementary pupils transferred to 'modern' schools and many others moved across the playground to a separate senior department of an all-age elementary school.

Yet both were still part of the elementary system. They did not teach languages and had poor arrangements for science. Most of their teachers had been to training college, not university, and all were paid less than grammar-school staff. Pupils were taught in larger classes, often with few books. They left without any qualification. Most went into unskilled jobs and many knew they would lose them when employers had to pay them adult wages. Sometimes the better job they might have had went to a young person who had been to grammar school and then left at 14.

Streaming

So the scholarship test could decide a child's whole life. Junior schools began to divide children at 7 into 'A', 'B', and 'C' streams. 'A' classes were taught with the 11+ scholarship always in mind. Psychologists of the time encouraged this because they believed it was possible to measure a child's 'general intelligence' to pick out those who were suitable for academic studies. The aim was to be as fair as possible to children whatever their background.

But, even so, just 4 per cent of elementary pupils who went through grammar schools got to universities. This was a tiny proportion, considering that many new redbrick universities were opened in towns such as Nottingham, Hull and Leicester.

Spens Report, 1938

Many people, including leaders of the Labour Party and the teachers' unions, objected that the system was unfair. Chances of passing the scholarship could vary in different parts of the country from one in five to one in twenty. The biggest complaint was simply that modern schools and senior departments were not good enough. The demand grew for 'secondary education for all'. In 1938 the Spens Committee suggested there should be secondary technical schools as well as secondary grammar schools. Again, war came before anything could be done.

Children's health

Teaching and learning were only part of the inter-war story of education. The doctors and nurses of the School Medical Service, started in 1906, did much for children's health, especially at school clinics which cared for teeth, eyes and hearing. Their work went alongside general improvements in diet, housing and hygiene. In the School Medical Service's first full year, 1907, only 30 children out of every thousand were found to be clean enough for good health. In 1934 only 30 in a thousand were described as dirty.

Some local authorities gave meals and free milk to the children of the poorest families, especially in districts where there was high unemployment. But surveys in the 1930s showed that up to a quarter of all children were undernourished. In 1934 a new scheme gave each child a third of a pint of milk (supplied by the new Milk Marketing Board, see Unit 118) free or at reduced prices.

Change in the elementary school
A

Ida Rex taught in a London elementary school from 1916 to 1923 and gave this account fifty years later.

1 *Imagine you were the head teacher of the school where Ida Rex taught. Make a list of five aims you would expect the other teachers to have.*

"I started with the younger children and then specialised in art and special stencil work, and then the older children were taken on by Liberty's for stencilling and needlework. There weren't many that got scholarships to the grammar school. So they specialised in handwork and they did very well.... There were about 500–600 children and every day at playtime, in turn, a week at a time, we had to take drill in the open air with these whole lot for five minutes, so that they had their communal drill ...

There were free dinners for those who needed them in a special school nearby. It was not for those who could afford dinners. The Head said who should go, in conjunction with the Social Care Committee. Quite a lot of children went. They had to be deloused. There were some very, very poor children."
Ida Rex interviewed for 'Working Lives' (Hackney WEA), 1973

B

A domestic science class in a London school in the 1930s

2 *How does this photograph show progress and lack of progress in elementary education by the 1930s?*
3 *Describe the equipment being used by the three girls on the left of the photograph.*

The Scholarship
C

Norman Fell recalls how he failed the 11+ scholarship in 1931.

4 *If you had had Norman Fell's experience in the early 1930s which side would you have taken in the debate in the 1970s about whether to make education comprehensive?*
5 *What do you think are the strengths and weaknesses as historical evidence of oral accounts such as Ida Rex's in Source A and Norman Fell's in Source C?*

"We were sitting for the exam and I went in the morning, and there was a teacher Mabel Briggs. She was a wonderful teacher and I were in her class. And she said, prior to starting the exams, she said, Now you must concentrate because I think you've a good chance of going to the Grammar School. So we had the first part of the exams in the morning and oh I tried hard, and I felt I was doing exceptionally well. Until I went home, dinnertime. And my elder brother said, Under no circumstances must you pass for a scholarship because, he says, if you do, we'll never be able to clothe you to go to that school. And when I went back in the afternoon I just didn't try.... And that is the position. Then Mabel Briggs, the school mistress, said, What have you been doing this afternoon? When the exam results were known she said that she knew there was something wrong, and the wrong part about it were that I didn't try at all, because I knew the fact was that I wouldn't be able to go – I couldn't dress to go to the school."
Interviewed by Melvyn Bragg for *Speak for England*, 1976

123
Secondary education for all

The 1944 Education Act led to a tripartite division between grammar, technical and modern schools. From the 1960s increasing numbers of pupils attended comprehensives. By the 1980s there were new issues including the need for new kinds of education and training.

The 1944 Education Act

As in 1914–18, there was a great deal of planning in 1939–45 for a better post-war world. In education this meant dealing with the unfinished business of providing secondary education for all. It came in the 1944 Education Act drawn up by the Minister of Education, R.A. Butler:

1 All pupils must leave primary school at 11 (or 12 in Scotland) and go on to a free secondary school, suitable for their age, ability and aptitude.
2 The leaving age should be raised to 15.
3 Each LEA must continue to provide school meals and free milk.

Tripartite system

The Act did not say what sorts of secondary school would be suitable. But the Ministry and the LEAs agreed on a 'tripartite' system which was based on ideas in the pre-war Hadow and Spens Reports. It assumed that there were three types of child: bookish, technical or practical. They would be divided among three types of school: grammar, technical and modern. The fairest way of fitting children into the new system was still thought to be the 11+ examination with its intelligence tests. About one in five passed to go on to a grammar school, where pupils took the School Certificate at 15 or 16. The rest went to a Secondary Modern. For some there was then a chance to sit another test for technical school at 13. In half the LEAs these schools were never built so the system was more truthfully dual rather than tripartite.

New examinations

Secondary modern schools met strong pressure from parents (and many teachers) to enter pupils for public examinations. This was made easier in 1951 when the School Certificate, which had to be taken in five subjects at one time, was replaced by the GCE which could be taken in a single subject. From 1964 pupils could also take subjects in a new 'second tier' examination, the CSE. The number staying on for a voluntary extra year to 16 tripled between 1951 and 1964. It was one reason for calls to end the tripartite system. Some educationists gave others. Their researches showed that the 11+ scholarship tests measured differences in social background more than intelligence.

Crowther and Robbins Reports

The idea that only a limited number of pupils were suitable for grammar schools was weakened by three reports. The Crowther Report on education for 15–19-year-olds said that many 15-year-olds were not allowed to develop as much as they could. It recommended a steady movement to a new leaving age of 16. In 1963 the Robbins Report on higher education pointed to a large pool of untapped ability among pupils who should be helped to qualify for places at university or college. Both Crowther and Robbins were concerned that Britain was lagging behind other countries in educating skilled workers, technologists and scientists. Their reports were followed by a spurt in university building so that, by 1979, there were forty-five instead of the seventeen of 1945. In the 1960s the new universities were joined by Polytechnics and in the 1970s by Colleges of Higher Education.

Plowden Report

In 1963 the Plowden Report said that primary pupils should be encouraged to learn through activities which arose from their interests rather than being trained for tests. It also said that there should be a major effort to help socially disadvantaged children by giving more money and teachers to schools in 'educational priority' areas. It was another argument in the growing belief that everyone can do more if given a proper chance.

Circular 10/65

In 1965 the Labour government sent out Circular 10/65 saying it wished to end selection at 11+. It asked LEAs to send in plans for reorganising secondary schools on comprehensive lines. Many did so willingly because they had already built comprehensive schools. Others, such as Leicestershire, sent all 11-year-olds to junior high schools with a chance of moving to a senior high school at 13.

Comprehensive schools

Many Conservative voters wanted to keep grammar schools and the new Conservative government withdrew Circular 10/65 in 1970. Yet many new comprehensives and no new grammar schools were built. In 1974 the next Labour government also abolished the 'direct grant' arrangement which meant LEAs could no longer pay fees for pupils going to private grammar schools. In the 1980s more than 90 per cent of pupils outside the private or independent sector went to comprehensives. But by then the number of secondary school pupils began to shrink and many schools found it hard to run sixth-form classes in all subjects. One way of dealing with this was to have a two-tier system with school followed at 16 by sixth-form college.

The GCSE

In the late 1970s and 1980s there were many schemes to up-date studies. Some reflected the fact that Britain had become a multi-cultural society. Others were intended to give girls equal chances to qualify for all jobs. Still others aimed to prepare young people for the shift in jobs away from the craft trades towards technology and service industries. In 1984 the Minister of Education, Keith Joseph, agreed to a new single examination at 16+, which teachers had wanted for years. He said that the GCSE could only begin after the curriculum in each subject was thoroughly examined. The examining boards and teachers had to agree on 'national criteria' for what should be learned.

Tripartite schools – and children!
A

A Ministry of Education handbook set out the ideas behind 'tripartite' secondary education.

1 *Take three sheets of paper, one for each kind of child described here, and try to divide all the students in your class among them. Use a fourth sheet for any which you cannot place – or those who object to the placing you suggest! What do the results tell you about the educational ideas of the 1940s?*

New issues for the 1960s
B

From the Crowther Report.

Sources B–C

2 *What weaknesses did the Crowther Report see in the leaving age of the time?*

3 *Do you think the arguments about comprehensive schools in the 1960s have any relevance today?*

C

From a guide to the English school system.

What this book has been all about!
D

Part of the National Criteria for syllabuses in British social and economic history.

4 *Which of the topics would you rank as first, second and third in importance? Give your reasons.*

5 *Are there topics not in the Criteria which you think you should have studied? Give your reasons.*

"The majority of children learn most easily by dealing with concrete things and following a course rooted in their own day-to-day experience. . . . It is for this majority that the secondary *modern* school will cater.

Some children, on the other hand, will have decided at quite an early stage to make their careers in branches of industry or agriculture requiring a special kind of aptitude in science or mathematics. Others may need a course, longer, more exacting, and more specialised than that provided in the modern school, with a particular emphasis on commercial subjects, music or art. All these boys and girls will find their best outlet in the secondary *technical* school.

Finally, there will be a proportion whose ability and aptitude require the kind of course with the emphasis on books and ideas that is provided at secondary *grammar* school."
Ministry of Education Pamphlet No. 12, 1947

"*671. Chapter 12. Why the School-Leaving Age should be Raised: (2) The National Interest*
(a) The country is a long way from tapping all the available supply of talent by present methods – half the National Service recruits to the Army who were rated in the two highest ability groups had left school at 15.
(e) The demand both for more educated workers and for more deeply educated workers is growing at almost all levels of industry – raising the school leaving age to 16 would give those near the bottom a better foundation, and would be reflected in larger numbers receiving full-time education to 18 or beyond."
Report of the Central Advisory Committee for Education, vol. 1, 1959

"COMPREHENSIVE SCHOOLS
Their advocates see them as a way of abolishing social and academic segregation at 11 and of giving all children the chance to come up against 'grammar school' standards of staff, curriculum, and aspirations. Opponents of comprehensive schools argue that they have to be unnecessarily large, unwieldy, and impersonal, and that the bright children in them are bound to be held back."
T. Burgess, *A Guide to English Schools*, 1964

"The syllabus should include economic (e.g. changes in government policy concerning taxation and trade), social (e.g. attitudes and policy about poverty and public health) and technological aspects (e.g. impact of invention in the textile industry). Political aspects (such as the widening of the franchise and local government growth), religious and cultural developments (exemplified in attitudes to education and involvement in philanthropic movements) and scientific changes (such as the impact of Pasteur's work on medical and public health practices) could all be included. The importance of world trade and the impact of foreign competition should be studied so that British developments are fitted into a wider context."

Index

A page number followed by a letter in brackets directs you to the source which has that letter. Numbers in bold type show pages where there is information in the narrative and one or more sources on that topic.